Shojo Beat

yona of the Dawn

13

Story & Art by

Mizuho Kusanagi

yona of the Dawn

Volume 13

CONTENTS

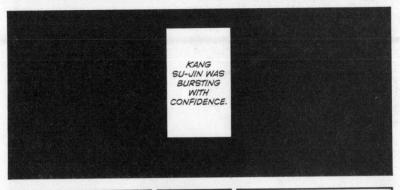

KANG SU-JIN WAS BURSTING WITH CONFIDENCE.
CAVALRY SQUAD 1, FORWARD!
THE ROYAL REGI-MENT'S* POWER ...
...AND SU-WON'S LEADER-SHIP SKILLS ...
...HAD BEEN CAREFULLY ACCOUNTED FOR WHEN HE MADE HIS PLANS.
HE HAD NO CAUSE FOR CONCERN.
*THE KING'S PERSONAL TROOPS

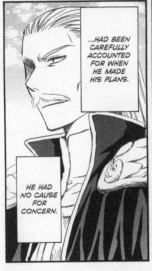

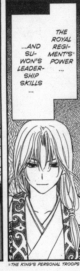

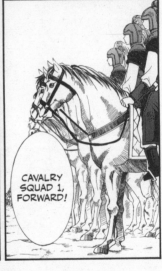

I have a blog where I post things about my day and my work.
You can send me web claps and messages.
I hope you'll drop by!

Mizuho Kusanagi's NG Life
http://yaplog.jp/sanaginonaka/

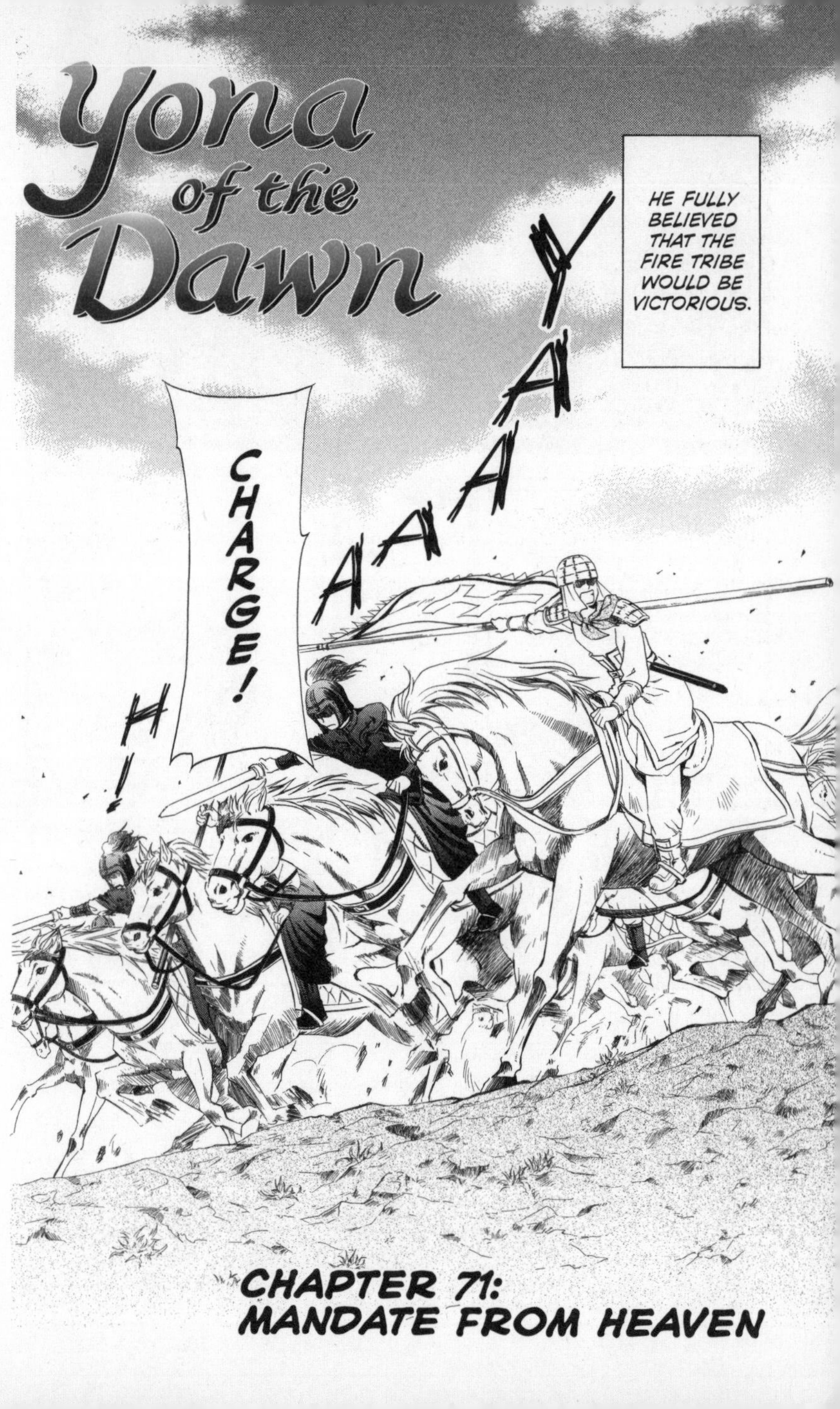
Yona of the Dawn
HE FULLY BELIEVED THAT THE FIRE TRIBE WOULD BE VICTORIOUS.
YAAAAH!
CHARGE!
CHAPTER 71: MANDATE FROM HEAVEN

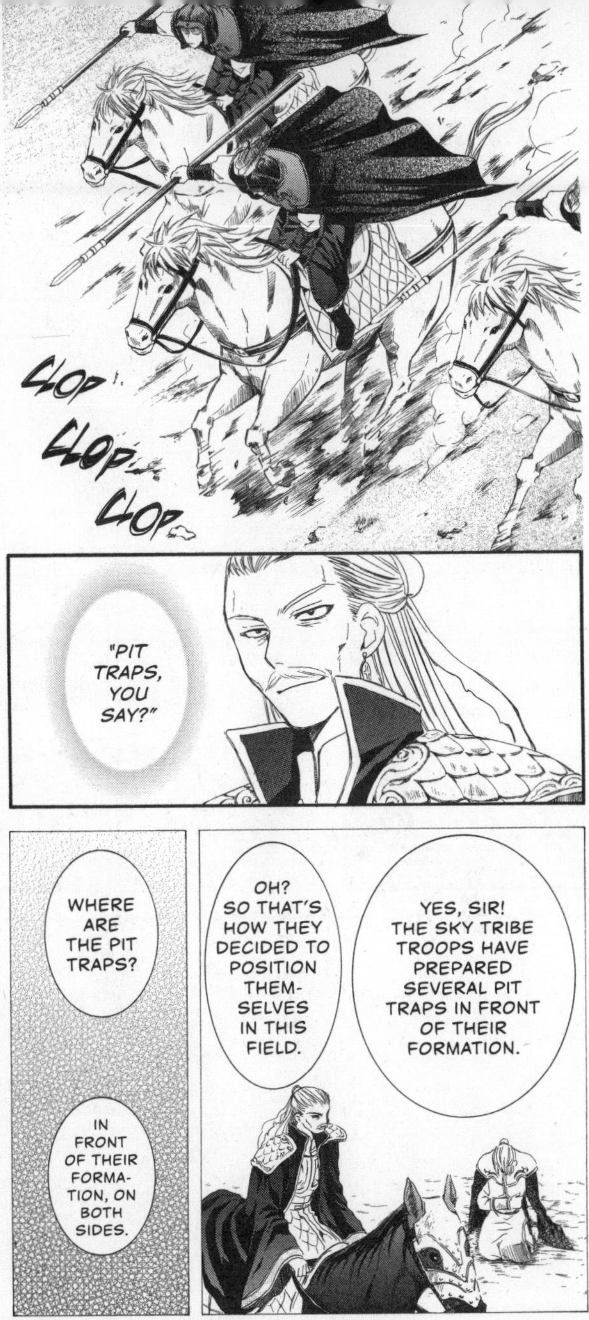
CLOP
CLOP
CLOP
"PIT TRAPS, YOU SAY?"
YES, SIR! THE SKY TRIBE TROOPS HAVE PREPARED SEVERAL PIT TRAPS IN FRONT OF THEIR FORMATION.
OH? SO THAT'S HOW THEY DECIDED TO POSITION THEMSELVES IN THIS FIELD.
WHERE ARE THE PIT TRAPS?
IN FRONT OF THEIR FORMATION, ON BOTH SIDES.

Hello! This is Mizuho Kusanagi. We've reached volume 13, chapter 71 of Yona of the Dawn. The story's been going on for quite a while, hasn't it? My last series, *NG Life*, was only nine volumes long, and it felt like Yona quickly overtook it.

This volume opens with a battle. Yona herself doesn't make an appearance, but bear with me!

While I was planning this part, I thought of things like "charging armies" and "soldiers and horses trying to escape." But then, while actually writing it, I thought "Who's going to draw all that?" I knew I wouldn't have enough time, so I sketched the soldiers and horses and got my assistants to ink them. Thank you so much...!

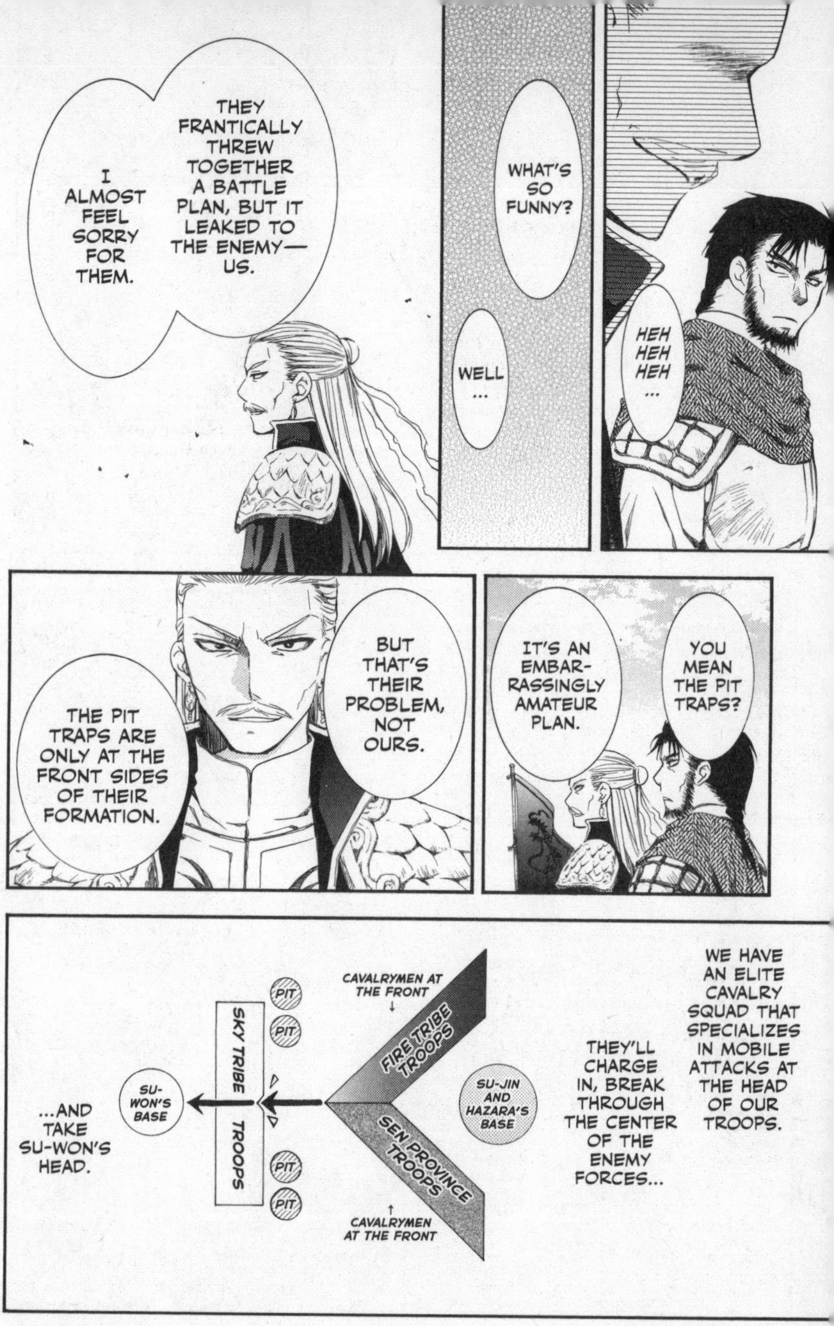
HEH HEH HEH ...
WHAT'S SO FUNNY?
WELL ...
THEY FRANTICALLY THREW TOGETHER A BATTLE PLAN, BUT IT LEAKED TO THE ENEMY—US.
I ALMOST FEEL SORRY FOR THEM.
YOU MEAN THE PIT TRAPS?
IT'S AN EMBAR-RASSINGLY AMATEUR PLAN.
BUT THAT'S THEIR PROBLEM, NOT OURS.
THE PIT TRAPS ARE ONLY AT THE FRONT SIDES OF THEIR FORMATION.
WE HAVE AN ELITE CAVALRY SQUAD THAT SPECIALIZES IN MOBILE ATTACKS AT THE HEAD OF OUR TROOPS.
THEY'LL CHARGE IN, BREAK THROUGH THE CENTER OF THE ENEMY FORCES...
SU-JIN AND HAZARA'S BASE
CAVALRYMEN AT THE FRONT
FIRE TRIBE TROOPS
SEN PROVINCE TROOPS
CAVALRYMEN AT THE FRONT
PIT
PIT
PIT
PIT
SKY TRIBE TROOPS
SU-WON'S BASE
...AND TAKE SU-WON'S HEAD.

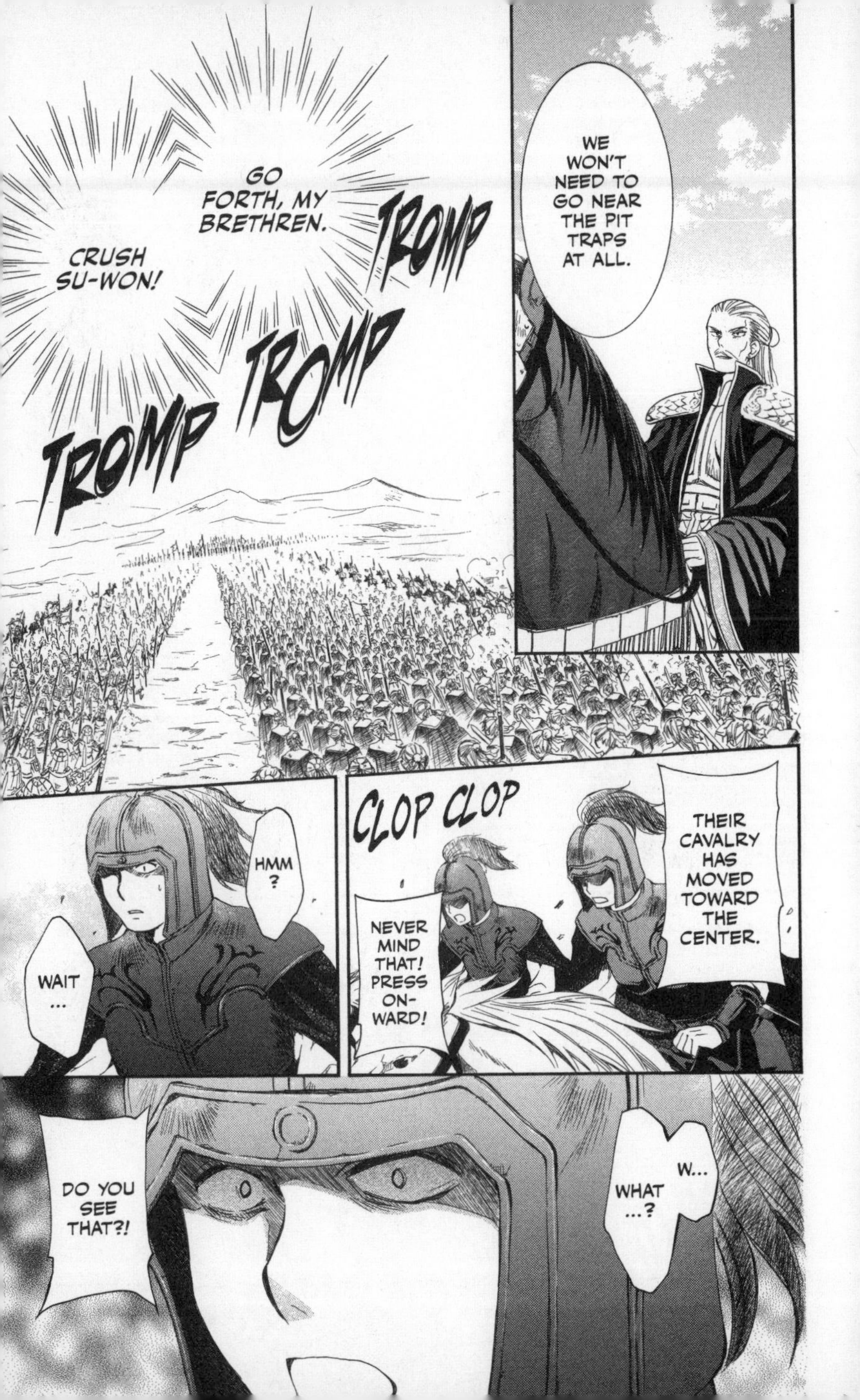
WE WON'T NEED TO GO NEAR THE PIT TRAPS AT ALL.
TROMP
GO FORTH, MY BRETHREN.
CRUSH SU-WON!
TROMP
TROMP
THEIR CAVALRY HAS MOVED TOWARD THE CENTER.
CLOP CLOP
NEVER MIND THAT! PRESS ON-WARD!
HMM?
WAIT...
W...
WHAT...?
DO YOU SEE THAT?!

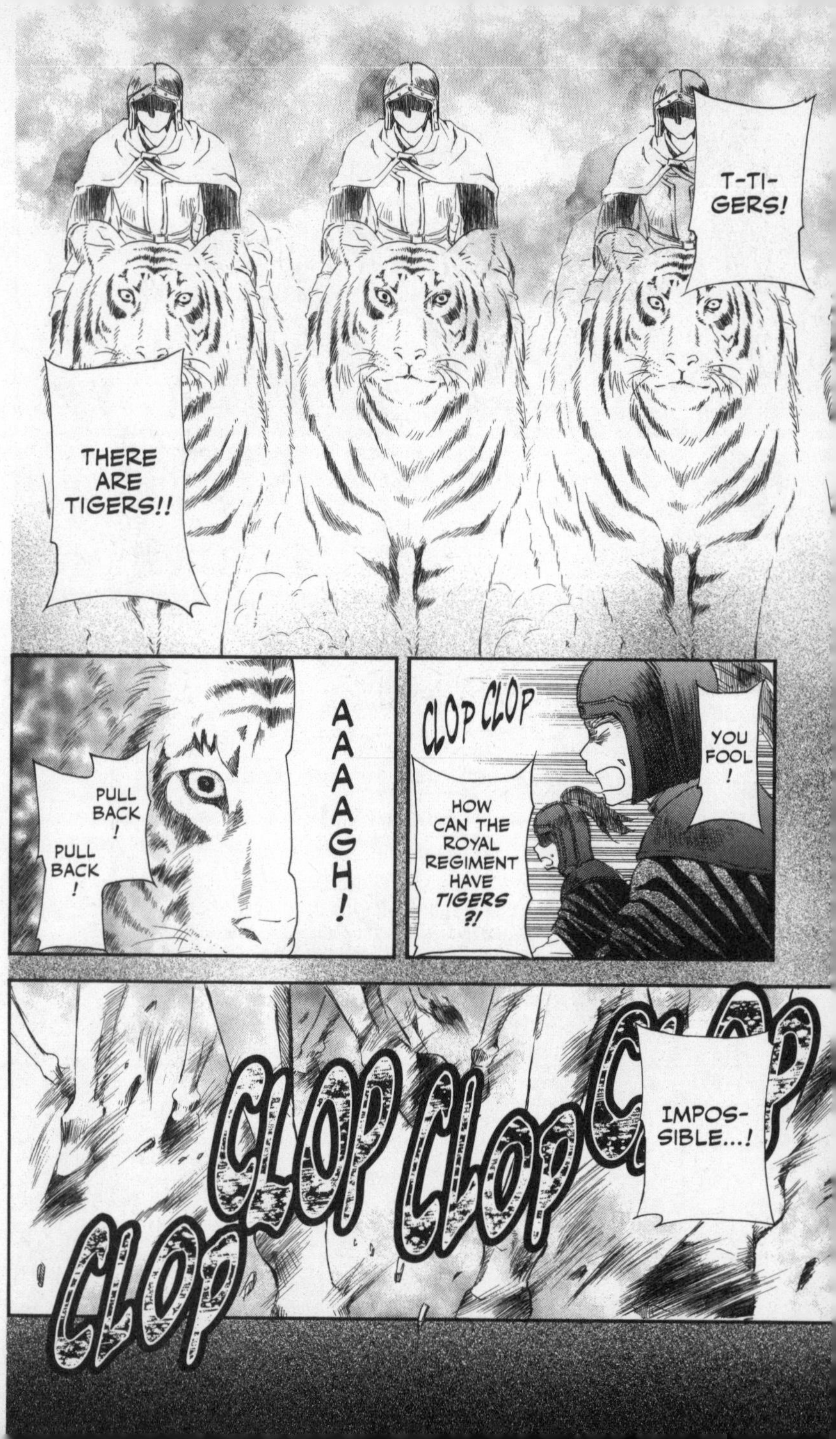
T-TI-
GERS!
THERE
ARE
TIGERS!!
CLOP CLOP
YOU
FOOL
!
HOW
CAN THE
ROYAL
REGIMENT
HAVE
TIGERS
?!
AAAAAGH!
PULL
BACK
!
PULL
BACK
!
IMPOS-
SIBLE...!
CLOP CLOP CLOP CLOP

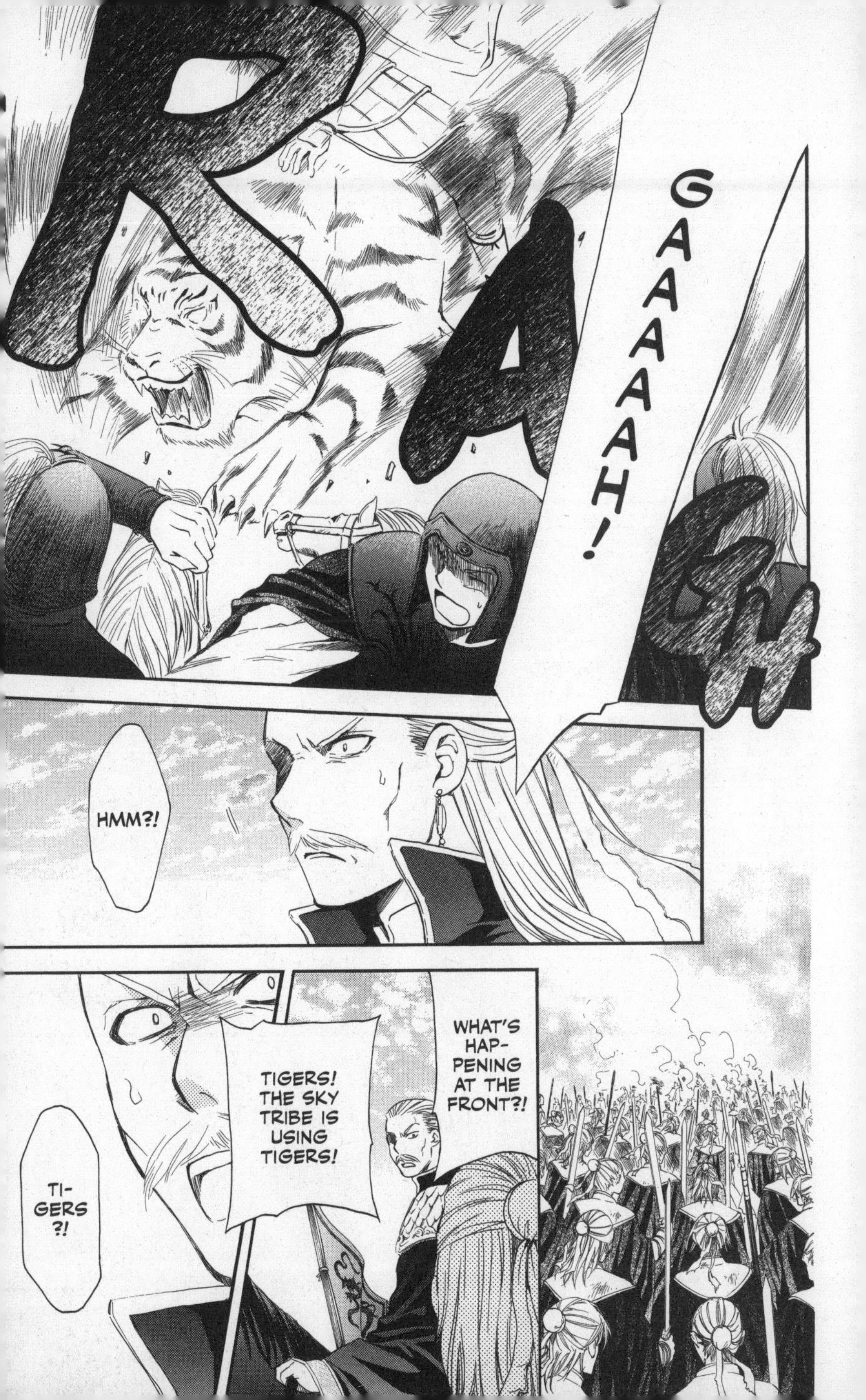
GAAAAAH!
HMM?!
WHAT'S HAP-PENING AT THE FRONT?!
TIGERS! THE SKY TRIBE IS USING TIGERS!
TI-GERS?!

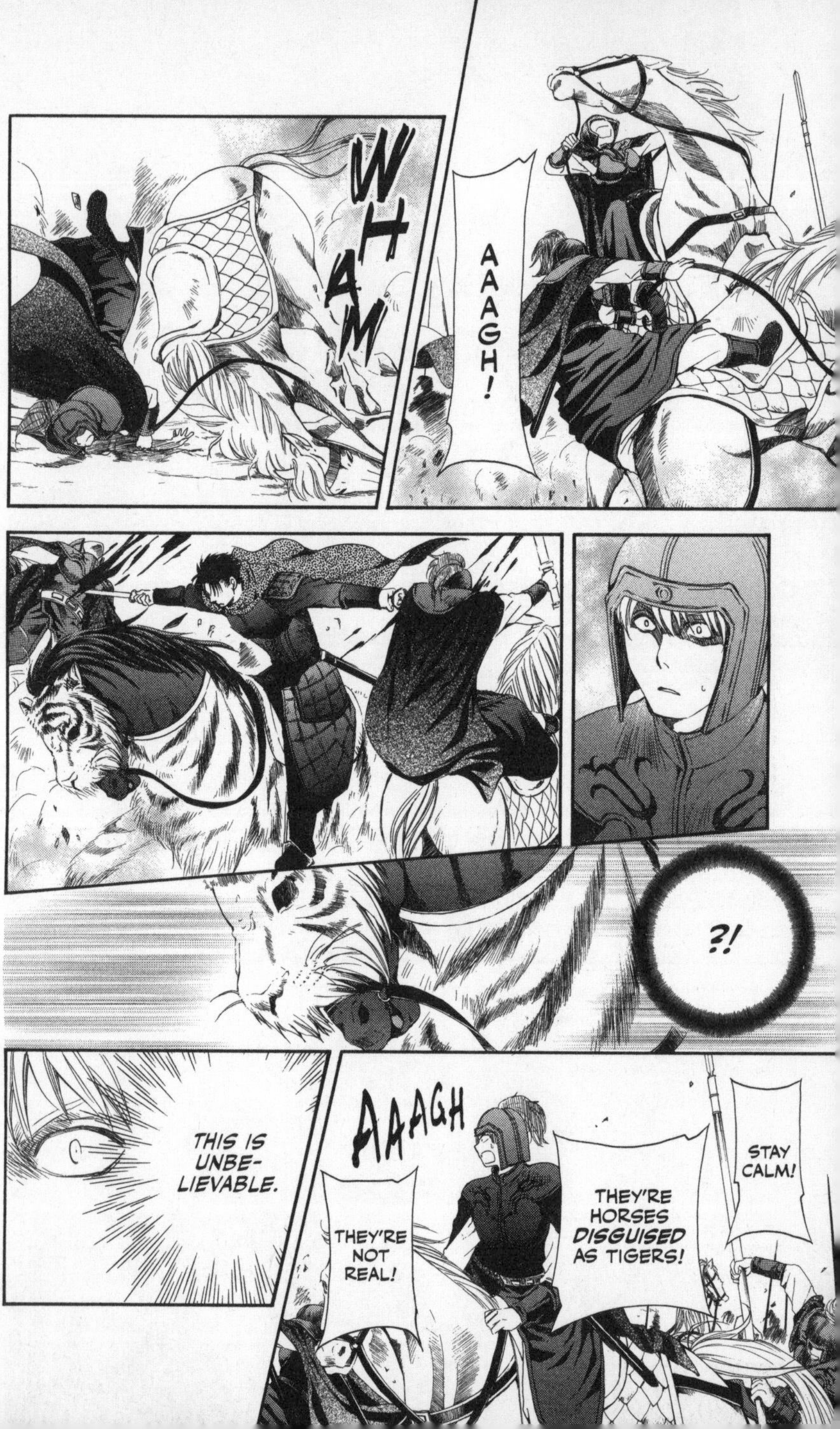
AAAGH!
WHAM
?!
STAY CALM!
AAAGH
THEY'RE HORSES DISGUISED AS TIGERS!
THEY'RE NOT REAL!
THIS IS UNBE-LIEVABLE.

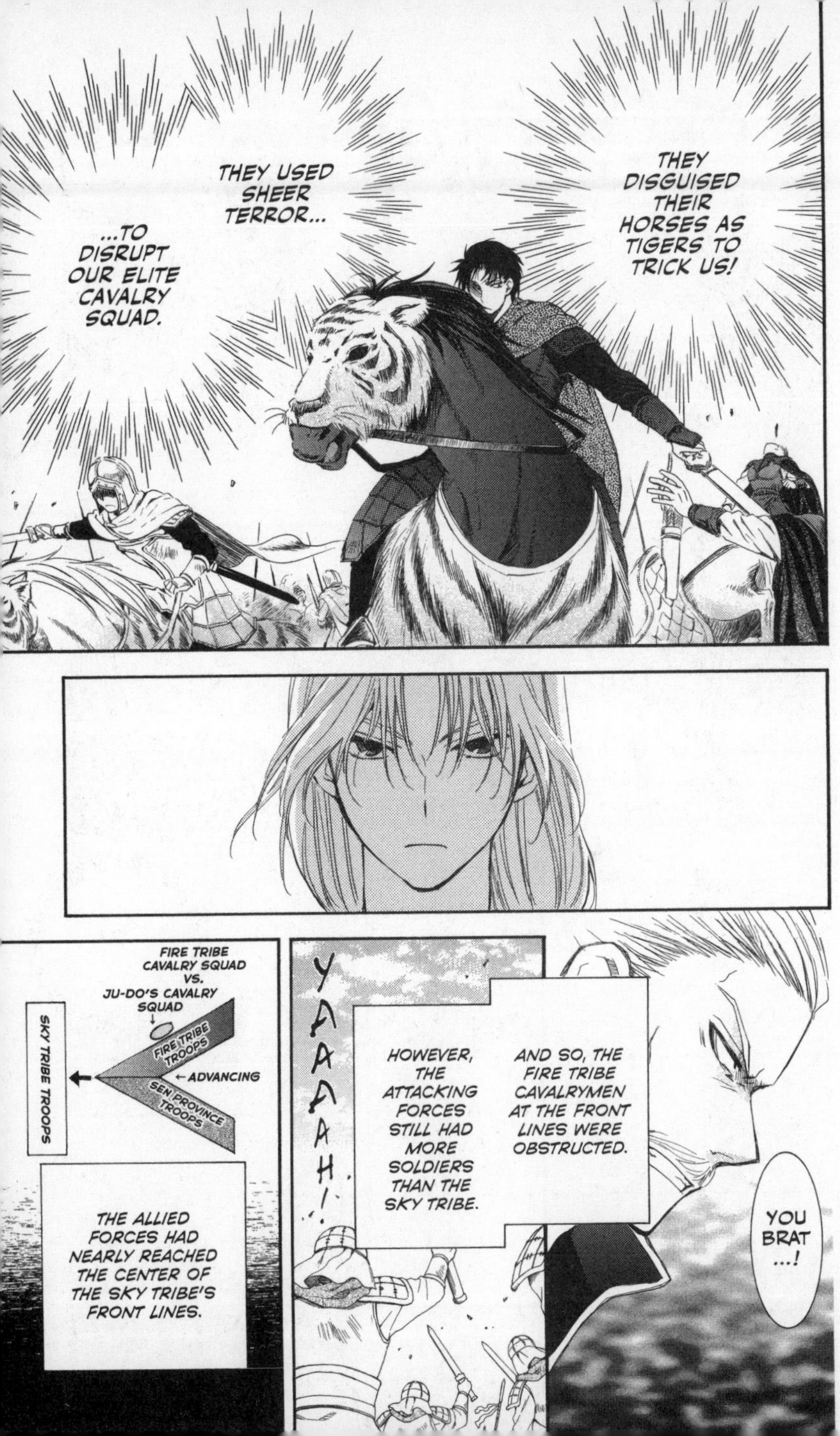

THEY DISGUISED THEIR HORSES AS TIGERS TO TRICK US!
THEY USED SHEER TERROR...
...TO DISRUPT OUR ELITE CAVALRY SQUAD.
AND SO, THE FIRE TRIBE CAVALRYMEN AT THE FRONT LINES WERE OBSTRUCTED.
HOWEVER, THE ATTACKING FORCES STILL HAD MORE SOLDIERS THAN THE SKY TRIBE.
YOU BRAT ...!
YAAAAH!
FIRE TRIBE CAVALRY SQUAD VS. JU-DO'S CAVALRY SQUAD
FIRE TRIBE TROOPS
← ADVANCING
SEN PROVINCE TROOPS
SKY TRIBE TROOPS
THE ALLIED FORCES HAD NEARLY REACHED THE CENTER OF THE SKY TRIBE'S FRONT LINES.

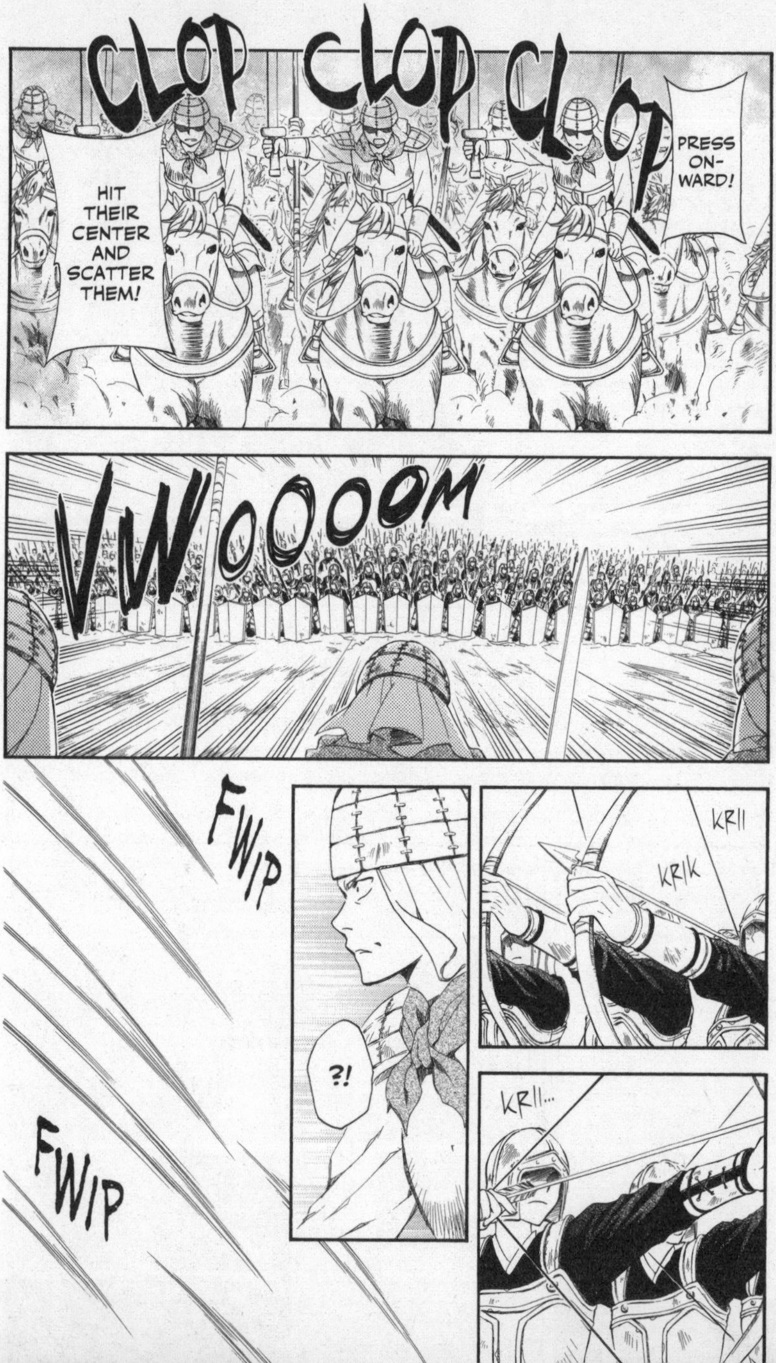
CLOP CLOP CLOP
PRESS ON-WARD!
HIT THEIR CENTER AND SCATTER THEM!
VWOOOOM
KRII
KRIK
KRII...
?!
FWIP
FWIP

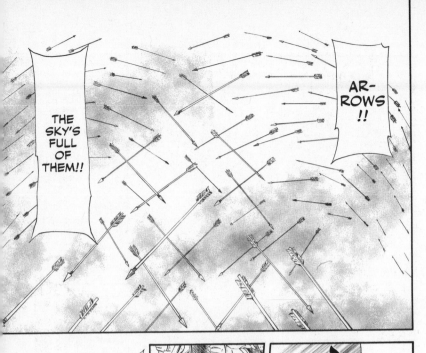

AR-
ROWS
!!

THE
SKY'S
FULL
OF
THEM!!

THEY'RE
FIRING
AT US
FROM
BOTH
SIDES!

FWSH

THOK THOK

AAAGH!

A
A
G
H
!

PULL
BACK
!

PULL
BACK!

FWSH

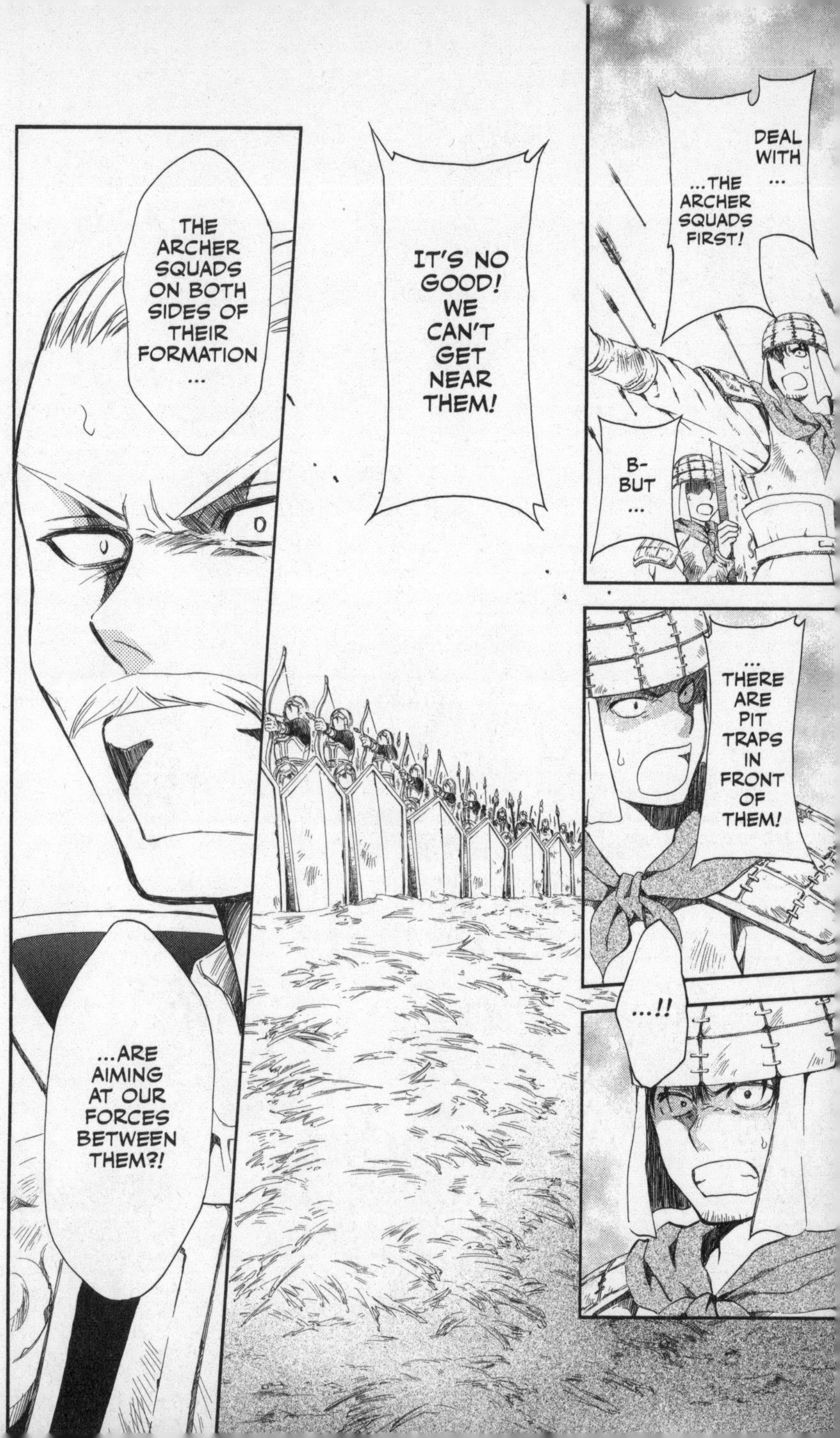
DEAL WITH...
...THE ARCHER SQUADS FIRST!
B-BUT...
IT'S NO GOOD! WE CAN'T GET NEAR THEM!
...THERE ARE PIT TRAPS IN FRONT OF THEM!
...!!
THE ARCHER SQUADS ON BOTH SIDES OF THEIR FORMATION...
...ARE AIMING AT OUR FORCES BETWEEN THEM?!

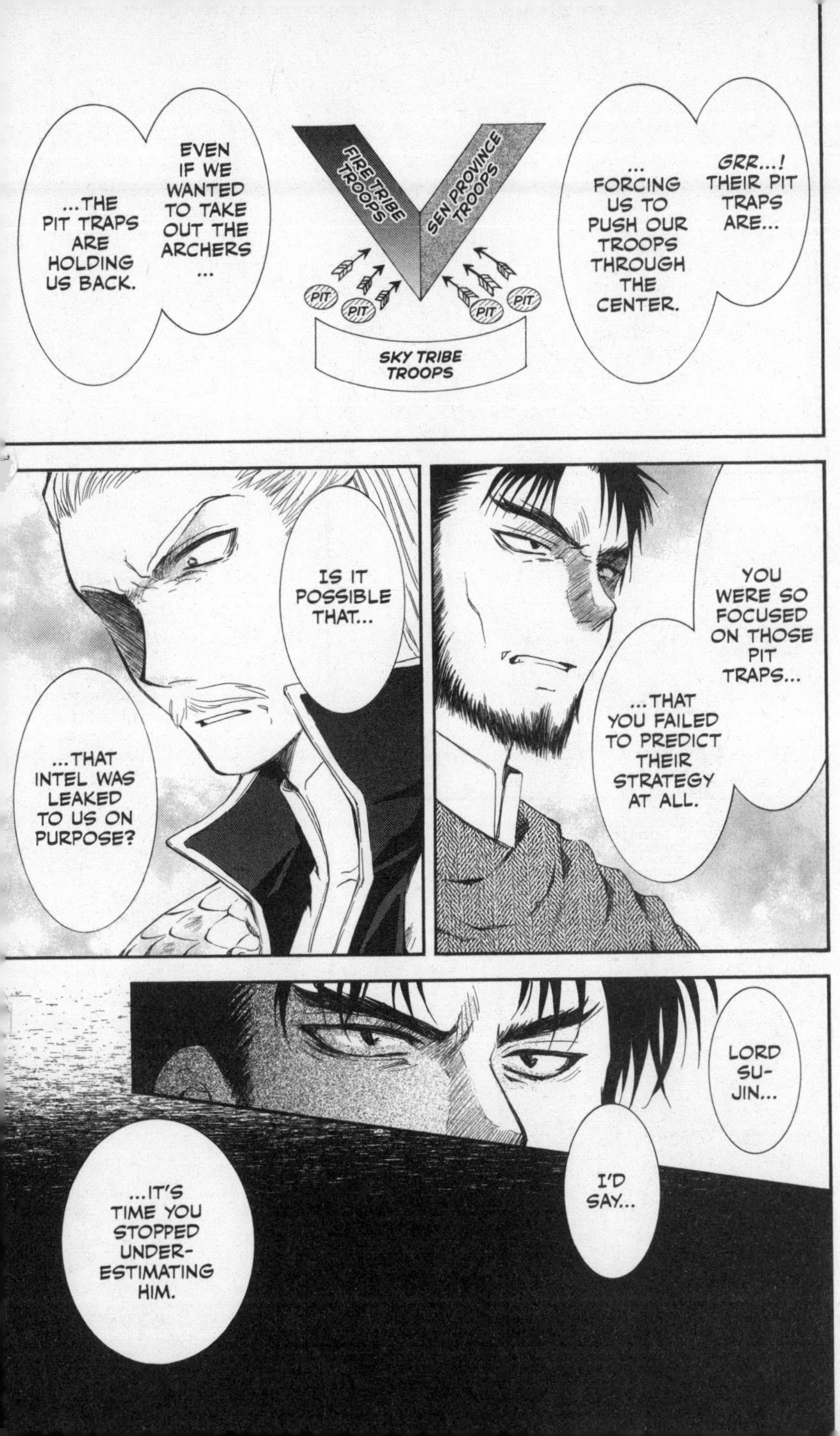
GRR...! THEIR PIT TRAPS ARE...
...FORCING US TO PUSH OUR TROOPS THROUGH THE CENTER.
SEN PROVINCE TROOPS
FIRE TRIBE TROOPS
PIT
PIT
PIT
PIT
SKY TRIBE TROOPS
EVEN IF WE WANTED TO TAKE OUT THE ARCHERS...
...THE PIT TRAPS ARE HOLDING US BACK.
YOU WERE SO FOCUSED ON THOSE PIT TRAPS...
...THAT YOU FAILED TO PREDICT THEIR STRATEGY AT ALL.
IS IT POSSIBLE THAT...
...THAT INTEL WAS LEAKED TO US ON PURPOSE?
LORD SU-JIN...
I'D SAY...
...IT'S TIME YOU STOPPED UNDER-ESTIMATING HIM.

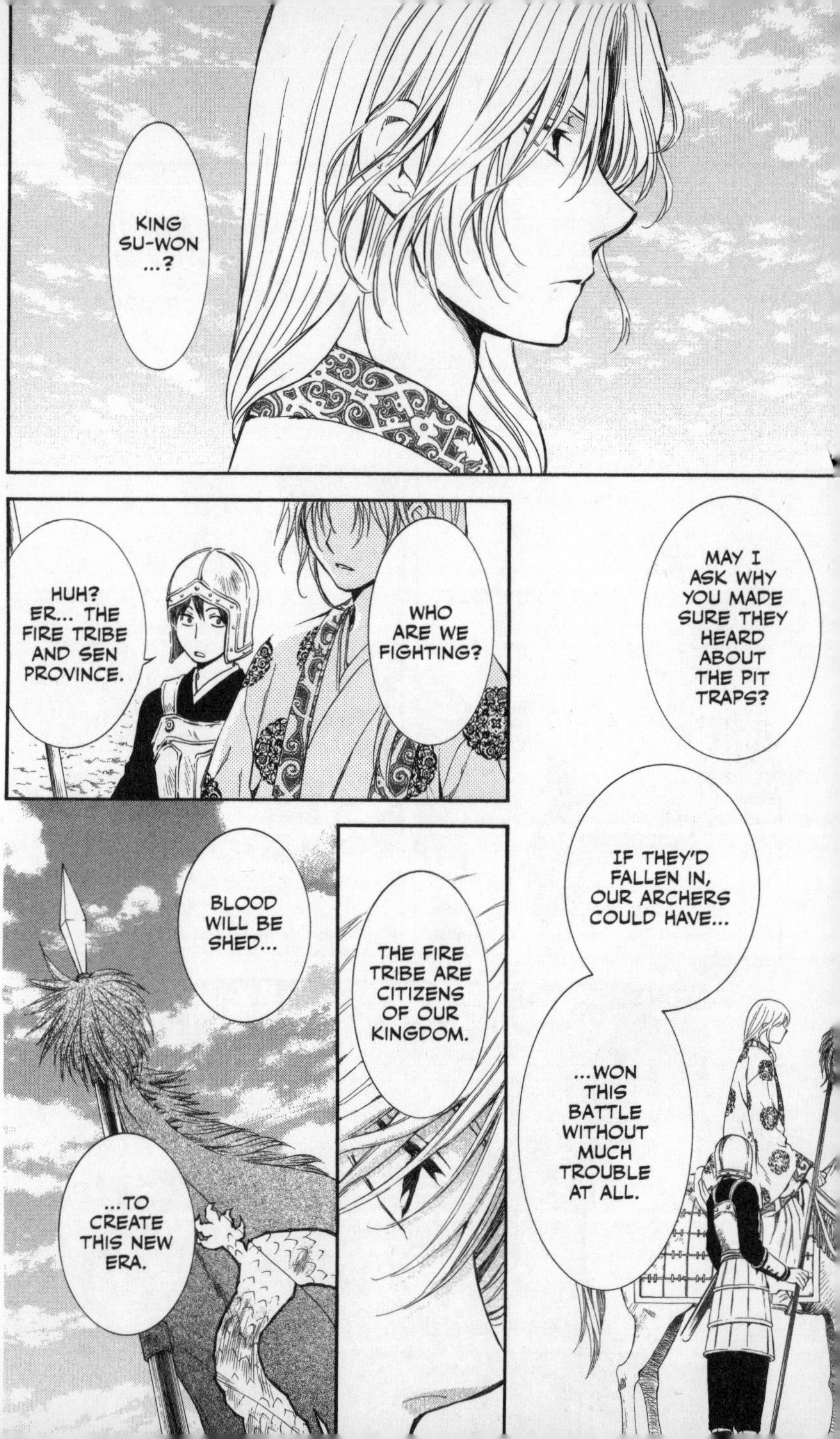
KING SU-WON ...?
WHO ARE WE FIGHTING?
HUH? ER... THE FIRE TRIBE AND SEN PROVINCE.
MAY I ASK WHY YOU MADE SURE THEY HEARD ABOUT THE PIT TRAPS?
IF THEY'D FALLEN IN, OUR ARCHERS COULD HAVE...
...WON THIS BATTLE WITHOUT MUCH TROUBLE AT ALL.
THE FIRE TRIBE ARE CITIZENS OF OUR KINGDOM.
BLOOD WILL BE SHED...
...TO CREATE THIS NEW ERA.

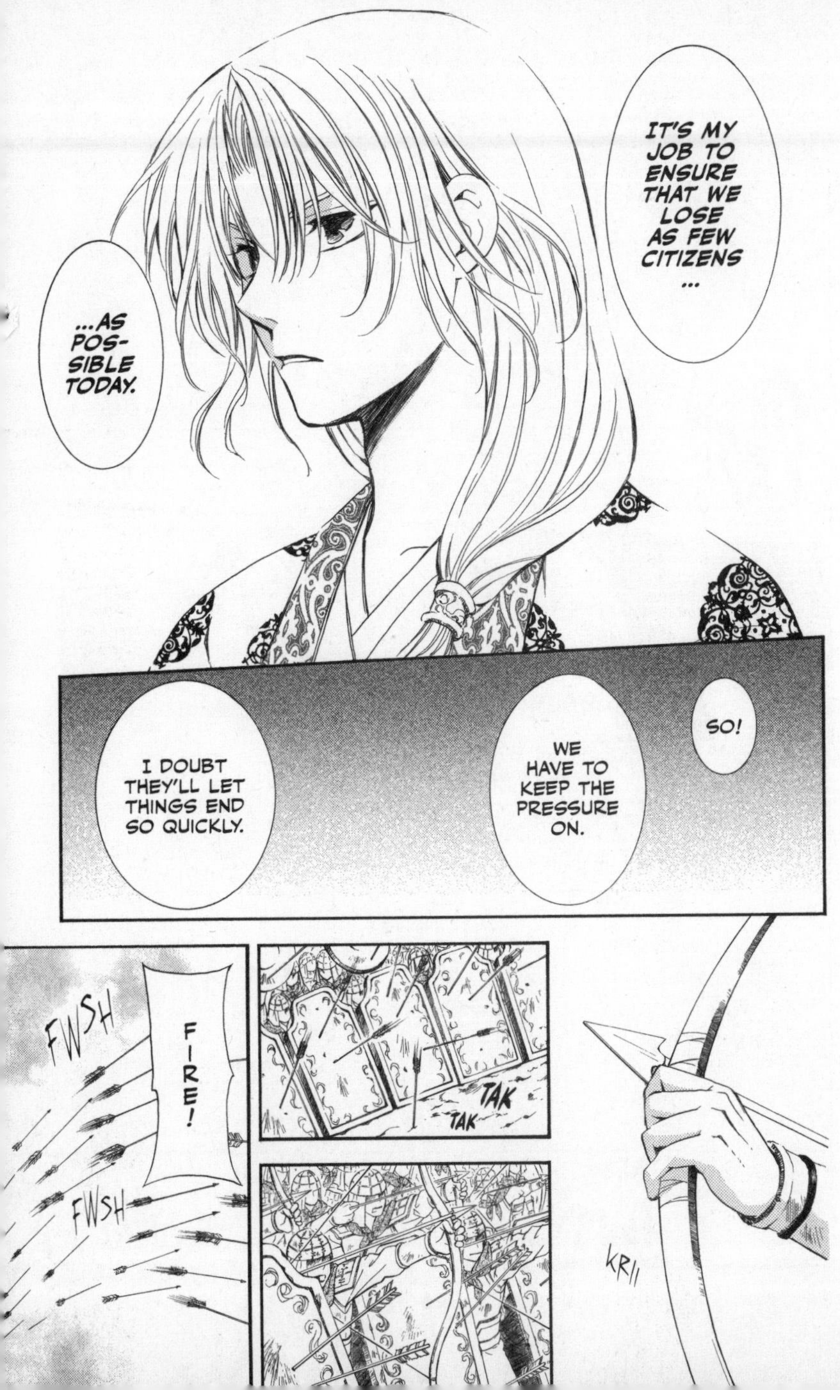
IT'S MY JOB TO ENSURE THAT WE LOSE AS FEW CITIZENS ...
...AS POS-SIBLE TODAY.
SO!
WE HAVE TO KEEP THE PRESSURE ON.
I DOUBT THEY'LL LET THINGS END SO QUICKLY.
KRII
TAK
TAK
FIRE!
FWSH
FWSH

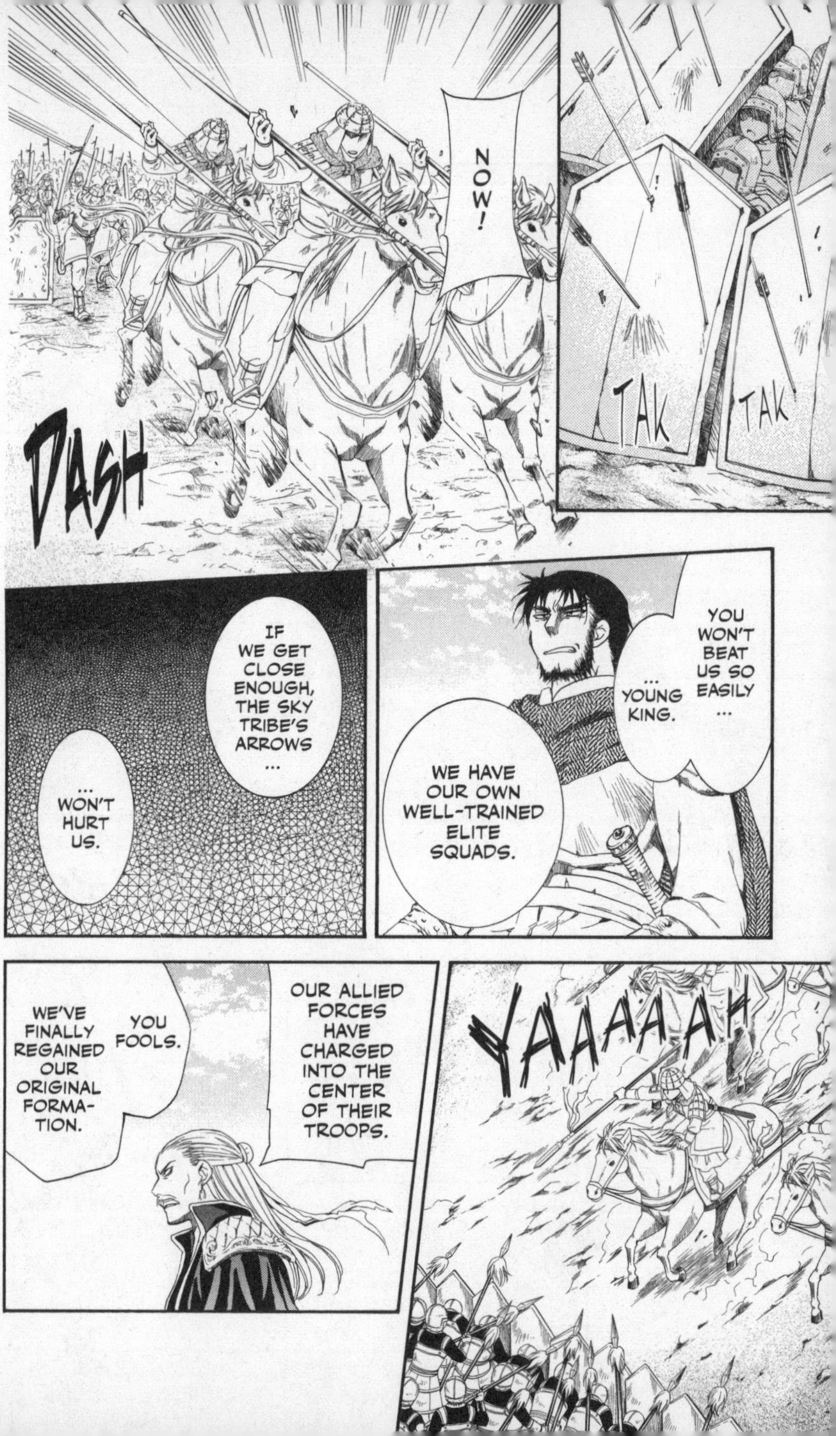
TAK TAK
NOW!
DASH
YOU WON'T BEAT US SO EASILY ...
... YOUNG KING.
WE HAVE OUR OWN WELL-TRAINED ELITE SQUADS.
IF WE GET CLOSE ENOUGH, THE SKY TRIBE'S ARROWS ...
... WON'T HURT US.
YAAAAAH
OUR ALLIED FORCES HAVE CHARGED INTO THE CENTER OF THEIR TROOPS.
YOU FOOLS.
WE'VE FINALLY REGAINED OUR ORIGINAL FORMA-TION.

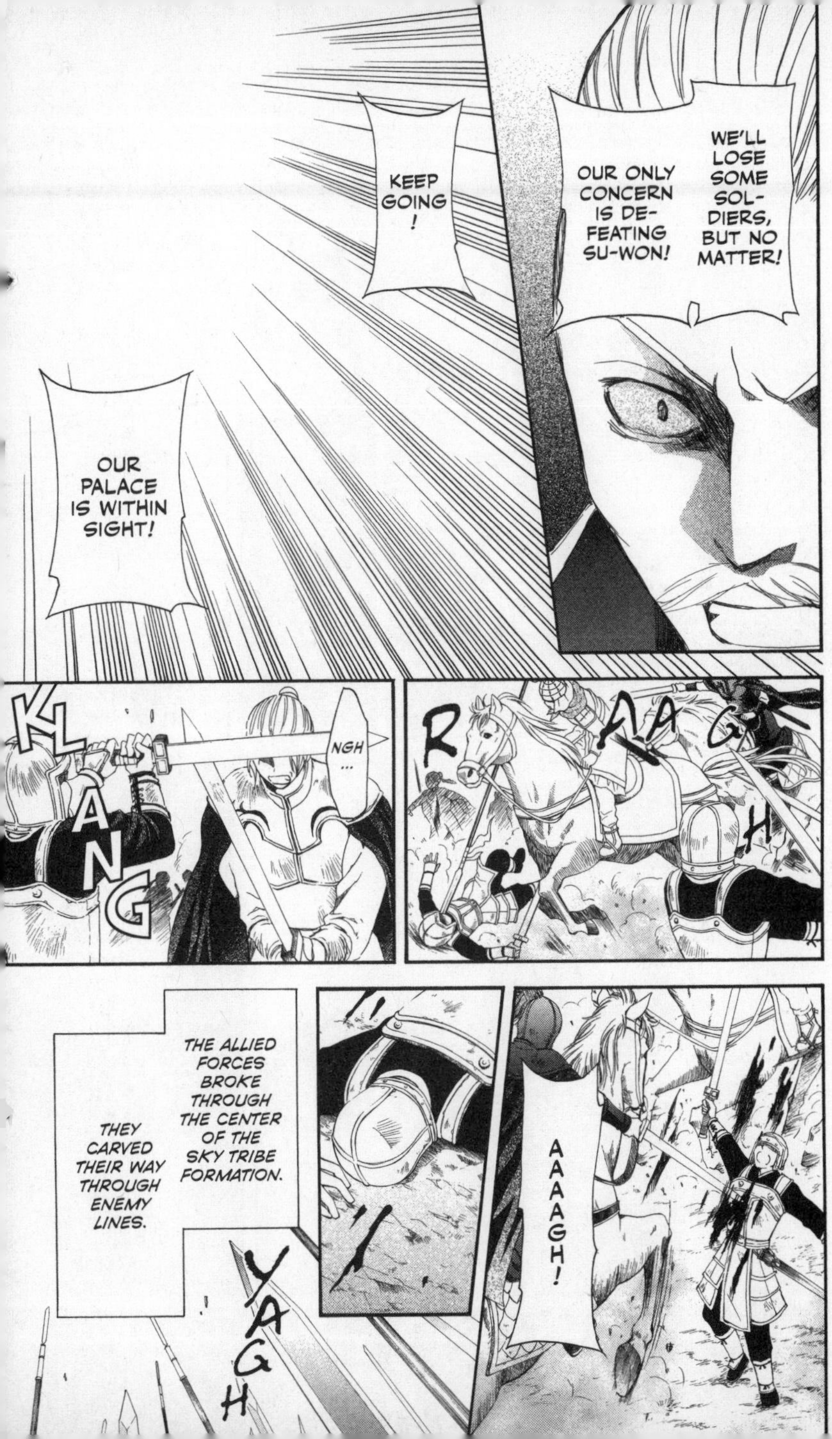
WE'LL LOSE SOME SOL-DIERS, BUT NO MATTER!
OUR ONLY CONCERN IS DE-FEATING SU-WON!
KEEP GOING!
OUR PALACE IS WITHIN SIGHT!
RAAGH
KLANG
NGH...
AAAAGH!
THE ALLIED FORCES BROKE THROUGH THE CENTER OF THE SKY TRIBE FORMATION.
THEY CARVED THEIR WAY THROUGH ENEMY LINES.
YAGH

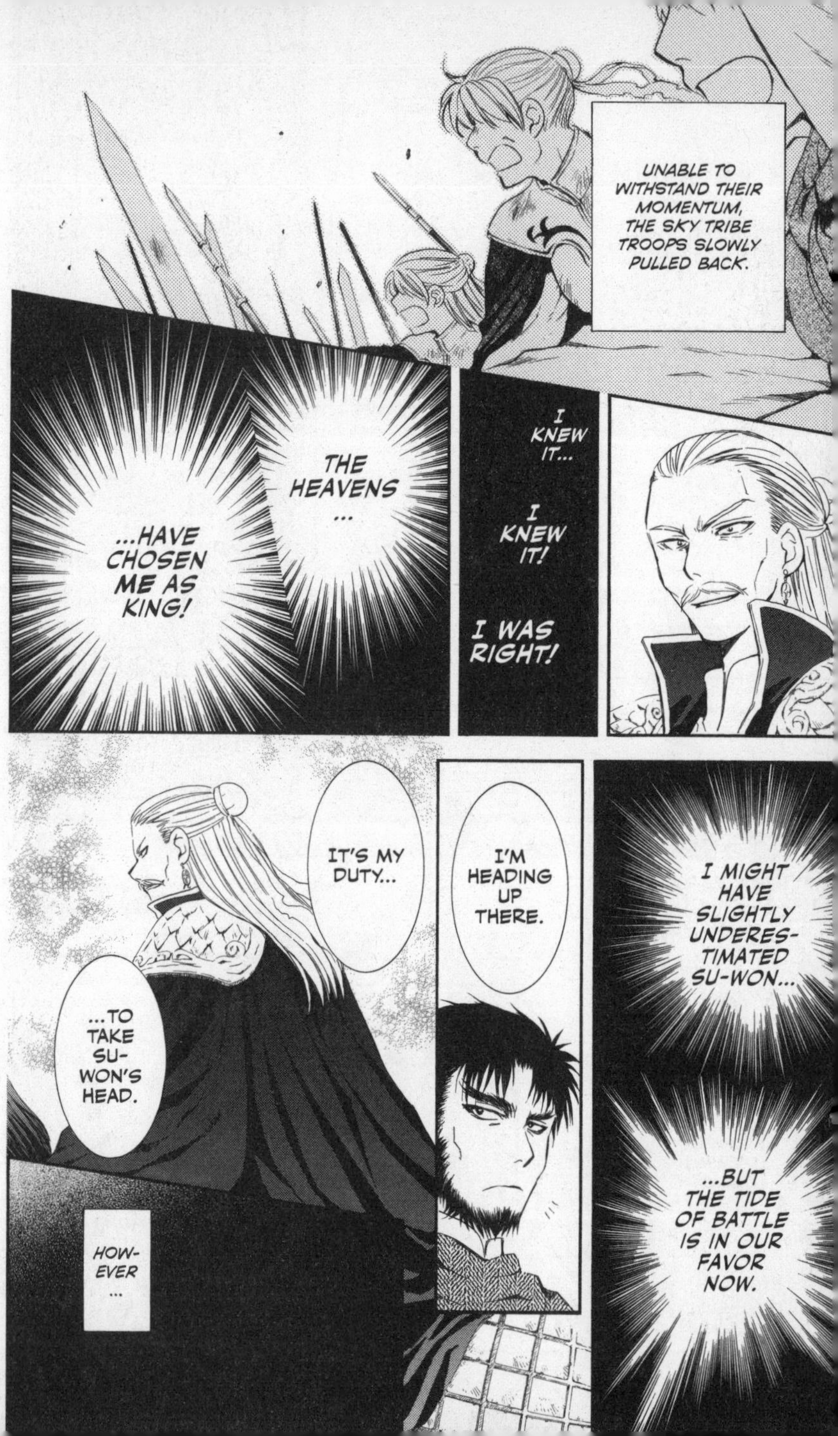
UNABLE TO WITHSTAND THEIR MOMENTUM, THE SKY TRIBE TROOPS SLOWLY PULLED BACK.
I KNEW IT...
I KNEW IT!
I WAS RIGHT!
THE HEAVENS...
...HAVE CHOSEN ME AS KING!
I MIGHT HAVE SLIGHTLY UNDERES-TIMATED SU-WON...
...BUT THE TIDE OF BATTLE IS IN OUR FAVOR NOW.
I'M HEADING UP THERE.
IT'S MY DUTY...
...TO TAKE SU-WON'S HEAD.
HOW-EVER...

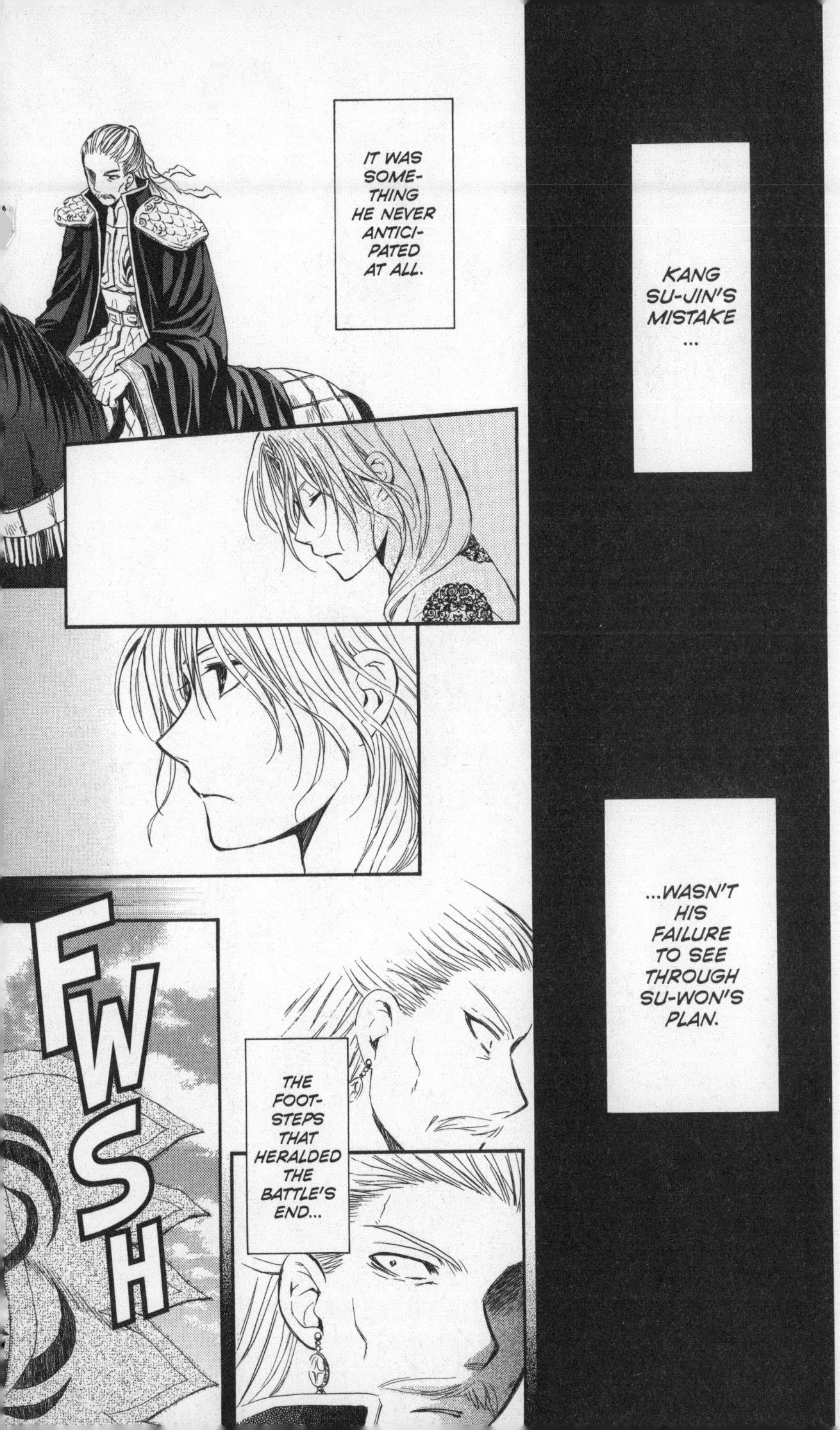
KANG SU-JIN'S MISTAKE ...
...WASN'T HIS FAILURE TO SEE THROUGH SU-WON'S PLAN.
IT WAS SOME-THING HE NEVER ANTICI-PATED AT ALL.
THE FOOT-STEPS THAT HERALDED THE BATTLE'S END...
FWSH

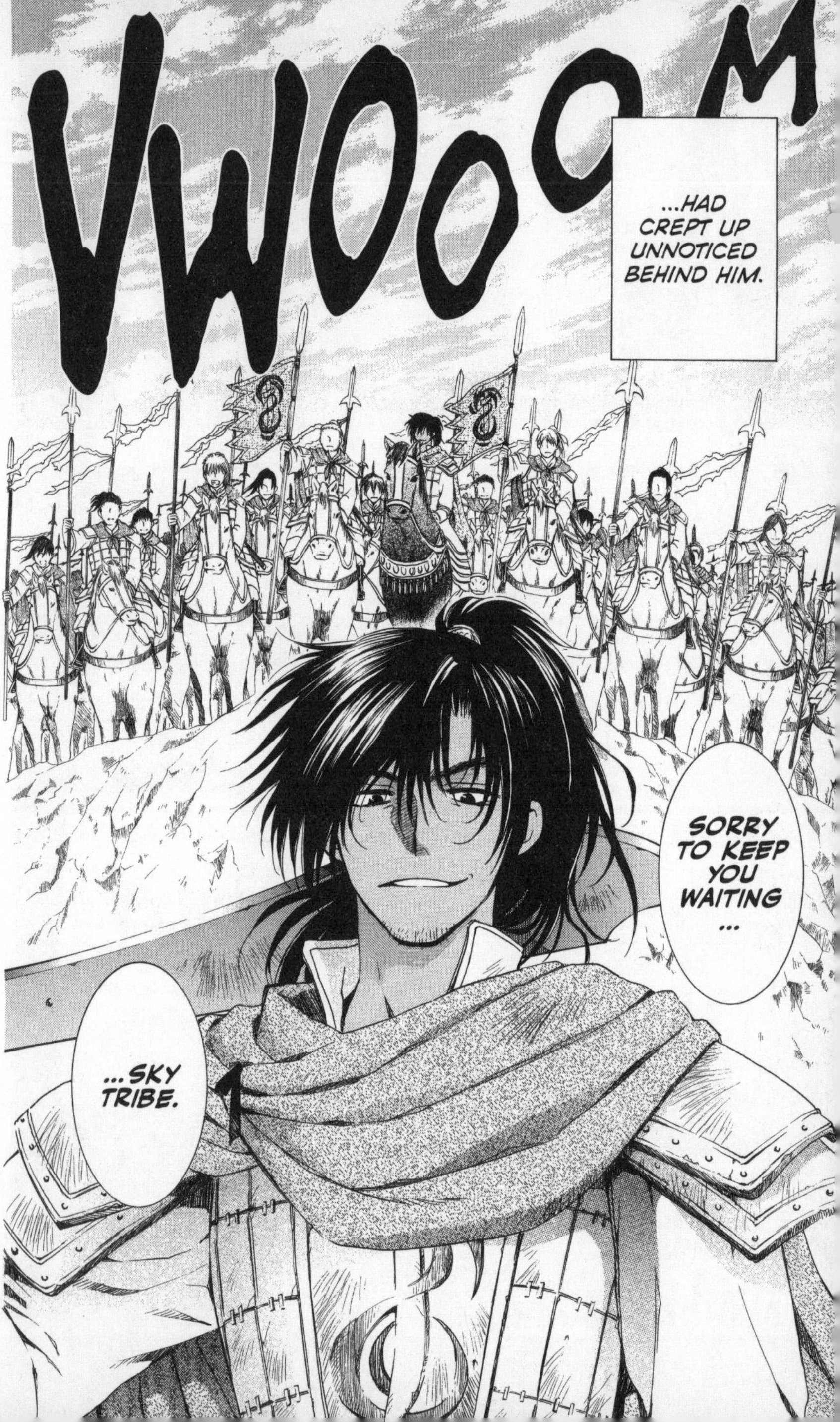
VWOOOM
...HAD CREPT UP UNNOTICED BEHIND HIM.
SORRY TO KEEP YOU WAITING ...
...SKY TRIBE.

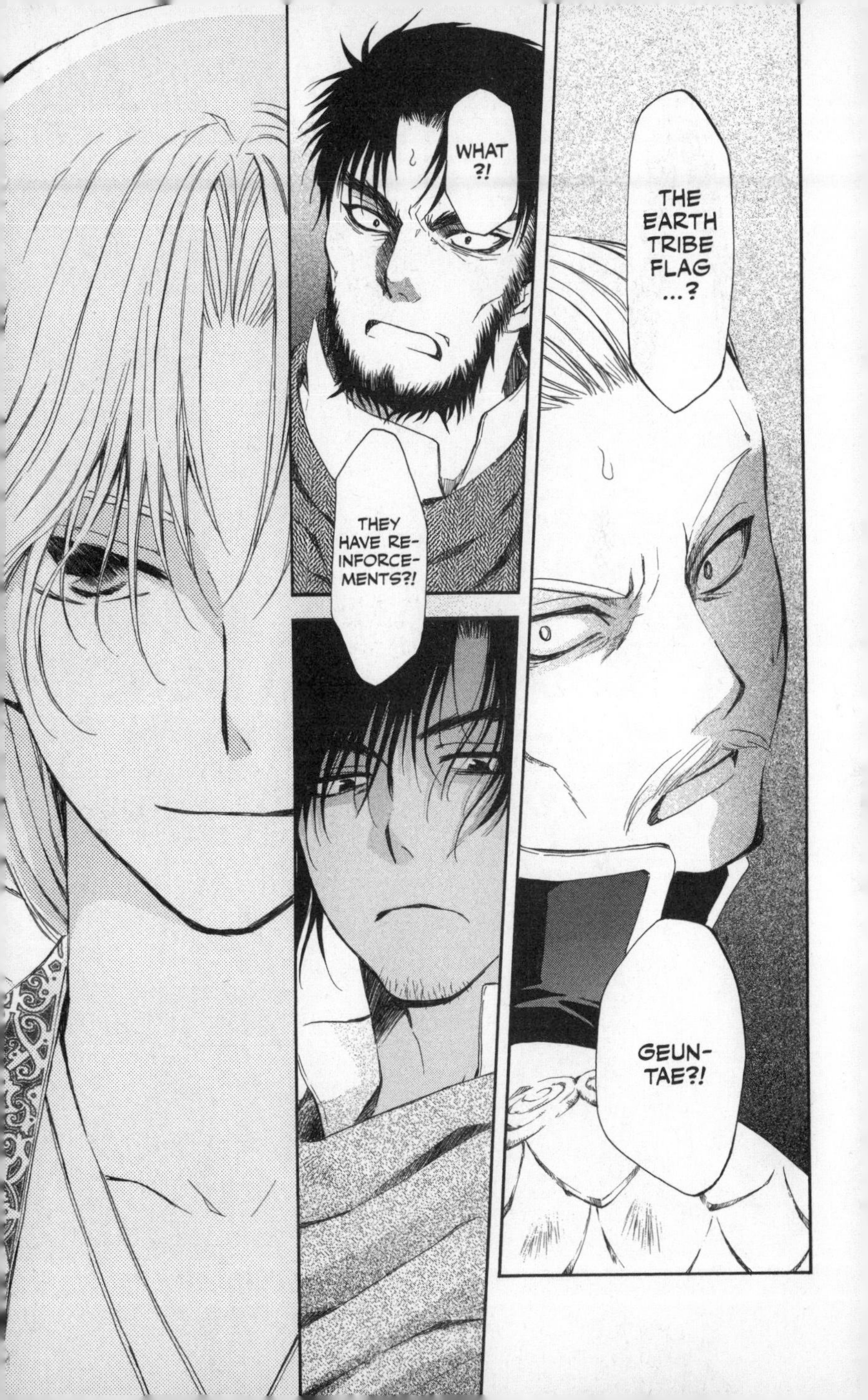
THE EARTH TRIBE FLAG ...?
GEUN-TAE?!
WHAT ?!
THEY HAVE RE-INFORCEMENTS?!

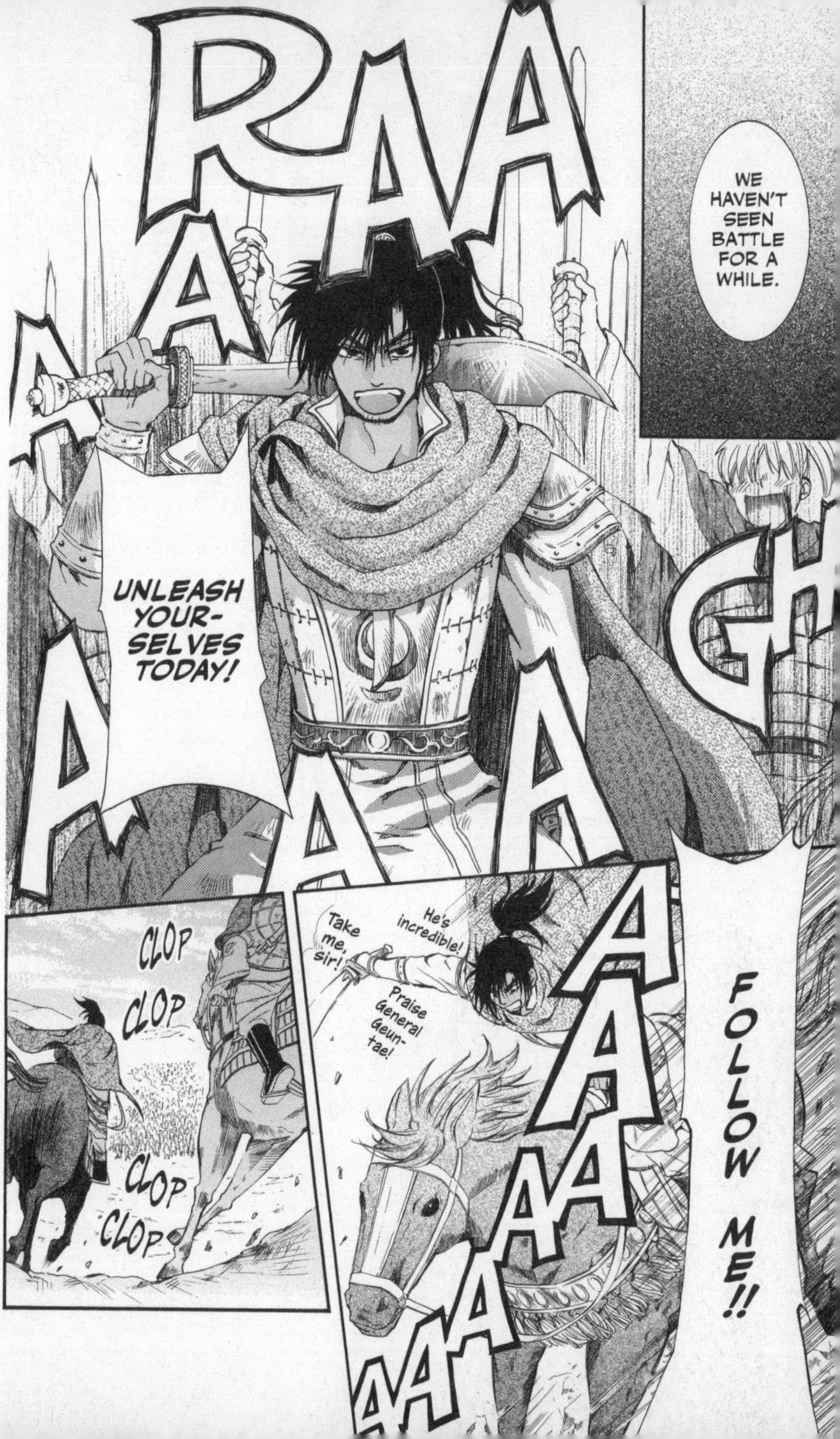
WE HAVEN'T SEEN BATTLE FOR A WHILE.
GH
RAAAAAA
UNLEASH YOUR-SELVES TODAY!
FOLLOW ME!!
AAAAAAA
He's incredible!
Take me, sir!
Praise General Geun-tae!
CLOP
CLOP
CLOP
CLOP

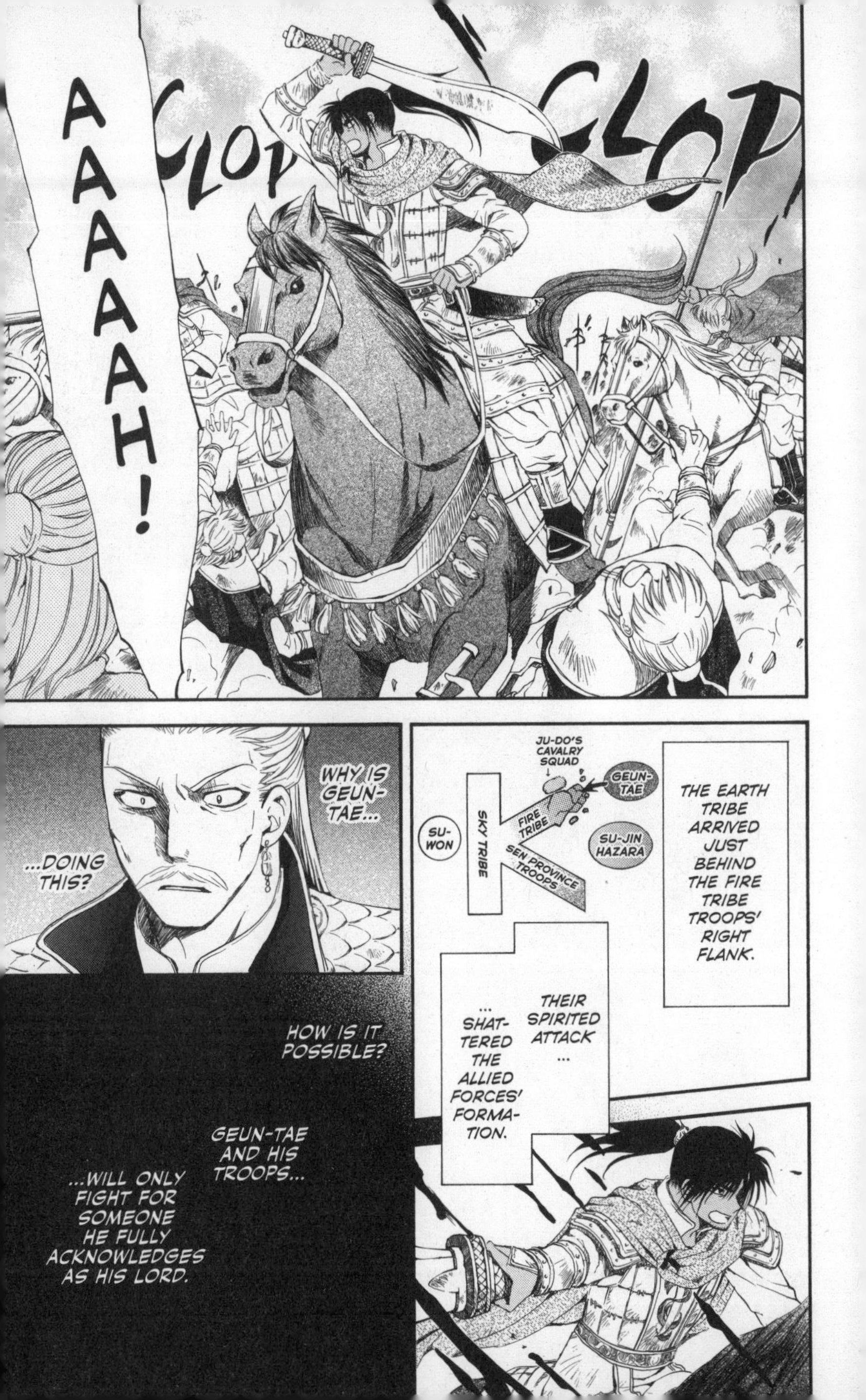
CLOP
CLOP
AAAAAH!
THE EARTH TRIBE ARRIVED JUST BEHIND THE FIRE TRIBE TROOPS' RIGHT FLANK.
JU-DO'S CAVALRY SQUAD
GEUN-TAE
FIRE TRIBE
SU-JIN HAZARA
SKY TRIBE
SU-WON
SEN PROVINCE TROOPS
WHY IS GEUN-TAE...
...DOING THIS?
THEIR SPIRITED ATTACK...
...SHATTERED THE ALLIED FORCES' FORMATION.
HOW IS IT POSSIBLE?
GEUN-TAE AND HIS TROOPS...
...WILL ONLY FIGHT FOR SOMEONE HE FULLY ACKNOWLEDGES AS HIS LORD.

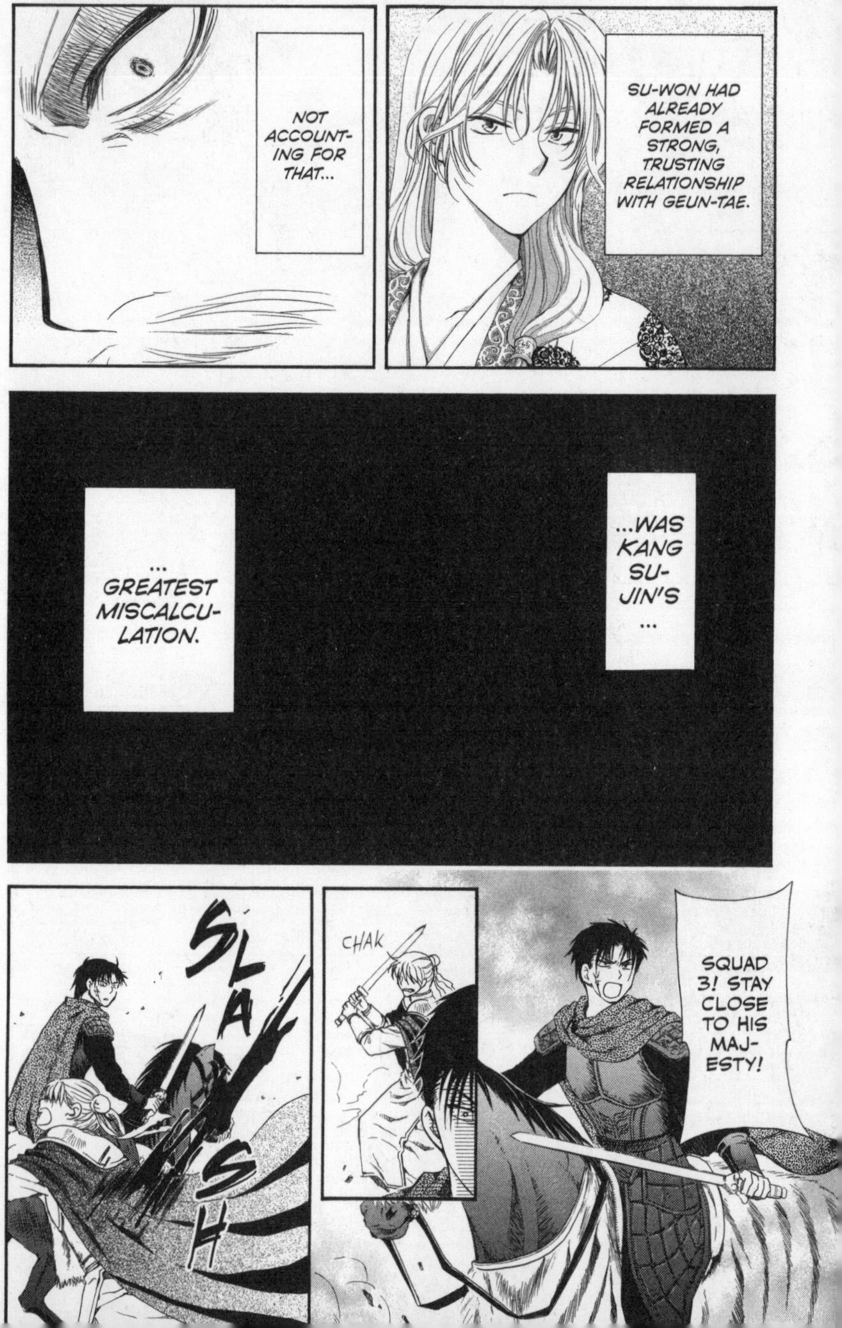
SU-WON HAD ALREADY FORMED A STRONG, TRUSTING RELATIONSHIP WITH GEUN-TAE.
NOT ACCOUNT-ING FOR THAT...
...WAS KANG SU-JIN'S ...
... GREATEST MISCALCU-LATION.
SQUAD 3! STAY CLOSE TO HIS MAJ-ESTY!
CHAK
SLASH

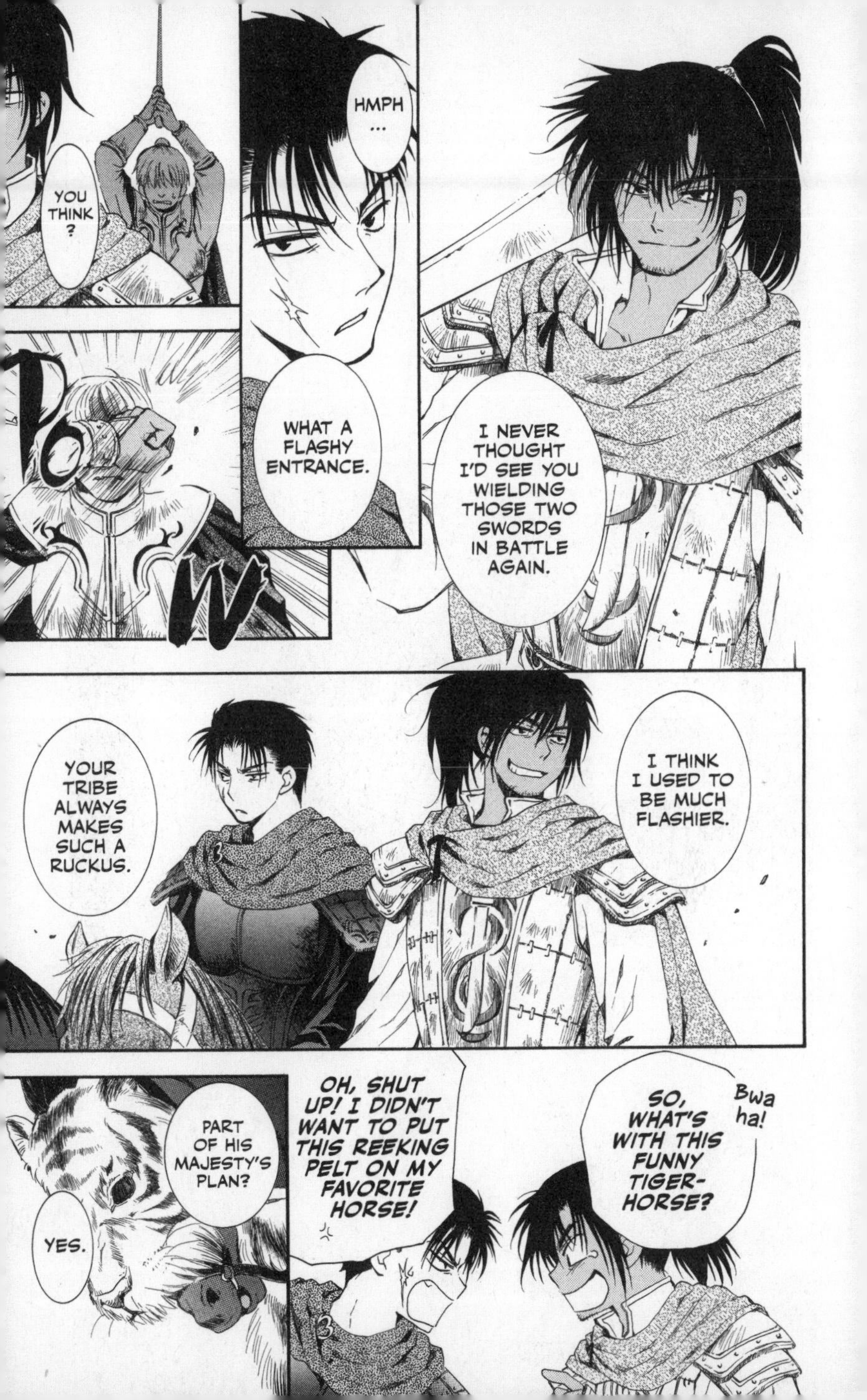
I NEVER THOUGHT I'D SEE YOU WIELDING THOSE TWO SWORDS IN BATTLE AGAIN.
HMPH ...
WHAT A FLASHY ENTRANCE.
YOU THINK?
POW
I THINK I USED TO BE MUCH FLASHIER.
YOUR TRIBE ALWAYS MAKES SUCH A RUCKUS.
Bwa ha!
SO, WHAT'S WITH THIS FUNNY TIGER-HORSE?
OH, SHUT UP! I DIDN'T WANT TO PUT THIS REEKING PELT ON MY FAVORITE HORSE!
PART OF HIS MAJESTY'S PLAN?
YES.

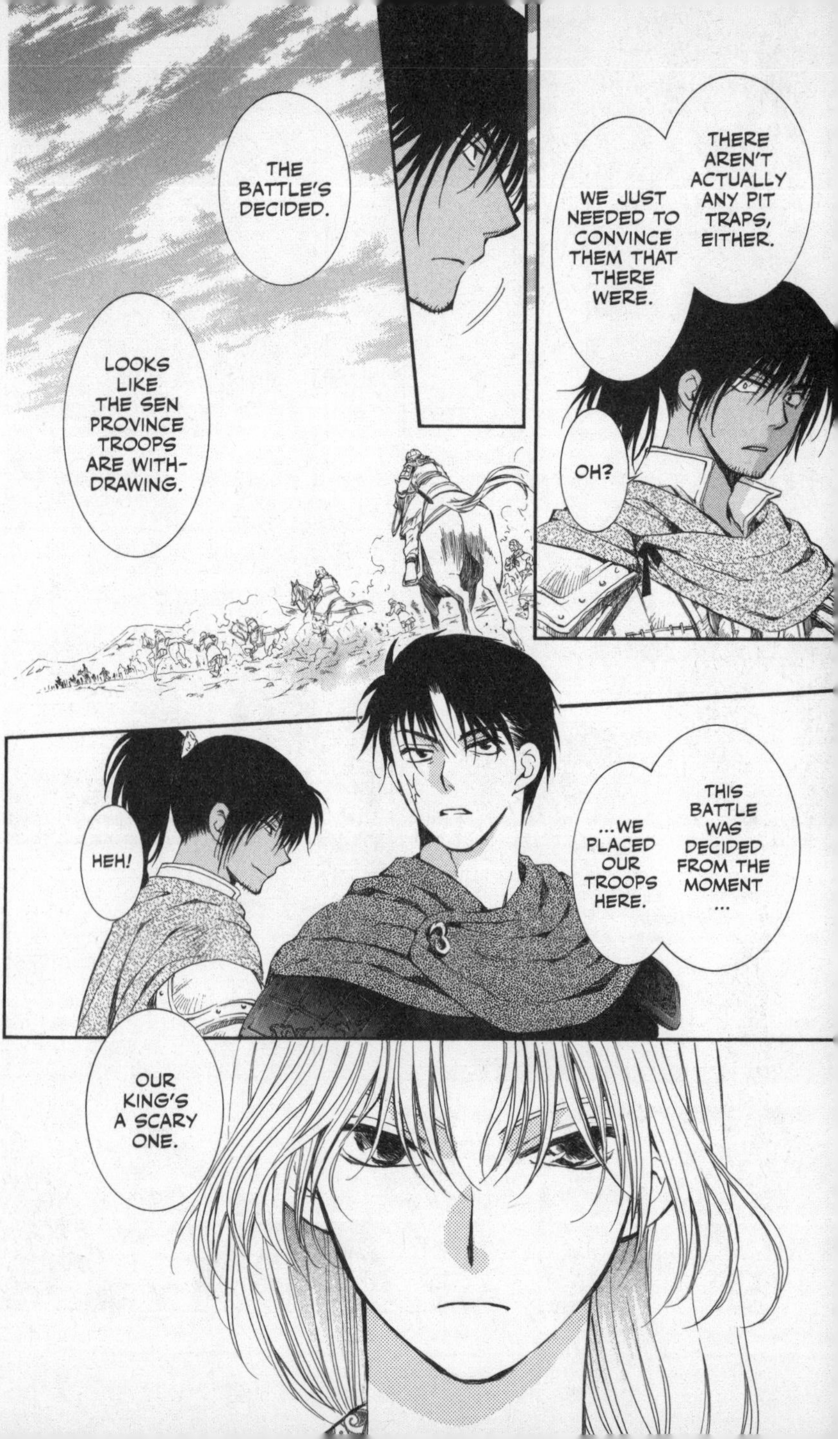
THERE AREN'T ACTUALLY ANY PIT TRAPS, EITHER.
WE JUST NEEDED TO CONVINCE THEM THAT THERE WERE.
OH?
THE BATTLE'S DECIDED.
LOOKS LIKE THE SEN PROVINCE TROOPS ARE WITH-DRAWING.
THIS BATTLE WAS DECIDED FROM THE MOMENT ...
...WE PLACED OUR TROOPS HERE.
HEH!
OUR KING'S A SCARY ONE.

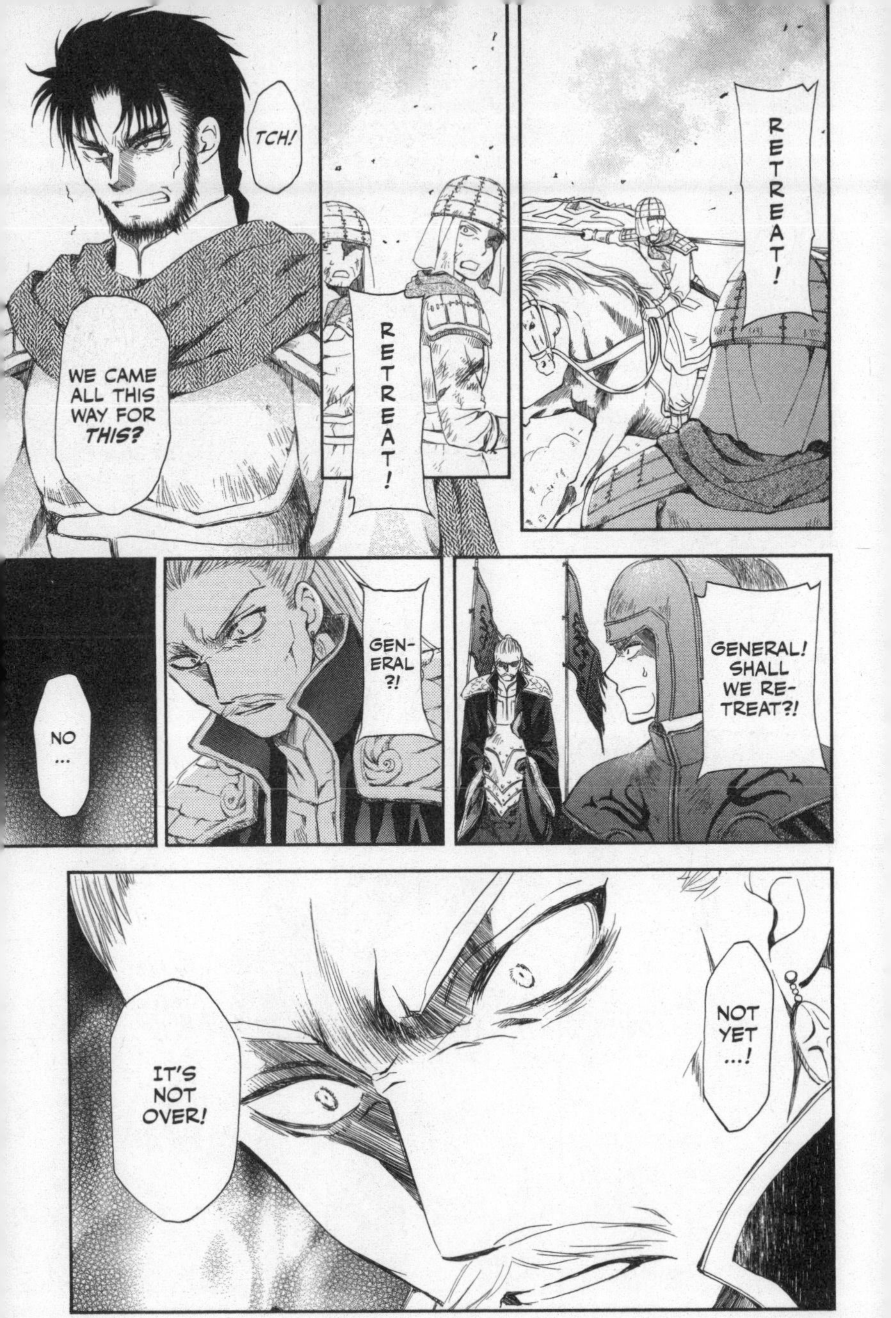
RETREAT!
RETREAT!
TCH!
WE CAME ALL THIS WAY FOR *THIS?*
GENERAL! SHALL WE RE-TREAT?!
GEN-ERAL ?!
NO ...
NOT YET ...!
IT'S NOT OVER!

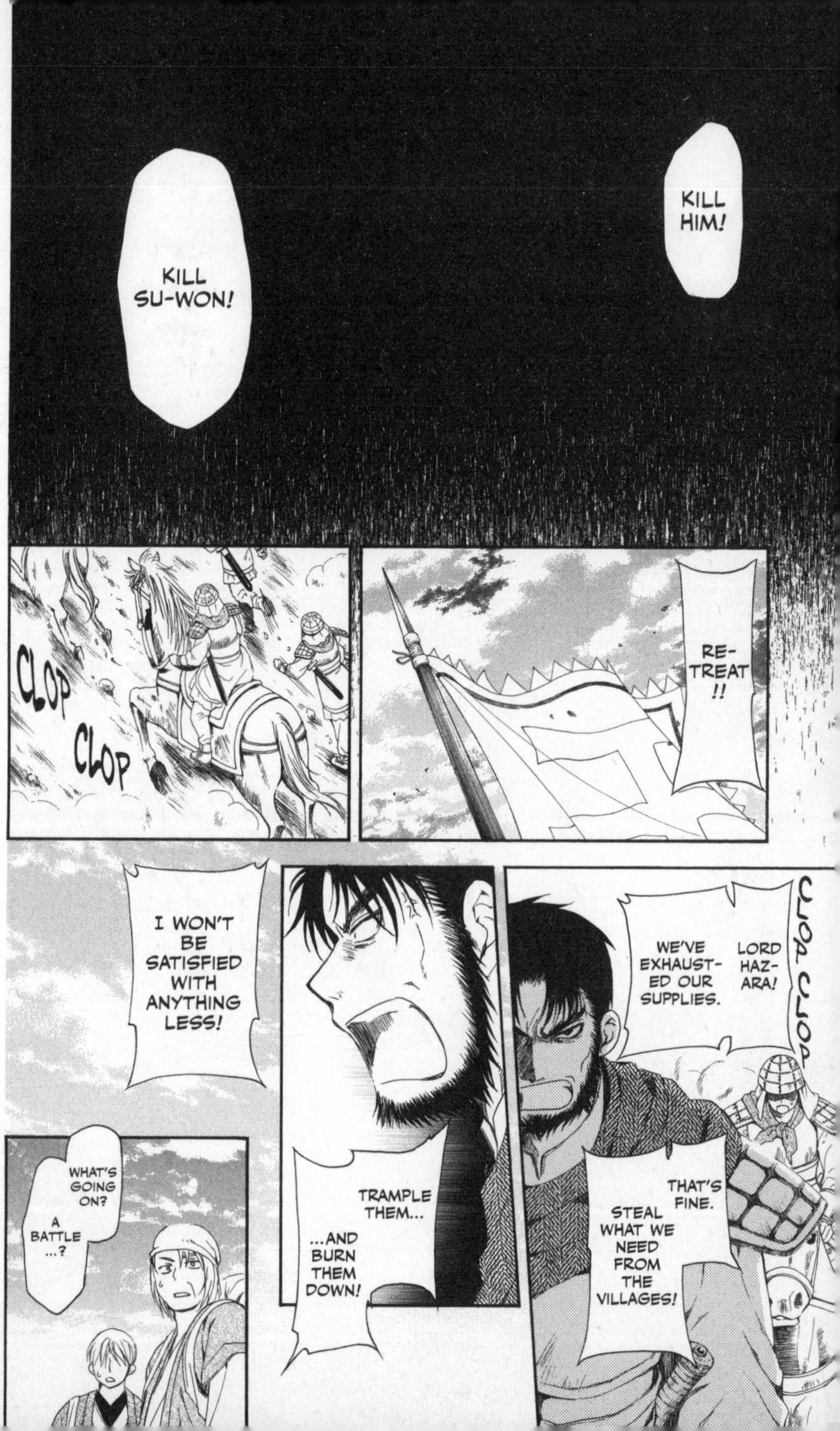
KILL HIM!
KILL SU-WON!
RE-TREAT!!
CLOP
CLOP
LORD HAZ-ARA!
WE'VE EXHAUST-ED OUR SUPPLIES.
CLOP CLOP
THAT'S FINE.
STEAL WHAT WE NEED FROM THE VILLAGES!
TRAMPLE THEM...
...AND BURN THEM DOWN!
I WON'T BE SATISFIED WITH ANYTHING LESS!
WHAT'S GOING ON?
A BATTLE ...?

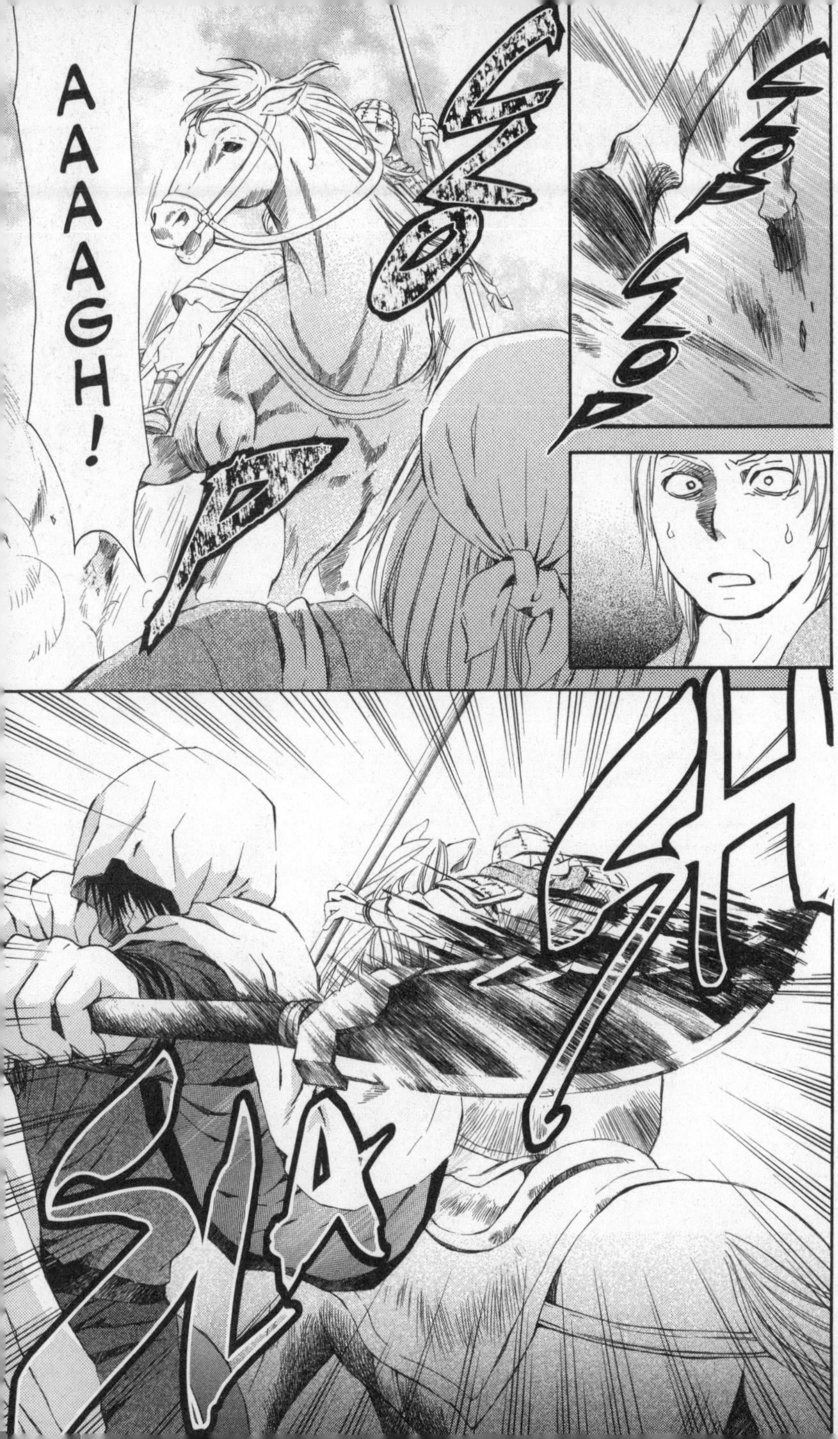
CLOP
CLOP
CLOP
AAAAGH!
SHA

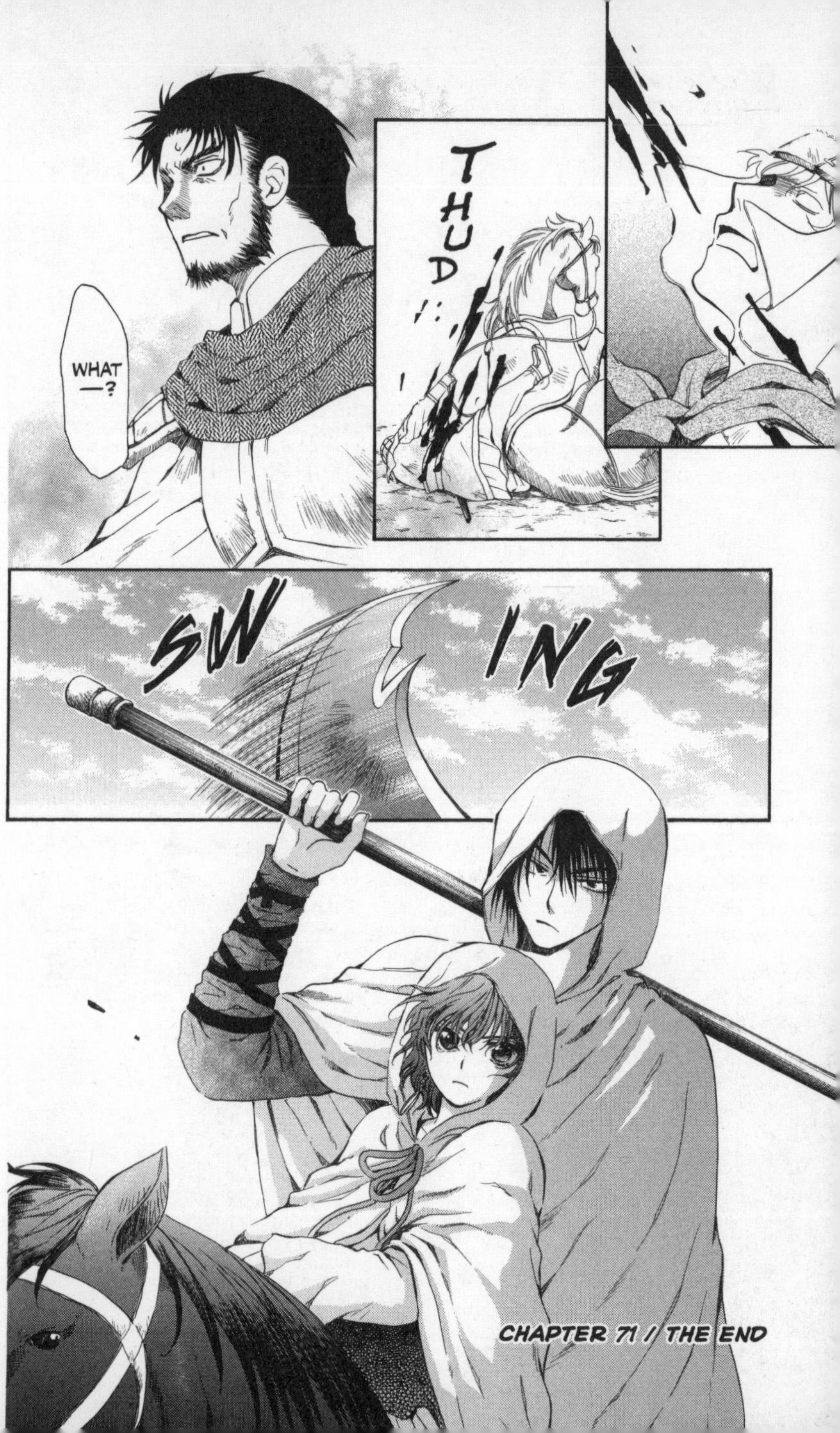
THUD!!
WHAT—?
SWING
CHAPTER 71 / THE END

CHAPTER 72: THE ONE WHO LEADS

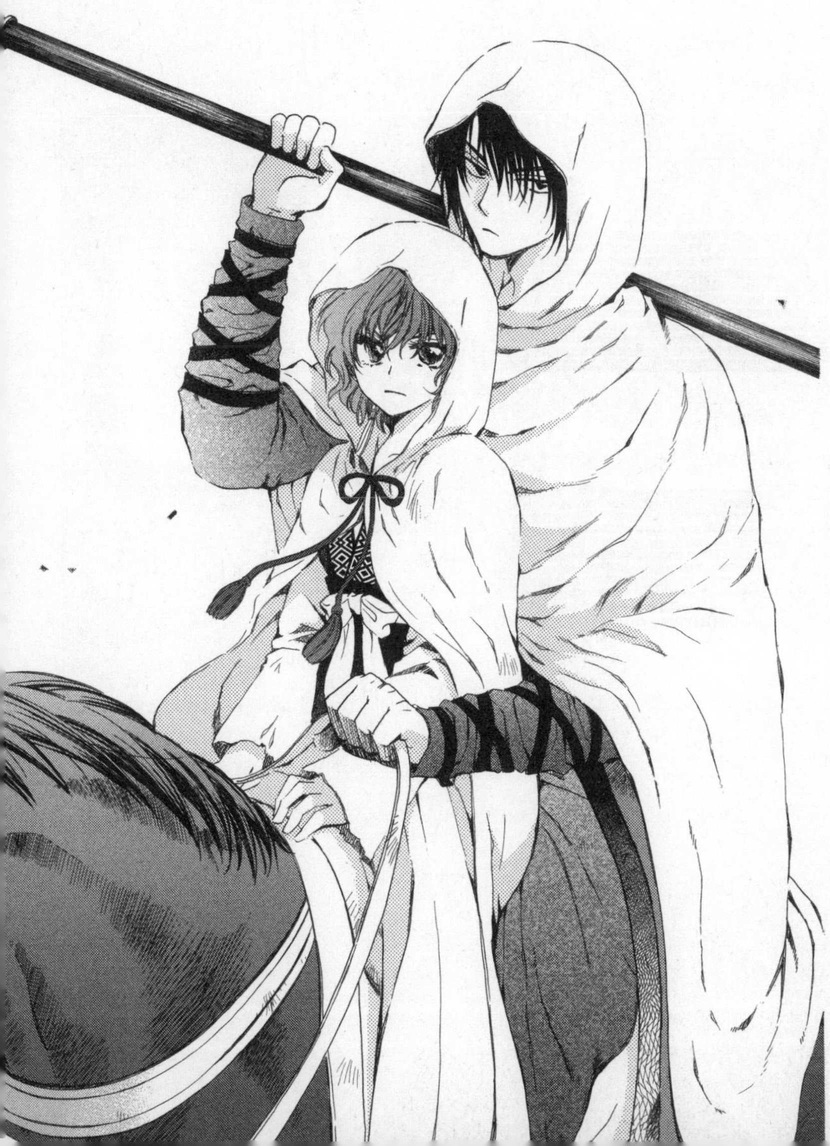

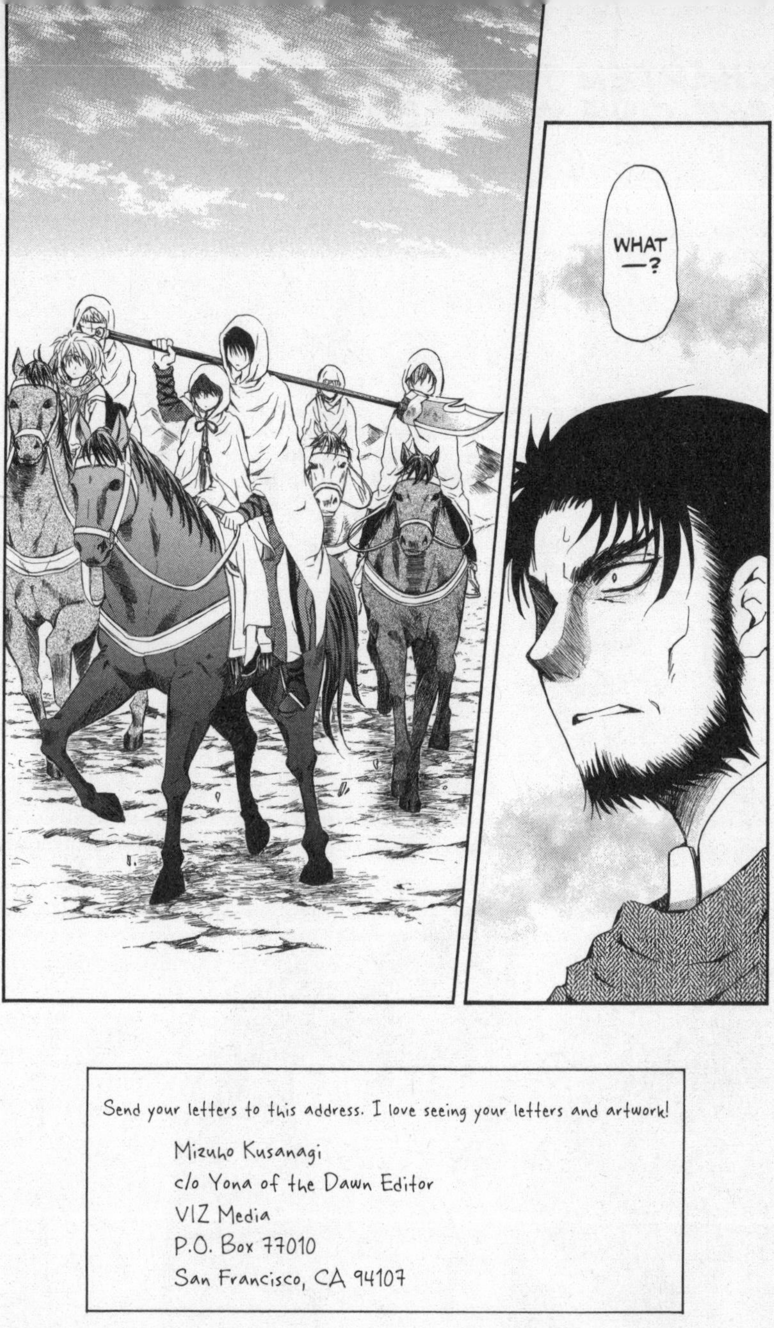
WHAT—?

Send your letters to this address. I love seeing your letters and artwork!

Mizuho Kusanagi
c/o Yona of the Dawn Editor
VIZ Media
P.O. Box 77010
San Francisco, CA 94107

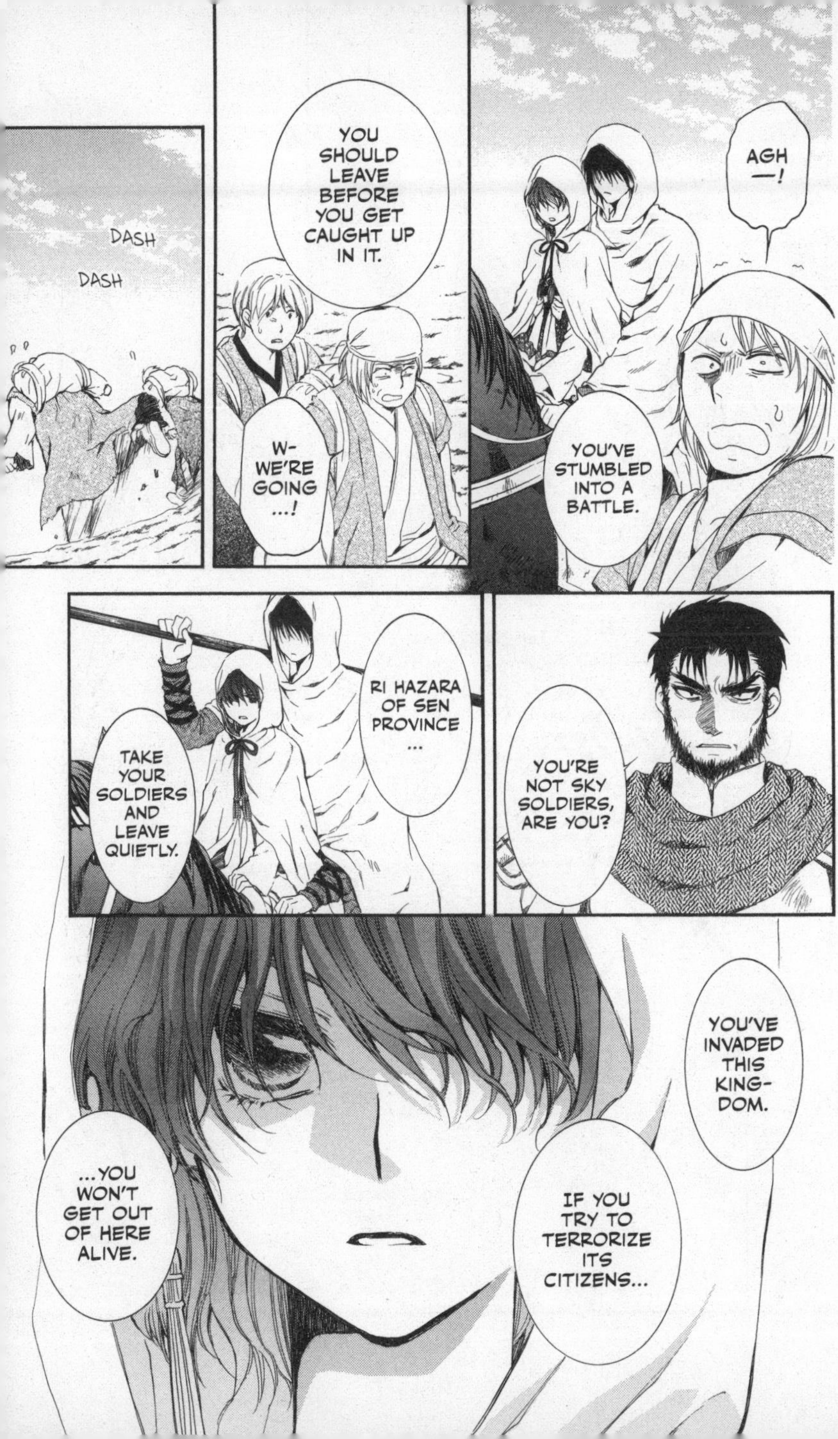
AGH—!
YOU'VE STUMBLED INTO A BATTLE.
YOU SHOULD LEAVE BEFORE YOU GET CAUGHT UP IN IT.
W-WE'RE GOING...!
DASH
DASH
YOU'RE NOT SKY SOLDIERS, ARE YOU?
RI HAZARA OF SEN PROVINCE...
TAKE YOUR SOLDIERS AND LEAVE QUIETLY.
YOU'VE INVADED THIS KING-DOM.
IF YOU TRY TO TERRORIZE ITS CITIZENS...
...YOU WON'T GET OUT OF HERE ALIVE.

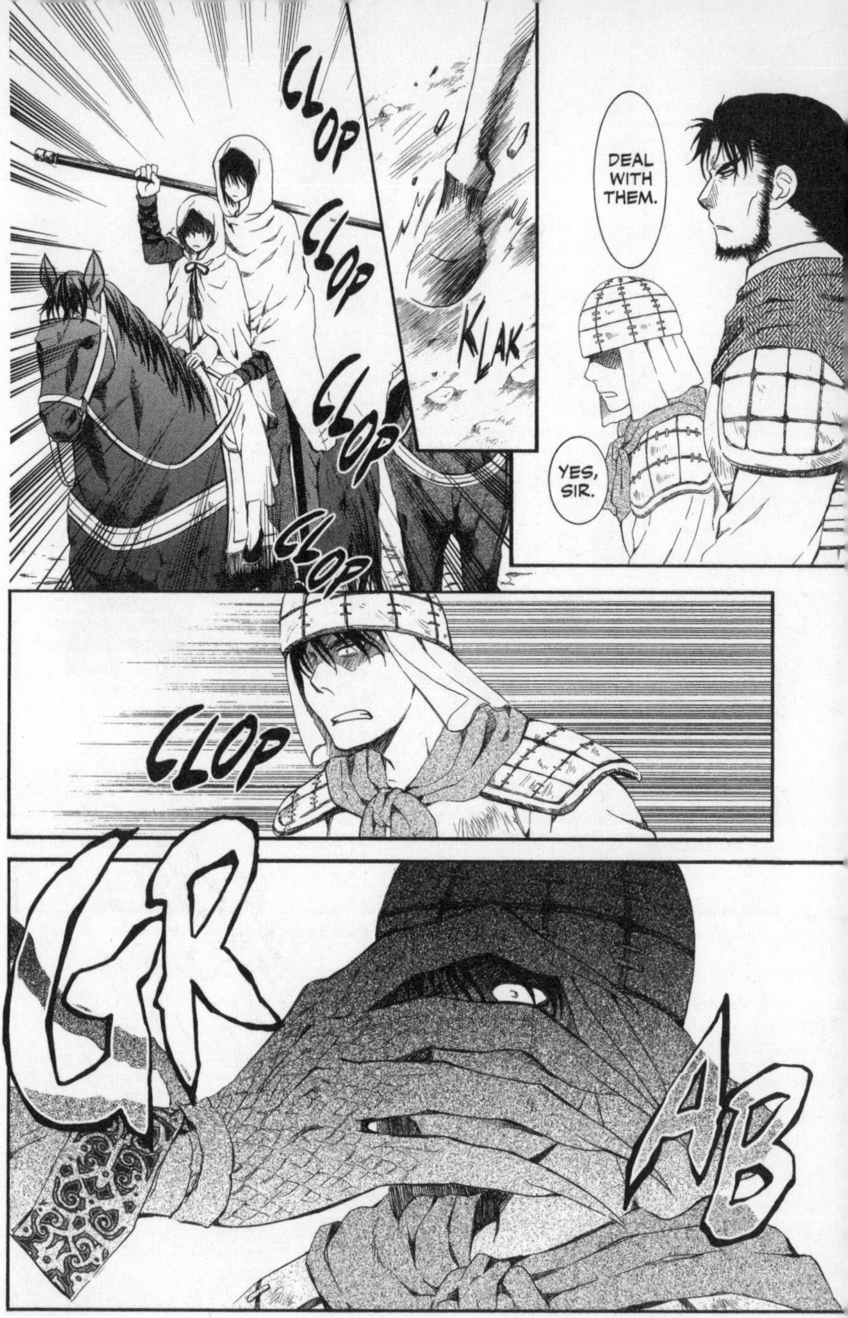
DEAL WITH THEM.
YES, SIR.
KLAK
CLOP
CLOP
CLOP
CLOP
CLOP
GR
AB

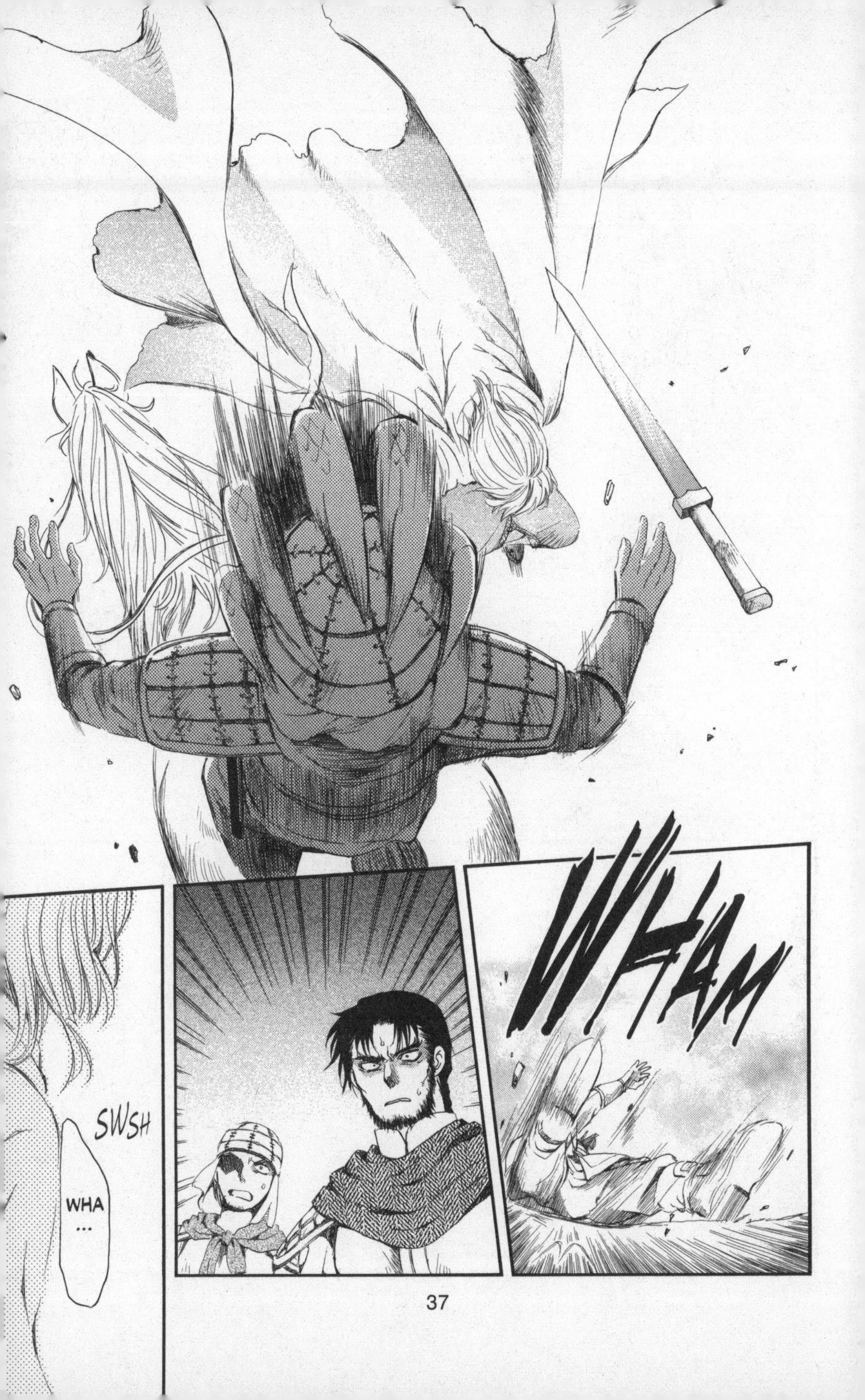
WHAM
SWSH
WHA ...

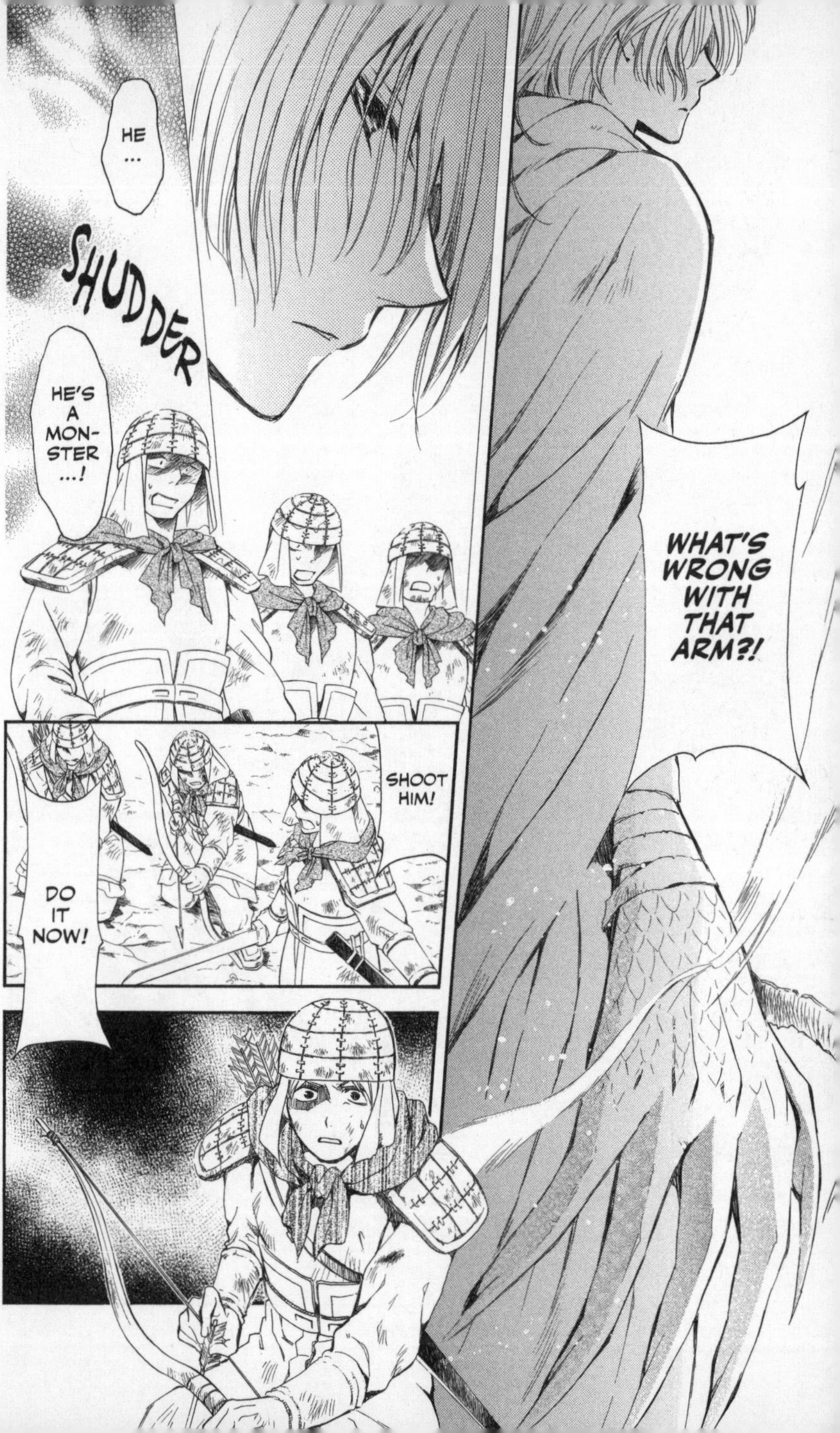
WHAT'S WRONG WITH THAT ARM?!
HE ...
SHUDDER
HE'S A MON-STER ...!
SHOOT HIM!
DO IT NOW!

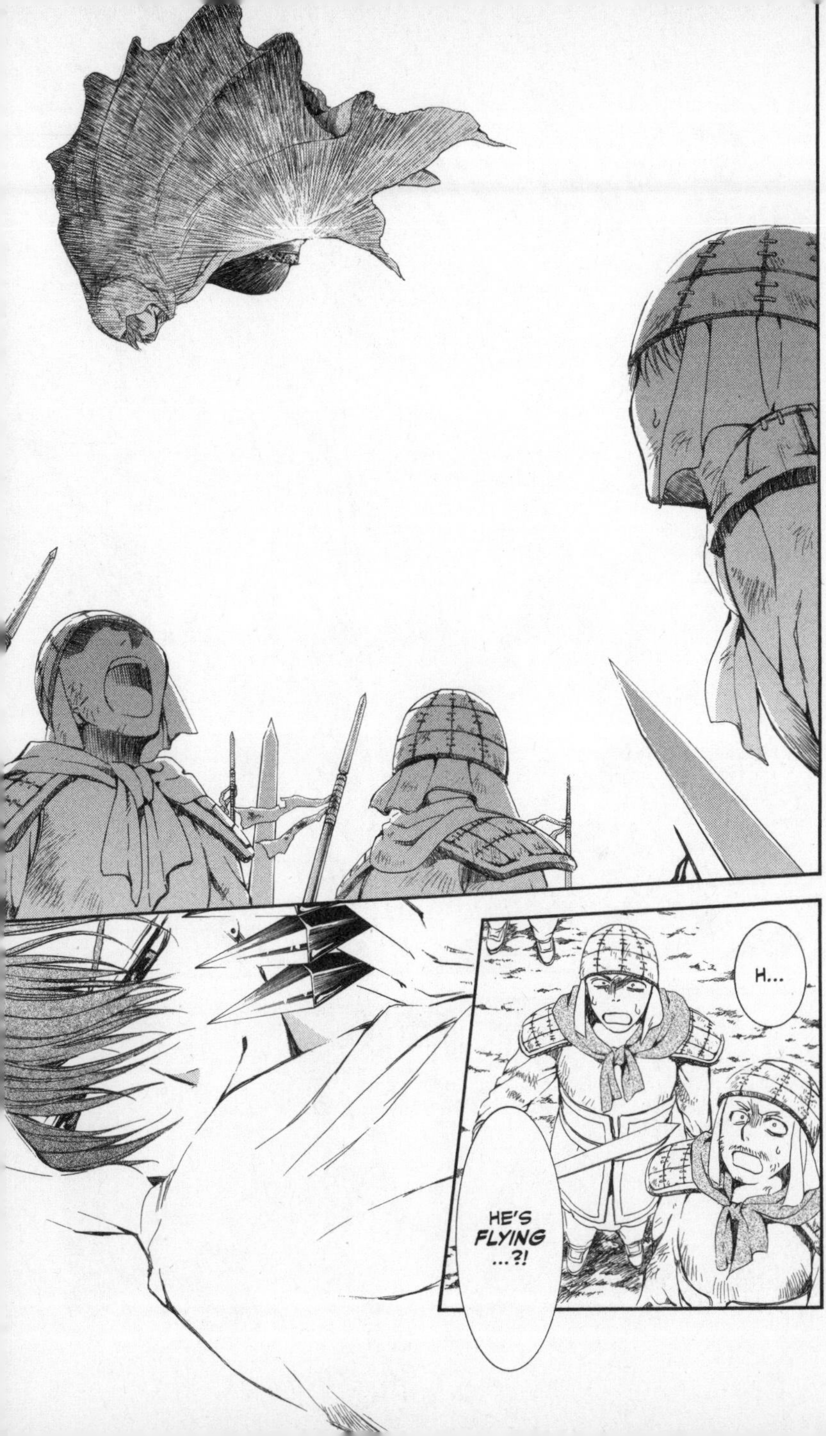
H...
HE'S FLYING ...?!

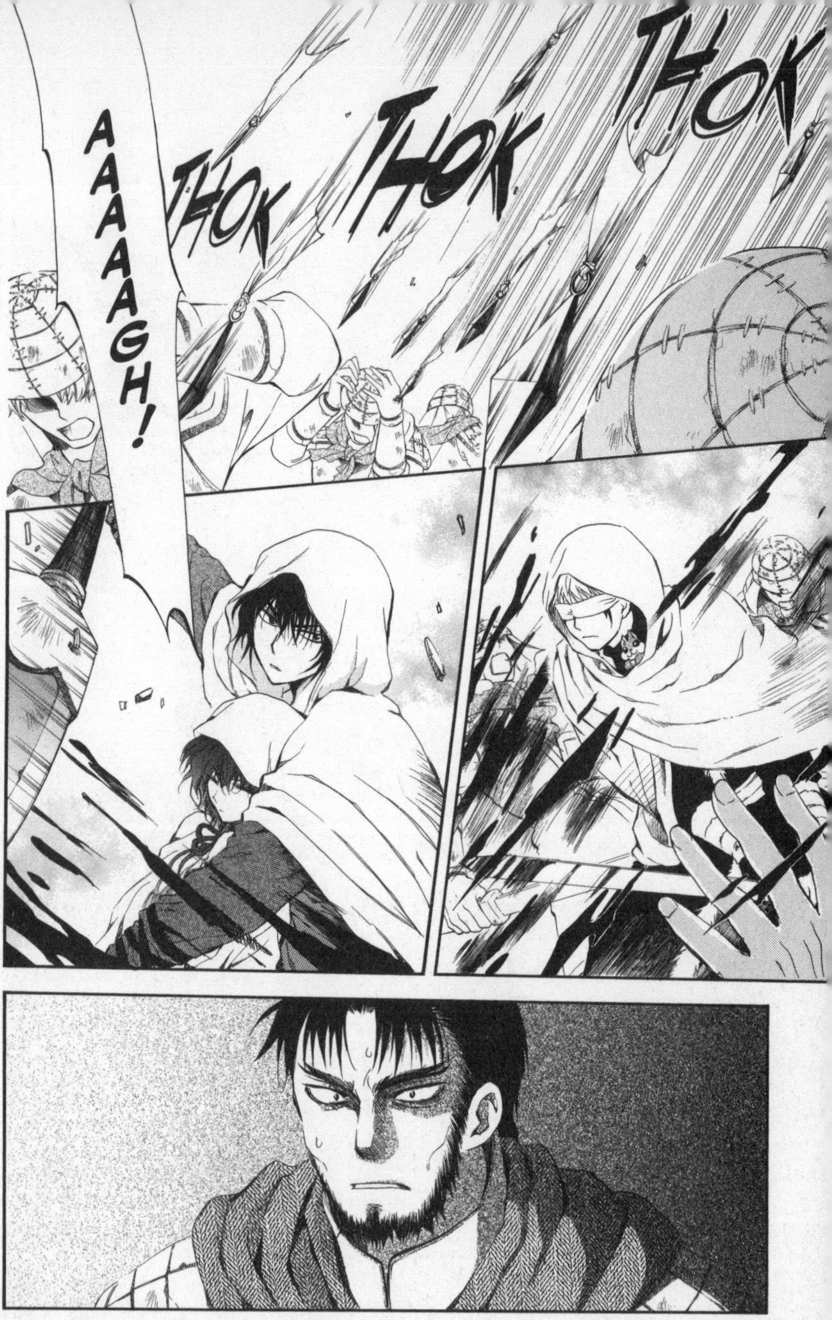
THOK
THOK
THOK
AAAAAAGH!

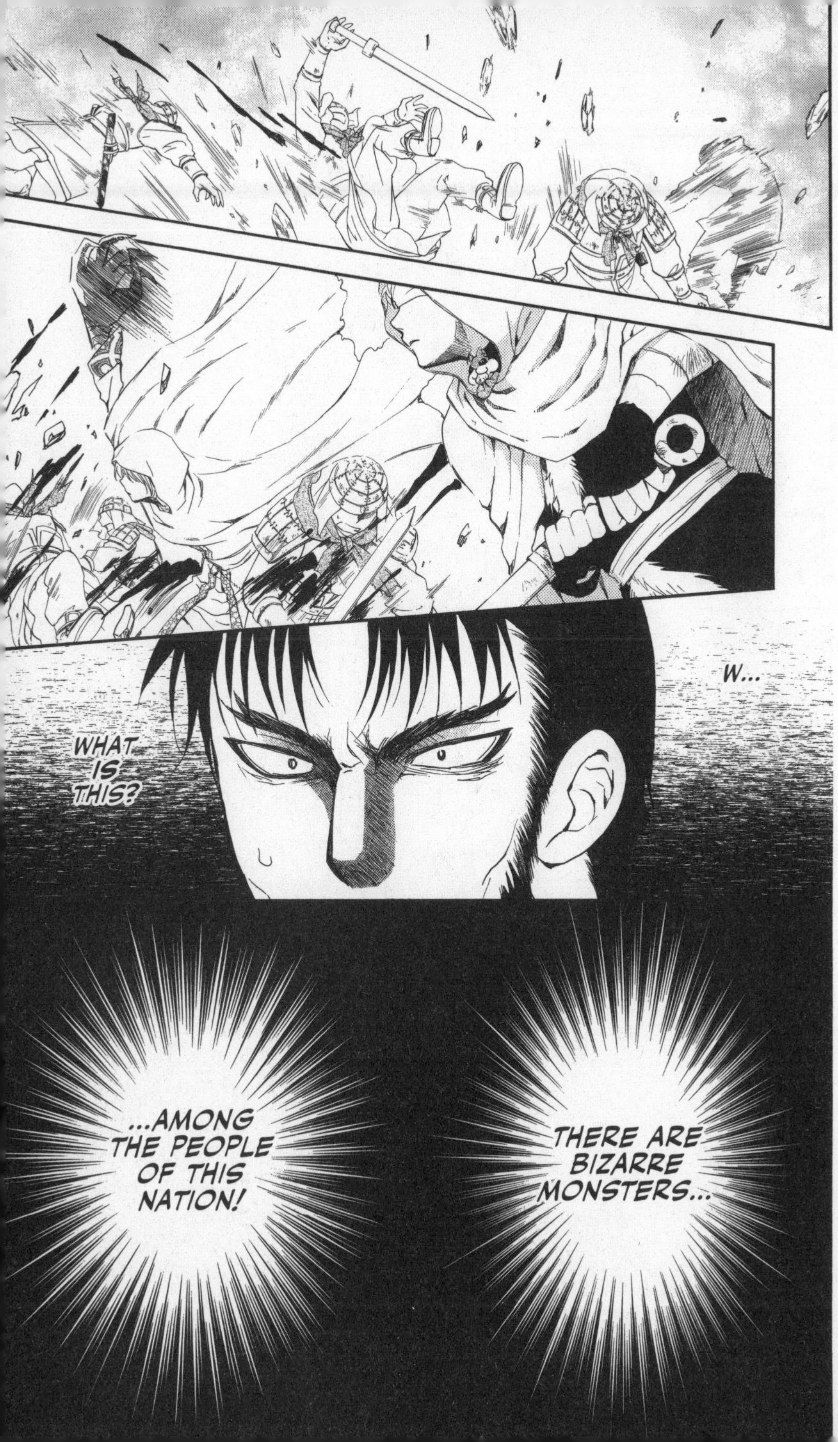
W...
WHAT IS THIS?
THERE ARE BIZARRE MONSTERS...
...AMONG THE PEOPLE OF THIS NATION!

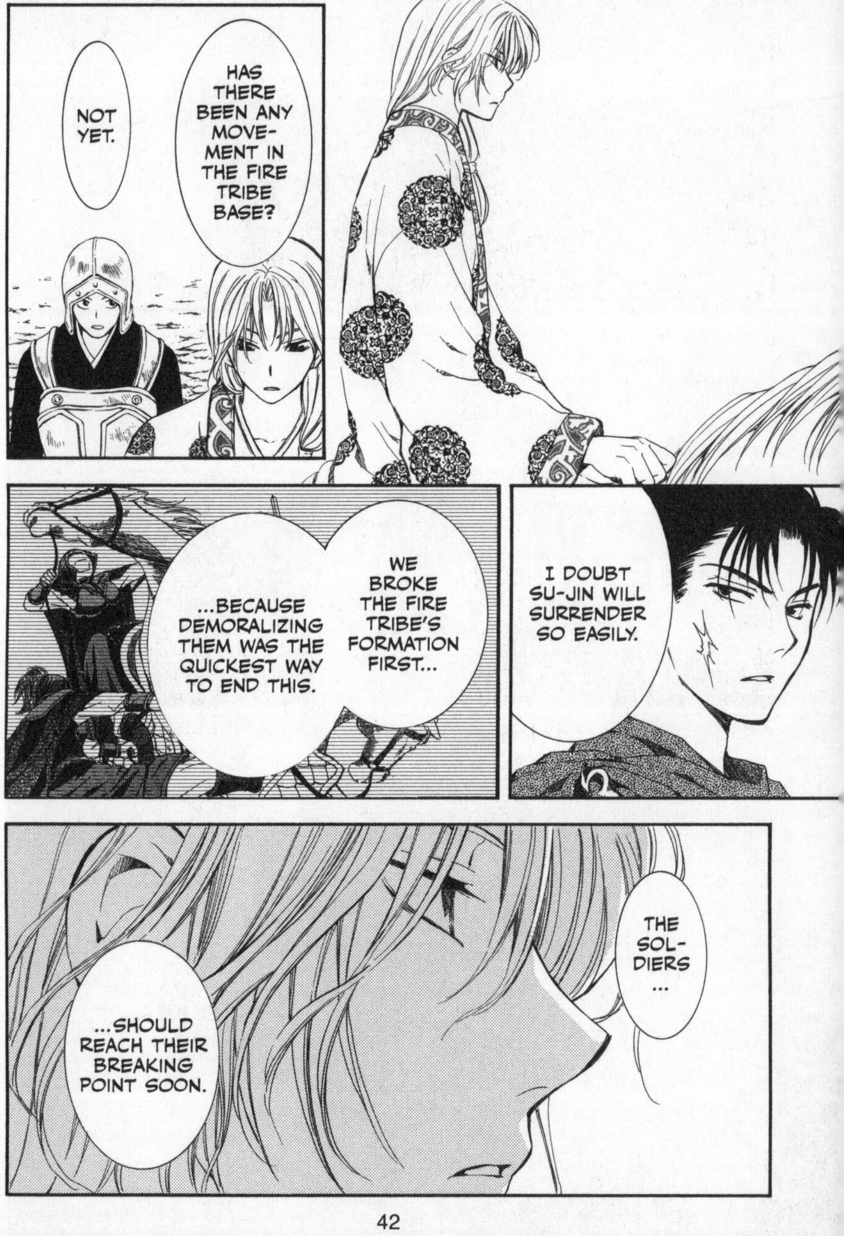
HAS THERE BEEN ANY MOVEMENT IN THE FIRE TRIBE BASE?
NOT YET.
I DOUBT SU-JIN WILL SURRENDER SO EASILY.
WE BROKE THE FIRE TRIBE'S FORMATION FIRST...
...BECAUSE DEMORALIZING THEM WAS THE QUICKEST WAY TO END THIS.
THE SOLDIERS...
...SHOULD REACH THEIR BREAKING POINT SOON.

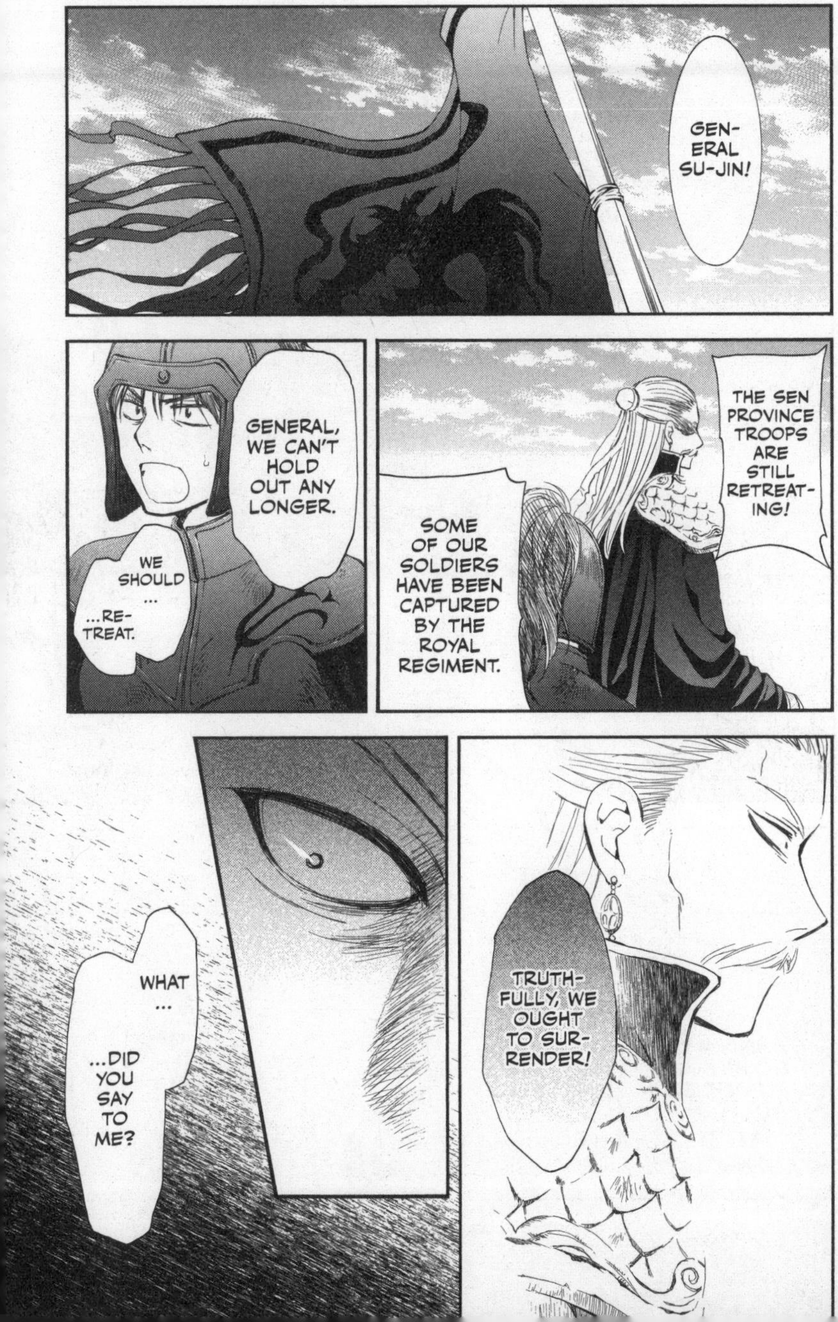
GEN-
ERAL
SU-JIN!
THE SEN
PROVINCE
TROOPS
ARE
STILL
RETREAT-
ING!
SOME
OF OUR
SOLDIERS
HAVE BEEN
CAPTURED
BY THE
ROYAL
REGIMENT.
GENERAL,
WE CAN'T
HOLD
OUT ANY
LONGER.
WE
SHOULD
...
...RE-
TREAT.
TRUTH-
FULLY, WE
OUGHT
TO SUR-
RENDER!
WHAT
...
...DID
YOU
SAY
TO
ME?

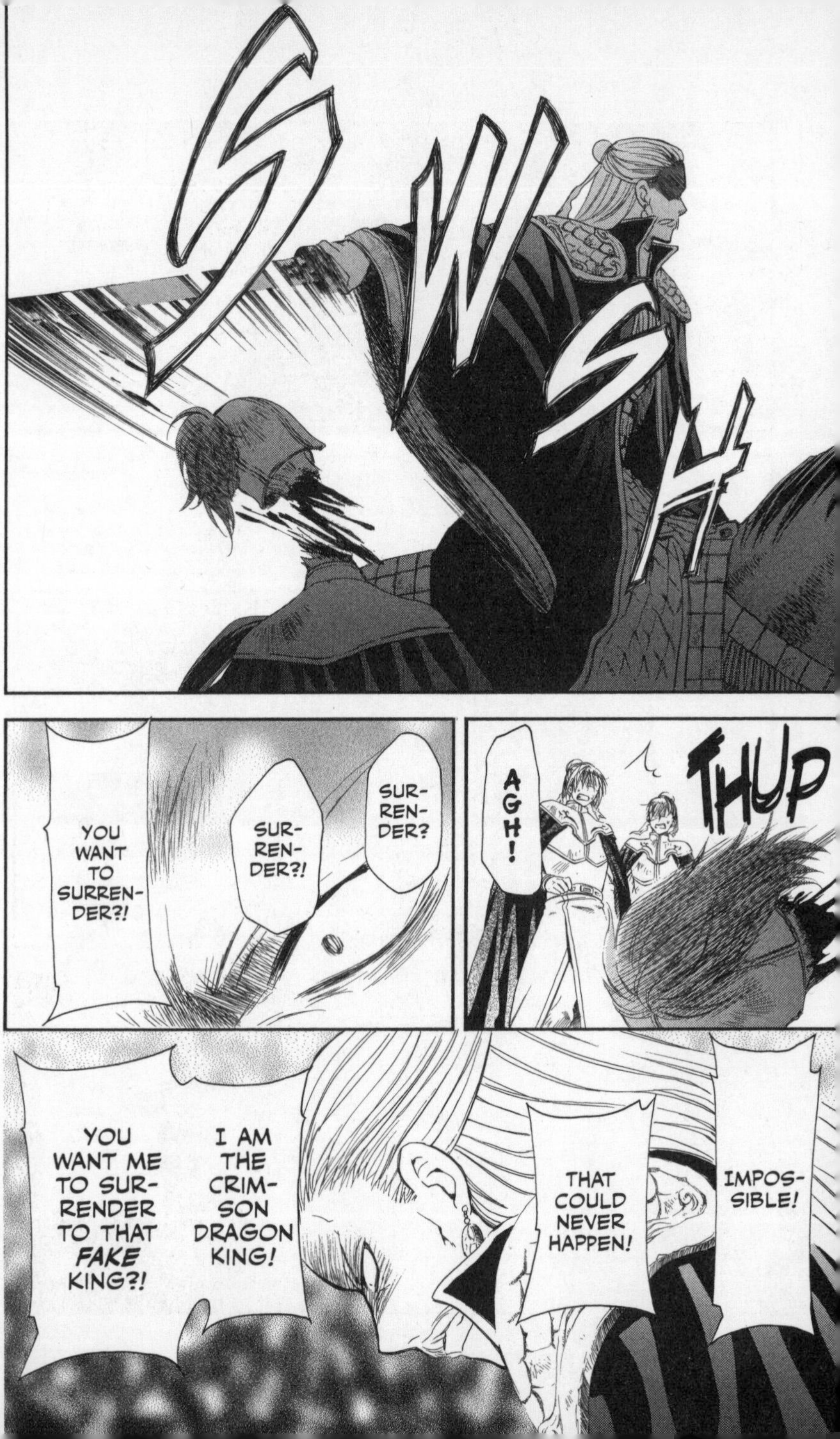
SWISH
THUP
AGH!
SUR-REN-DER?
SUR-REN-DER?!
YOU WANT TO SURREN-DER?!
IMPOS-SIBLE!
THAT COULD NEVER HAPPEN!
I AM THE CRIM-SON DRAGON KING!
YOU WANT ME TO SUR-RENDER TO THAT *FAKE* KING?!

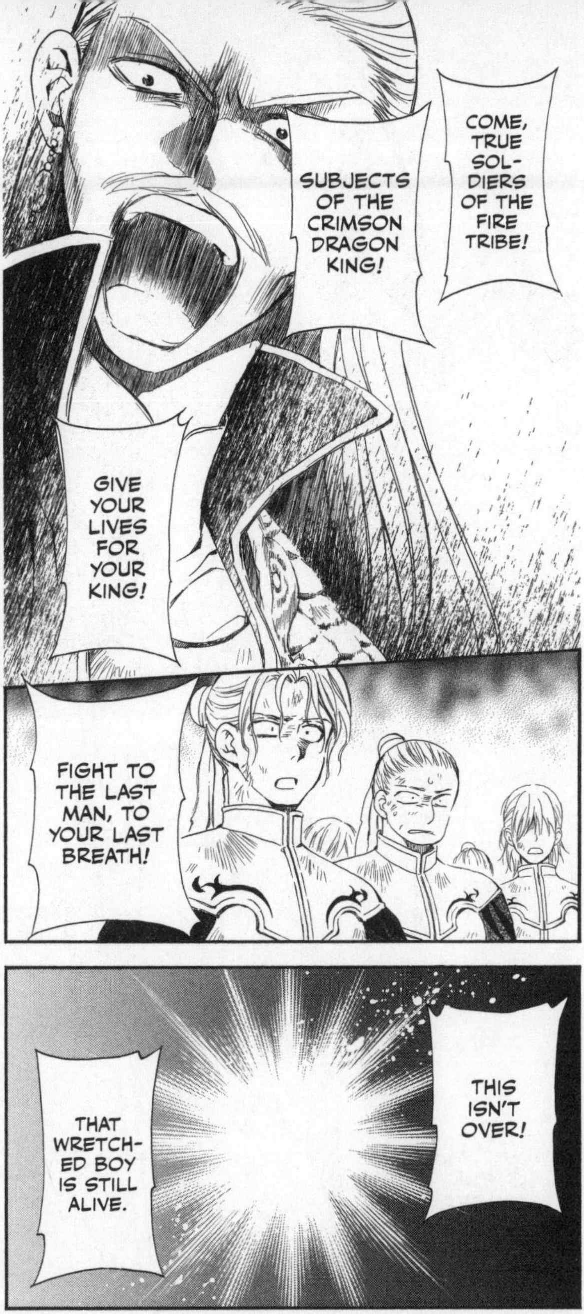
COME, TRUE SOL- DIERS OF THE FIRE TRIBE!
SUBJECTS OF THE CRIMSON DRAGON KING!
GIVE YOUR LIVES FOR YOUR KING!
FIGHT TO THE LAST MAN, TO YOUR LAST BREATH!
THIS ISN'T OVER!
THAT WRETCH- ED BOY IS STILL ALIVE.

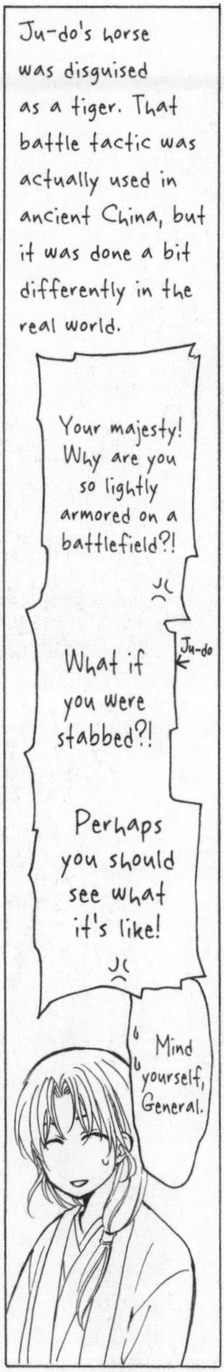
Ju-do's horse was disguised as a tiger. That battle tactic was actually used in ancient China, but it was done a bit differently in the real world.
Your majesty! Why are you so lightly armored on a battlefield?!
Ju-do
What if you were stabbed?!
Perhaps you should see what it's like!
Mind yourself, General.

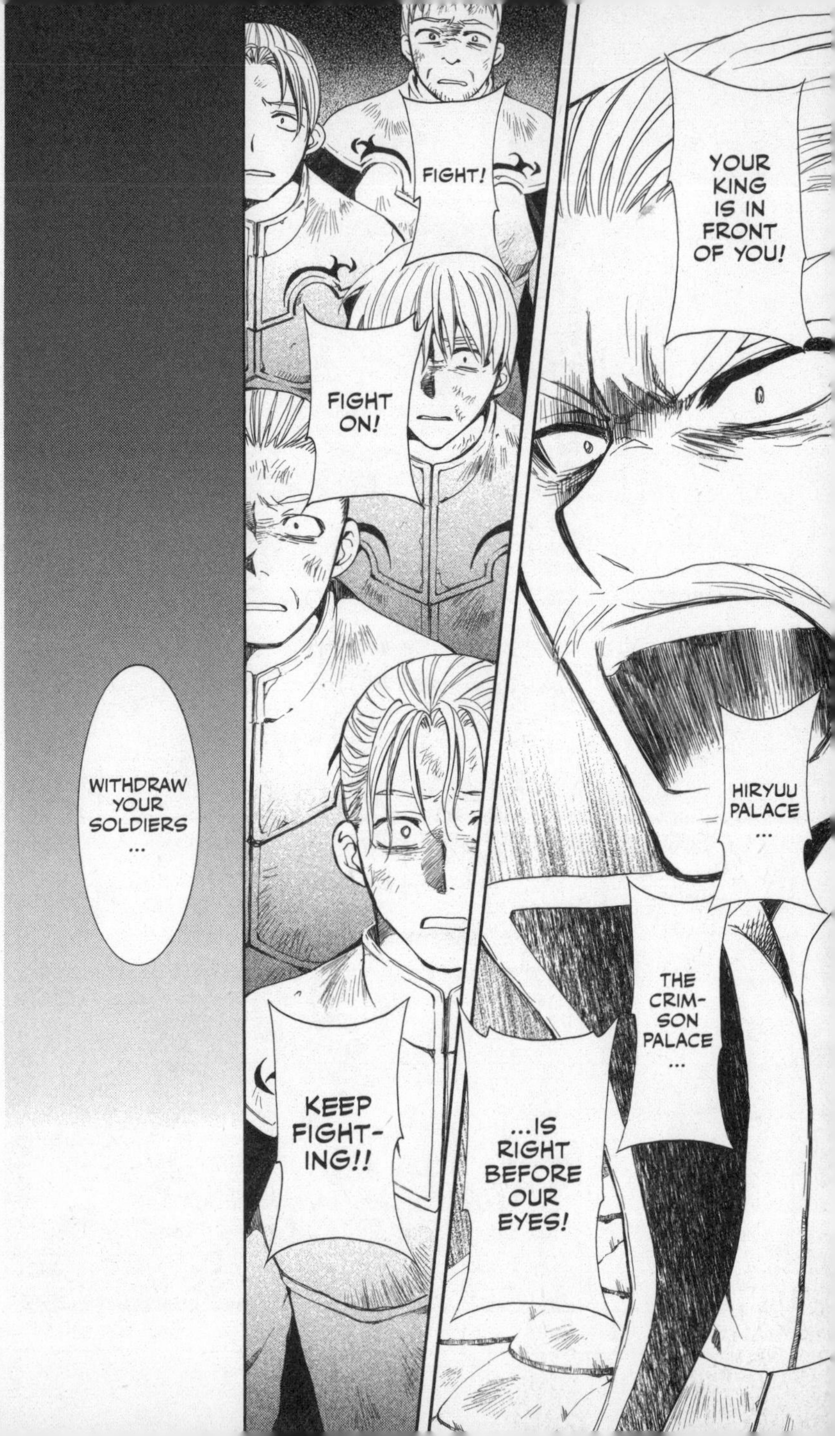

YOUR KING IS IN FRONT OF YOU!
HIRYUU PALACE ...
THE CRIMSON PALACE ...
...IS RIGHT BEFORE OUR EYES!
FIGHT!
FIGHT ON!
KEEP FIGHTING!!
WITHDRAW YOUR SOLDIERS ...

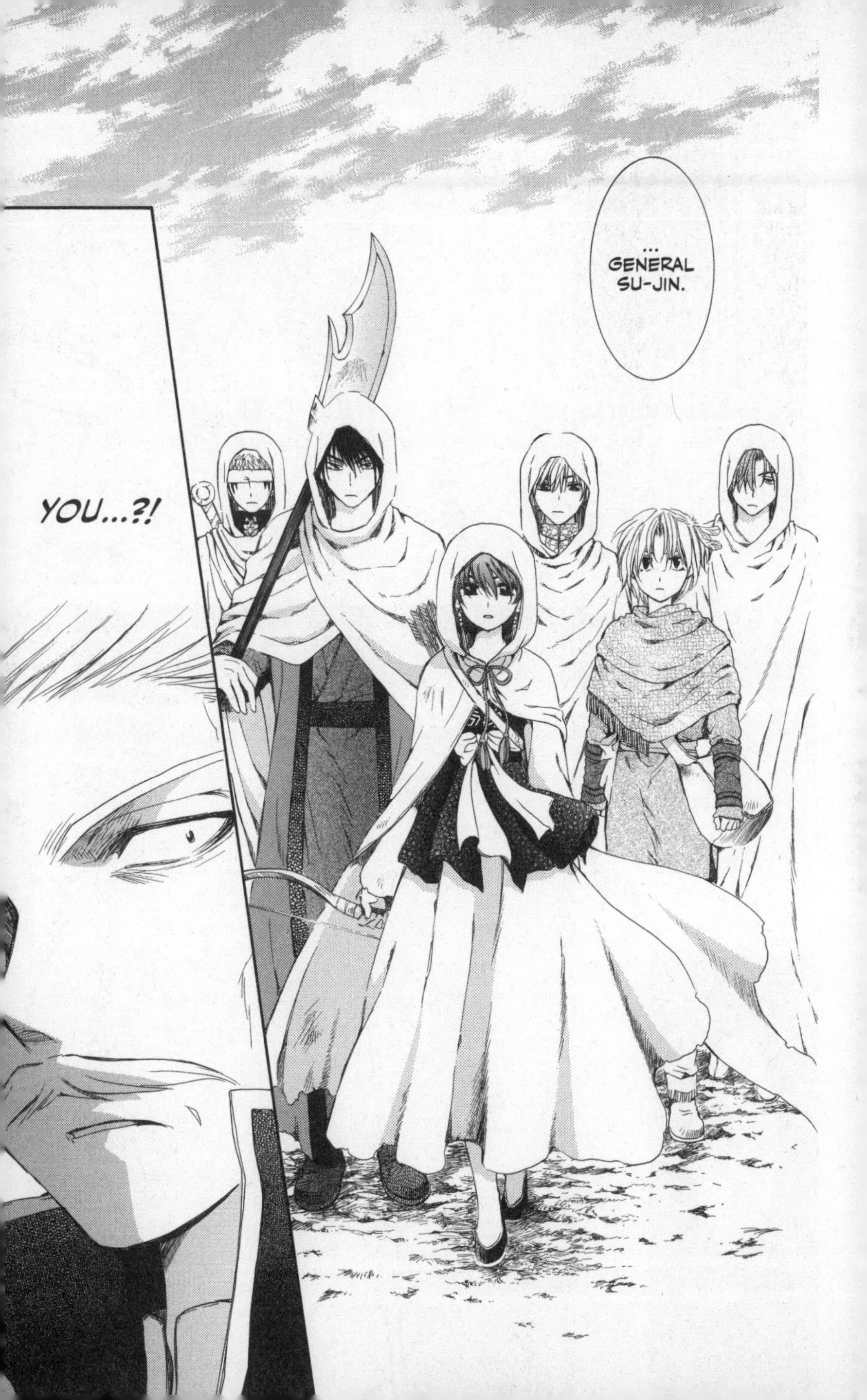
...GENERAL SU-JIN.
YOU...?!

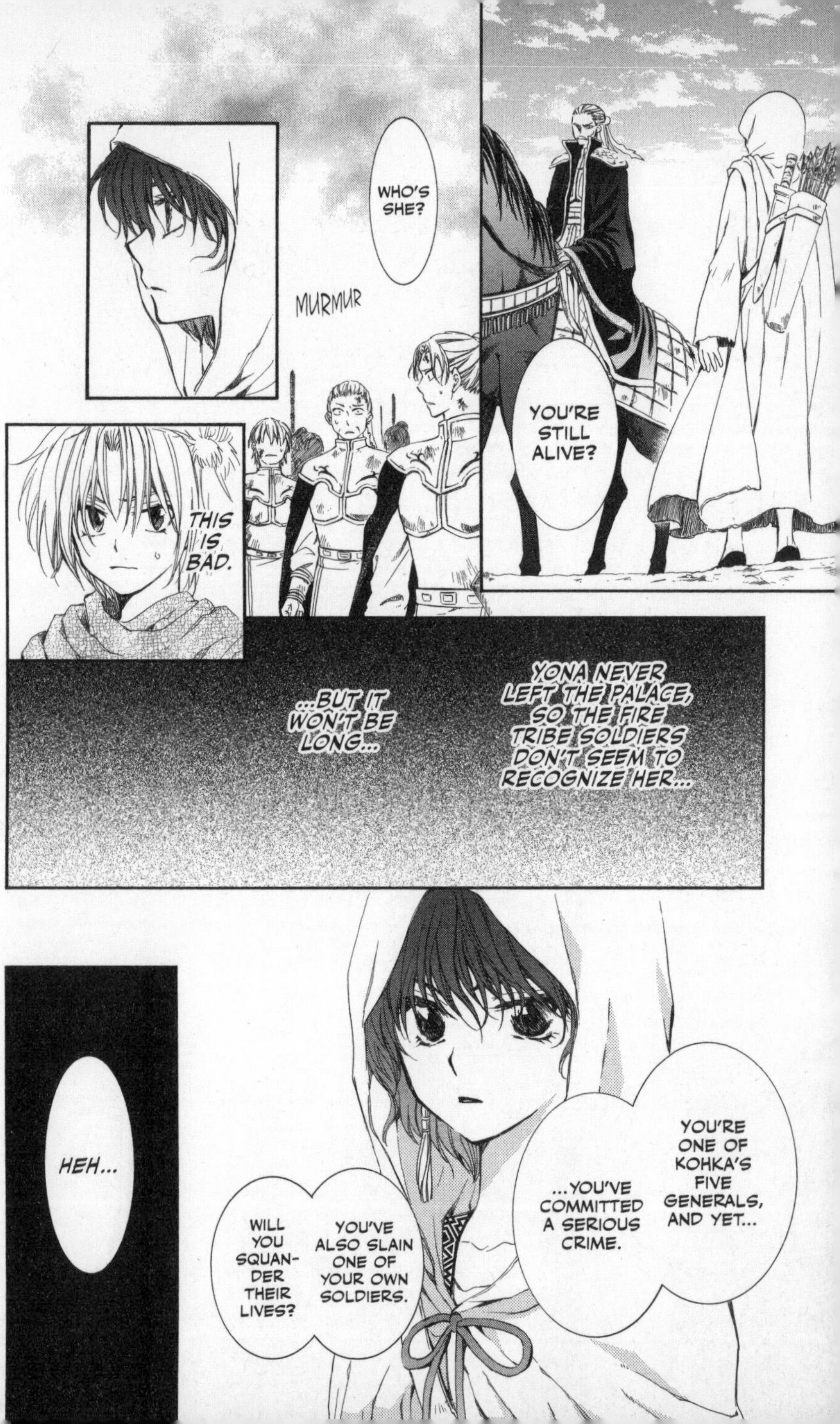
YOU'RE STILL ALIVE?
WHO'S SHE?
MURMUR
THIS IS BAD.
YONA NEVER LEFT THE PALACE, SO THE FIRE TRIBE SOLDIERS DON'T SEEM TO RECOGNIZE HER...
...BUT IT WON'T BE LONG...
YOU'RE ONE OF KOHKA'S FIVE GENERALS, AND YET...
...YOU'VE COMMITTED A SERIOUS CRIME.
YOU'VE ALSO SLAIN ONE OF YOUR OWN SOLDIERS.
WILL YOU SQUANDER THEIR LIVES?
HEH...

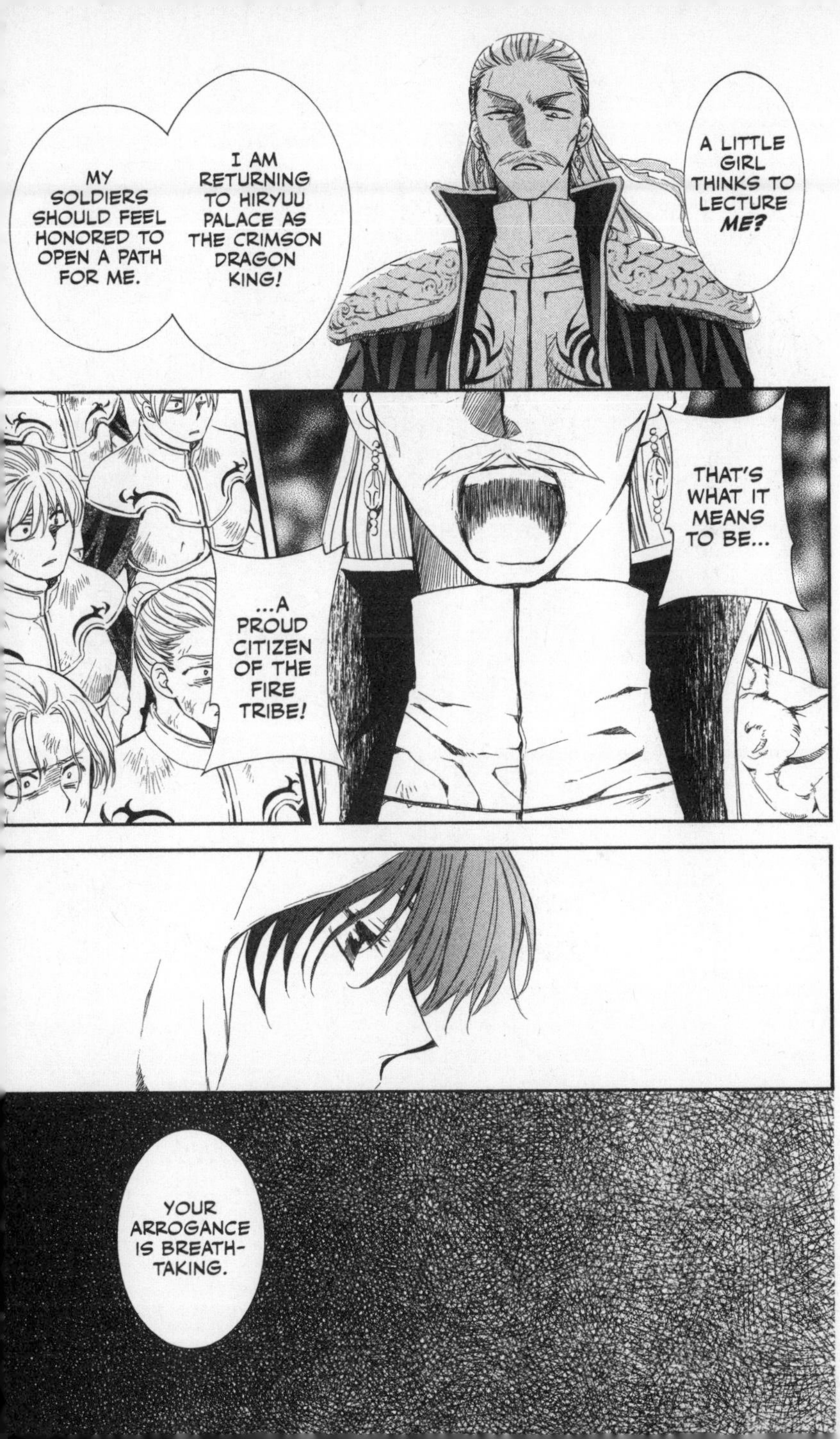
A LITTLE GIRL THINKS TO LECTURE *ME?*
I AM RETURNING TO HIRYUU PALACE AS THE CRIMSON DRAGON KING!
MY SOLDIERS SHOULD FEEL HONORED TO OPEN A PATH FOR ME.
THAT'S WHAT IT MEANS TO BE...
...A PROUD CITIZEN OF THE FIRE TRIBE!
YOUR ARROGANCE IS BREATH-TAKING.

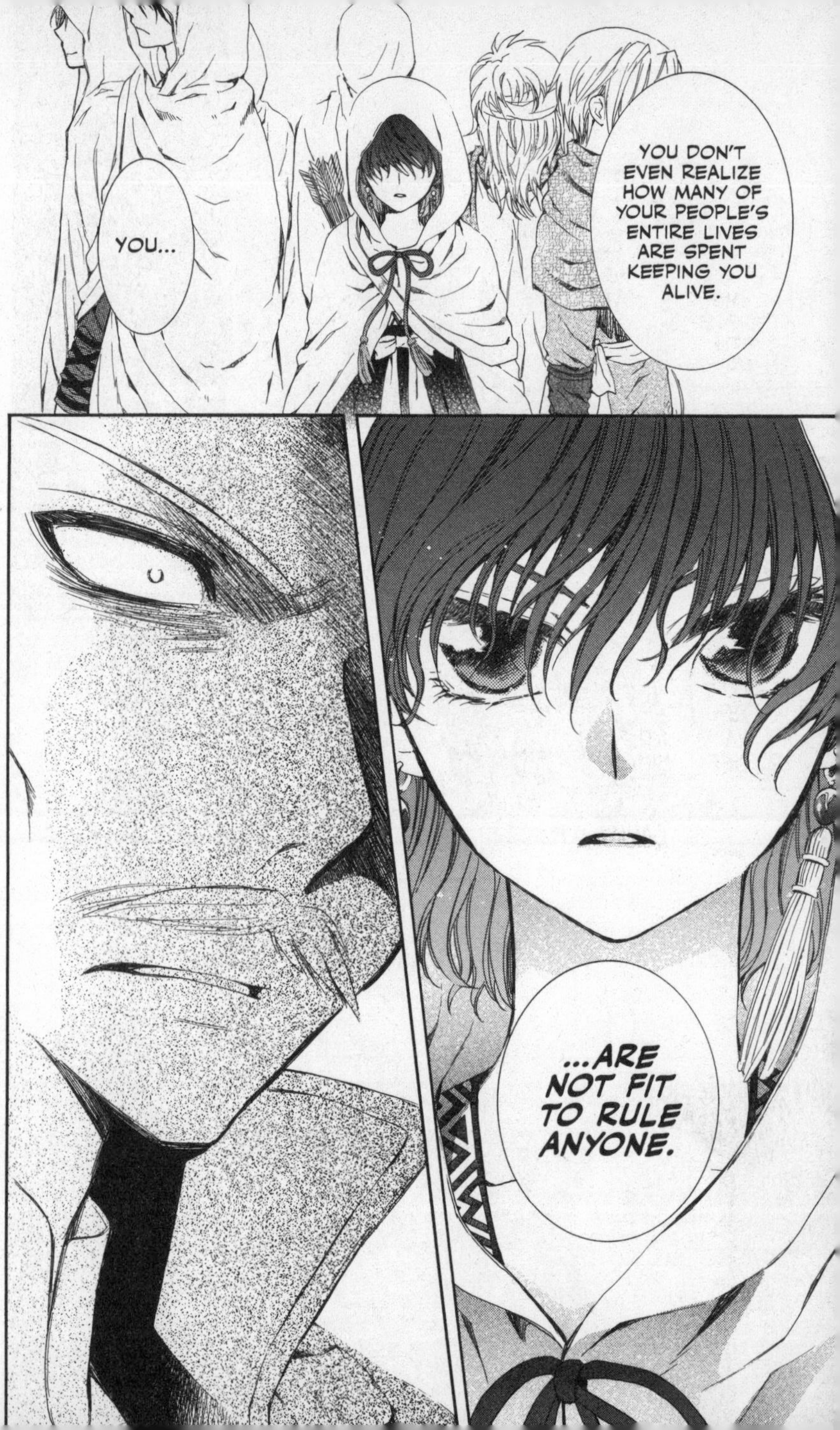
YOU DON'T EVEN REALIZE HOW MANY OF YOUR PEOPLE'S ENTIRE LIVES ARE SPENT KEEPING YOU ALIVE.
YOU...
...ARE NOT FIT TO RULE ANYONE.

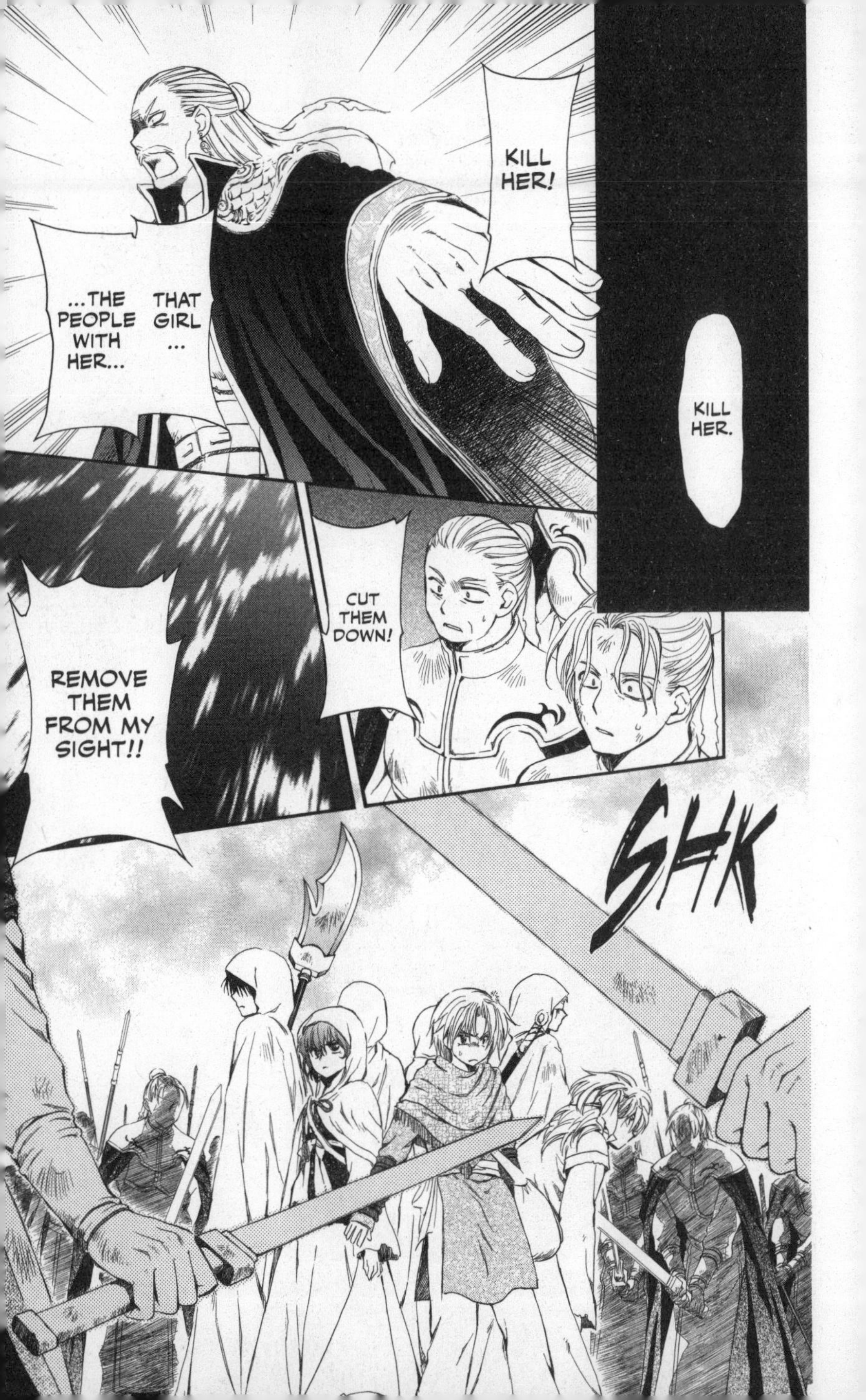
KILL HER.
KILL HER!
THAT GIRL...
...THE PEOPLE WITH HER...
CUT THEM DOWN!
REMOVE THEM FROM MY SIGHT!!
SHK

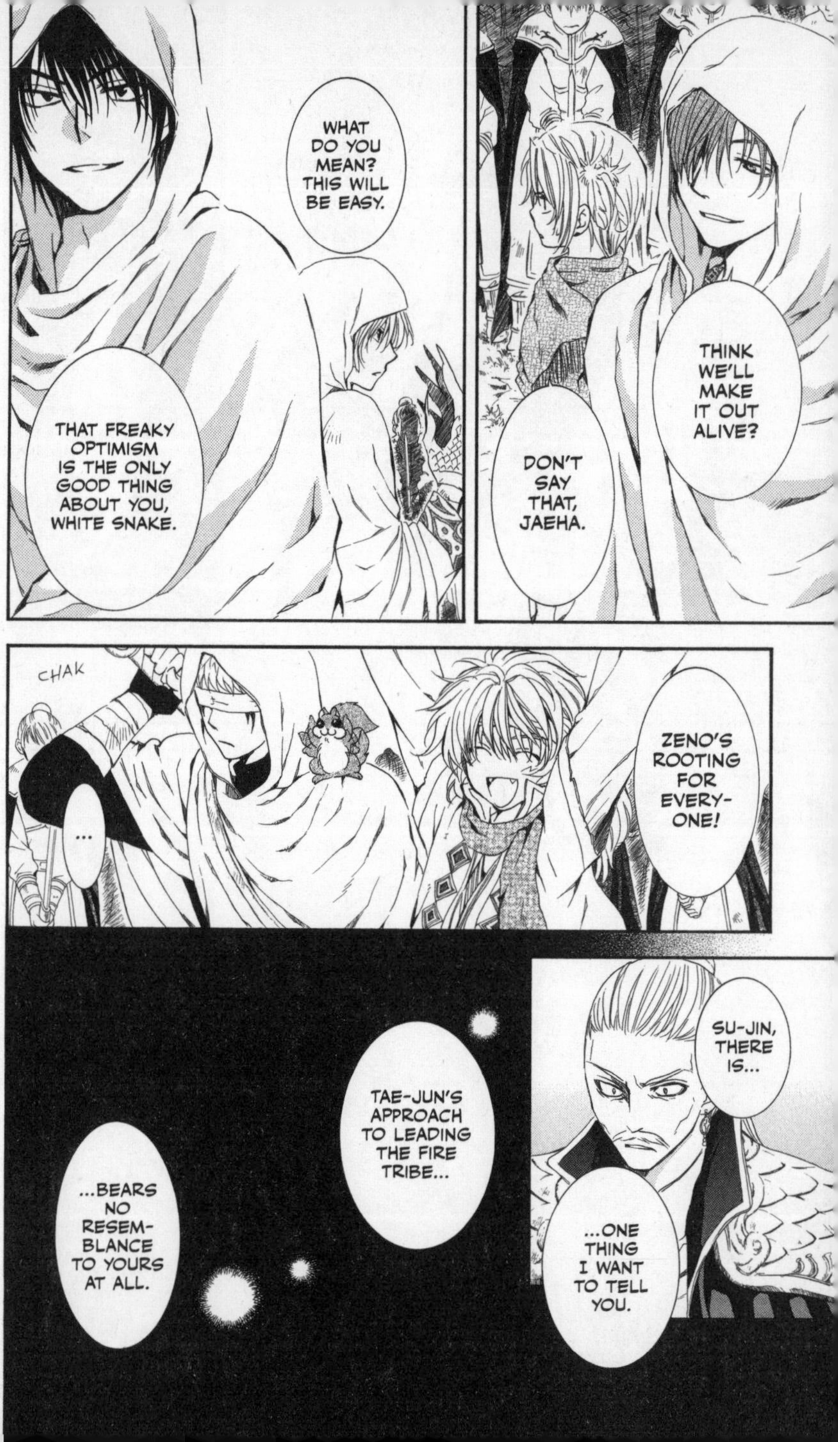
THINK WE'LL MAKE IT OUT ALIVE?
DON'T SAY THAT, JAEHA.
WHAT DO YOU MEAN? THIS WILL BE EASY.
THAT FREAKY OPTIMISM IS THE ONLY GOOD THING ABOUT YOU, WHITE SNAKE.
ZENO'S ROOTING FOR EVERY-ONE!
CHAK
...
SU-JIN, THERE IS...
...ONE THING I WANT TO TELL YOU.
TAE-JUN'S APPROACH TO LEADING THE FIRE TRIBE...
...BEARS NO RESEM-BLANCE TO YOURS AT ALL.

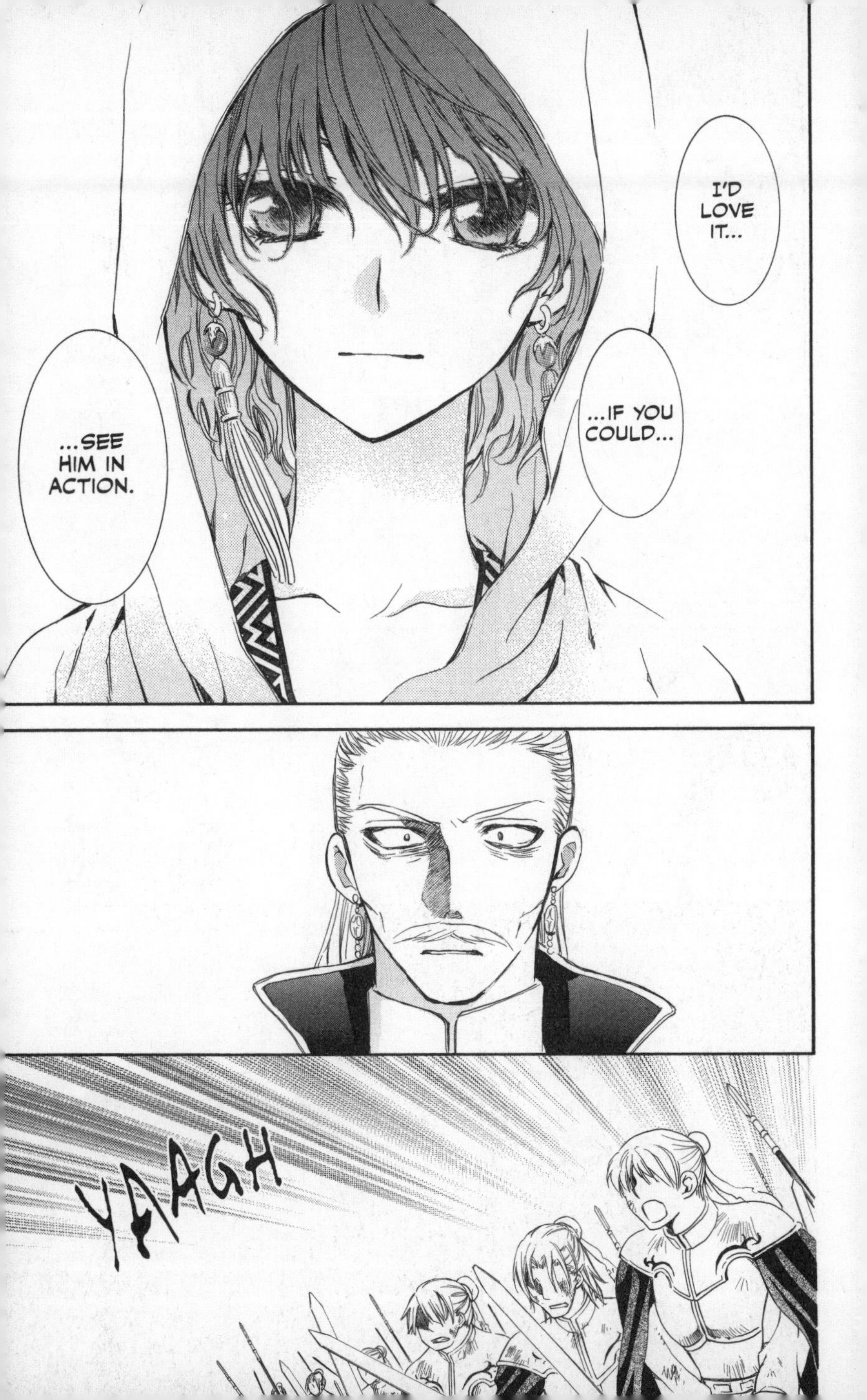
I'D LOVE IT...
...IF YOU COULD...
...SEE HIM IN ACTION.
YAAGH

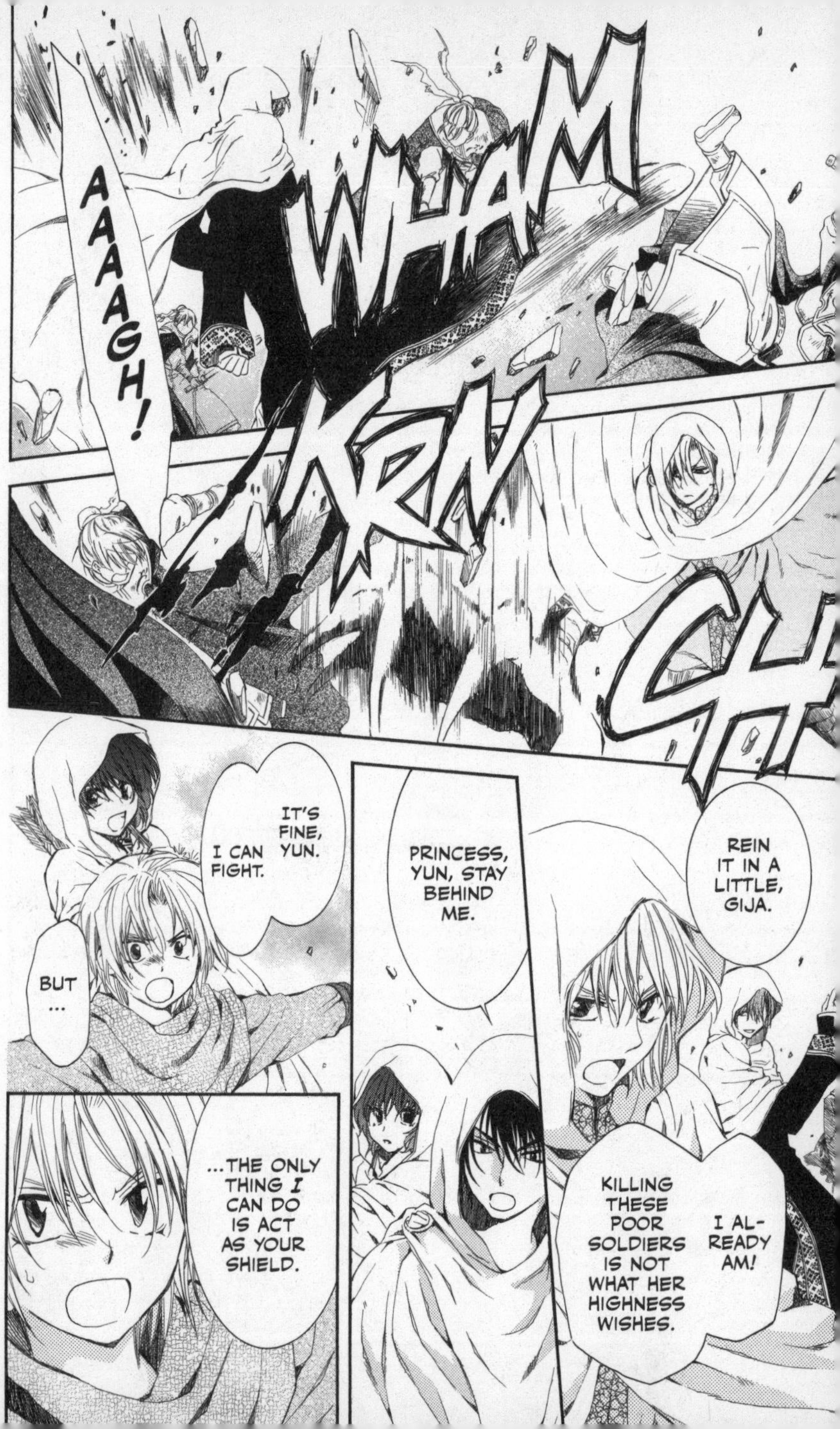
WHAM
AAAAGH!
KRN
REIN IT IN A LITTLE, GIJA.
PRINCESS, YUN, STAY BEHIND ME.
I AL-READY AM!
KILLING THESE POOR SOLDIERS IS NOT WHAT HER HIGHNESS WISHES.
IT'S FINE, YUN.
I CAN FIGHT.
BUT ...
...THE ONLY THING *I* CAN DO IS ACT AS YOUR SHIELD.

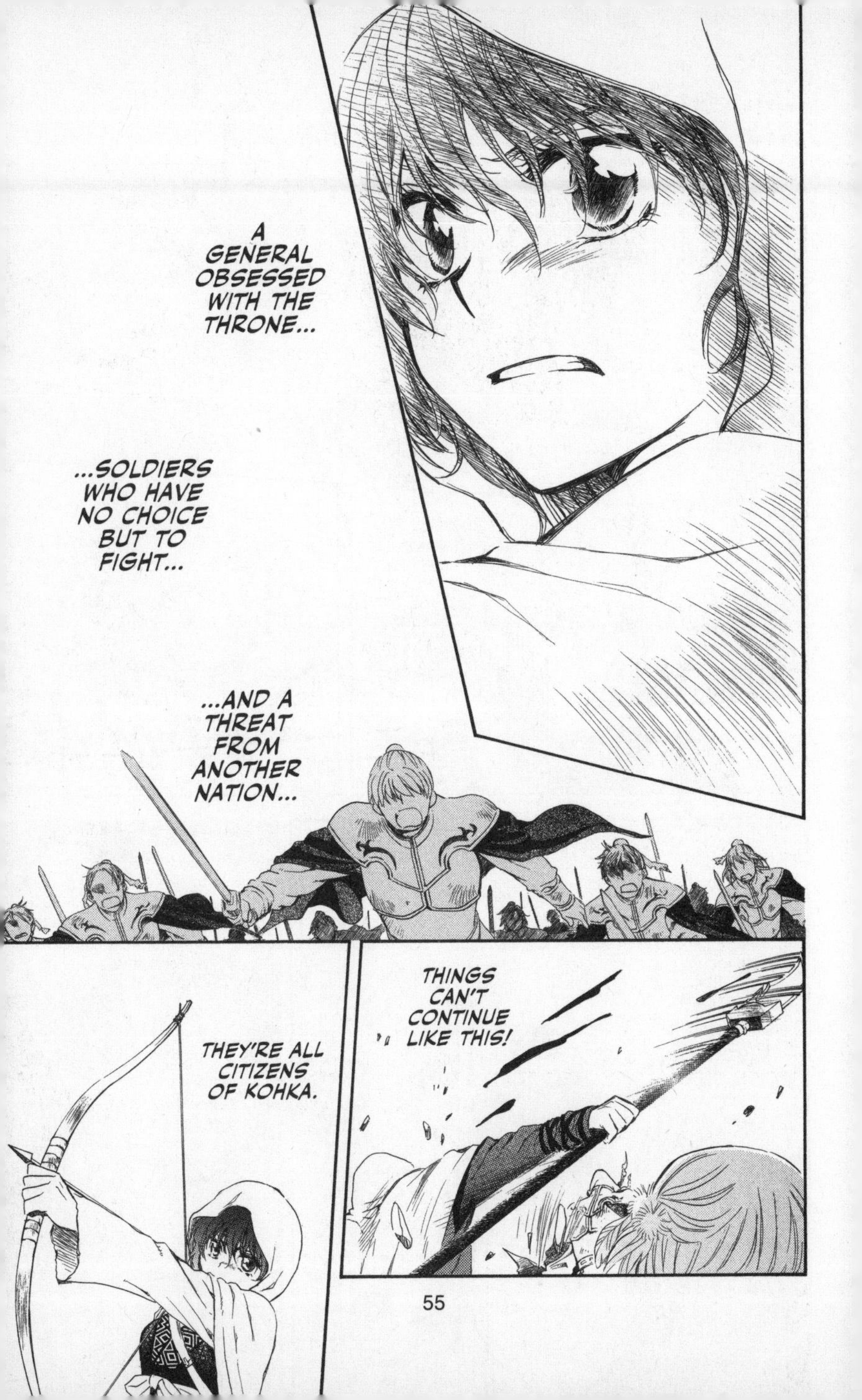
A GENERAL OBSESSED WITH THE THRONE...
...SOLDIERS WHO HAVE NO CHOICE BUT TO FIGHT...
...AND A THREAT FROM ANOTHER NATION...
THINGS CAN'T CONTINUE LIKE THIS!
THEY'RE ALL CITIZENS OF KOHKA.

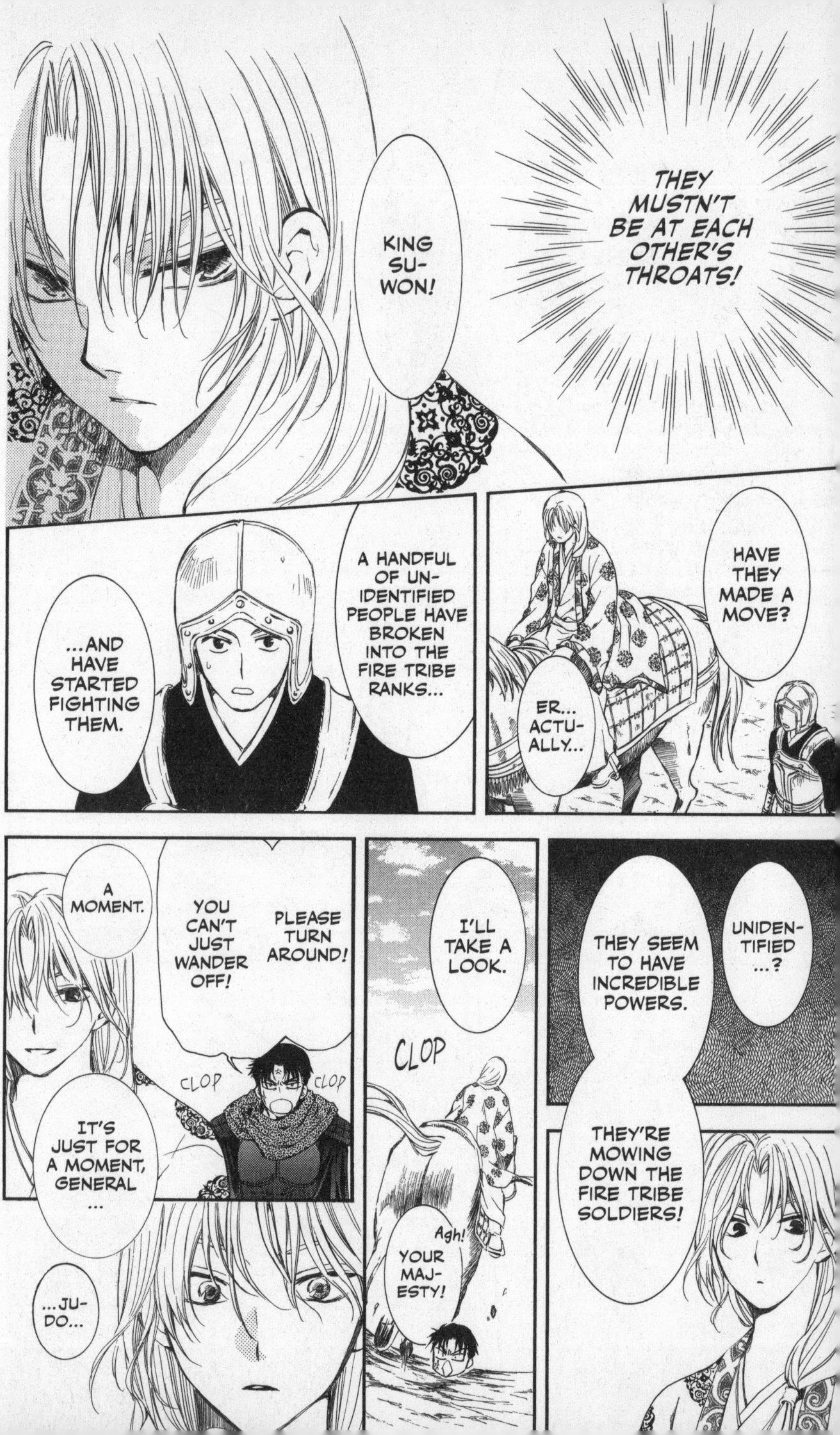
THEY MUSTN'T BE AT EACH OTHER'S THROATS!
KING SU-WON!
HAVE THEY MADE A MOVE?
ER... ACTUALLY...
A HANDFUL OF UNIDENTIFIED PEOPLE HAVE BROKEN INTO THE FIRE TRIBE RANKS...
...AND HAVE STARTED FIGHTING THEM.
UNIDENTIFIED...?
THEY SEEM TO HAVE INCREDIBLE POWERS.
THEY'RE MOWING DOWN THE FIRE TRIBE SOLDIERS!
I'LL TAKE A LOOK.
CLOP
Agh!
YOUR MAJESTY!
PLEASE TURN AROUND!
YOU CAN'T JUST WANDER OFF!
A MOMENT.
CLOP
CLOP
IT'S JUST FOR A MOMENT, GENERAL...
...JU-DO...

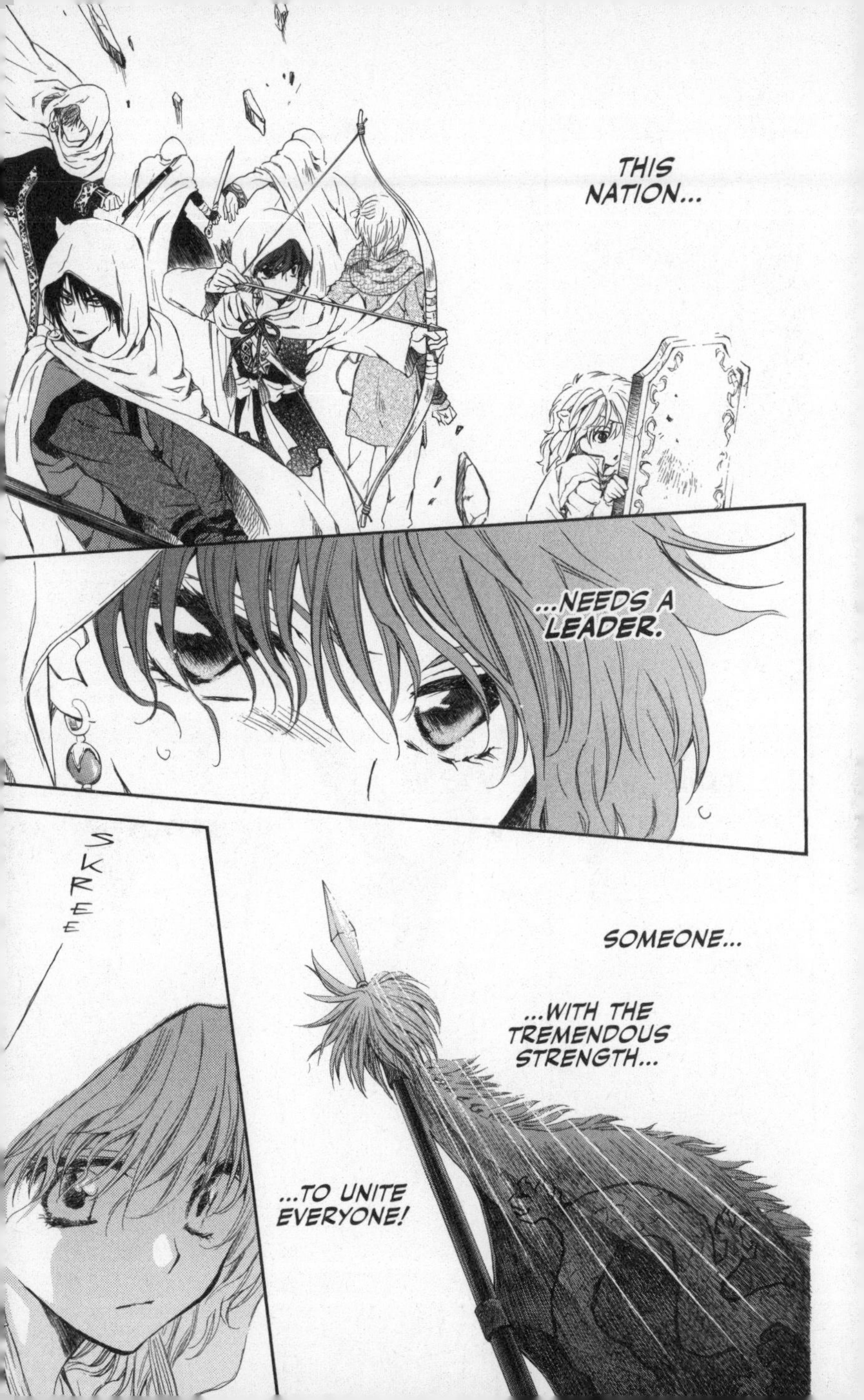
THIS NATION...
...NEEDS A LEADER.
SOMEONE...
...WITH THE TREMENDOUS STRENGTH...
...TO UNITE EVERYONE!
SKREE

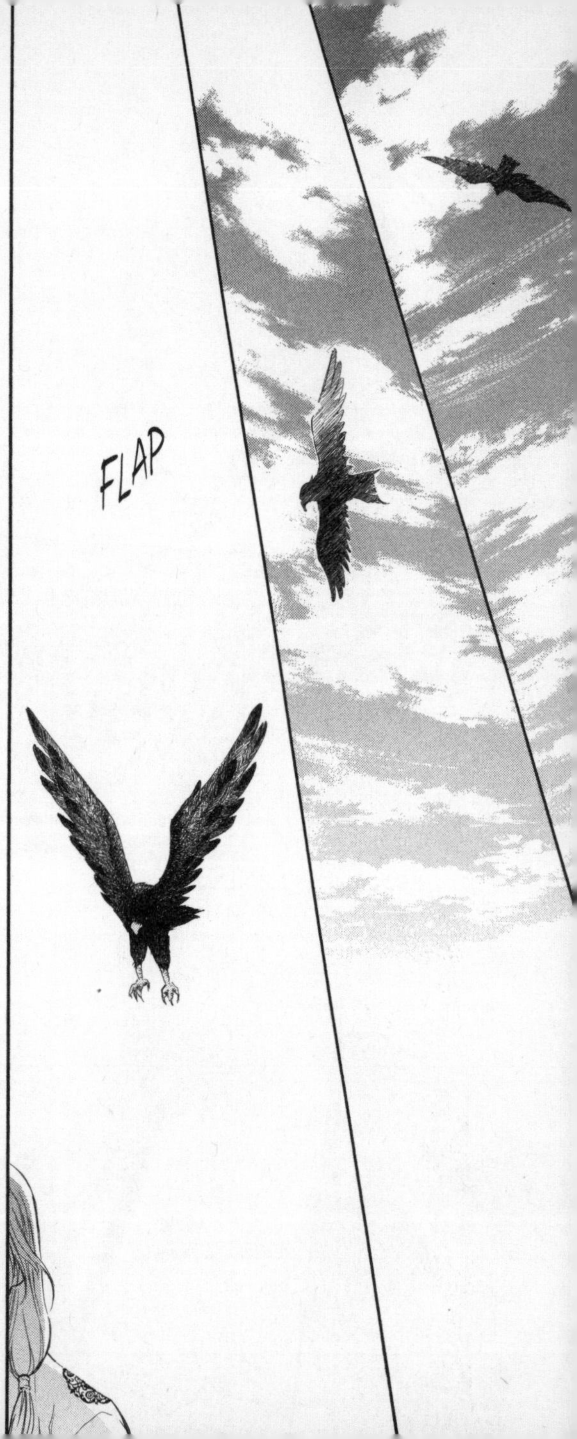
FLAP

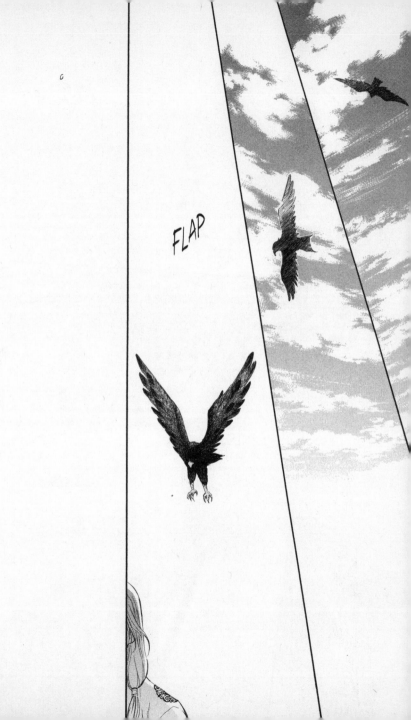

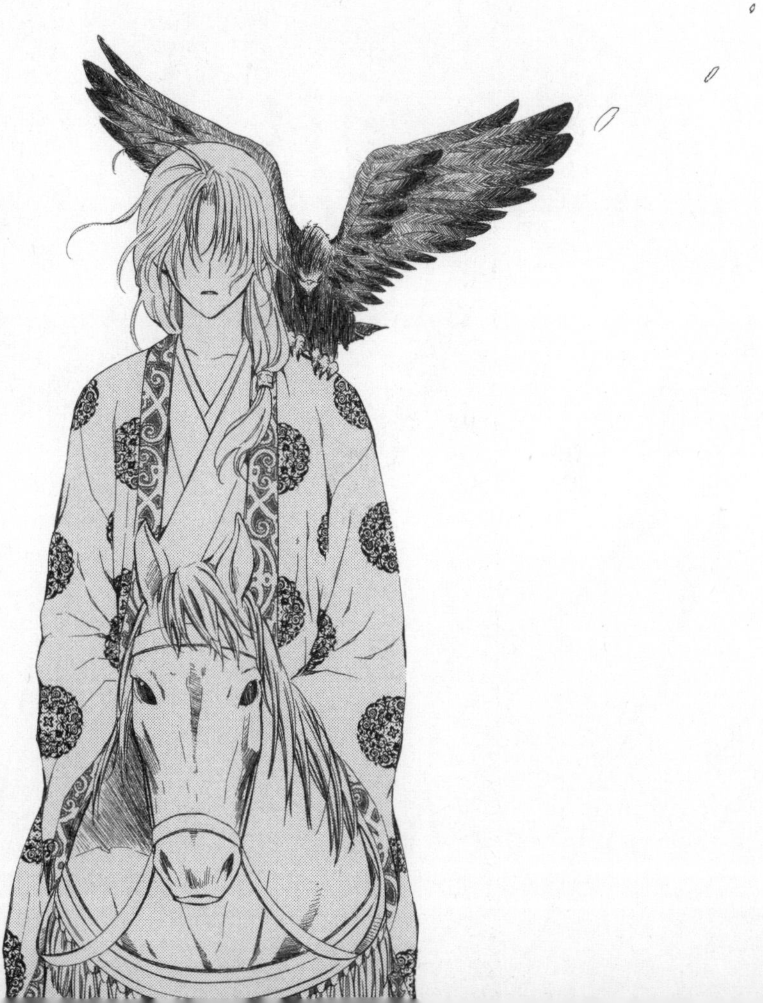

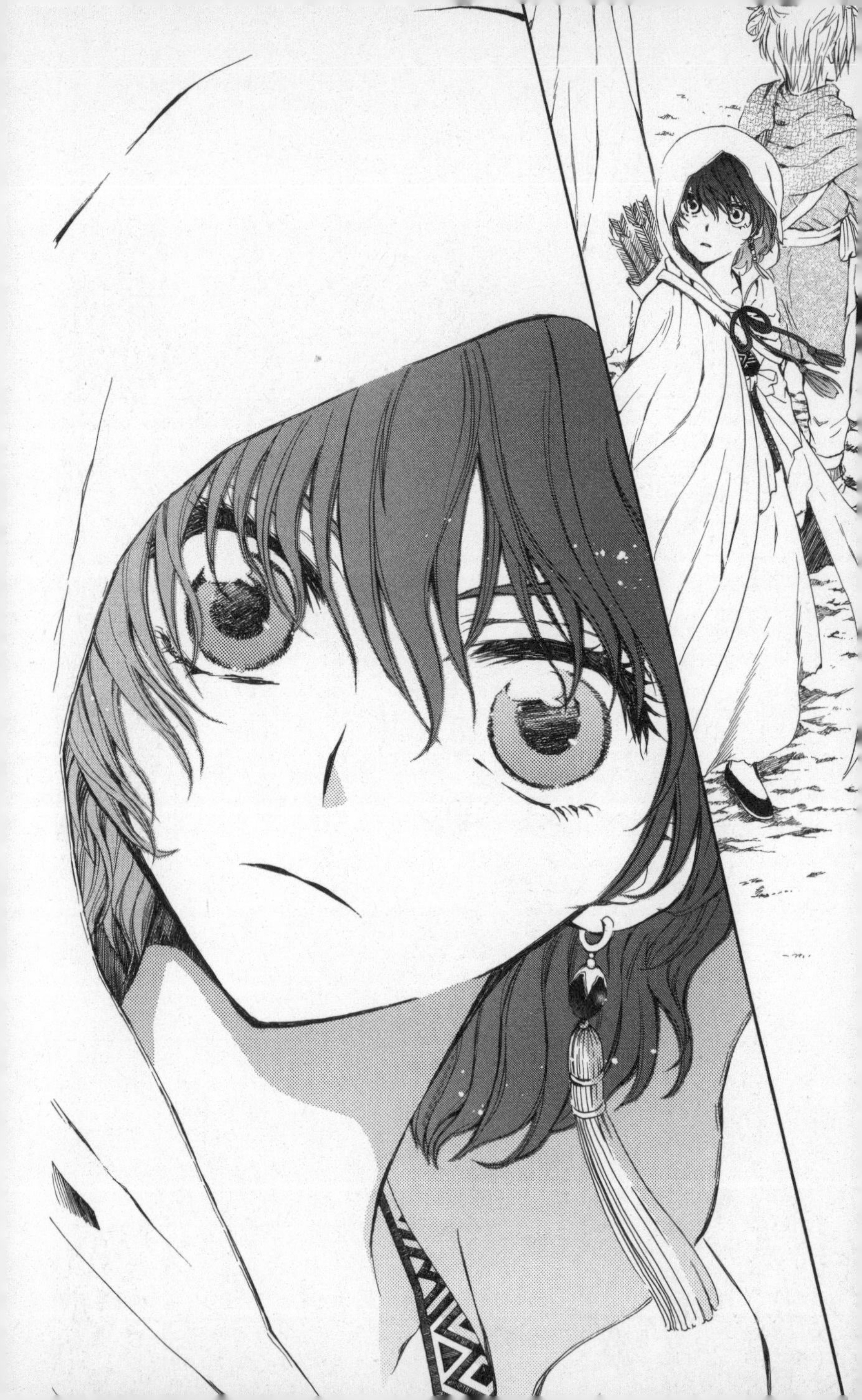

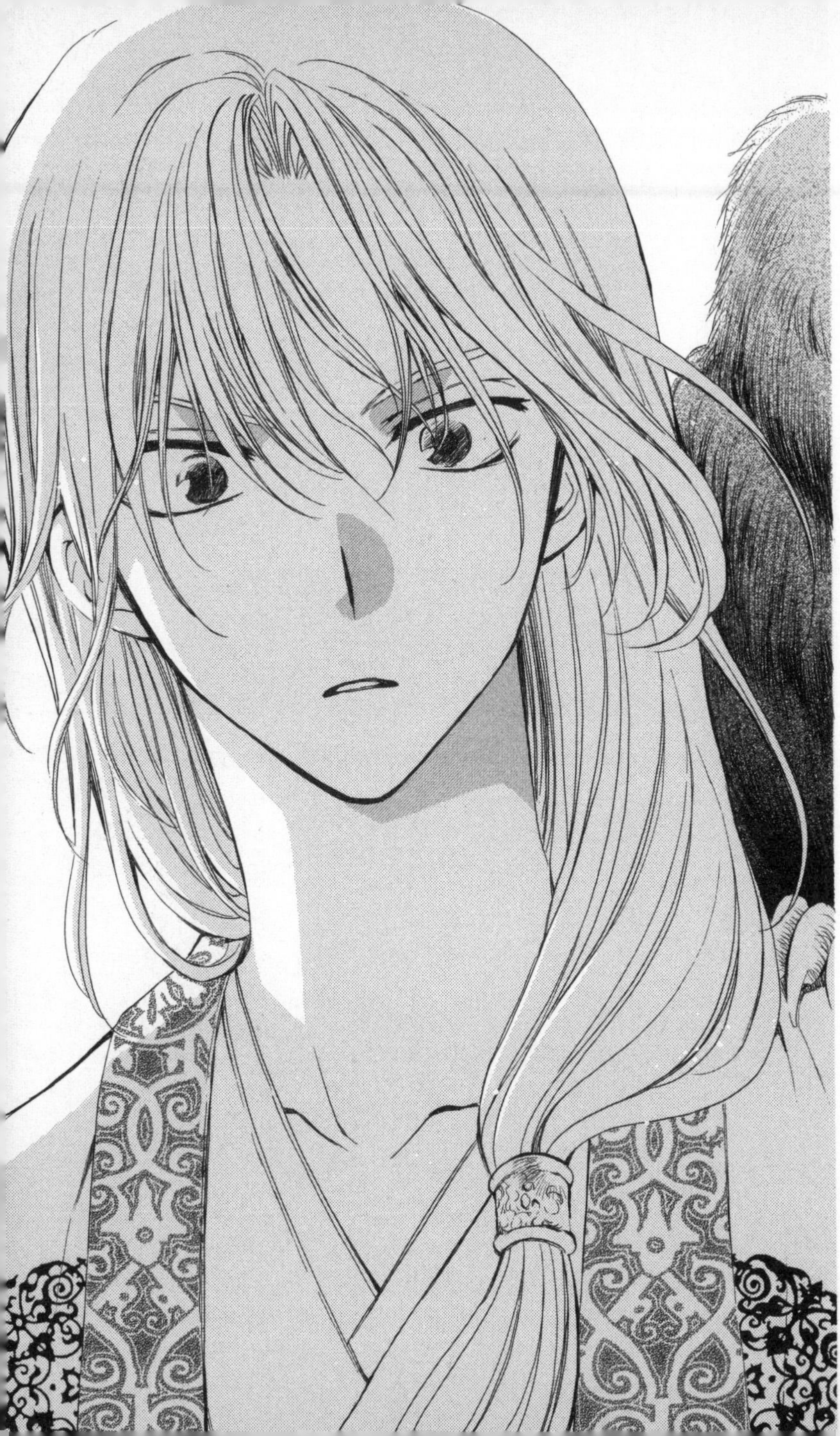

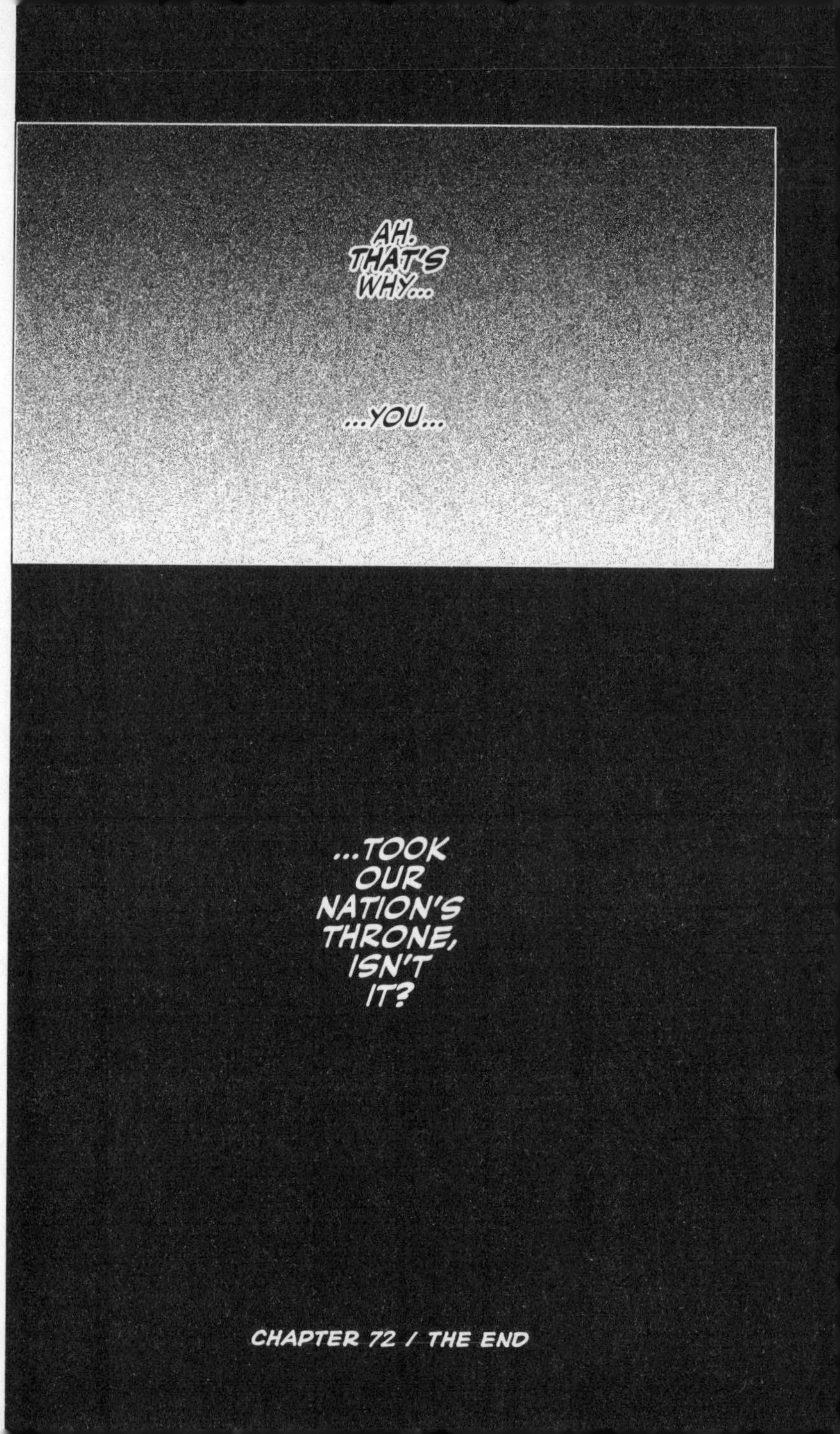
AH. THAT'S WHY...
...YOU...
...TOOK OUR NATION'S THRONE, ISN'T IT?
CHAPTER 72 / THE END

CHAPTER 73: DREAMS OF THE KING IN THE WILDERNESS

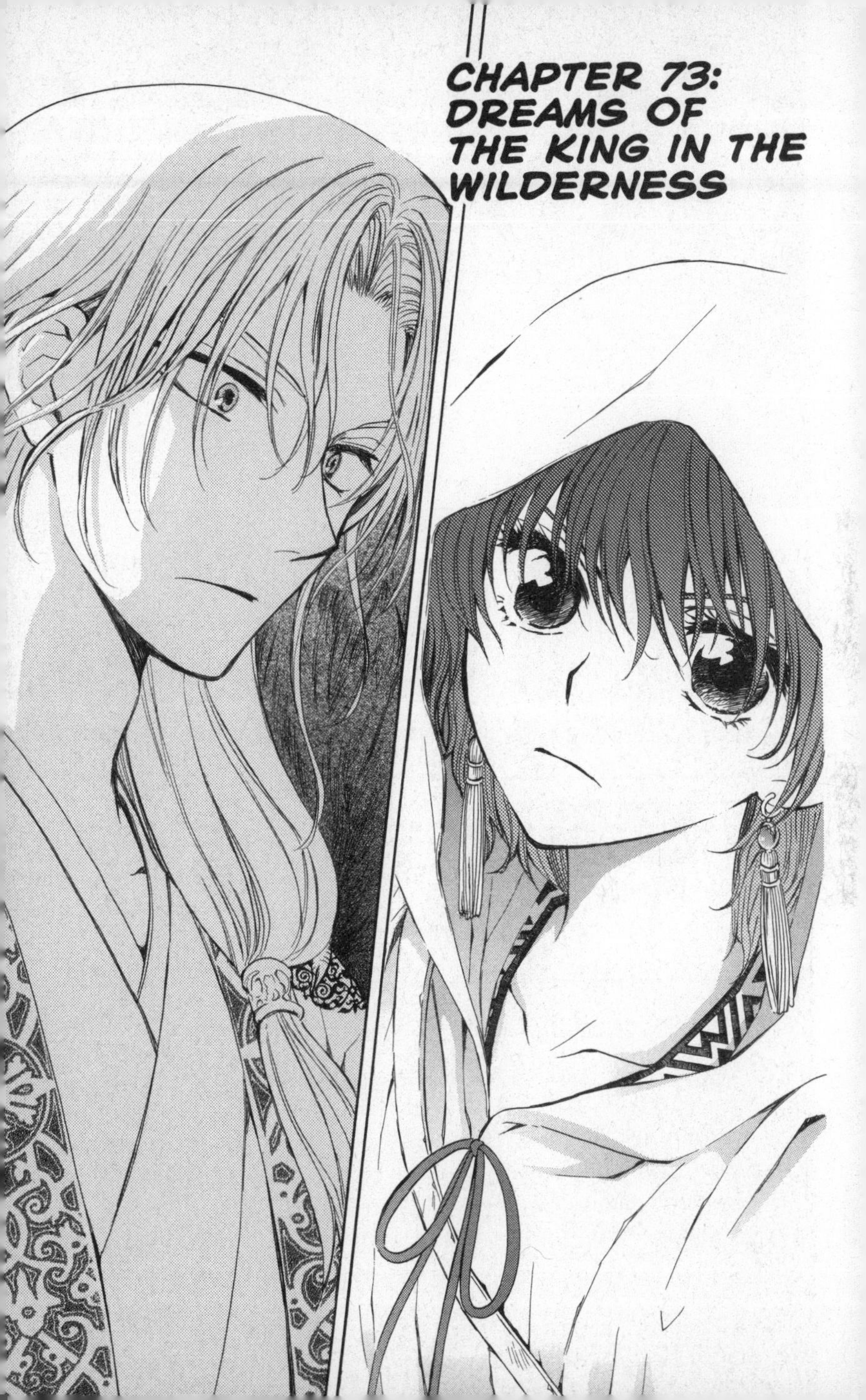

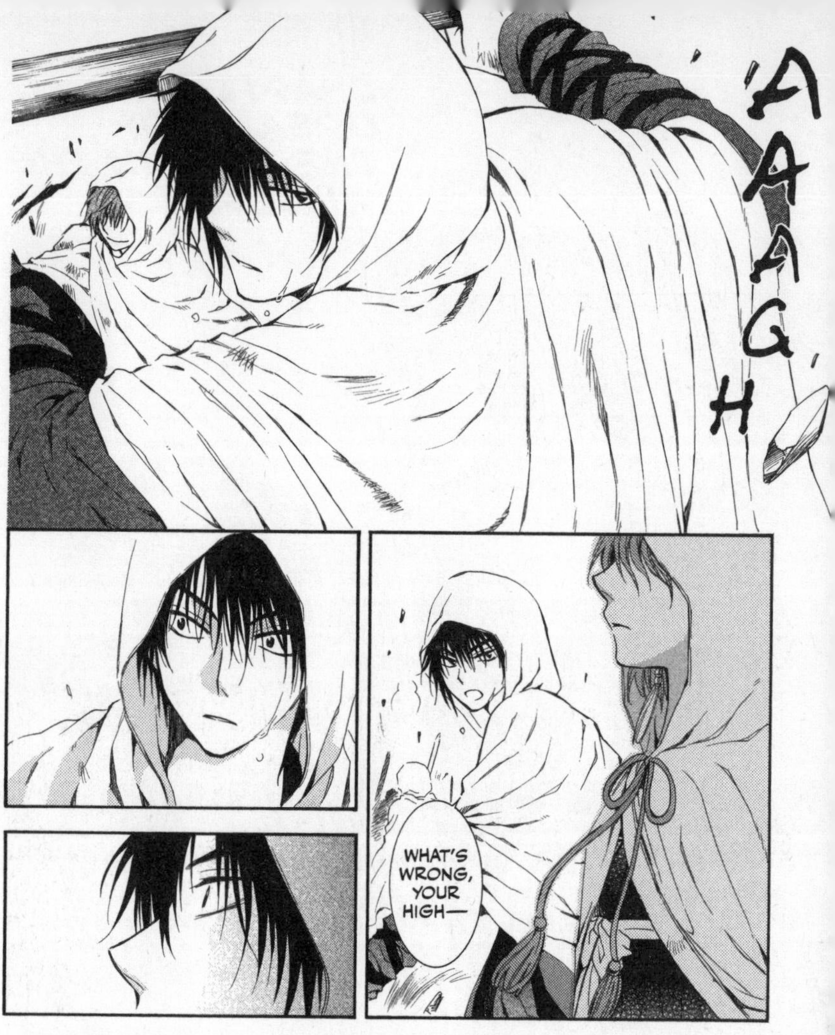
AAAGH
WHAT'S WRONG, YOUR HIGH—

Special thanks go out to so many people who make it possible for me to create *Yona of the Dawn.*
My assistants→Mikorun, Kyoko, Oka, Ryo, C.F., Awafuji and my little sister...
My editor Ishihara, my previous editors and the *Hana to Yume* editorial office...
Everyone who's helped me create and sell this manga...
Family, friends and readers who've always supported me...!
Thank you all so much! I'll keep doing my best and pouring all my energy into *Yona!*

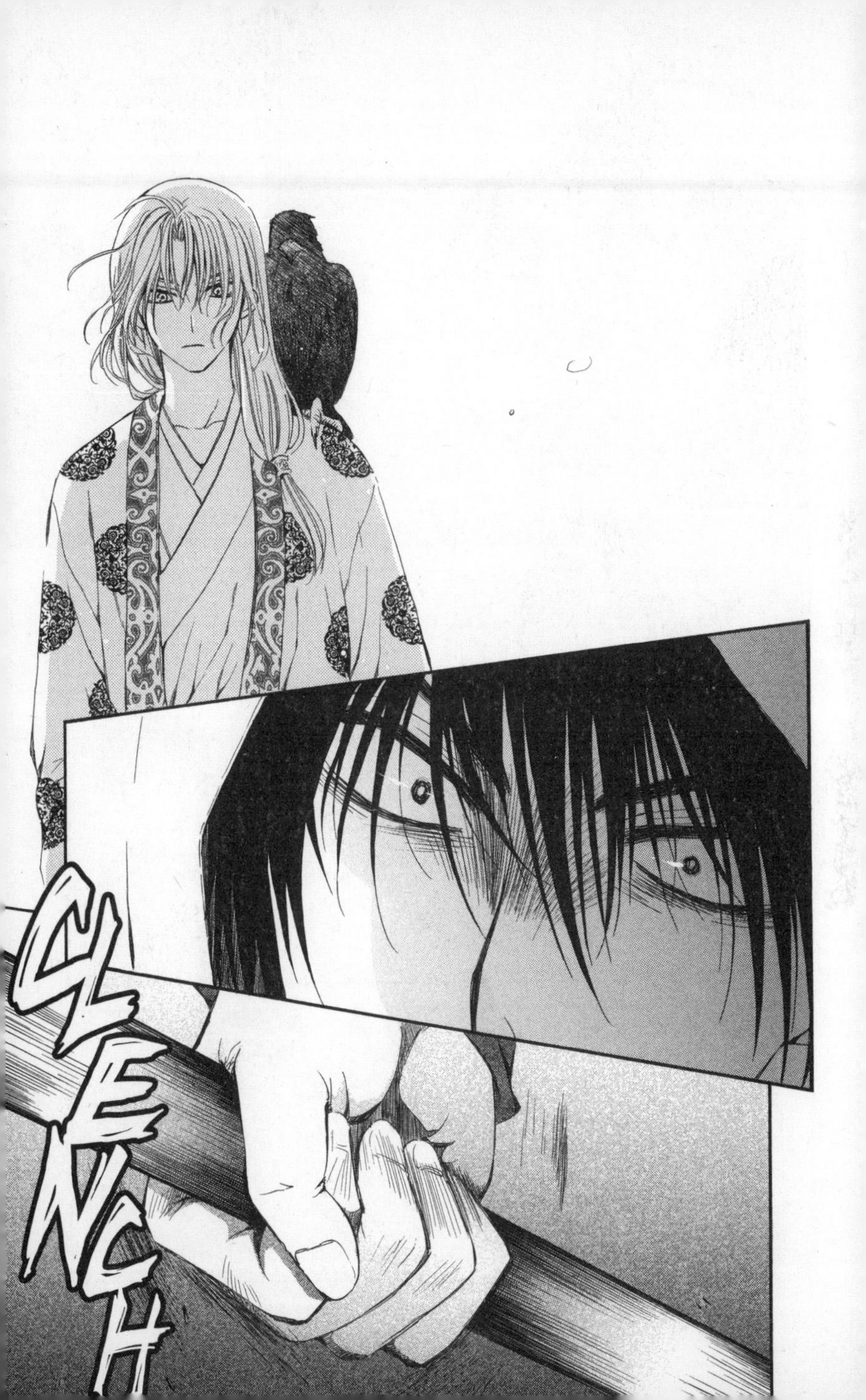
CLENCH

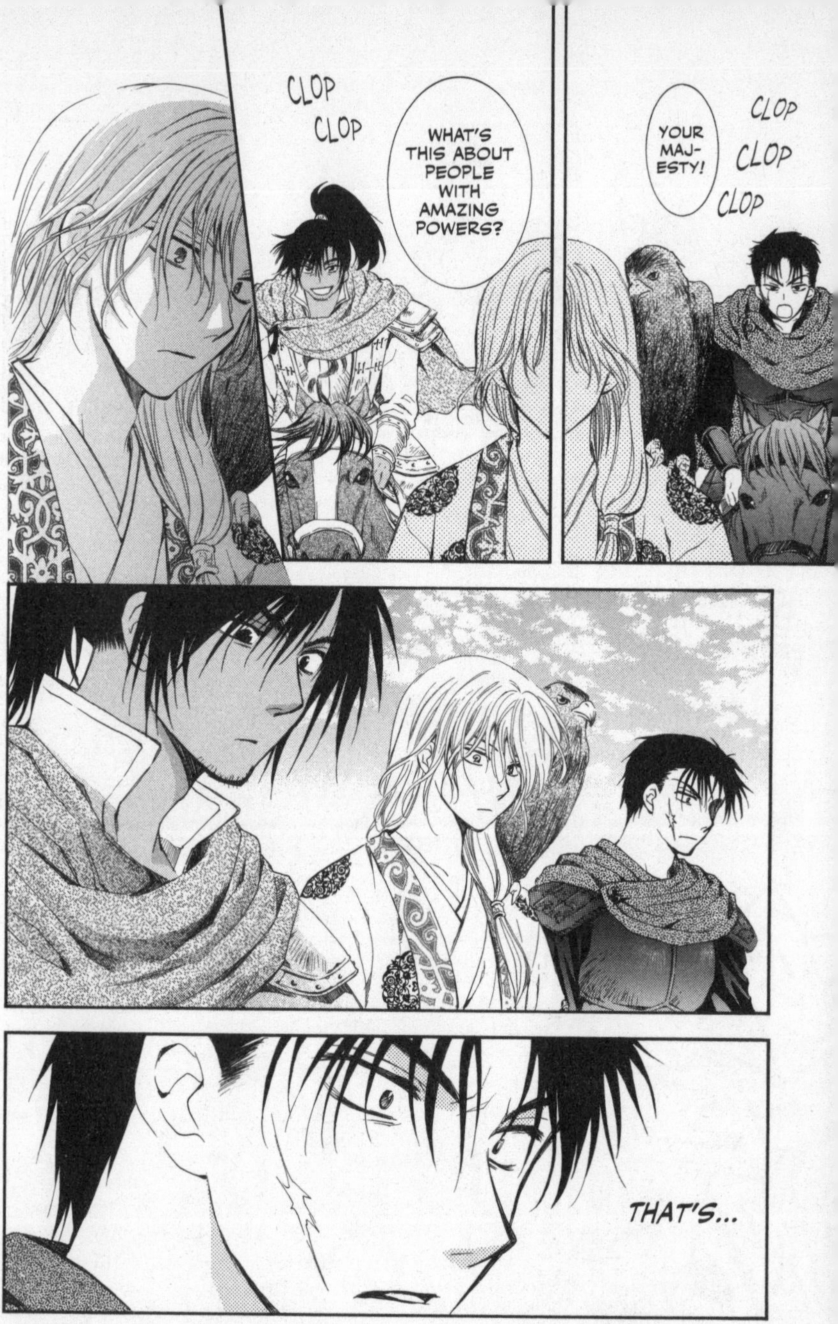
CLOP
CLOP
CLOP
YOUR MAJ-ESTY!
CLOP
CLOP
WHAT'S THIS ABOUT PEOPLE WITH AMAZING POWERS?
THAT'S...

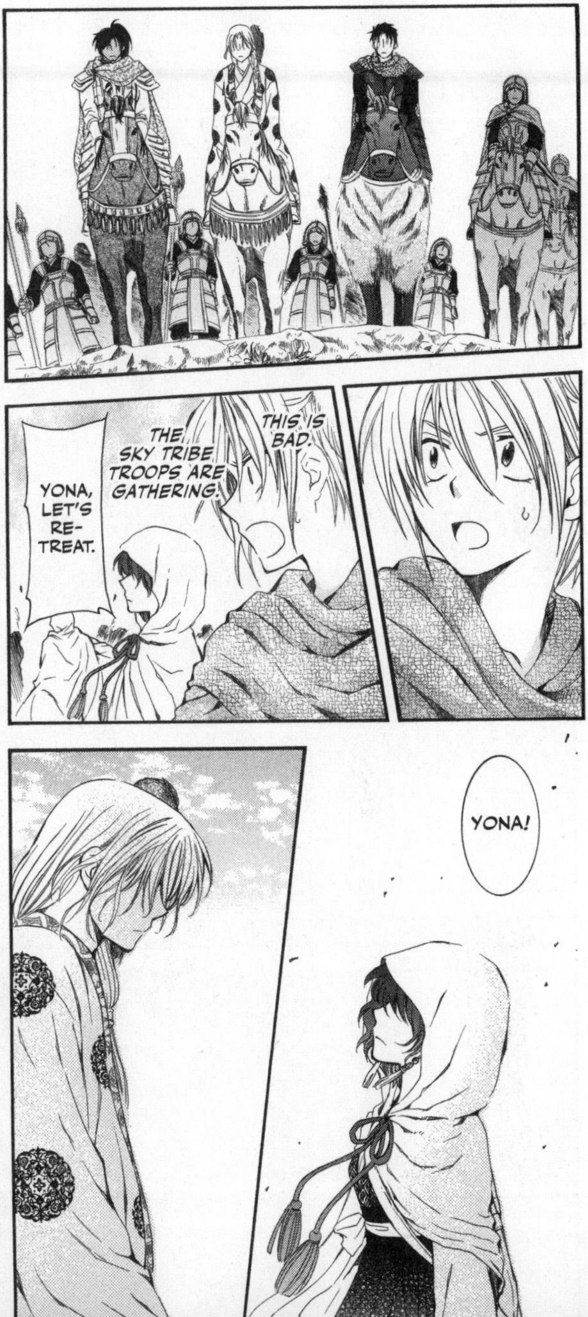
THIS IS BAD.
THE SKY TRIBE TROOPS ARE GATHERING.
YONA, LET'S RE-TREAT.
YONA!

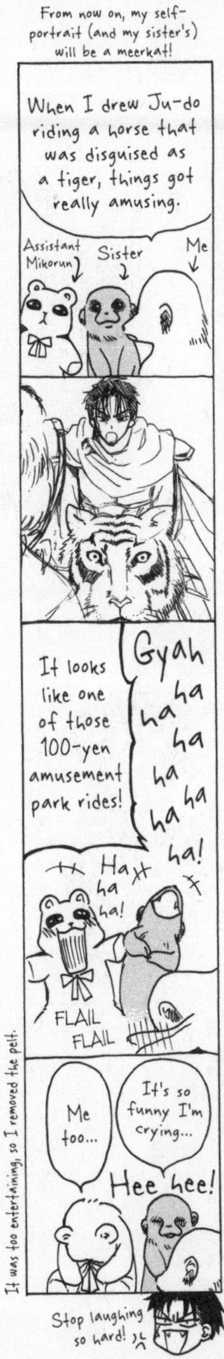
From now on, my self-portrait (and my sister's) will be a meerkat!
When I drew Ju-do riding a horse that was disguised as a tiger, things got really amusing.
Assistant Mikorun
Sister
Me
Gyah ha ha ha ha ha ha ha!
It looks like one of those 100-yen amusement park rides!
Ha ha ha!
FLAIL FLAIL
It's so funny I'm crying...
Me too...
Hee hee!
Stop laughing so hard!
It was too entertaining, so I removed the pelt.

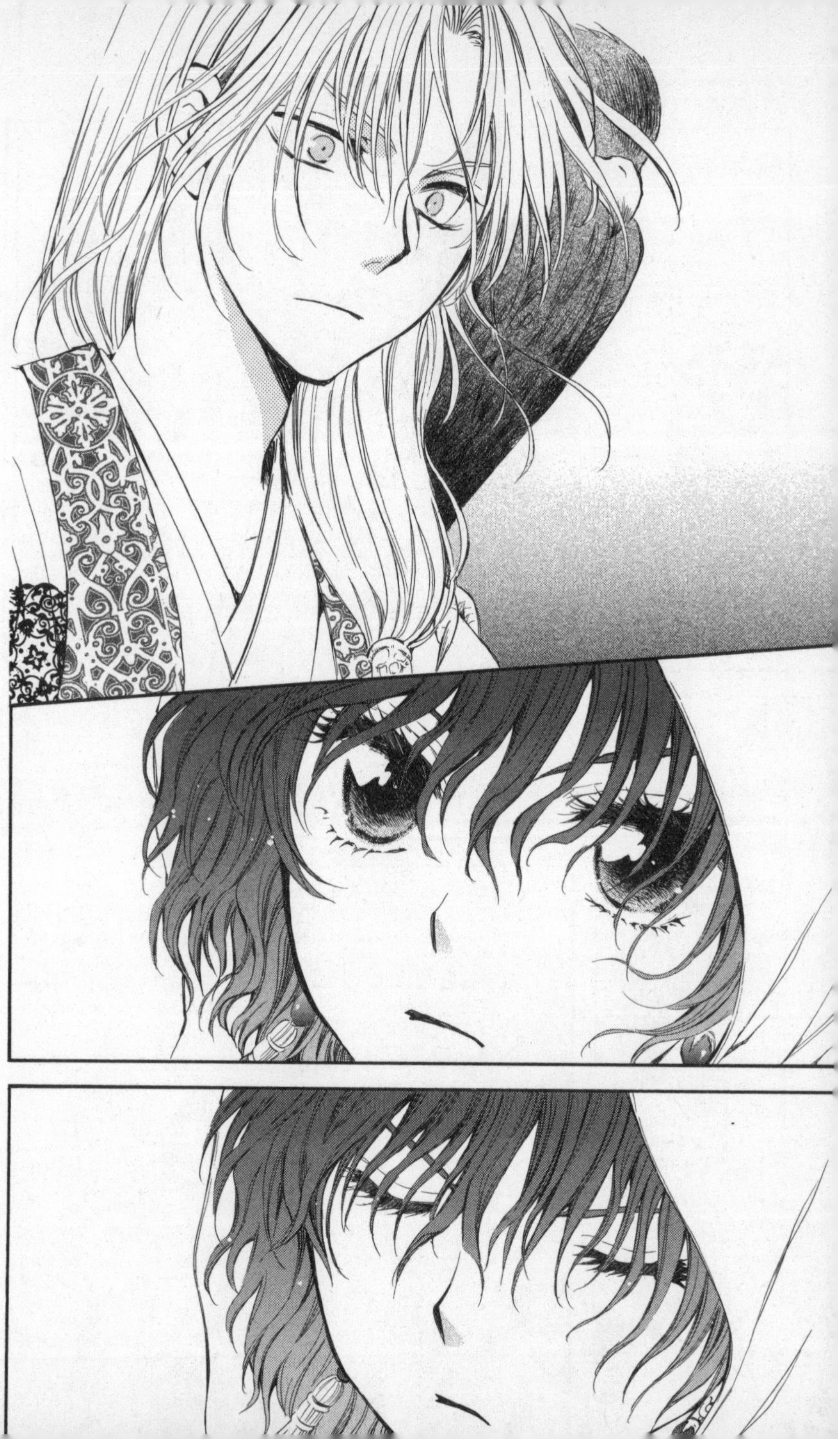

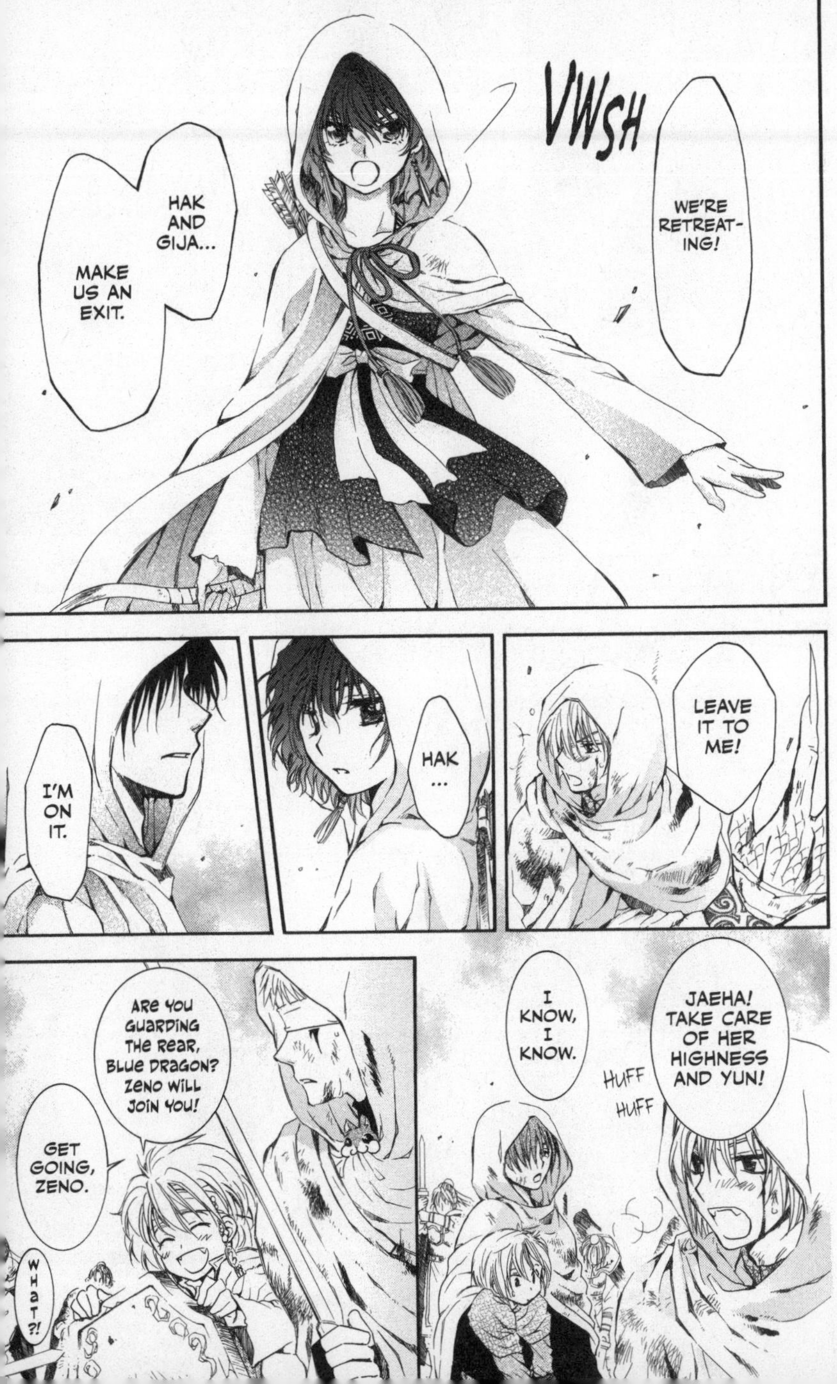
VWSH
WE'RE RETREATING!
HAK AND GIJA...
MAKE US AN EXIT.
LEAVE IT TO ME!
HAK...
I'M ON IT.
JAEHA! TAKE CARE OF HER HIGHNESS AND YUN!
I KNOW, I KNOW.
HUFF HUFF
ARE YOU GUARDING THE REAR, BLUE DRAGON? ZENO WILL JOIN YOU!
GET GOING, ZENO.
WHAT?!

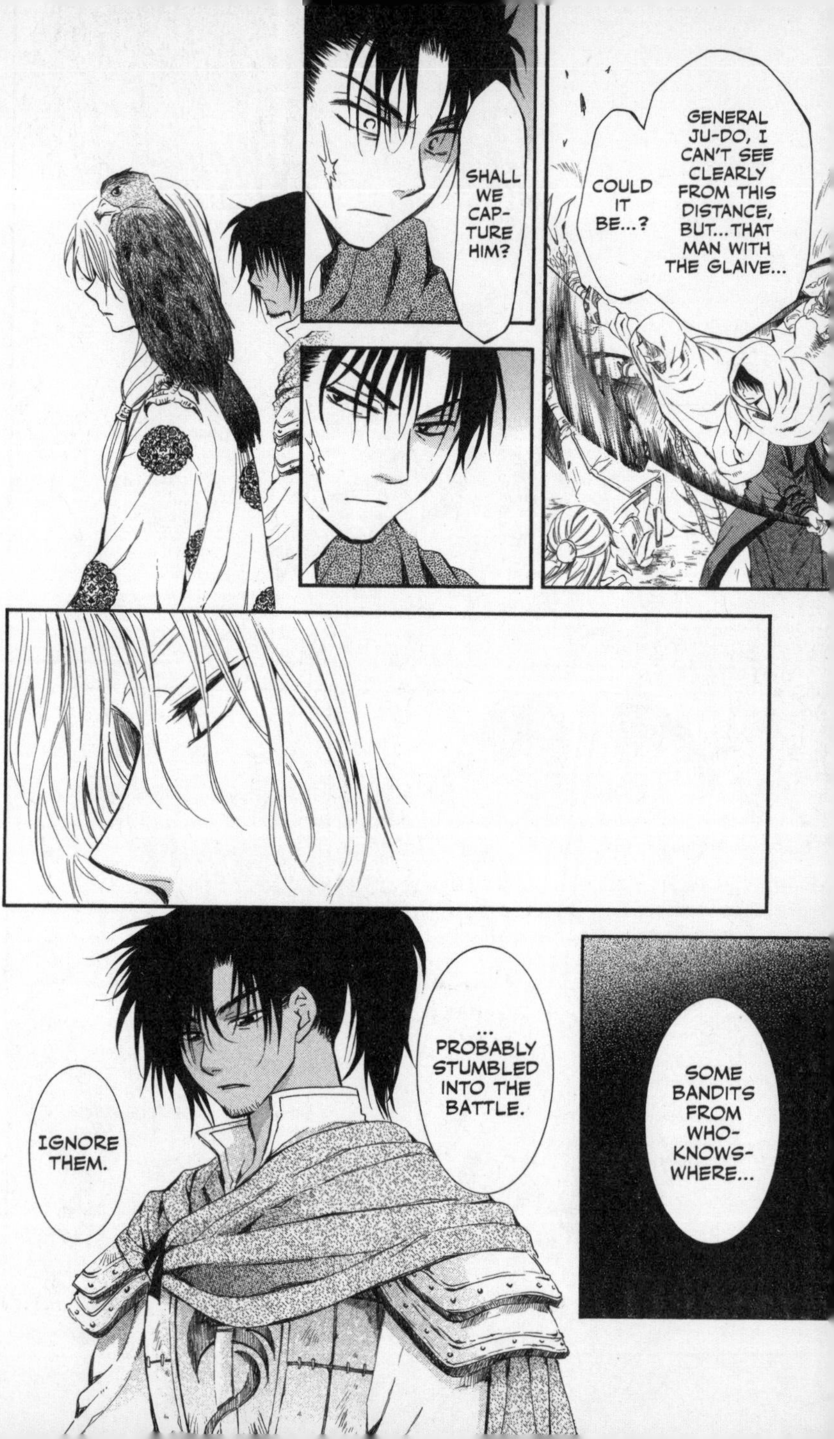
GENERAL JU-DO, I CAN'T SEE CLEARLY FROM THIS DISTANCE, BUT...THAT MAN WITH THE GLAIVE...
COULD IT BE...?
SHALL WE CAP-TURE HIM?
SOME BANDITS FROM WHO-KNOWS-WHERE...
...PROBABLY STUMBLED INTO THE BATTLE.
IGNORE THEM.

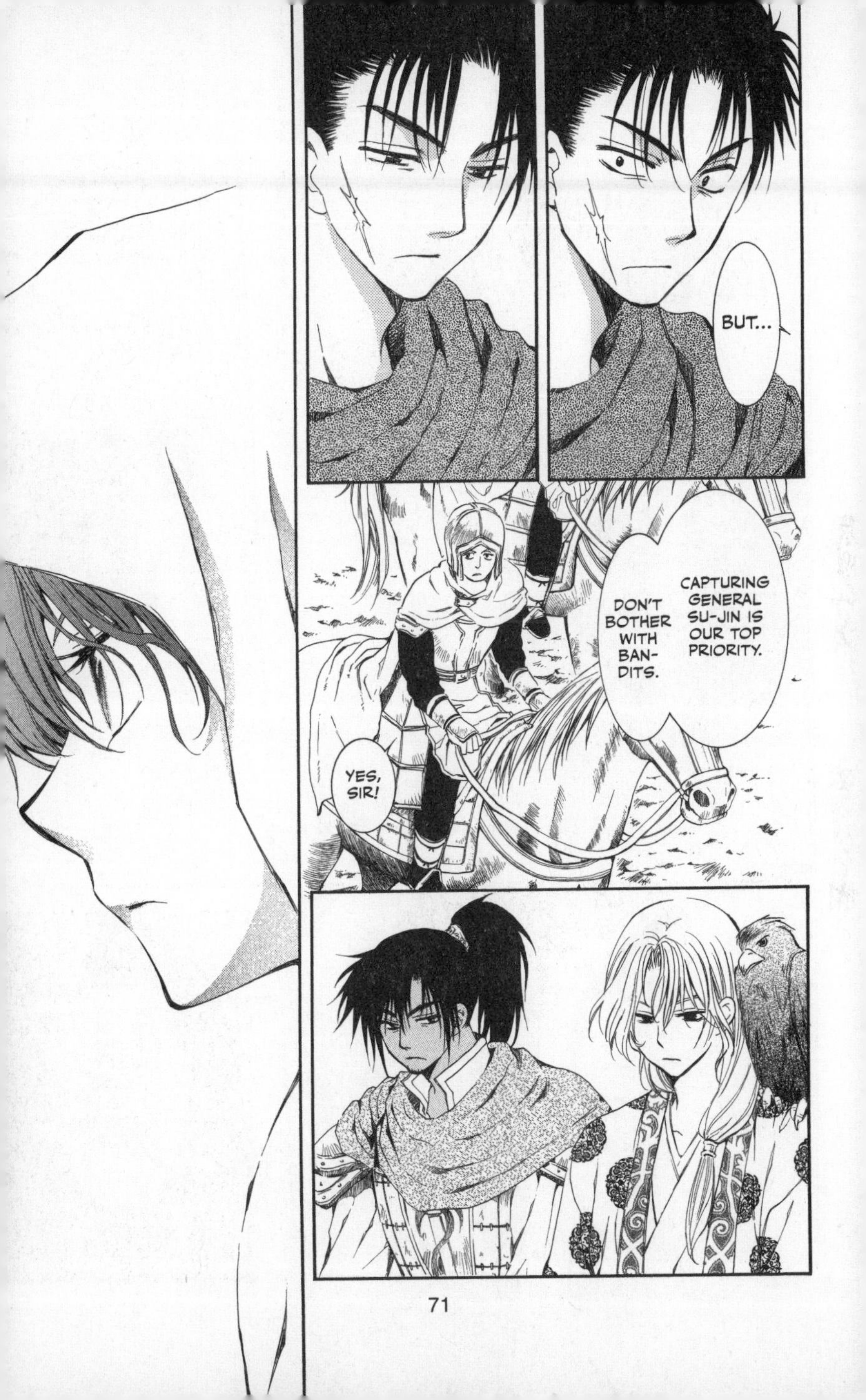
BUT...
CAPTURING GENERAL SU-JIN IS OUR TOP PRIORITY.
DON'T BOTHER WITH BAN-DITS.
YES, SIR!

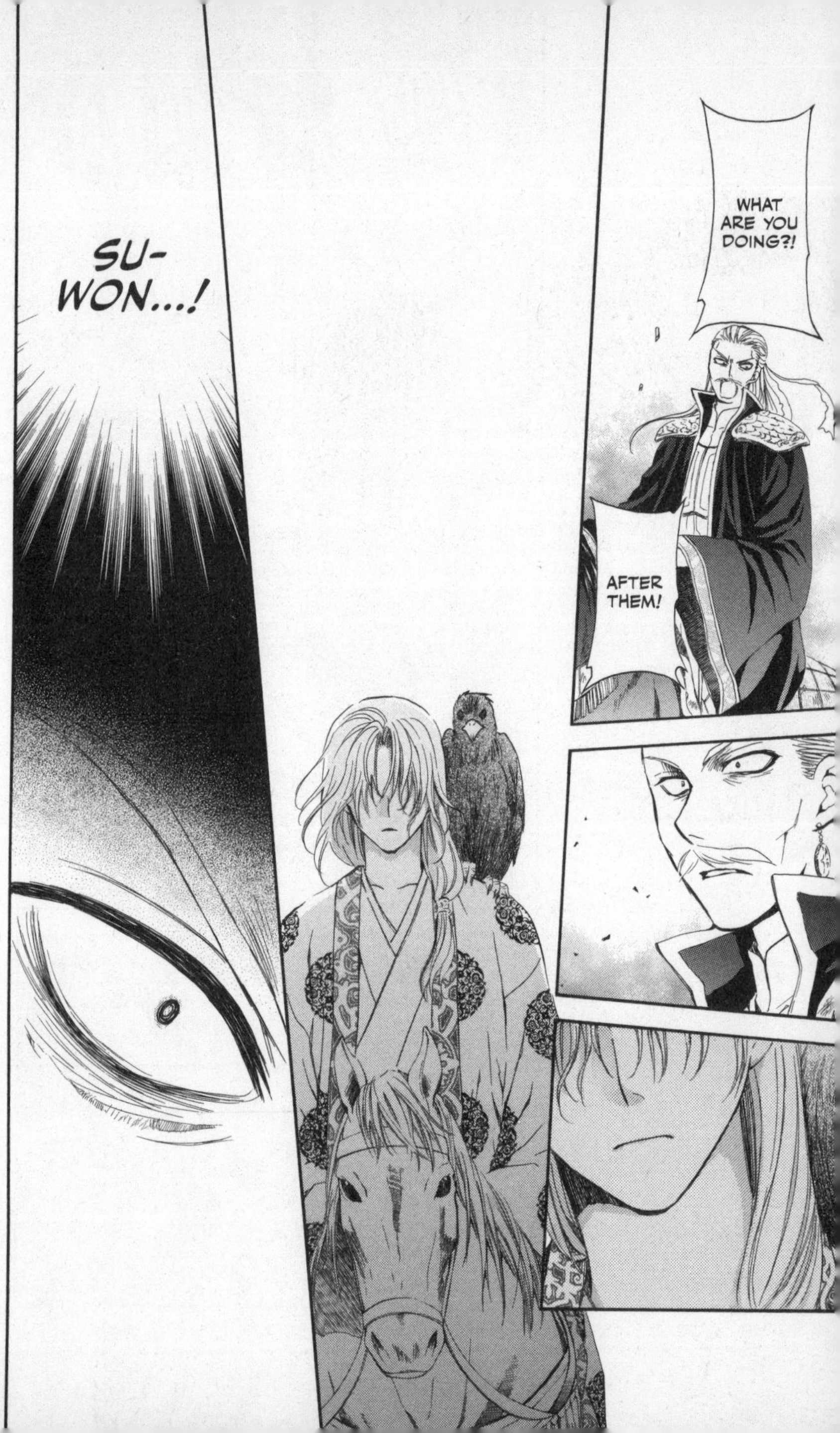
WHAT ARE YOU DOING?!
AFTER THEM!
SU-WON...!

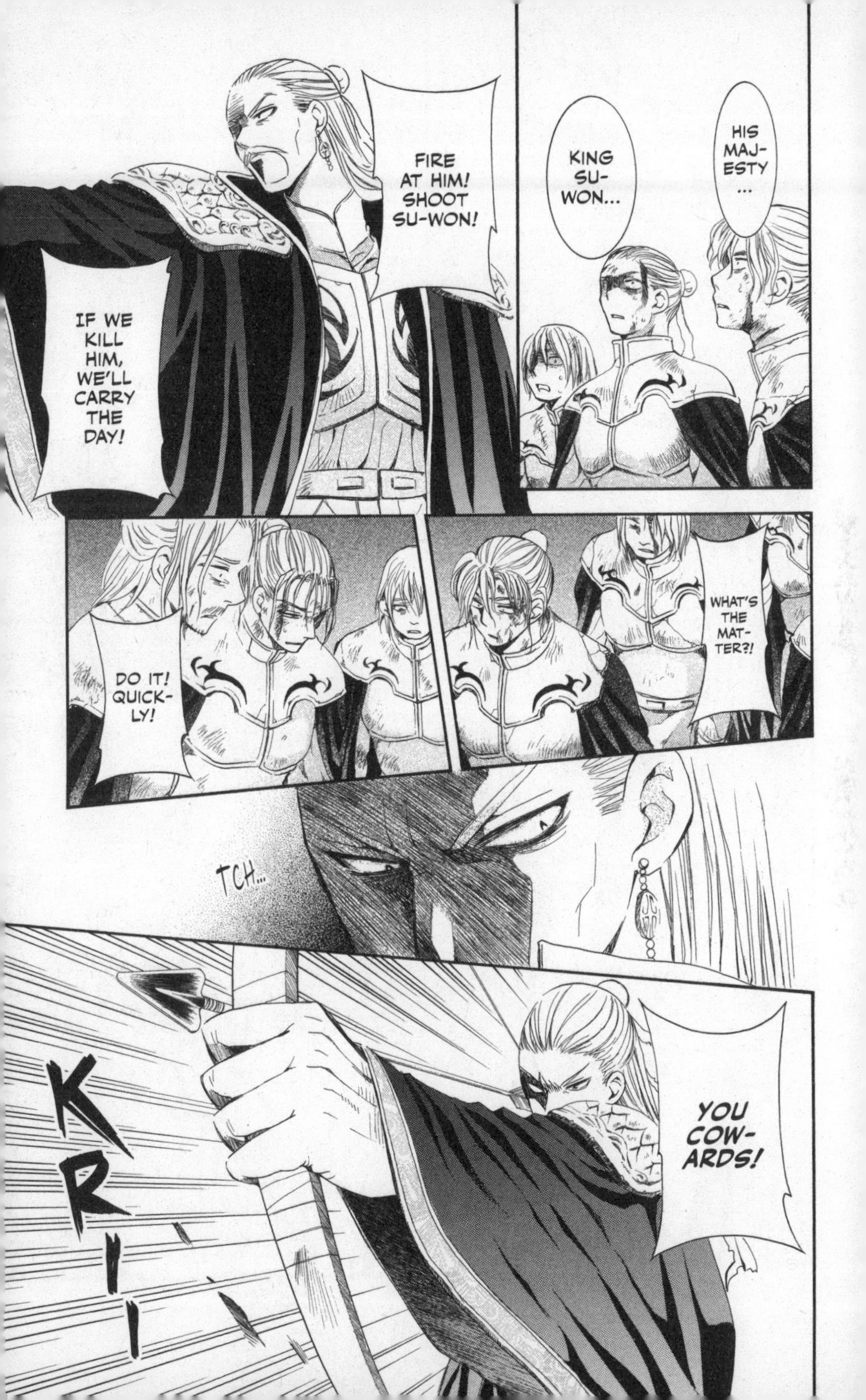
HIS MAJ-ESTY...
KING SU-WON...
FIRE AT HIM! SHOOT SU-WON!
IF WE KILL HIM, WE'LL CARRY THE DAY!
WHAT'S THE MAT-TER?!
DO IT! QUICK-LY!
TCH...
YOU COW-ARDS!
KRII

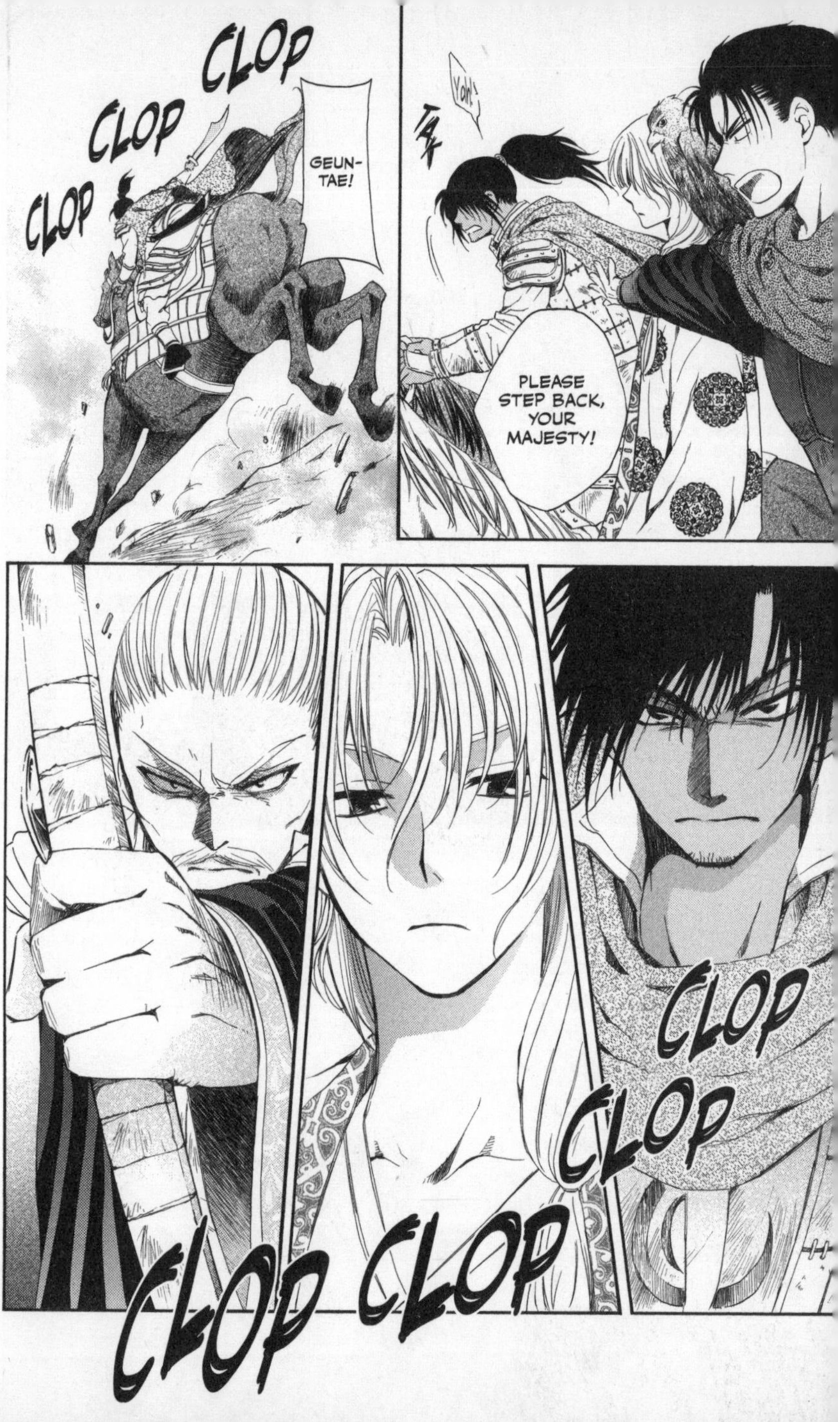
Yah!
PLEASE STEP BACK, YOUR MAJESTY!
CLOP
CLOP
CLOP
GEUN-TAE!
CLOP
CLOP
CLOP
CLOP
CLOP

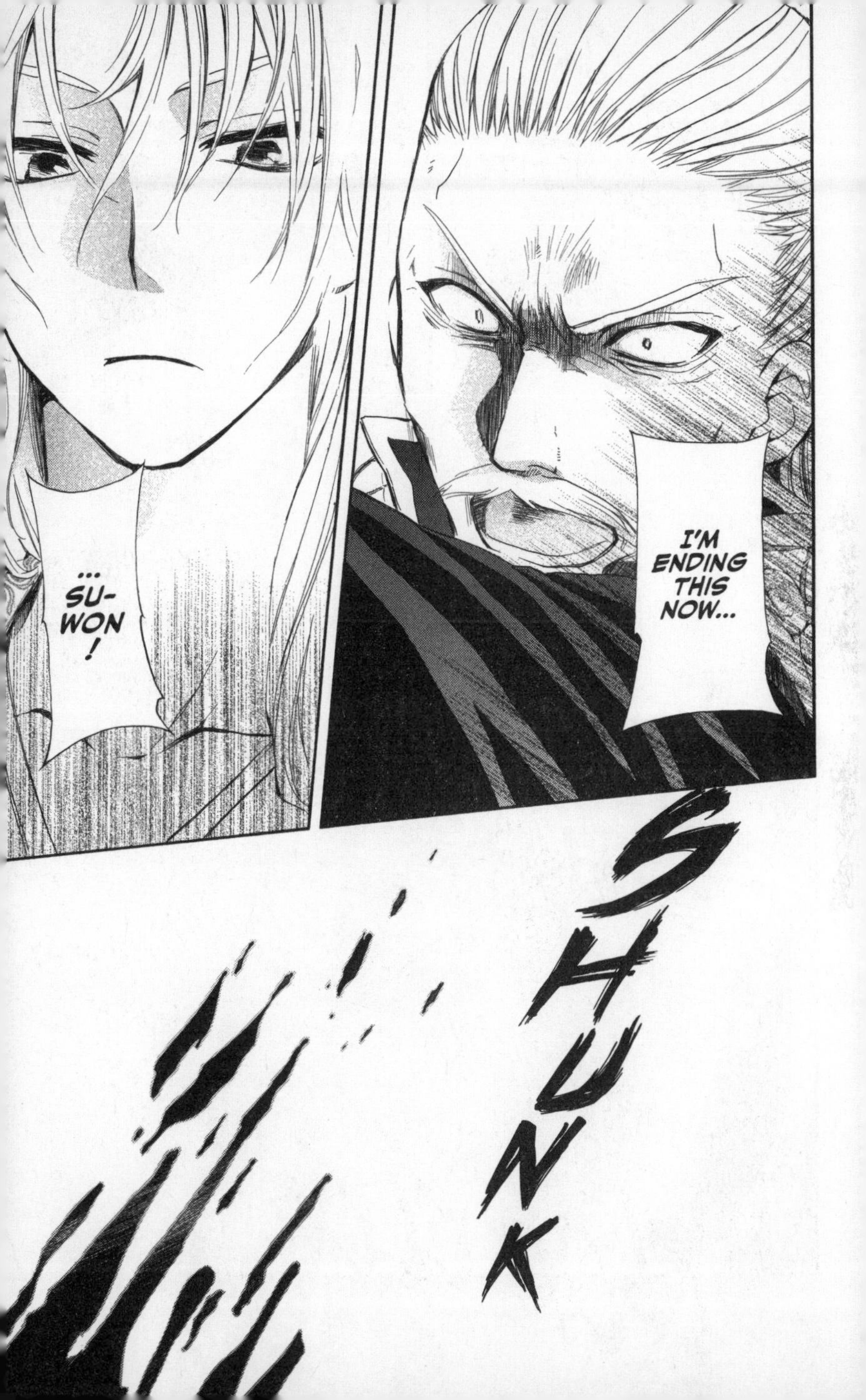
I'M ENDING THIS NOW...
... SU-WON!
SHUNK

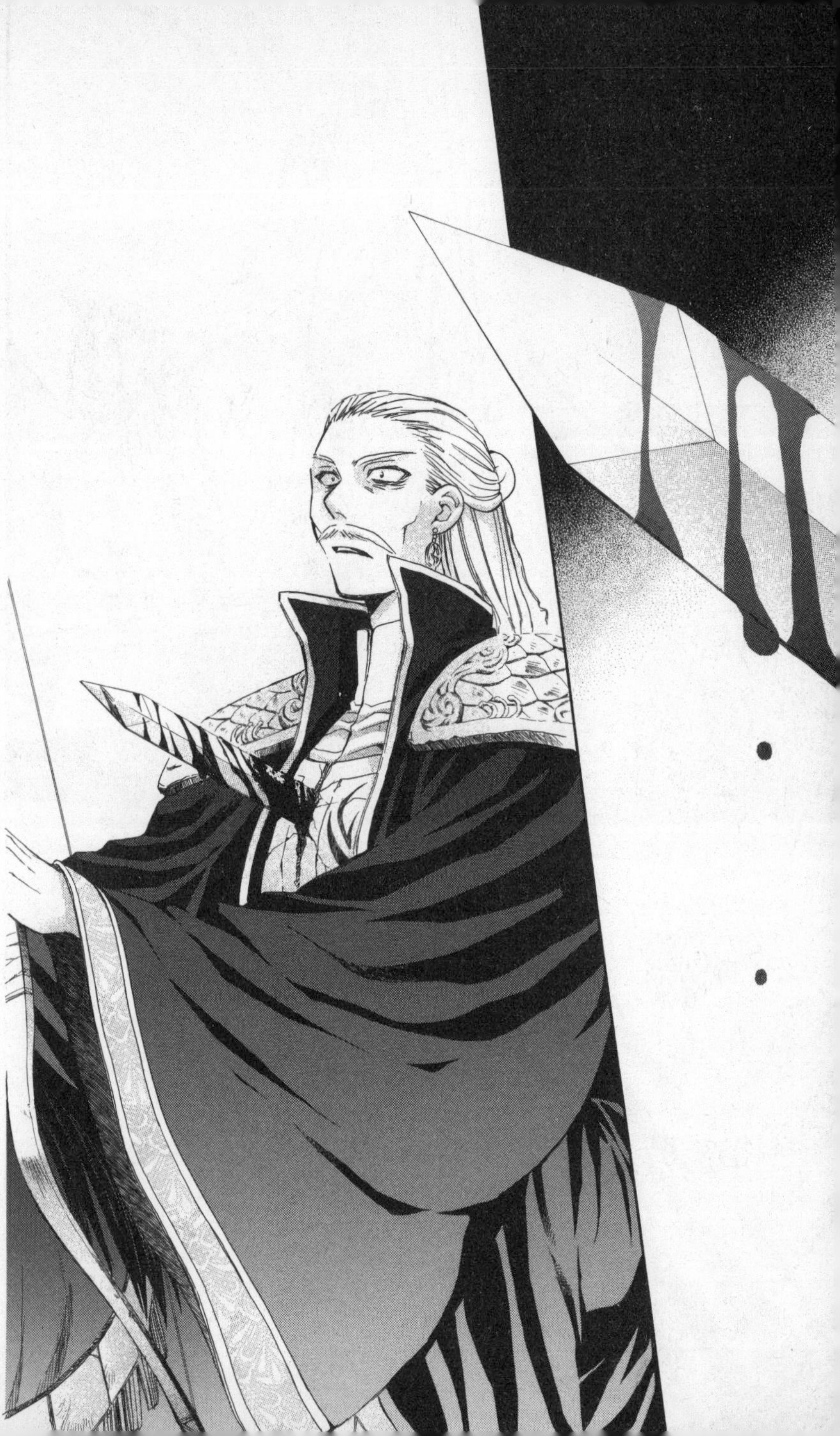

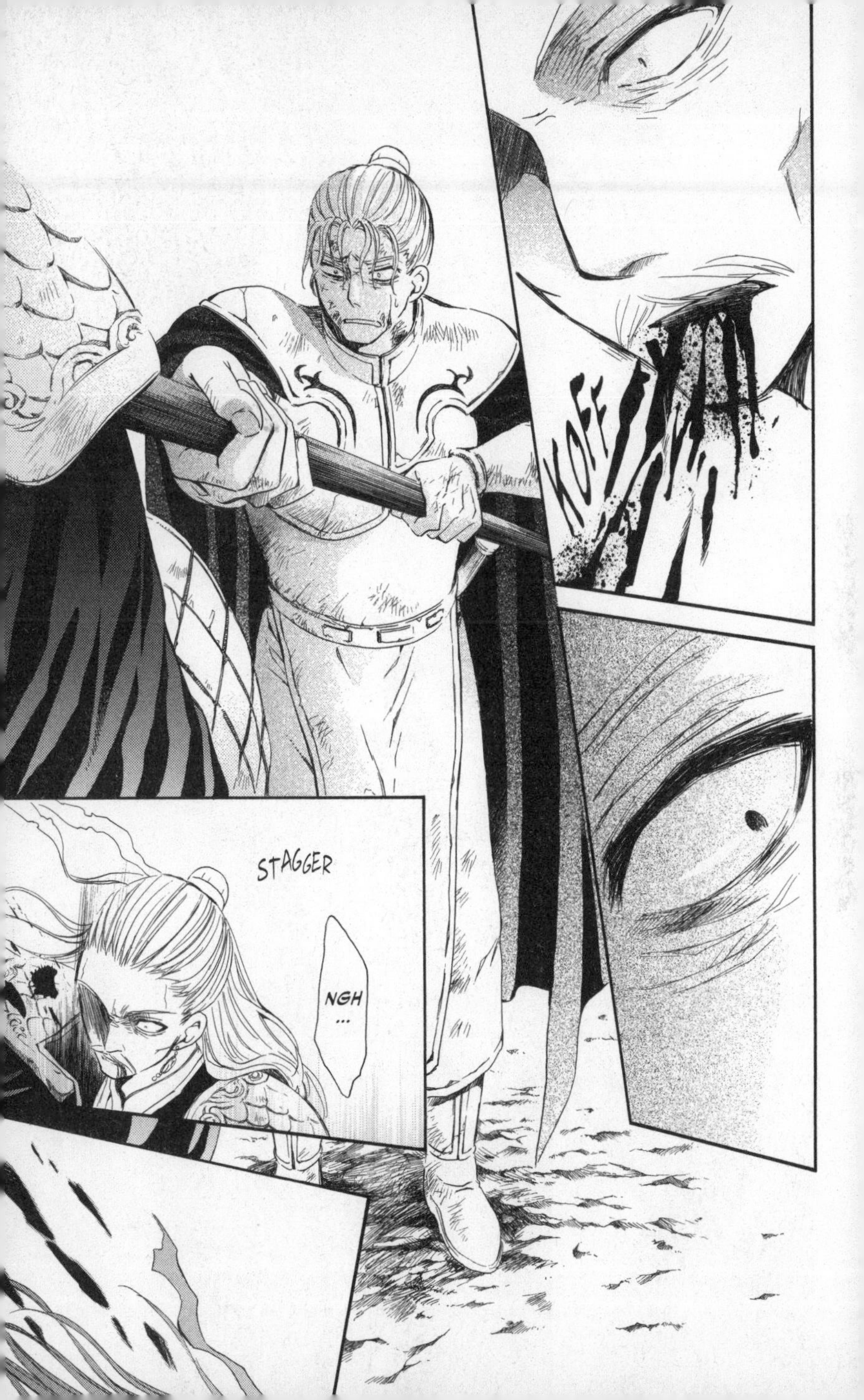
KOFF
STAGGER
NGH
...

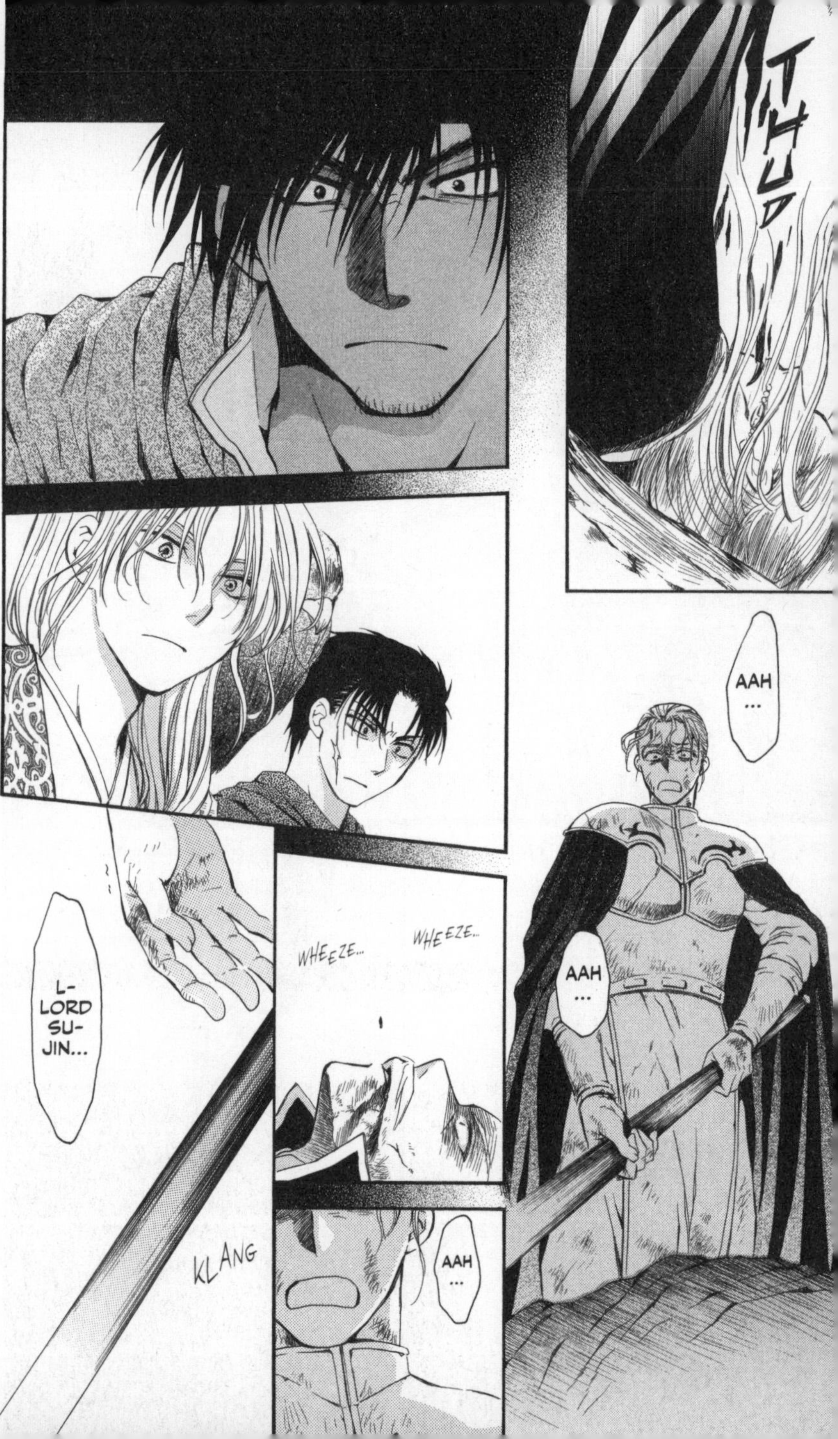
THUD
AAH...
AAH...
WHEEZE...
WHEEZE...
L-LORD SU-JIN...
AAH...
KLANG

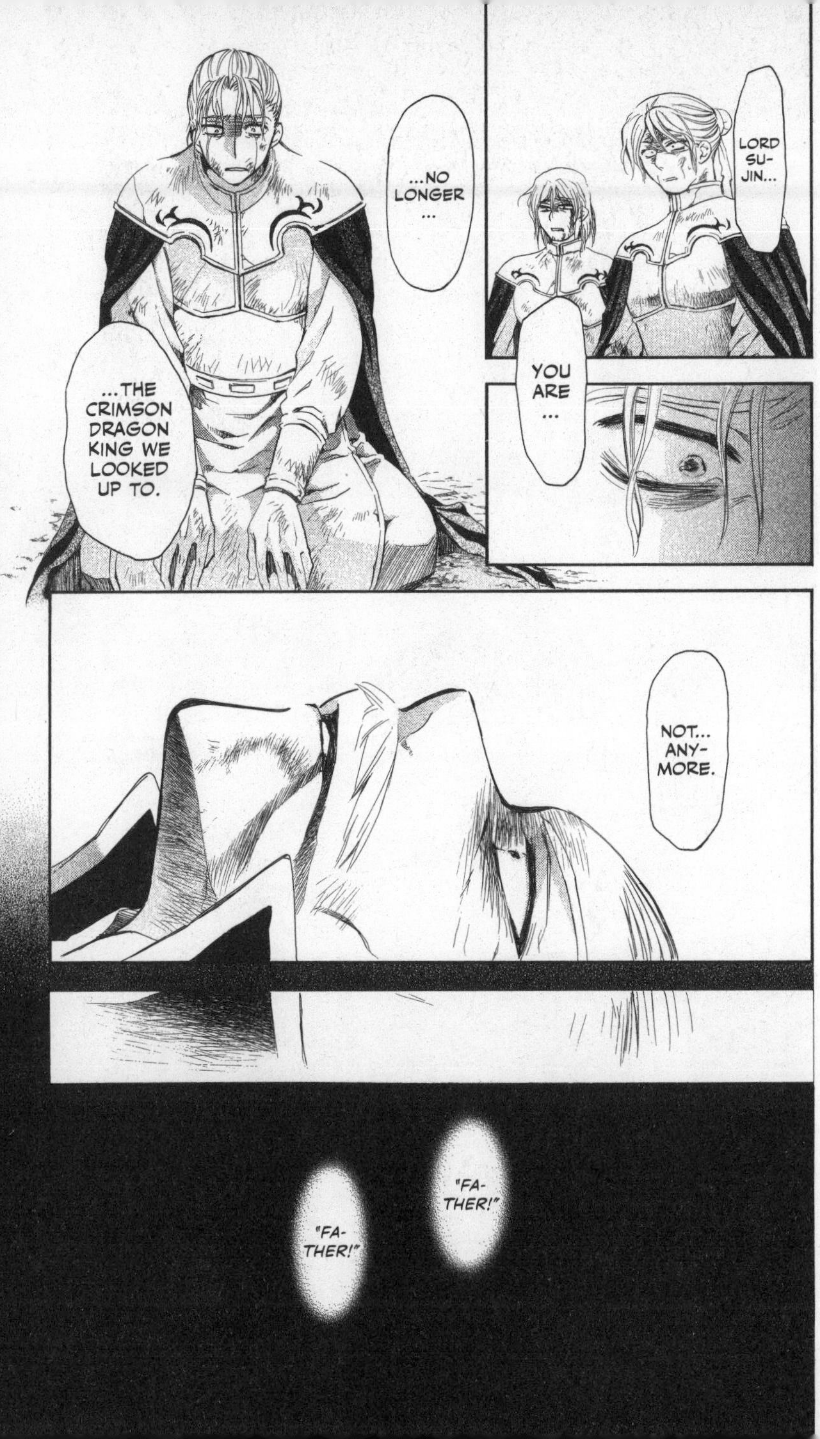
LORD SU-JIN...
YOU ARE...
...NO LONGER...
...THE CRIMSON DRAGON KING WE LOOKED UP TO.
NOT... ANYMORE.
"FATHER!"
"FATHER!"

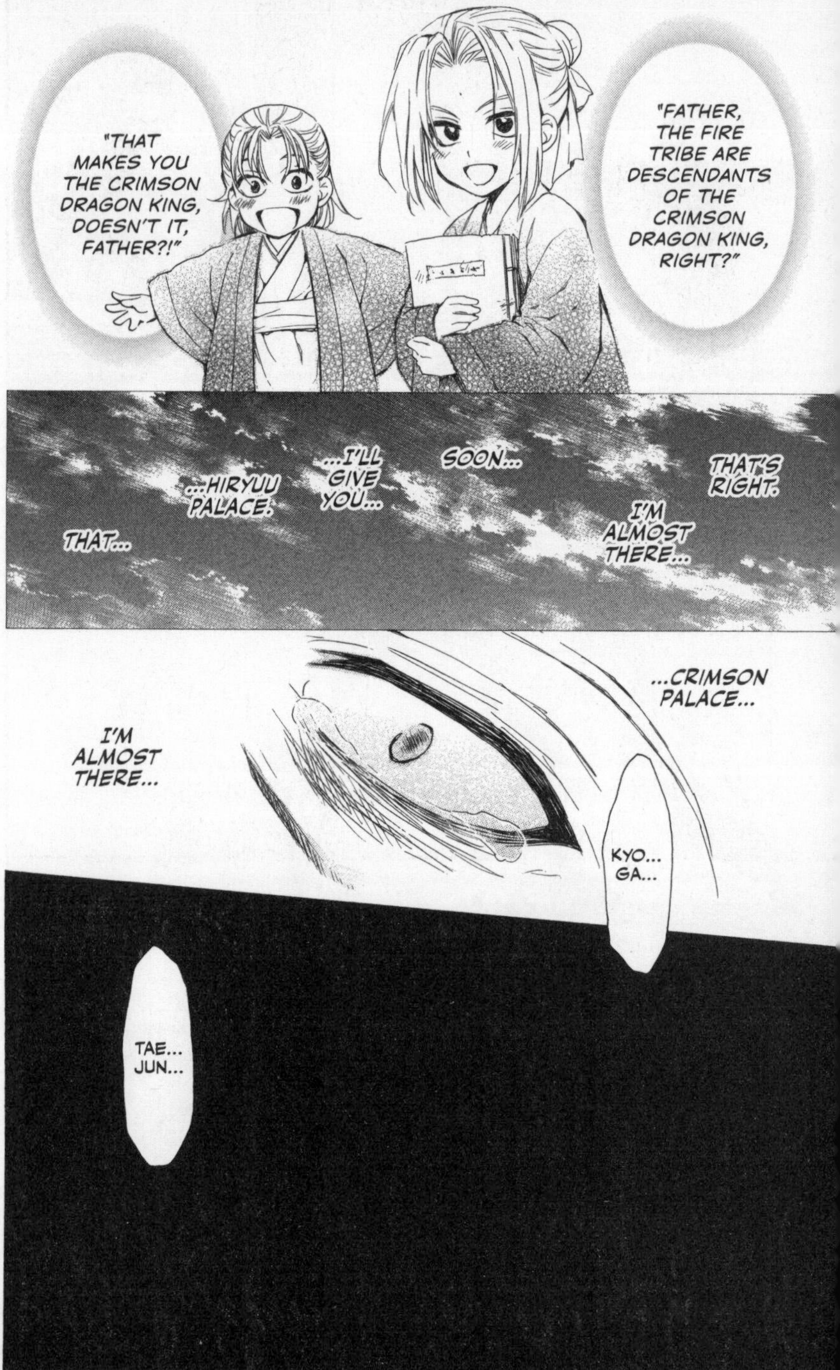
"FATHER, THE FIRE TRIBE ARE DESCENDANTS OF THE CRIMSON DRAGON KING, RIGHT?"
"THAT MAKES YOU THE CRIMSON DRAGON KING, DOESN'T IT, FATHER?!"
THAT'S RIGHT.
I'M ALMOST THERE...
SOON...
...I'LL GIVE YOU...
...HIRYUU PALACE.
THAT...
...CRIMSON PALACE...
I'M ALMOST THERE...
KYO... GA...
TAE... JUN...

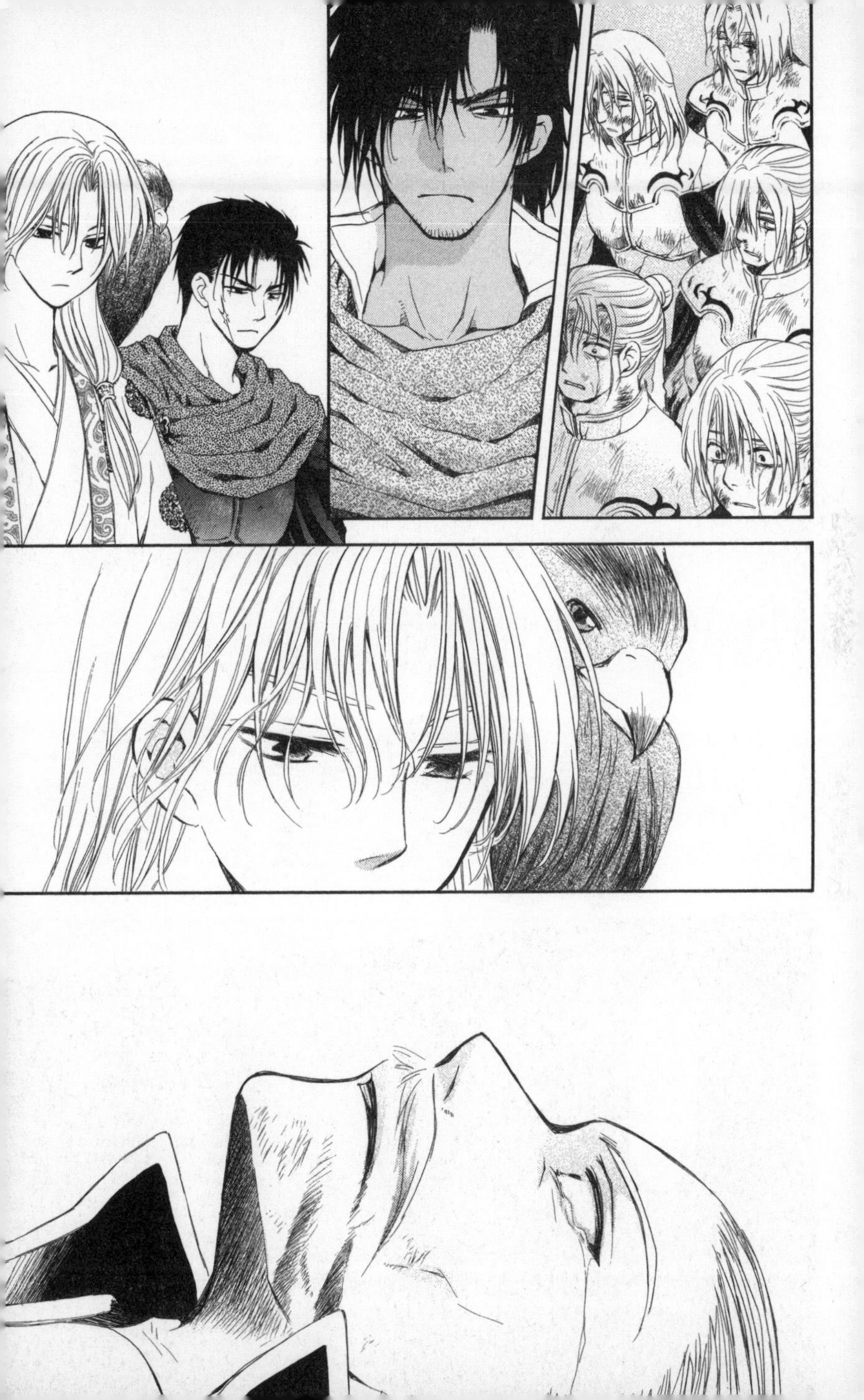

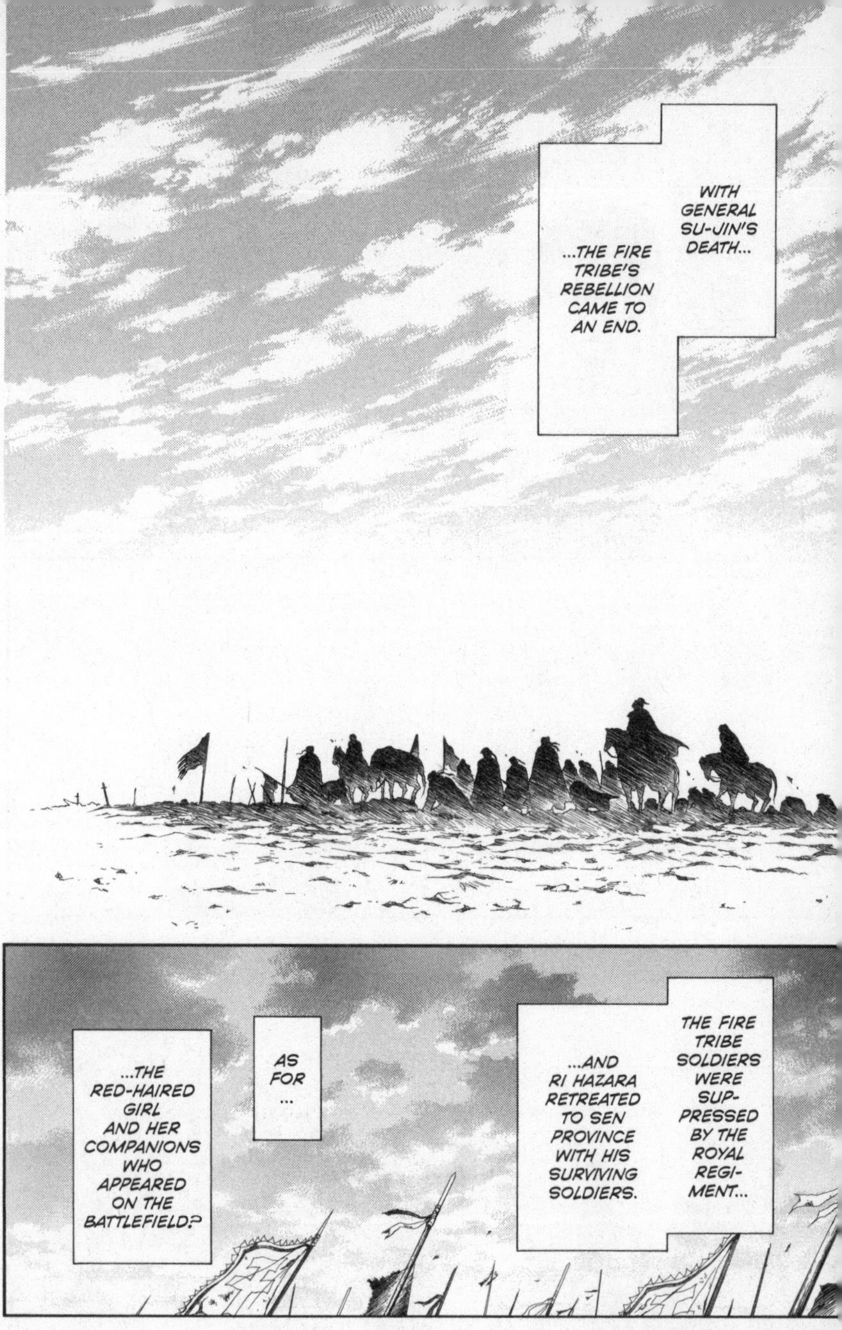
WITH GENERAL SU-JIN'S DEATH...
...THE FIRE TRIBE'S REBELLION CAME TO AN END.
THE FIRE TRIBE SOLDIERS WERE SUP-PRESSED BY THE ROYAL REGI-MENT...
...AND RI HAZARA RETREATED TO SEN PROVINCE WITH HIS SURVIVING SOLDIERS.
AS FOR ...
...THE RED-HAIRED GIRL AND HER COMPANIONS WHO APPEARED ON THE BATTLEFIELD?

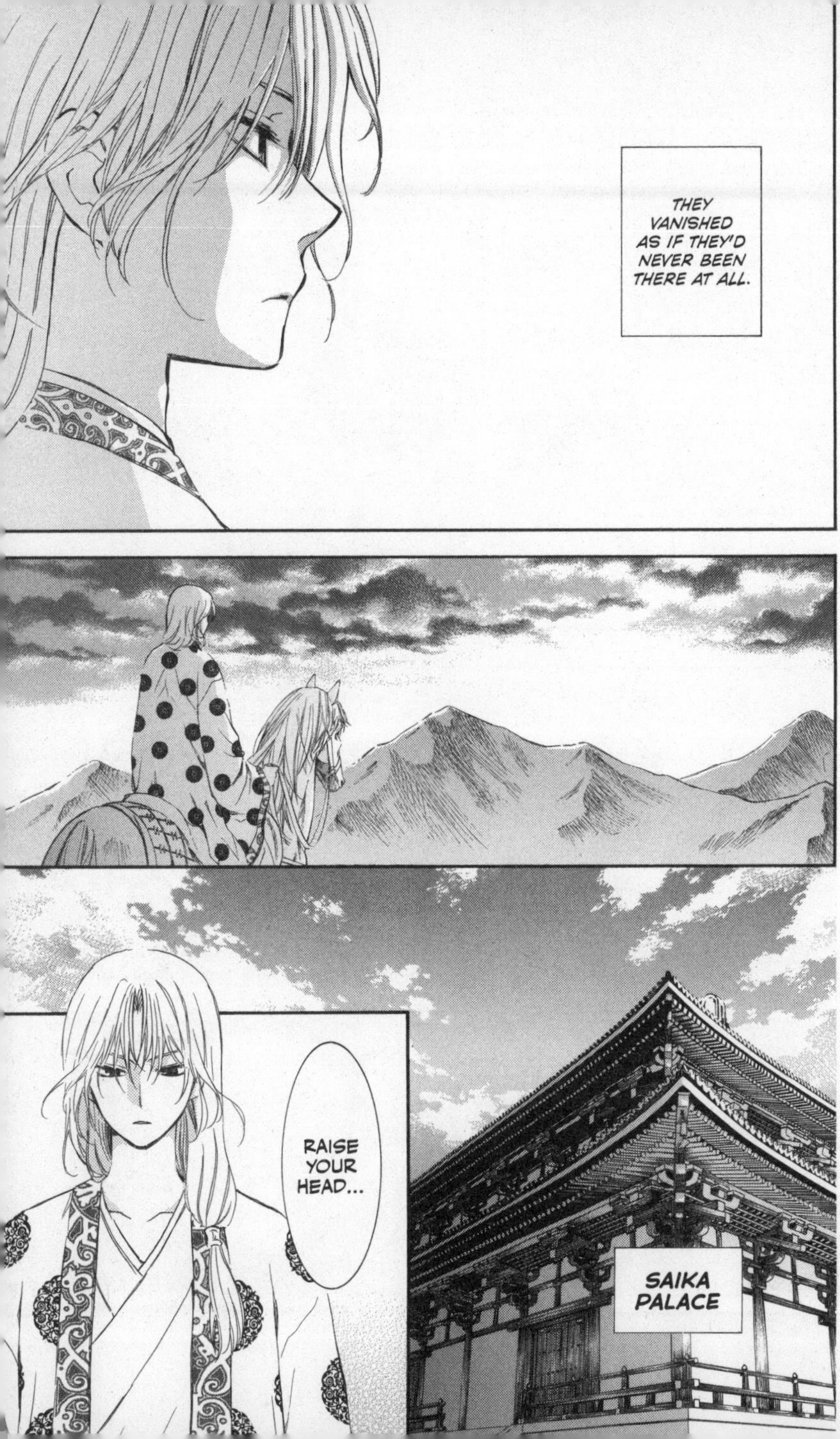
THEY VANISHED AS IF THEY'D NEVER BEEN THERE AT ALL.
SAIKA PALACE
RAISE YOUR HEAD...

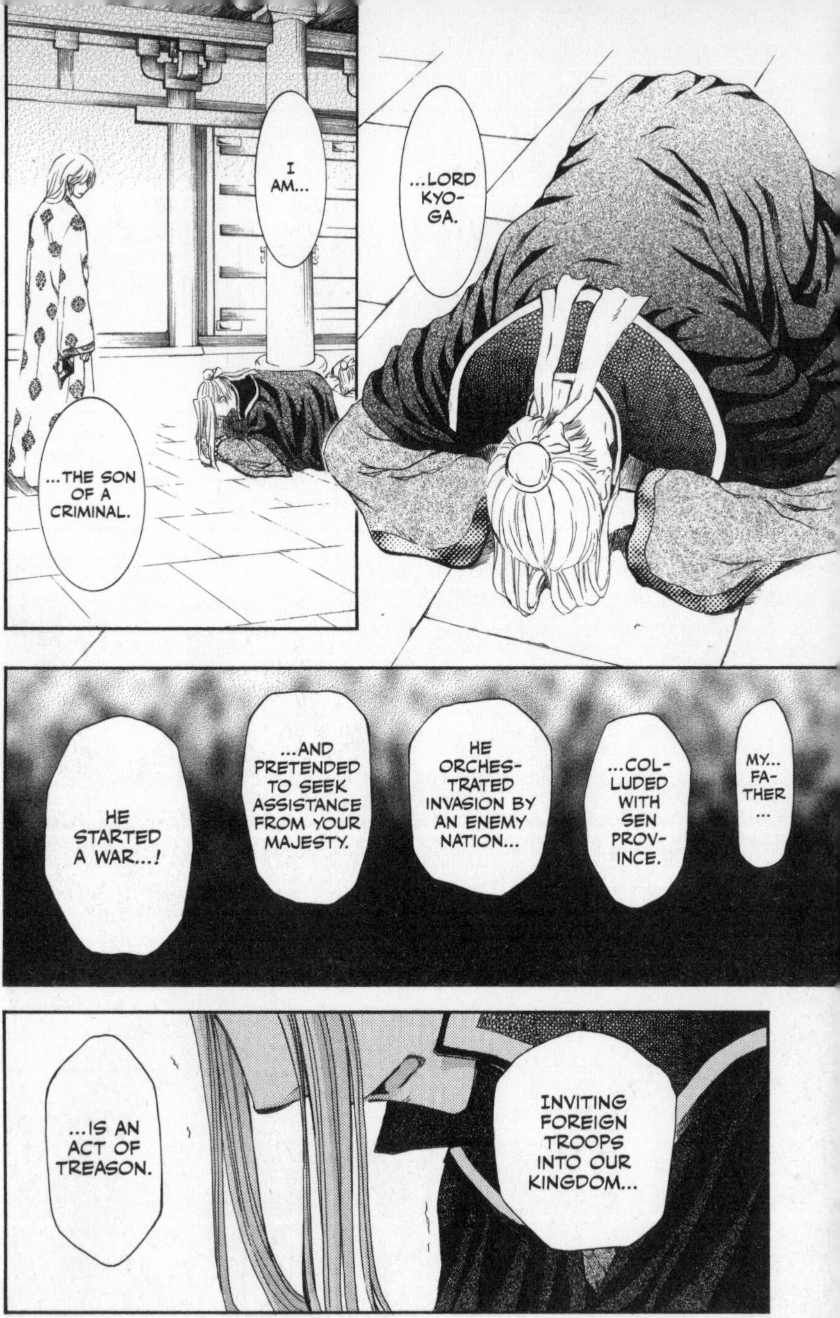
...LORD KYO- GA.
I AM...
...THE SON OF A CRIMINAL.
MY... FA- THER ...
...COL- LUDED WITH SEN PROV- INCE.
HE ORCHES- TRATED INVASION BY AN ENEMY NATION...
...AND PRETENDED TO SEEK ASSISTANCE FROM YOUR MAJESTY.
HE STARTED A WAR...!
INVITING FOREIGN TROOPS INTO OUR KINGDOM...
...IS AN ACT OF TREASON.

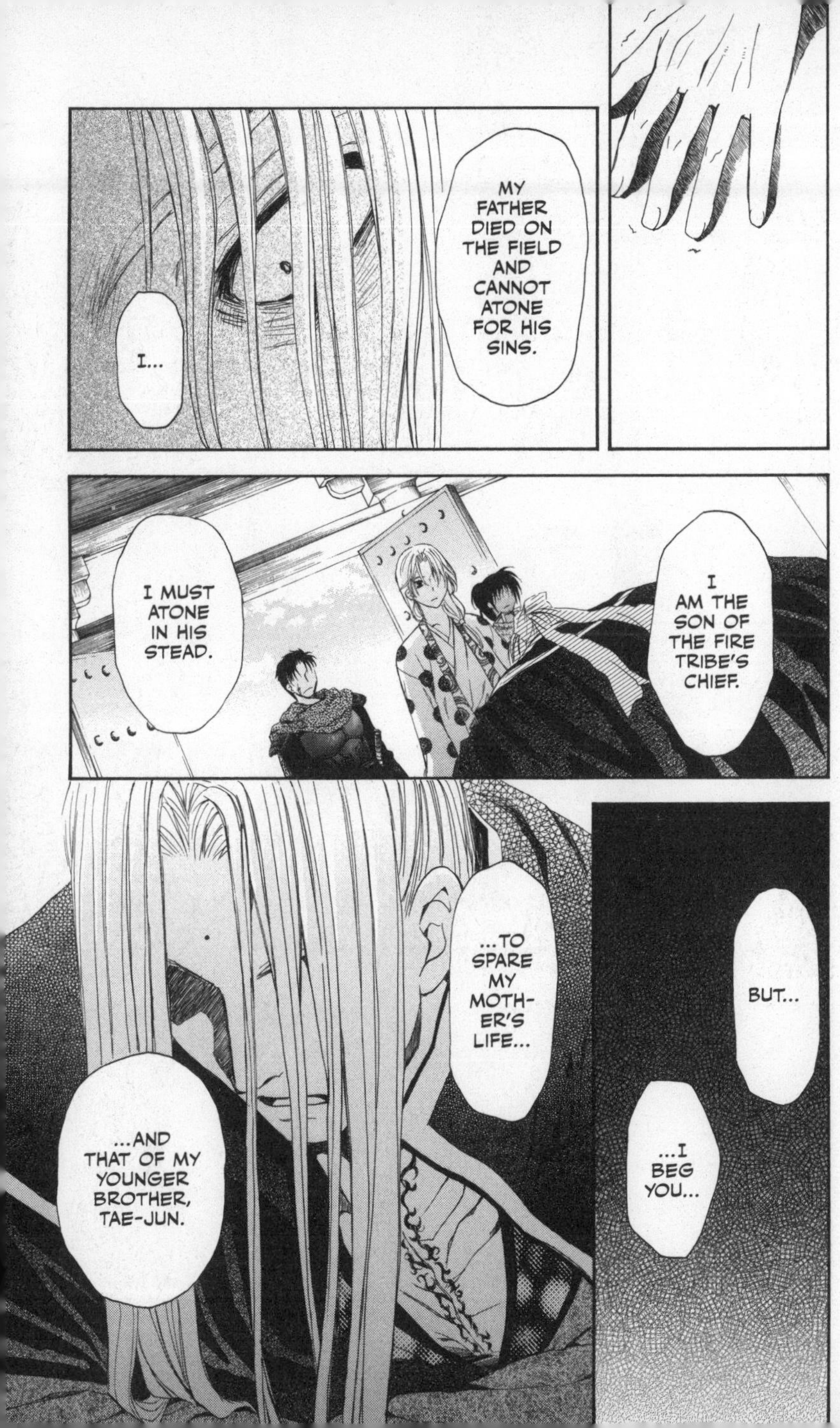
MY FATHER DIED ON THE FIELD AND CANNOT ATONE FOR HIS SINS.
I...
I AM THE SON OF THE FIRE TRIBE'S CHIEF.
I MUST ATONE IN HIS STEAD.
BUT...
...I BEG YOU...
...TO SPARE MY MOTHER'S LIFE...
...AND THAT OF MY YOUNGER BROTHER, TAE-JUN.

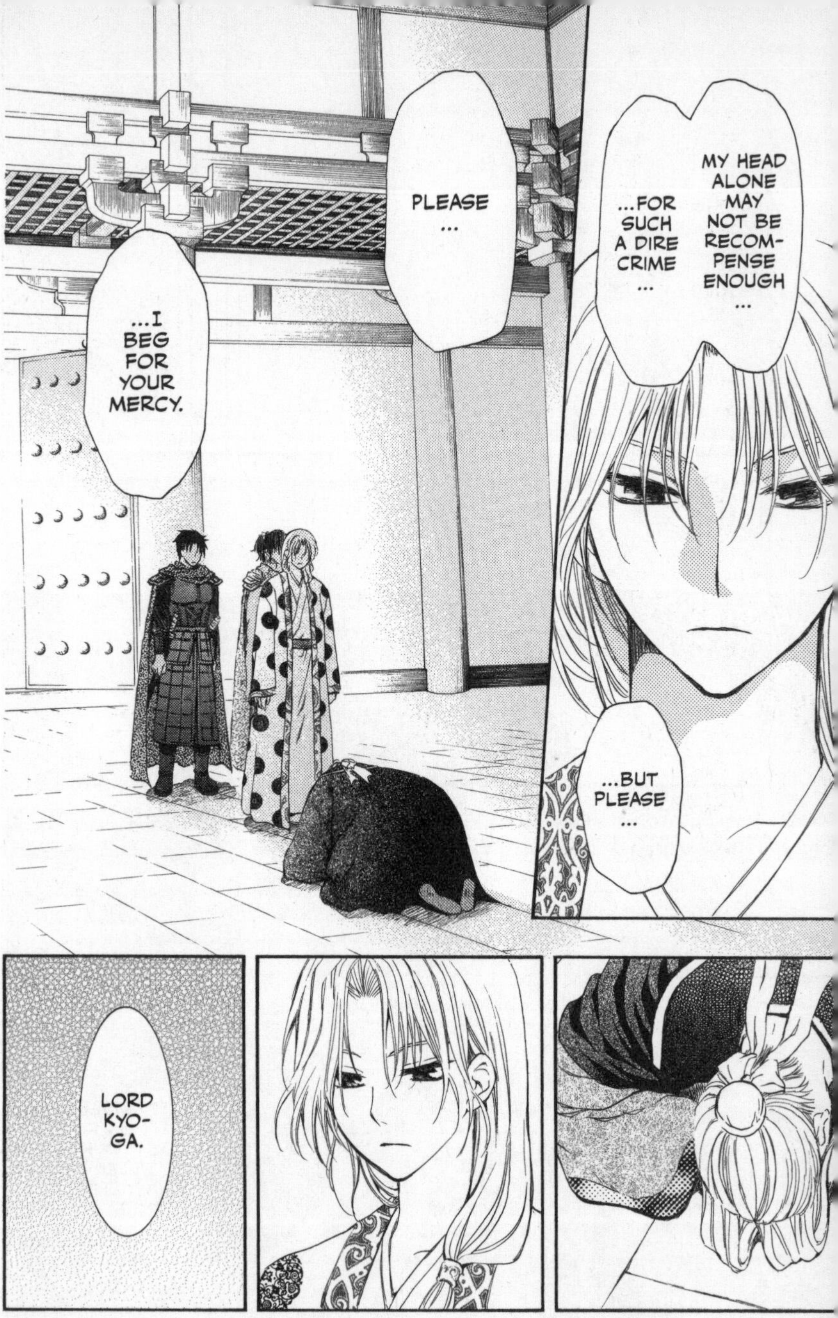
MY HEAD ALONE MAY NOT BE RECOMPENSE ENOUGH ...
...FOR SUCH A DIRE CRIME ...
...BUT PLEASE ...
PLEASE ...
...I BEG FOR YOUR MERCY.
LORD KYO-GA.

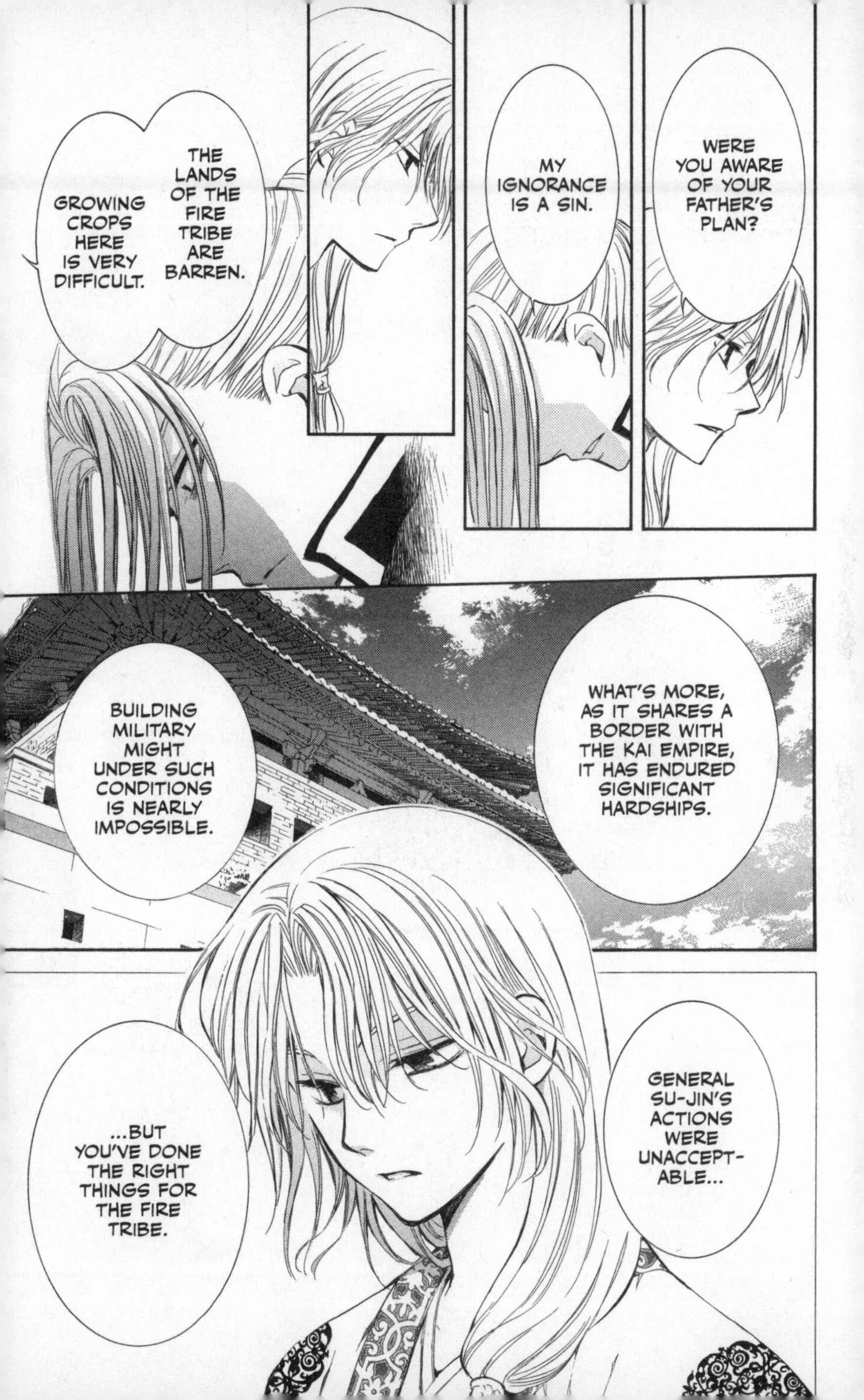
WERE YOU AWARE OF YOUR FATHER'S PLAN?
MY IGNORANCE IS A SIN.
THE LANDS OF THE FIRE TRIBE ARE BARREN.
GROWING CROPS HERE IS VERY DIFFICULT.
WHAT'S MORE, AS IT SHARES A BORDER WITH THE KAI EMPIRE, IT HAS ENDURED SIGNIFICANT HARDSHIPS.
BUILDING MILITARY MIGHT UNDER SUCH CONDITIONS IS NEARLY IMPOSSIBLE.
GENERAL SU-JIN'S ACTIONS WERE UNACCEPT-ABLE...
...BUT YOU'VE DONE THE RIGHT THINGS FOR THE FIRE TRIBE.

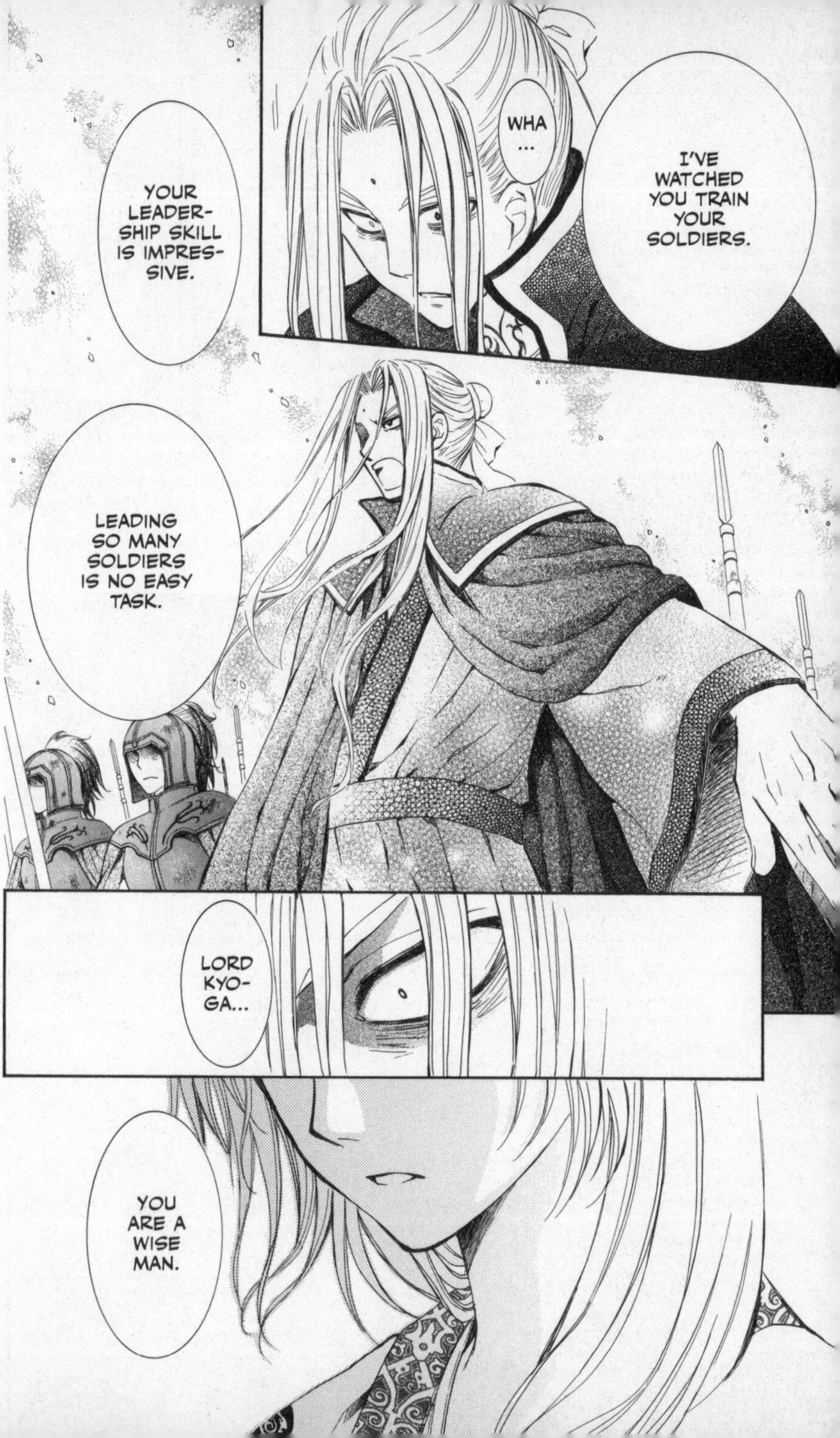
I'VE WATCHED YOU TRAIN YOUR SOLDIERS.
WHA ...
YOUR LEADER-SHIP SKILL IS IMPRES-SIVE.
LEADING SO MANY SOLDIERS IS NO EASY TASK.
LORD KYO-GA...
YOU ARE A WISE MAN.

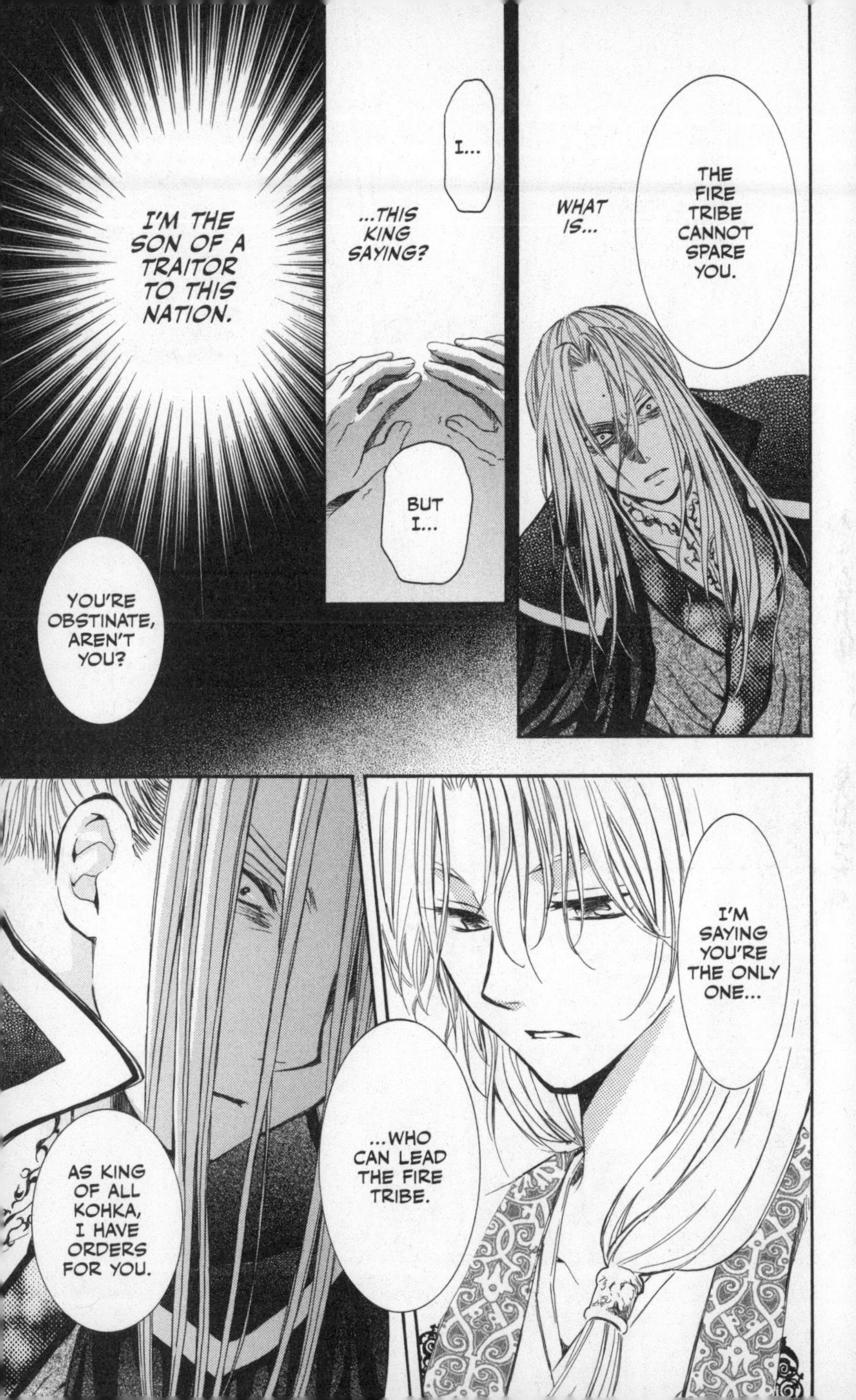
THE FIRE TRIBE CANNOT SPARE YOU.
WHAT IS...
I...
...THIS KING SAYING?
BUT I...
I'M THE SON OF A TRAITOR TO THIS NATION.
YOU'RE OBSTINATE, AREN'T YOU?
I'M SAYING YOU'RE THE ONLY ONE...
...WHO CAN LEAD THE FIRE TRIBE.
AS KING OF ALL KOHKA, I HAVE ORDERS FOR YOU.

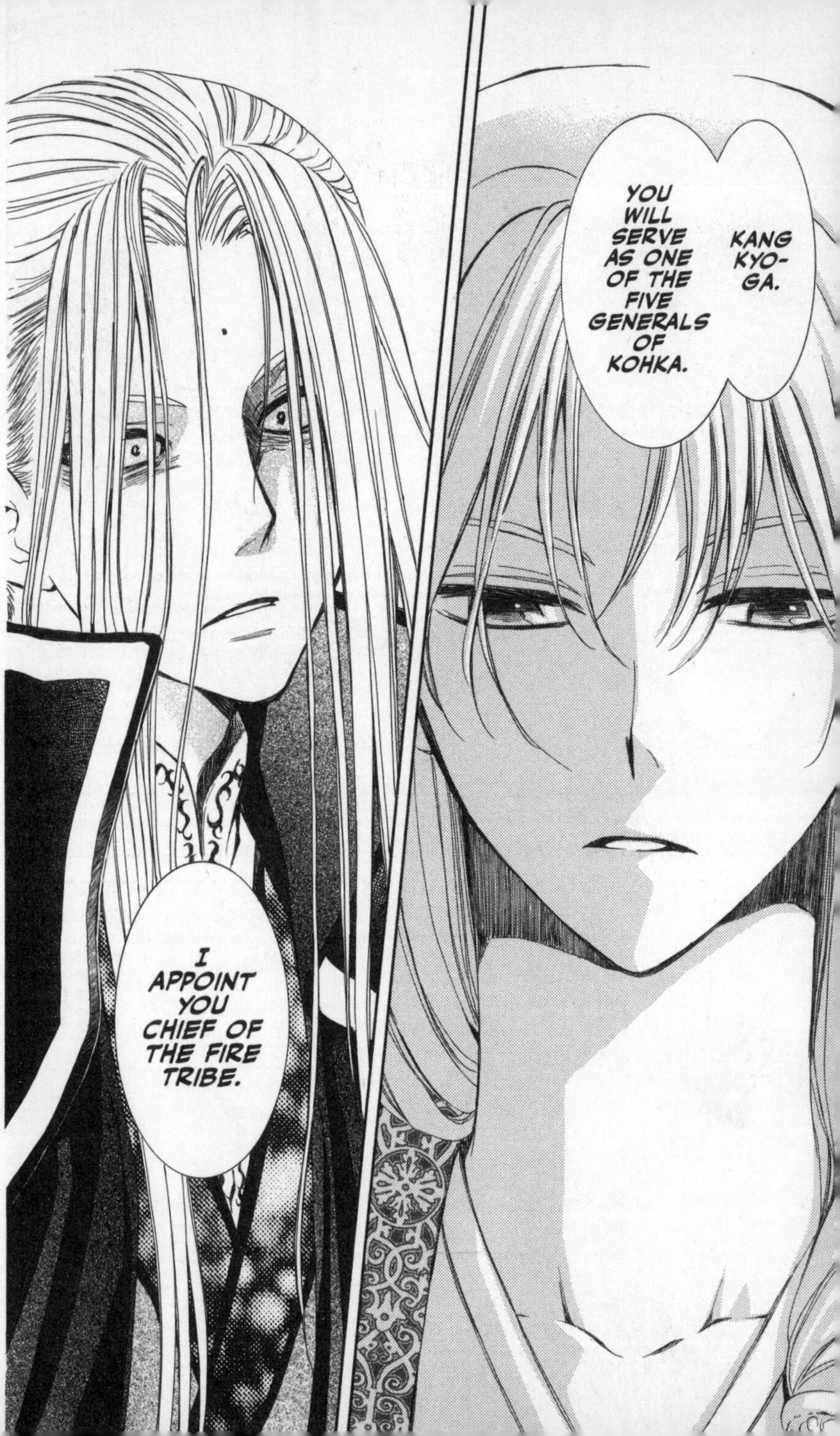
KANG KYO-GA.
YOU WILL SERVE AS ONE OF THE FIVE GENERALS OF KOHKA.
I APPOINT YOU CHIEF OF THE FIRE TRIBE.

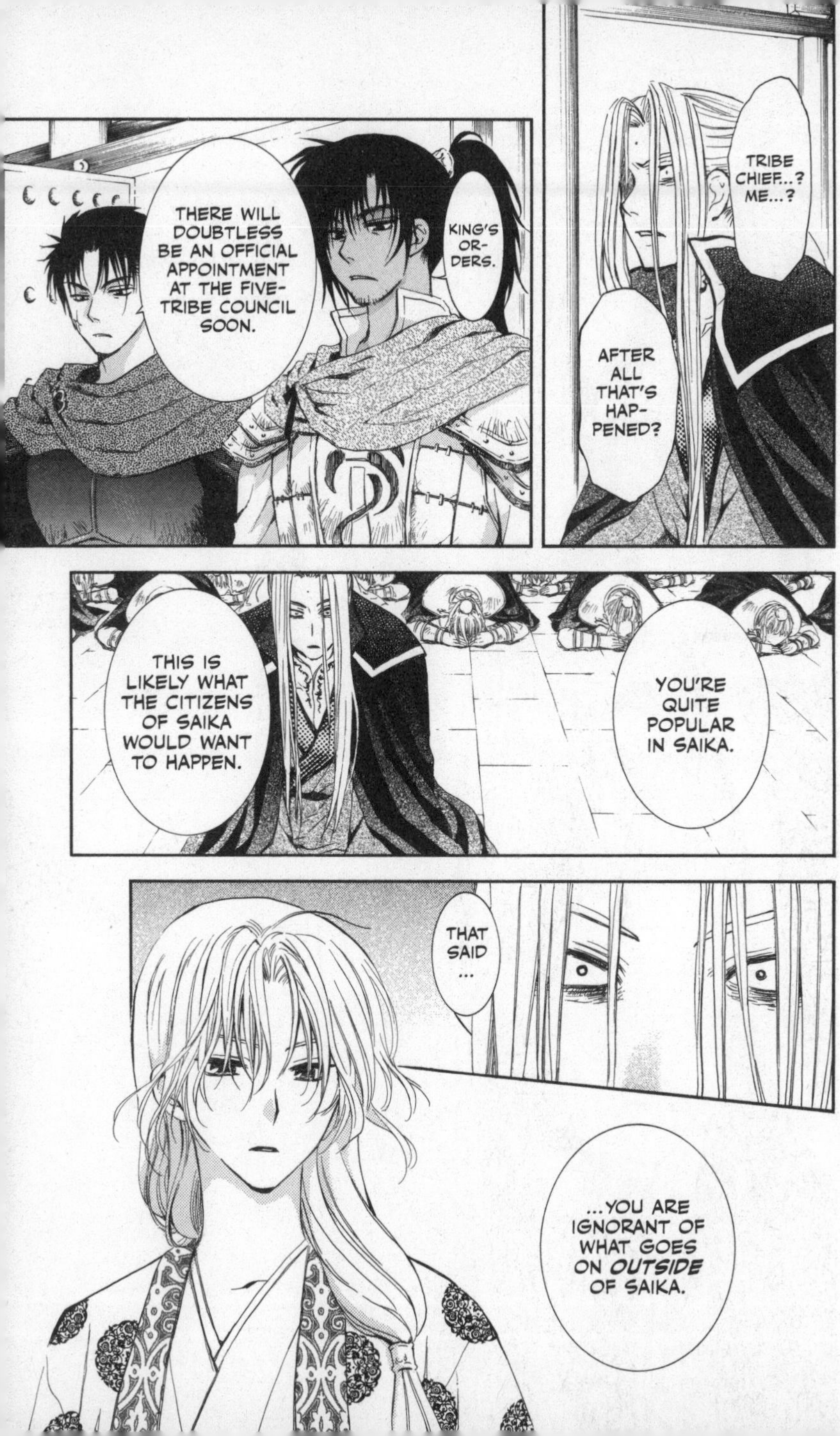
TRIBE CHIEF...? ME...?
AFTER ALL THAT'S HAPPENED?
KING'S ORDERS.
THERE WILL DOUBTLESS BE AN OFFICIAL APPOINTMENT AT THE FIVE-TRIBE COUNCIL SOON.
YOU'RE QUITE POPULAR IN SAIKA.
THIS IS LIKELY WHAT THE CITIZENS OF SAIKA WOULD WANT TO HAPPEN.
THAT SAID...
...YOU ARE IGNORANT OF WHAT GOES ON *OUTSIDE* OF SAIKA.

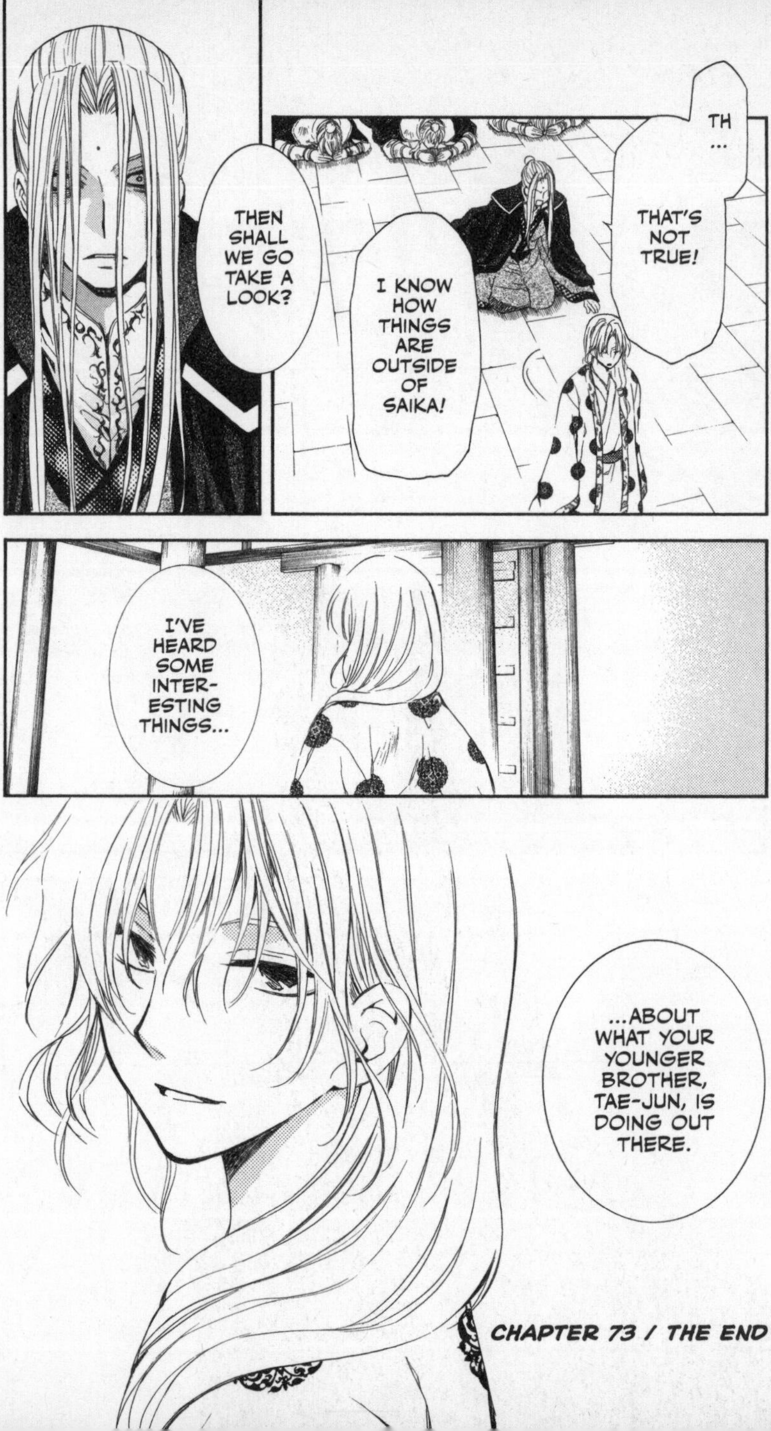
TH...
THAT'S NOT TRUE!
I KNOW HOW THINGS ARE OUTSIDE OF SAIKA!
THEN SHALL WE GO TAKE A LOOK?
I'VE HEARD SOME INTERESTING THINGS...
...ABOUT WHAT YOUR YOUNGER BROTHER, TAE-JUN, IS DOING OUT THERE.
CHAPTER 73 / THE END

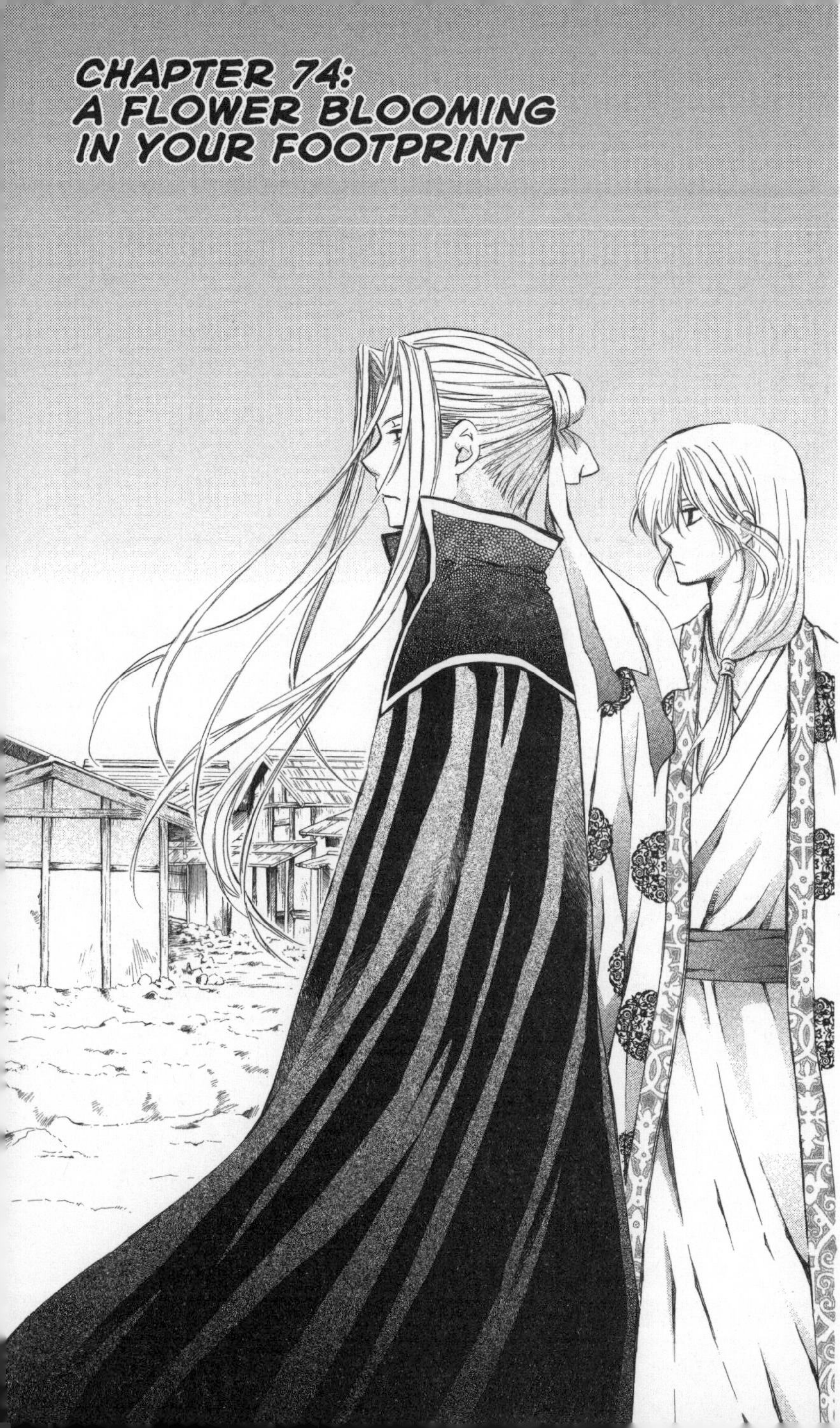
CHAPTER 74:
A FLOWER BLOOMING
IN YOUR FOOTPRINT

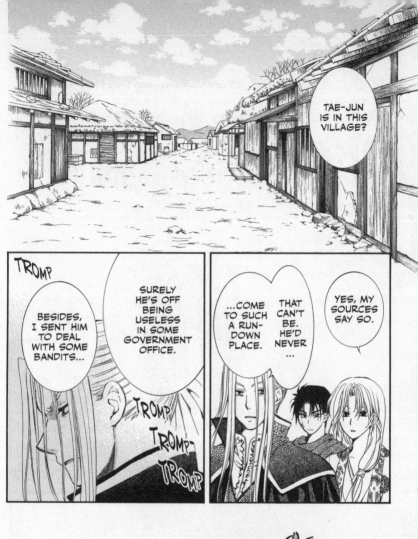

TAE-JUN IS IN THIS VILLAGE?
YES, MY SOURCES SAY SO.
THAT CAN'T BE. HE'D NEVER ...
...COME TO SUCH A RUN-DOWN PLACE.
SURELY HE'S OFF BEING USELESS IN SOME GOVERNMENT OFFICE.
TROMP
BESIDES, I SENT HIM TO DEAL WITH SOME BANDITS...
TROMP
TROMP
TROMP

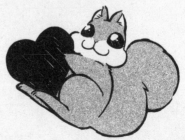

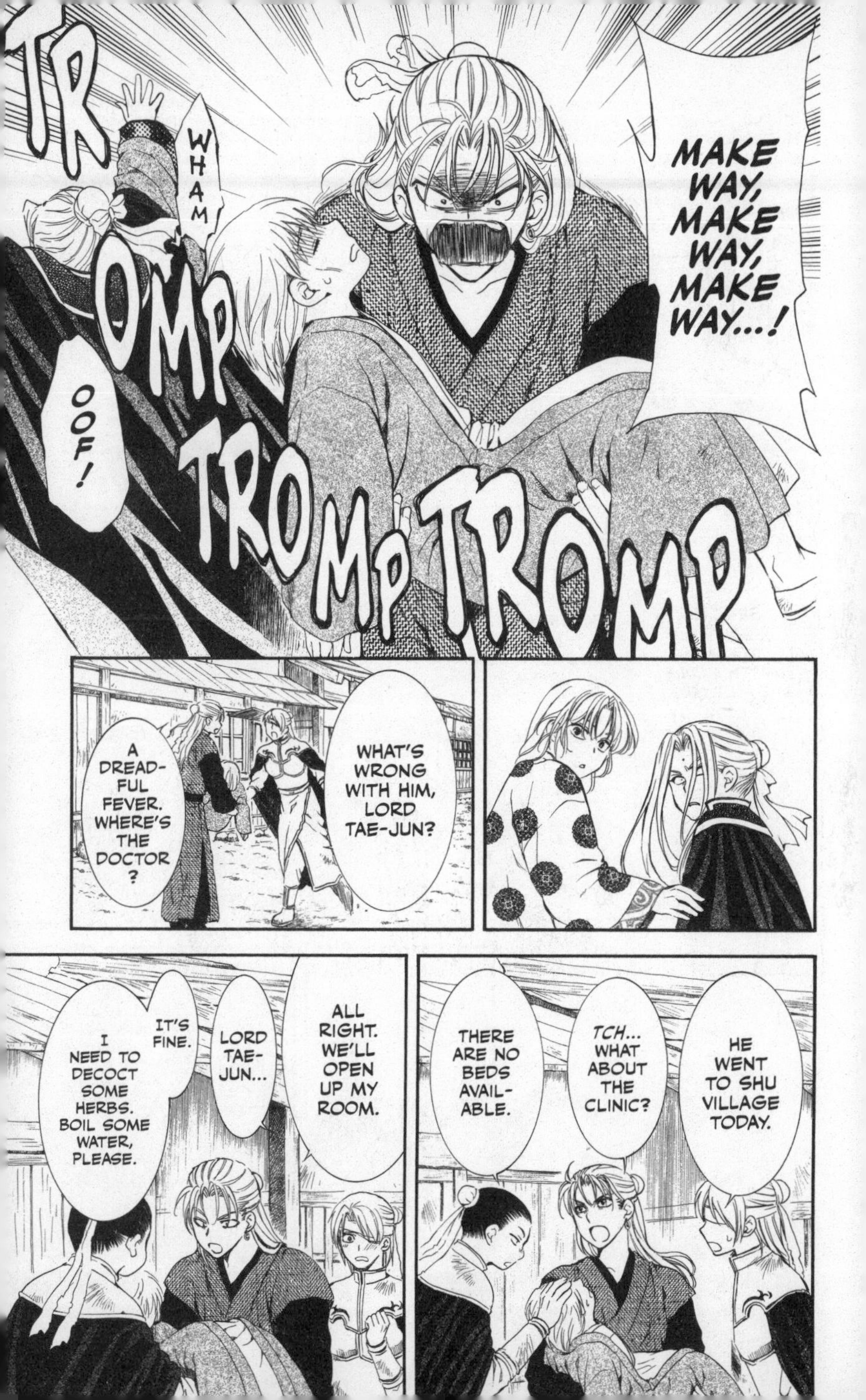
MAKE WAY, MAKE WAY, MAKE WAY...!
TROMP TROMP TROMP TROMP
WHAM
OOF!
WHAT'S WRONG WITH HIM, LORD TAE-JUN?
A DREADFUL FEVER. WHERE'S THE DOCTOR?
HE WENT TO SHU VILLAGE TODAY.
TCH... WHAT ABOUT THE CLINIC?
THERE ARE NO BEDS AVAIL-ABLE.
ALL RIGHT. WE'LL OPEN UP MY ROOM.
LORD TAE-JUN...
IT'S FINE.
I NEED TO DECOCT SOME HERBS. BOIL SOME WATER, PLEASE.

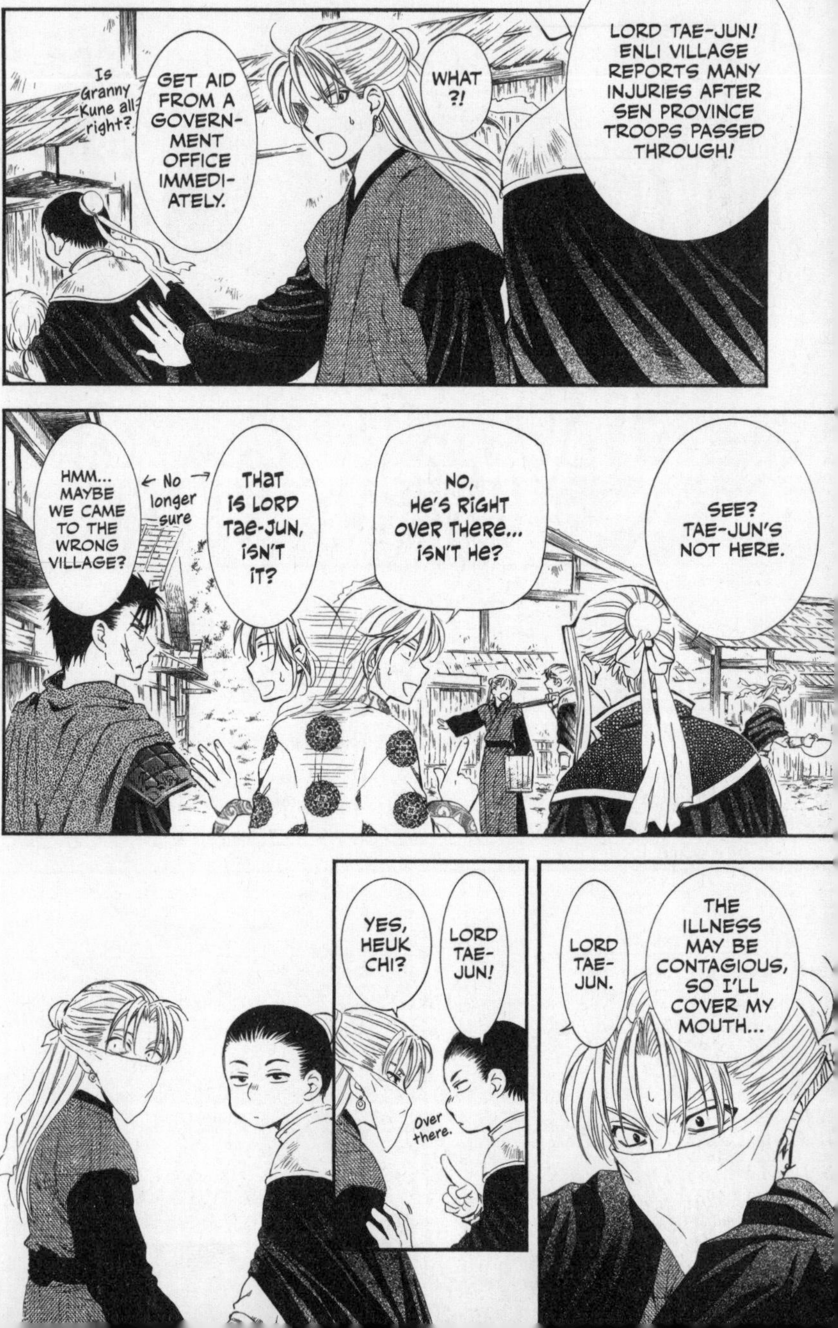
LORD TAE-JUN! ENLI VILLAGE REPORTS MANY INJURIES AFTER SEN PROVINCE TROOPS PASSED THROUGH!
WHAT ?!
GET AID FROM A GOVERN-MENT OFFICE IMMEDI-ATELY.
Is Granny Kune all right?
SEE? TAE-JUN'S NOT HERE.
NO, HE'S RIGHT OVER THERE... ISN'T HE?
THAT IS LORD TAE-JUN, ISN'T IT?
← No longer sure →
HMM... MAYBE WE CAME TO THE WRONG VILLAGE?
THE ILLNESS MAY BE CONTAGIOUS, SO I'LL COVER MY MOUTH...
LORD TAE-JUN.
LORD TAE-JUN!
YES, HEUK CHI?
Over there.

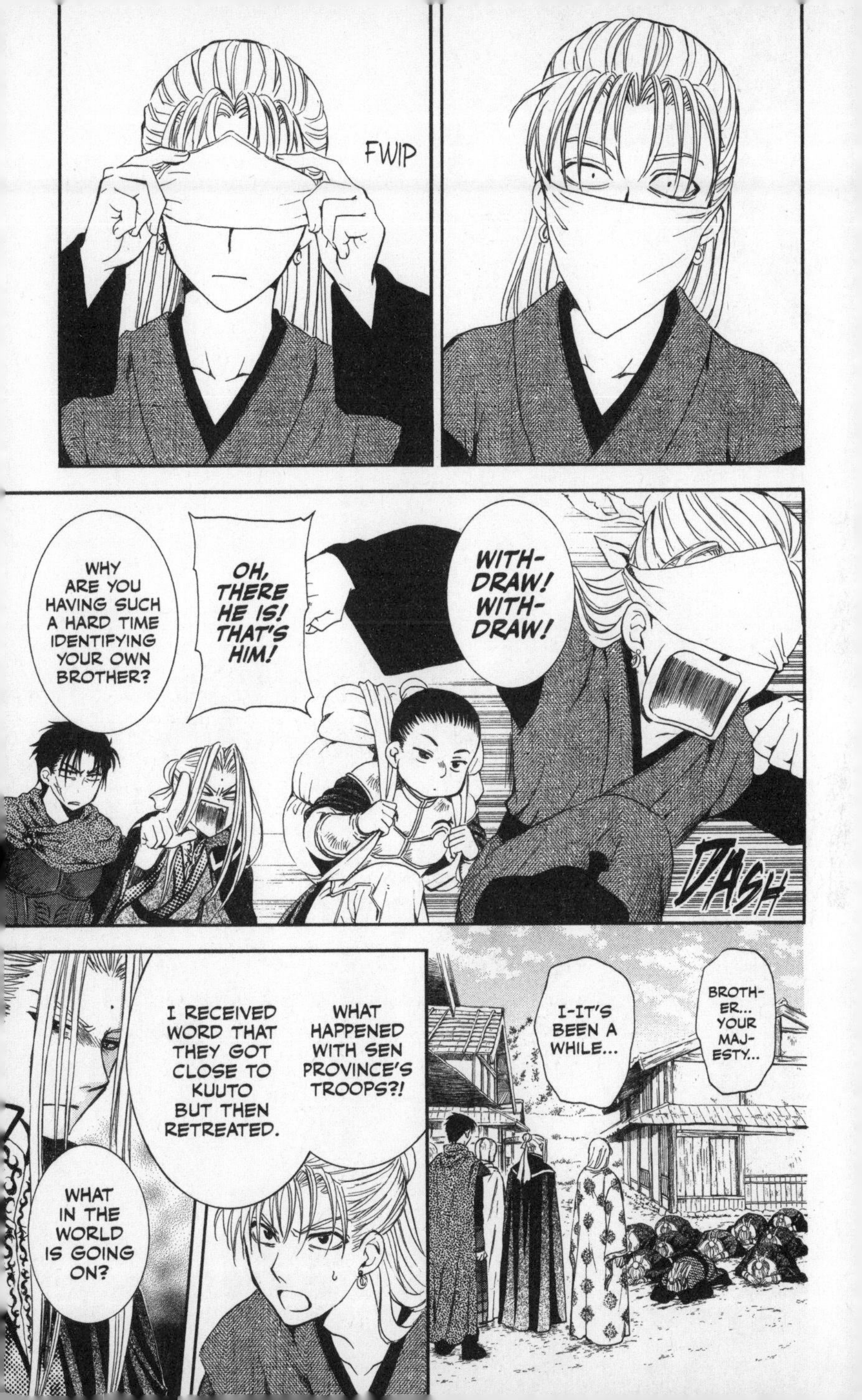
FWIP
WITH-DRAW! WITH-DRAW!
DASH
OH, THERE HE IS! THAT'S HIM!
WHY ARE YOU HAVING SUCH A HARD TIME IDENTIFYING YOUR OWN BROTHER?
BROTHER... YOUR MAJESTY...
I-IT'S BEEN A WHILE...
WHAT HAPPENED WITH SEN PROVINCE'S TROOPS?!
I RECEIVED WORD THAT THEY GOT CLOSE TO KUUTO BUT THEN RETREATED.
WHAT IN THE WORLD IS GOING ON?

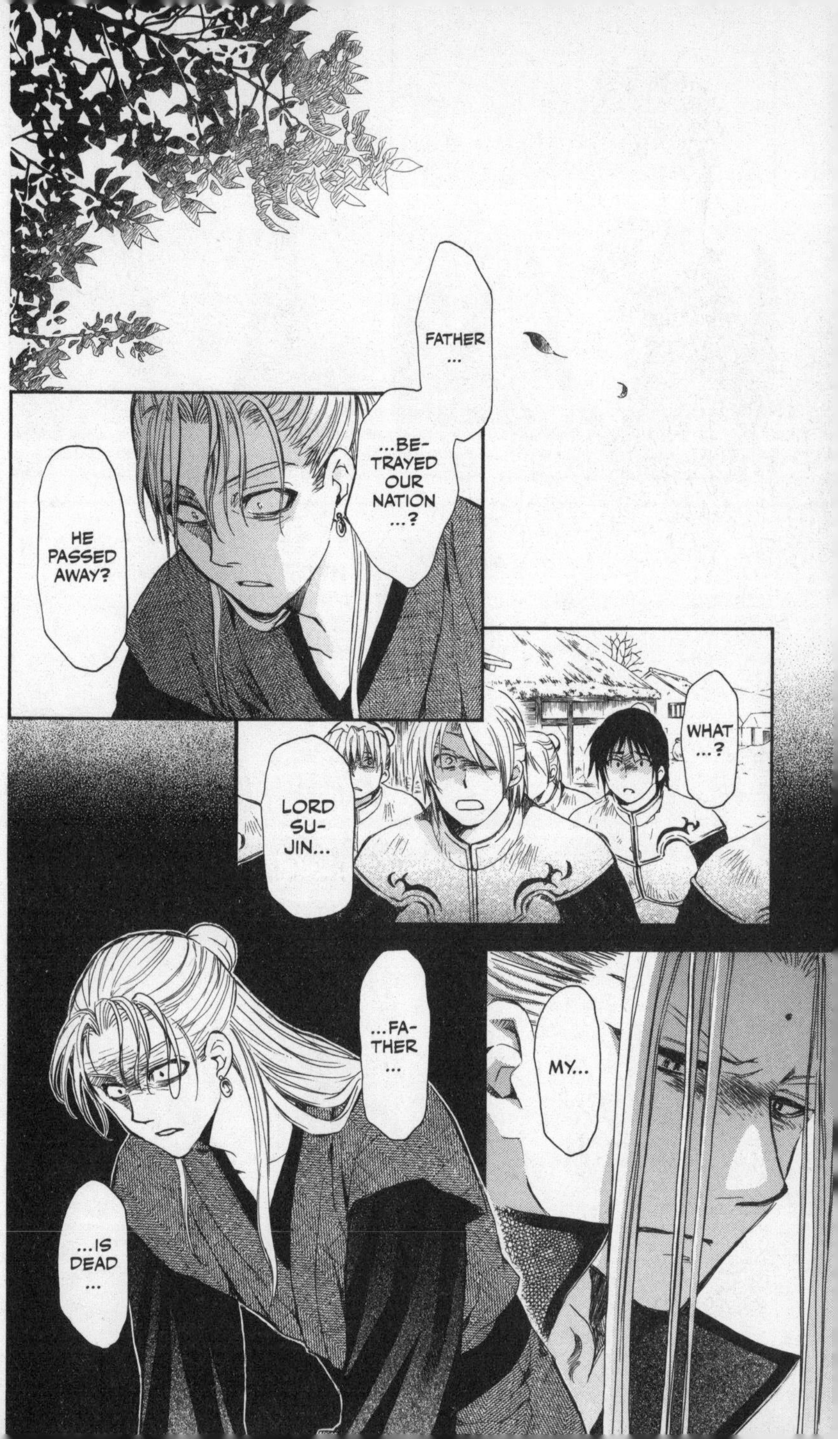

FATHER...
...BETRAYED OUR NATION...?
HE PASSED AWAY?
WHAT...?
LORD SU-JIN...
MY...
...FATHER...
...IS DEAD...

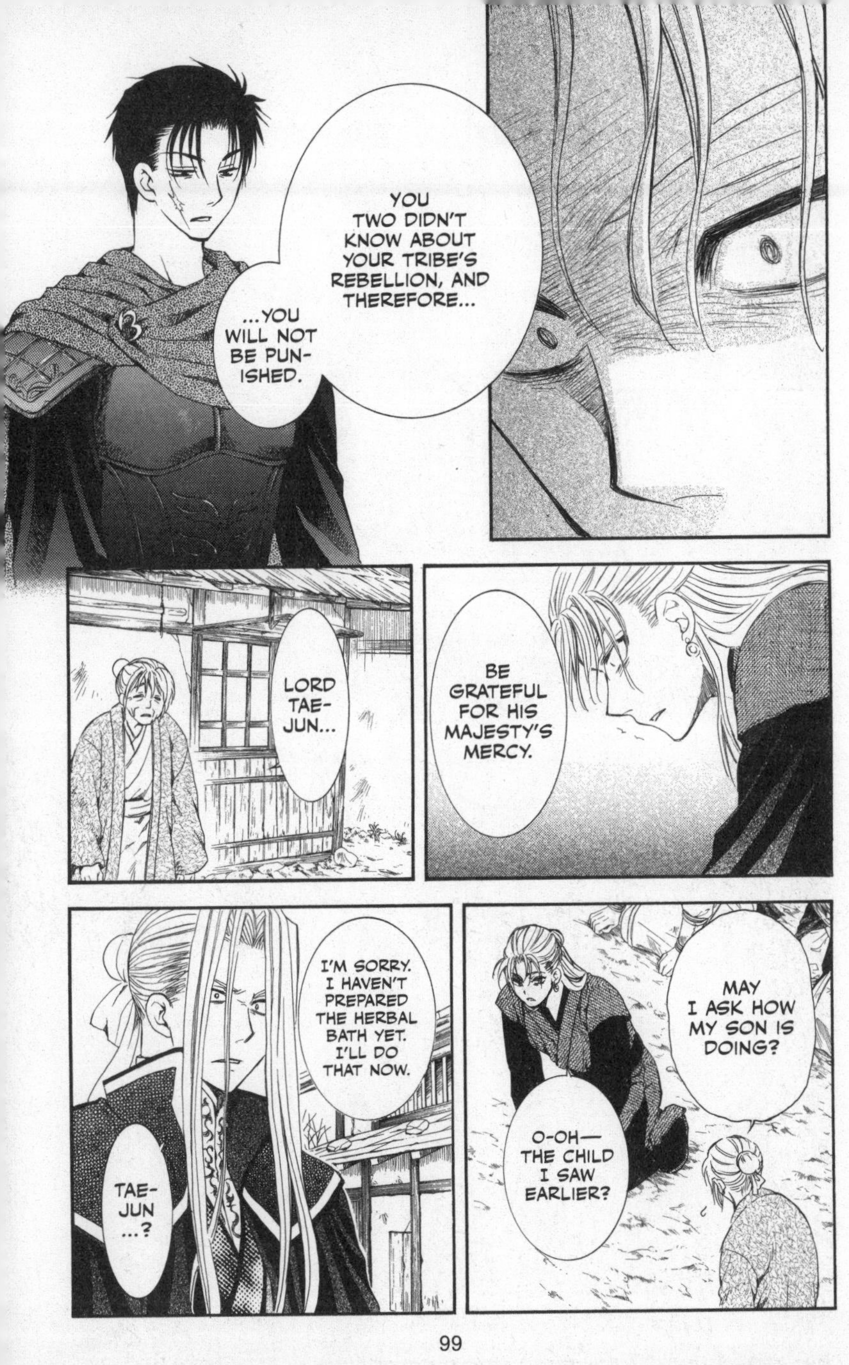
YOU TWO DIDN'T KNOW ABOUT YOUR TRIBE'S REBELLION, AND THEREFORE...
...YOU WILL NOT BE PUN-ISHED.
BE GRATEFUL FOR HIS MAJESTY'S MERCY.
LORD TAE-JUN...
MAY I ASK HOW MY SON IS DOING?
O-OH— THE CHILD I SAW EARLIER?
I'M SORRY. I HAVEN'T PREPARED THE HERBAL BATH YET. I'LL DO THAT NOW.
TAE-JUN ...?

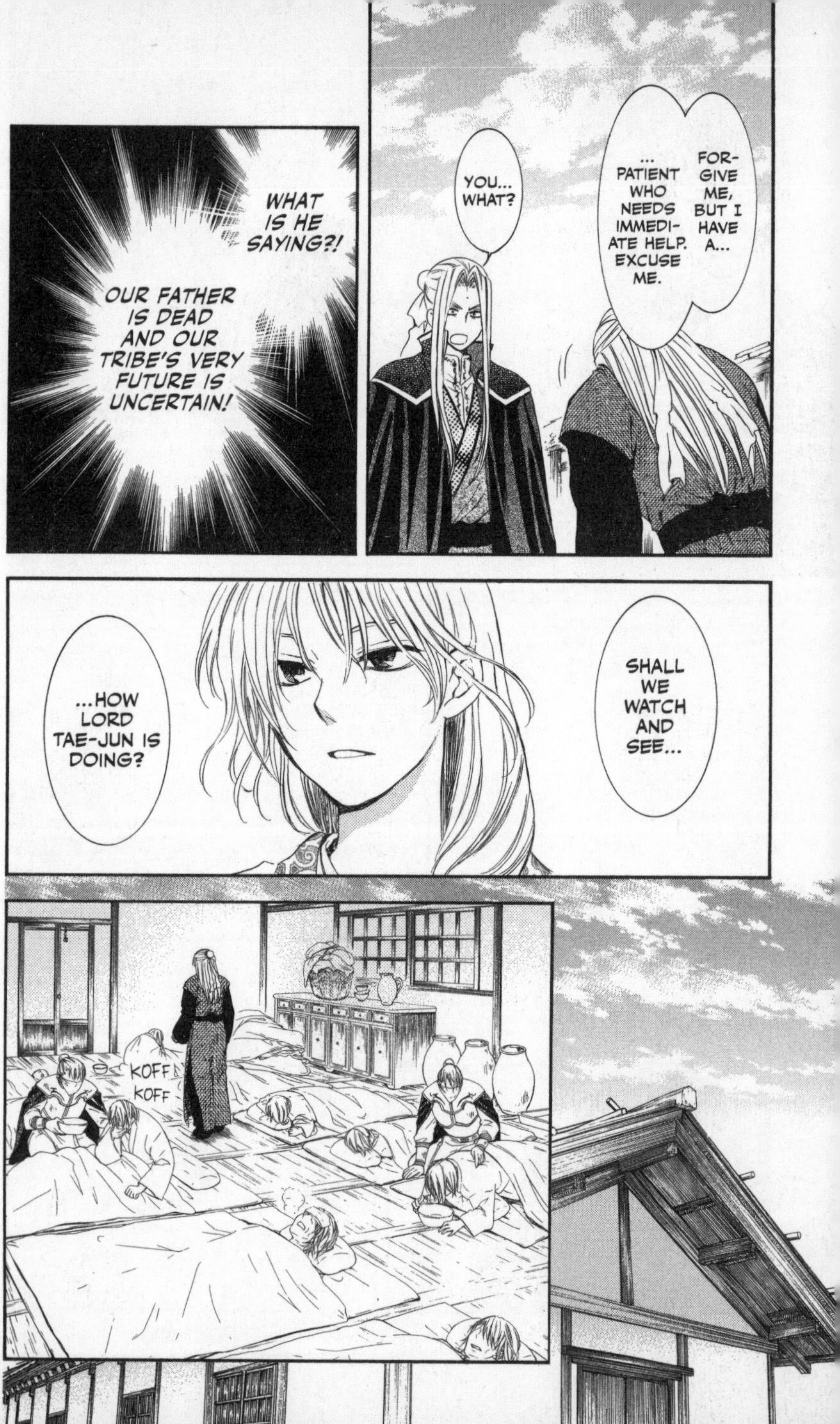
FOR-GIVE ME, BUT I HAVE A...
...PATIENT WHO NEEDS IMMEDIATE HELP. EXCUSE ME.
YOU... WHAT?
WHAT IS HE SAYING?!
OUR FATHER IS DEAD AND OUR TRIBE'S VERY FUTURE IS UNCERTAIN!
SHALL WE WATCH AND SEE...
...HOW LORD TAE-JUN IS DOING?
KOFF KOFF

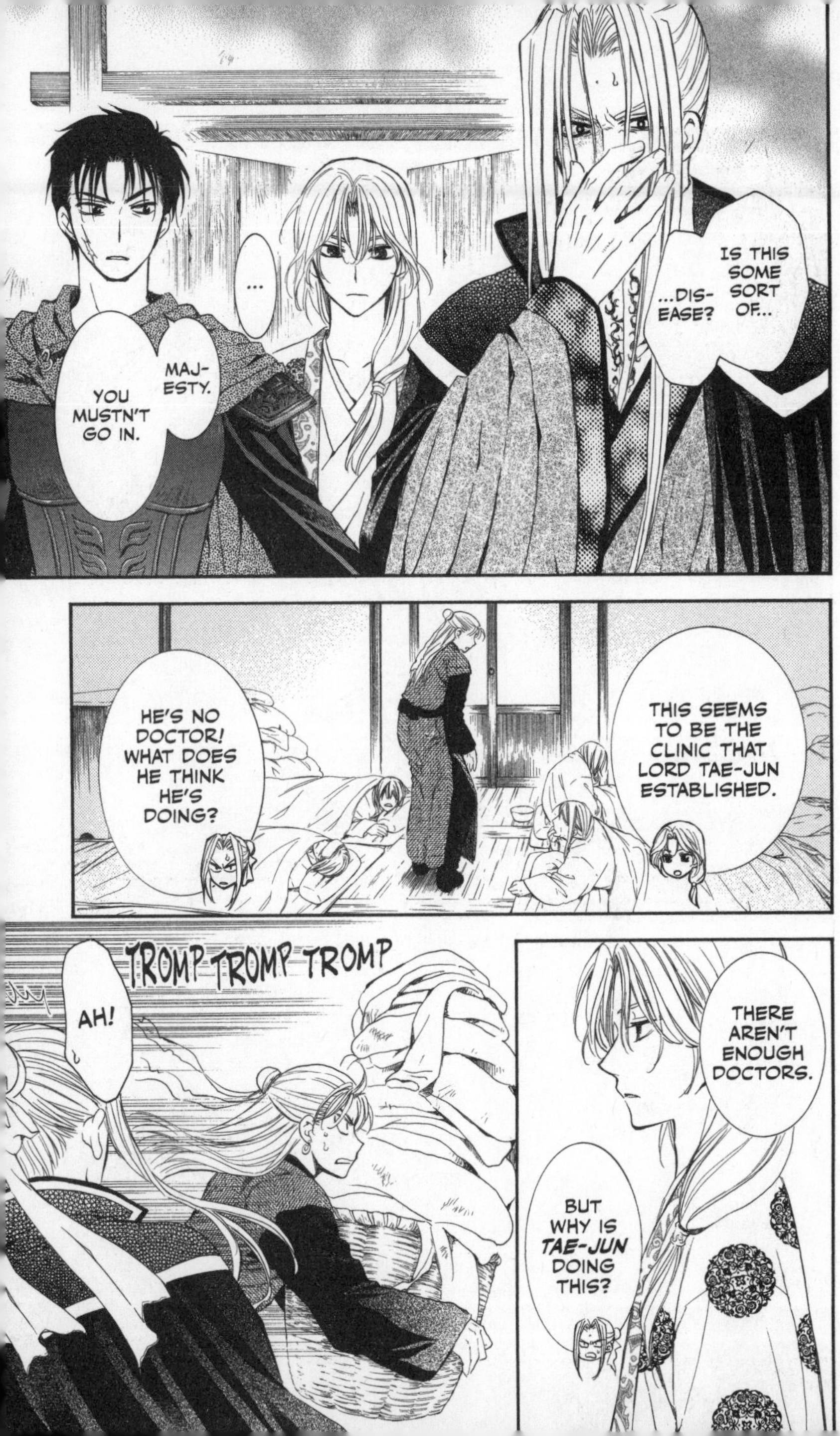
IS THIS SOME SORT OF... ...DIS-EASE?
...
MAJ-ESTY. YOU MUSTN'T GO IN.
THIS SEEMS TO BE THE CLINIC THAT LORD TAE-JUN ESTABLISHED.
HE'S NO DOCTOR! WHAT DOES HE THINK HE'S DOING?
THERE AREN'T ENOUGH DOCTORS.
BUT WHY IS TAE-JUN DOING THIS?
TROMP TROMP TROMP
AH!

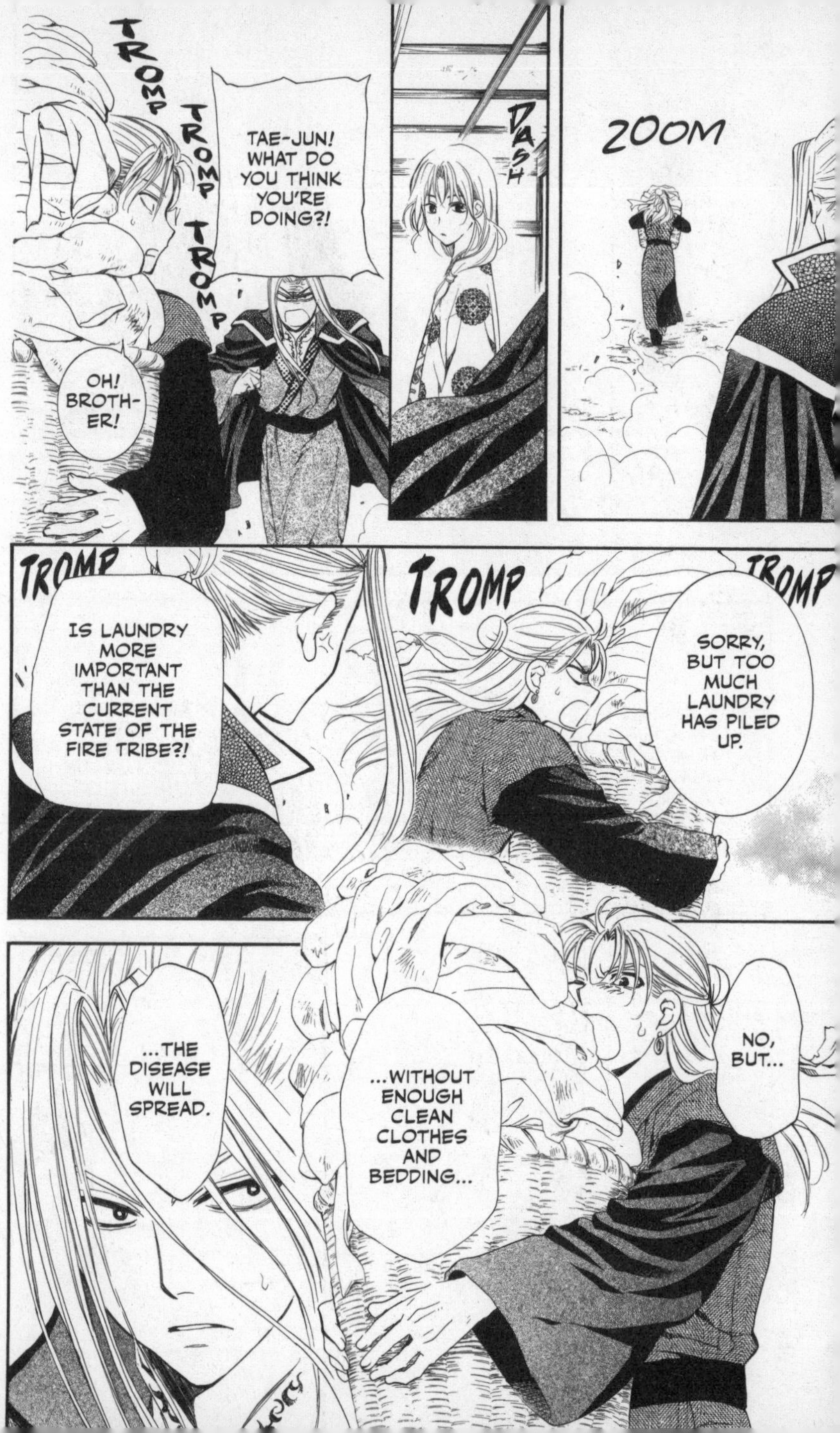
ZOOM
DASH
TAE-JUN! WHAT DO YOU THINK YOU'RE DOING?!
TROMP
TROMP
TROMP
TROMP
OH! BROTHER-ER!
TROMP
SORRY, BUT TOO MUCH LAUNDRY HAS PILED UP.
TROMP
IS LAUNDRY MORE IMPORTANT THAN THE CURRENT STATE OF THE FIRE TRIBE?!
TROMP
NO, BUT...
...WITHOUT ENOUGH CLEAN CLOTHES AND BEDDING...
...THE DISEASE WILL SPREAD.

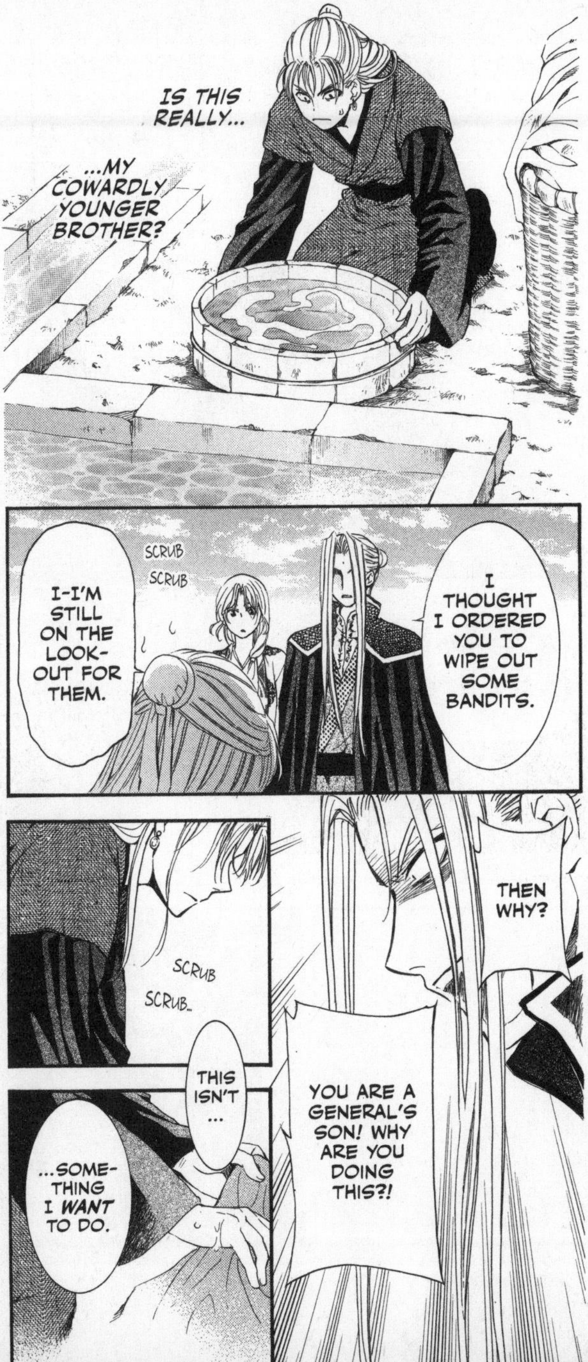
IS THIS REALLY...
...MY COWARDLY YOUNGER BROTHER?
I THOUGHT I ORDERED YOU TO WIPE OUT SOME BANDITS.
SCRUB SCRUB
I-I'M STILL ON THE LOOK-OUT FOR THEM.
THEN WHY?
YOU ARE A GENERAL'S SON! WHY ARE YOU DOING THIS?!
SCRUB SCRUB...
THIS ISN'T...
...SOME-THING I *WANT* TO DO.

Before the Battle

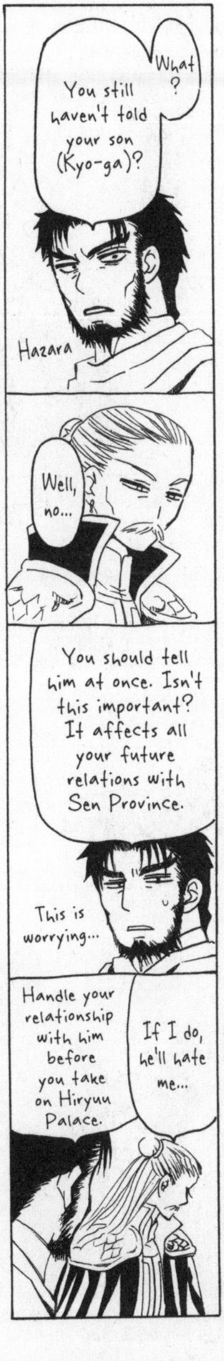
What?
You still haven't told your son (Kyo-ga)?
Hazara
Well, no...
You should tell him at once. Isn't this important? It affects all your future relations with Sen Province.
This is worrying...
Handle your relationship with him before you take on Hiryuu Palace.
If I do, he'll hate me...

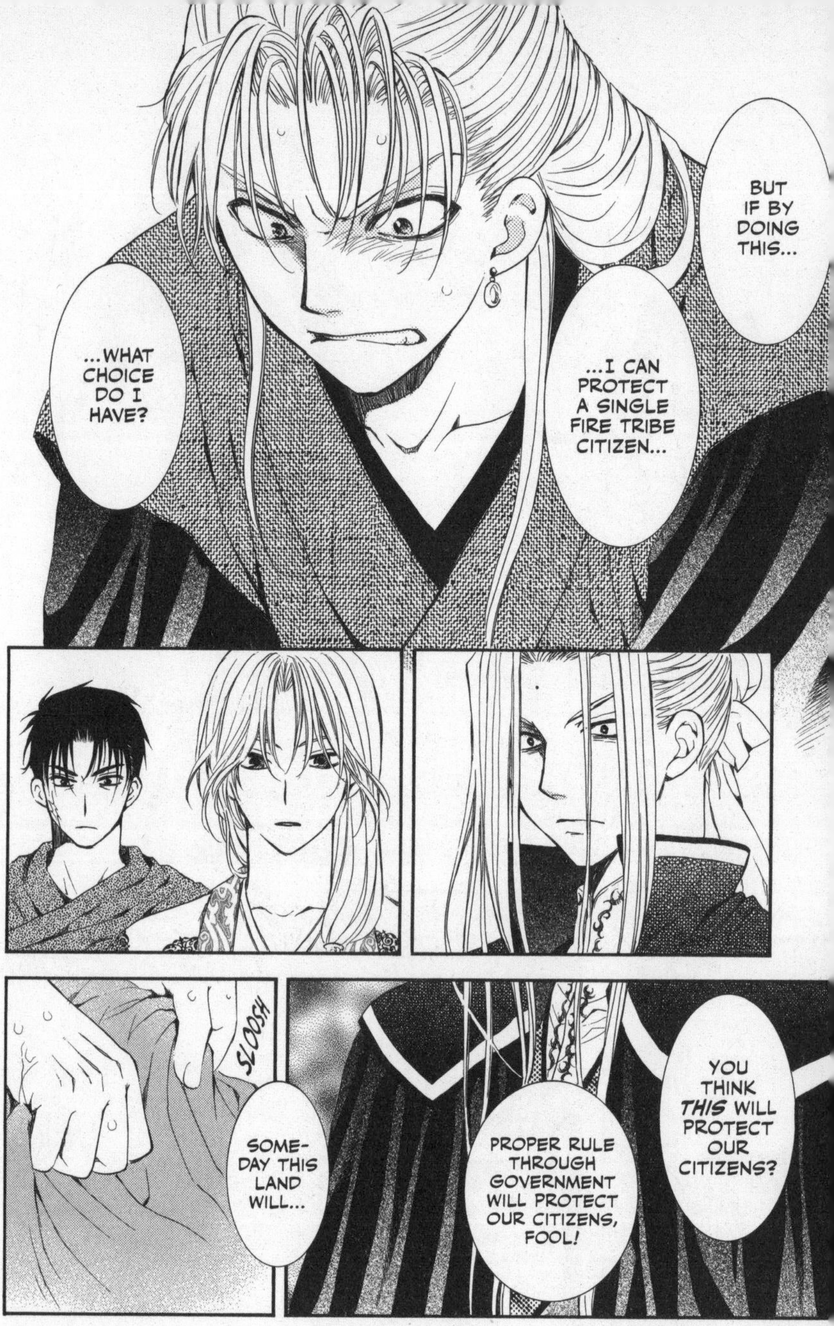
BUT IF BY DOING THIS...
...I CAN PROTECT A SINGLE FIRE TRIBE CITIZEN...
...WHAT CHOICE DO I HAVE?
YOU THINK *THIS* WILL PROTECT OUR CITIZENS?
PROPER RULE THROUGH GOVERNMENT WILL PROTECT OUR CITIZENS, FOOL!
SOMEDAY THIS LAND WILL...
SLOOSH

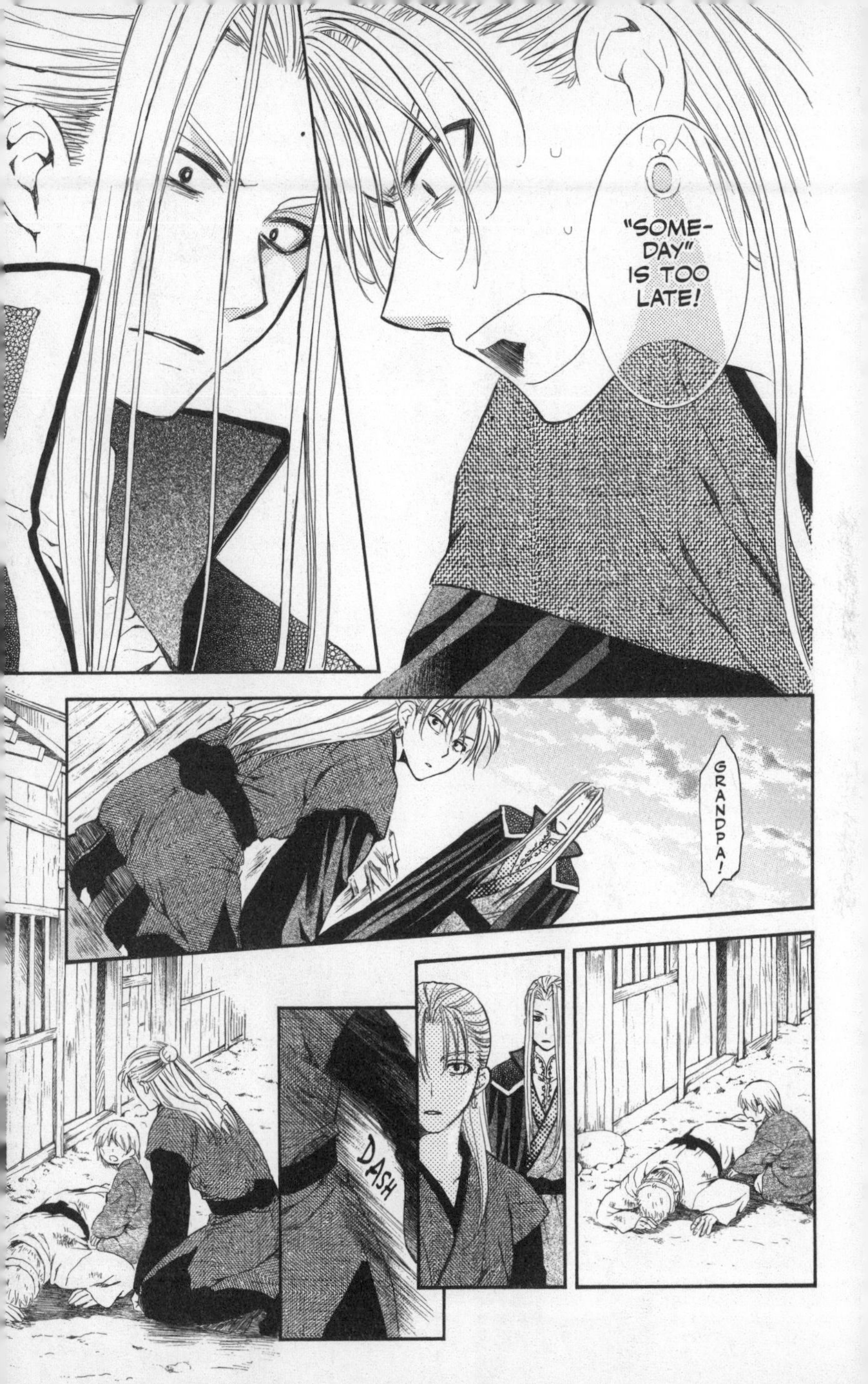
"SOME-DAY" IS TOO LATE!
GRANDPA!
DASH

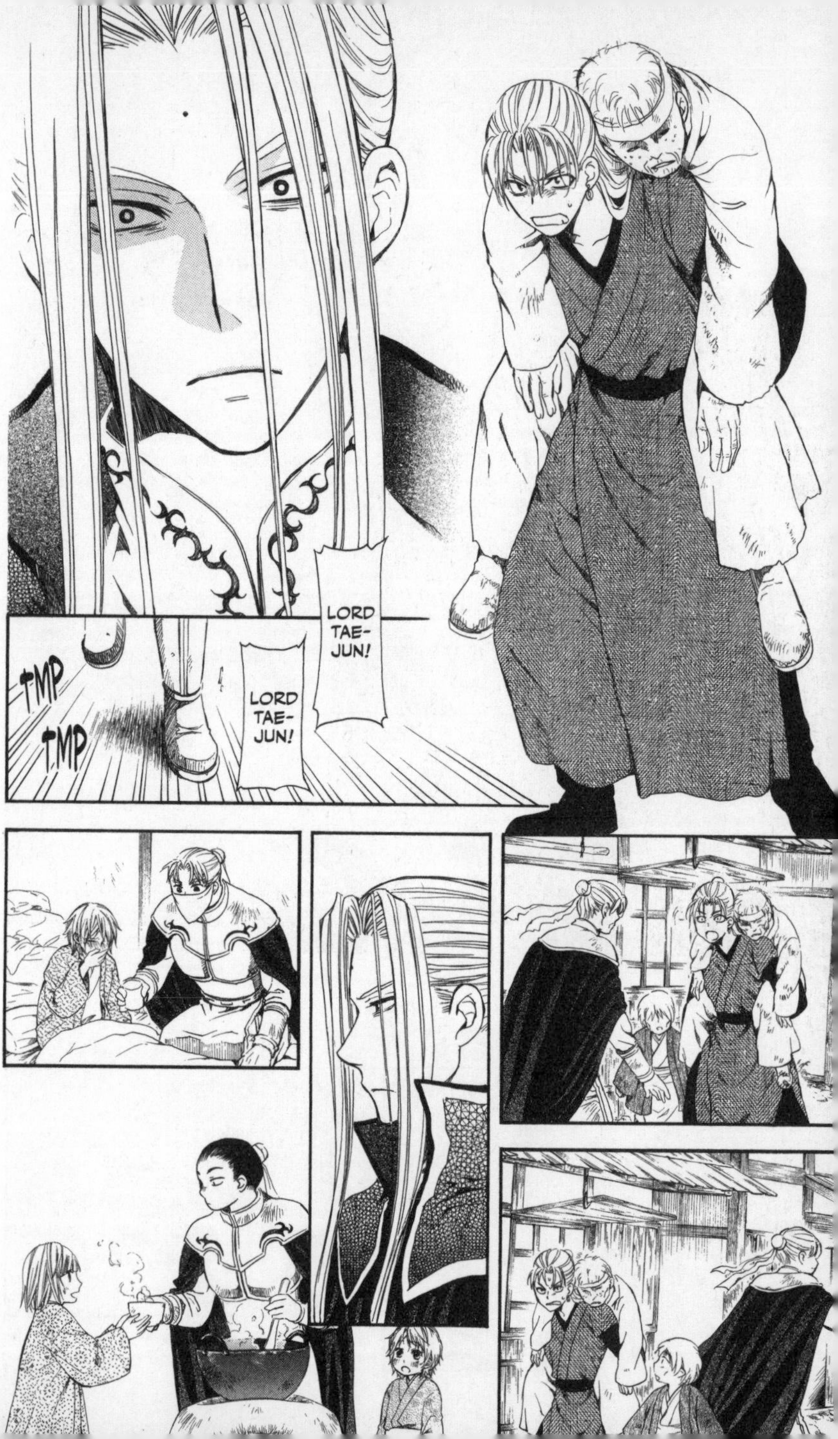
LORD TAE-JUN!
LORD TAE-JUN!
TMP
TMP

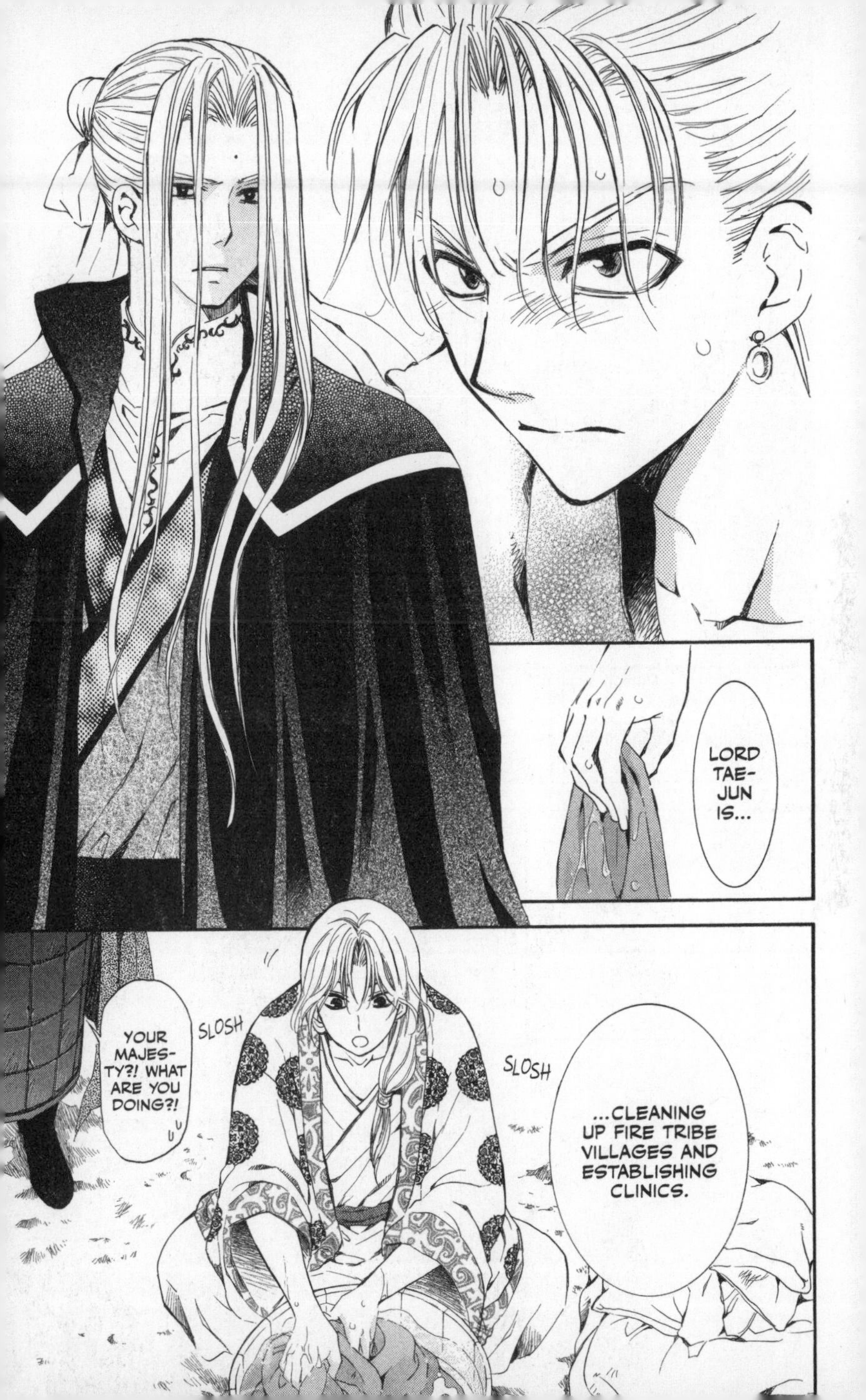
LORD TAE-JUN IS...
...CLEANING UP FIRE TRIBE VILLAGES AND ESTABLISHING CLINICS.
SLOSH
SLOSH
YOUR MAJESTY?! WHAT ARE YOU DOING?!

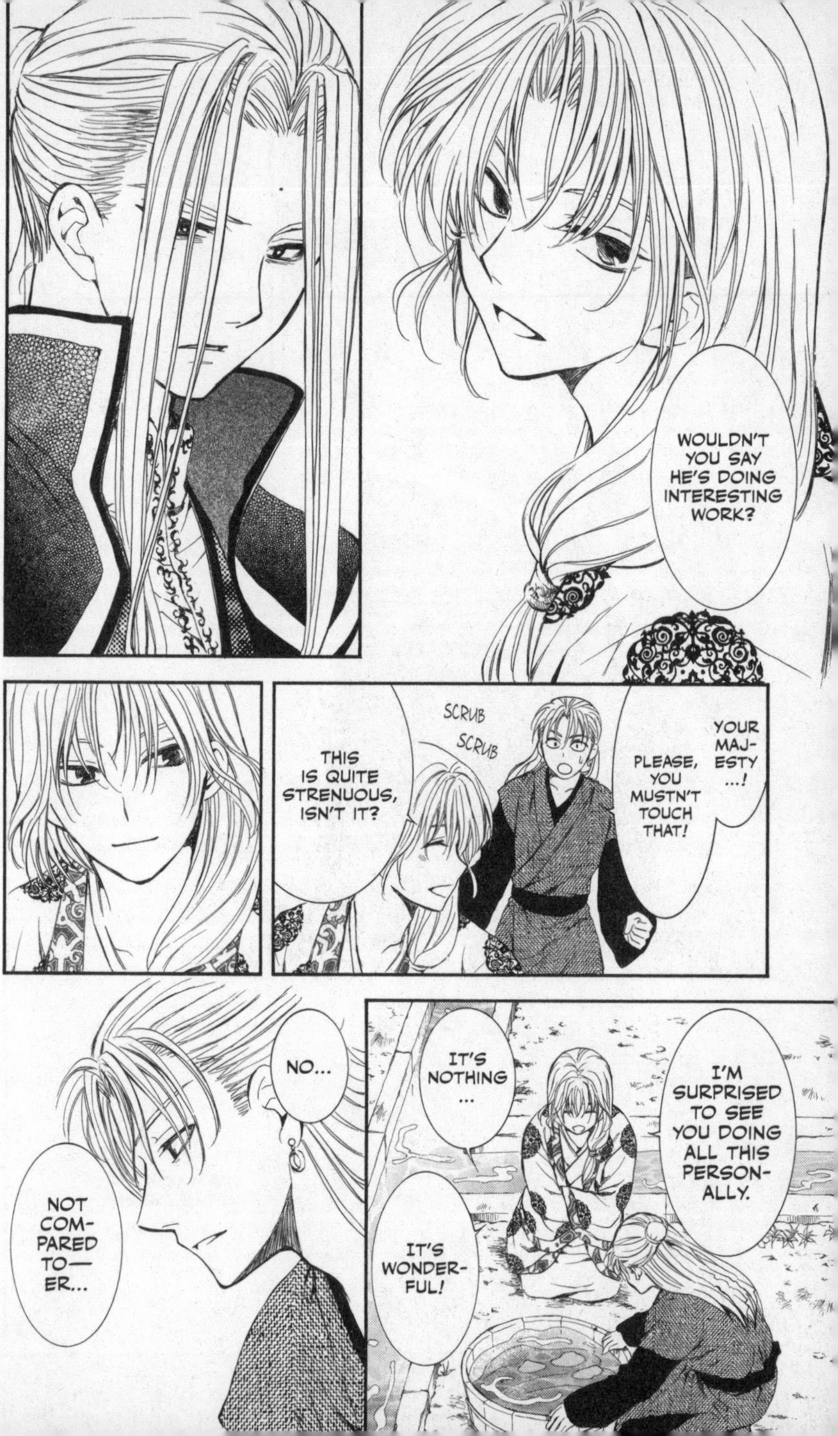
WOULDN'T YOU SAY HE'S DOING INTERESTING WORK?
YOUR MAJESTY ...!
PLEASE, YOU MUSTN'T TOUCH THAT!
SCRUB
SCRUB
THIS IS QUITE STRENUOUS, ISN'T IT?
I'M SURPRISED TO SEE YOU DOING ALL THIS PERSON-ALLY.
IT'S NOTHING ...
IT'S WONDER-FUL!
NO...
NOT COM-PARED TO— ER...

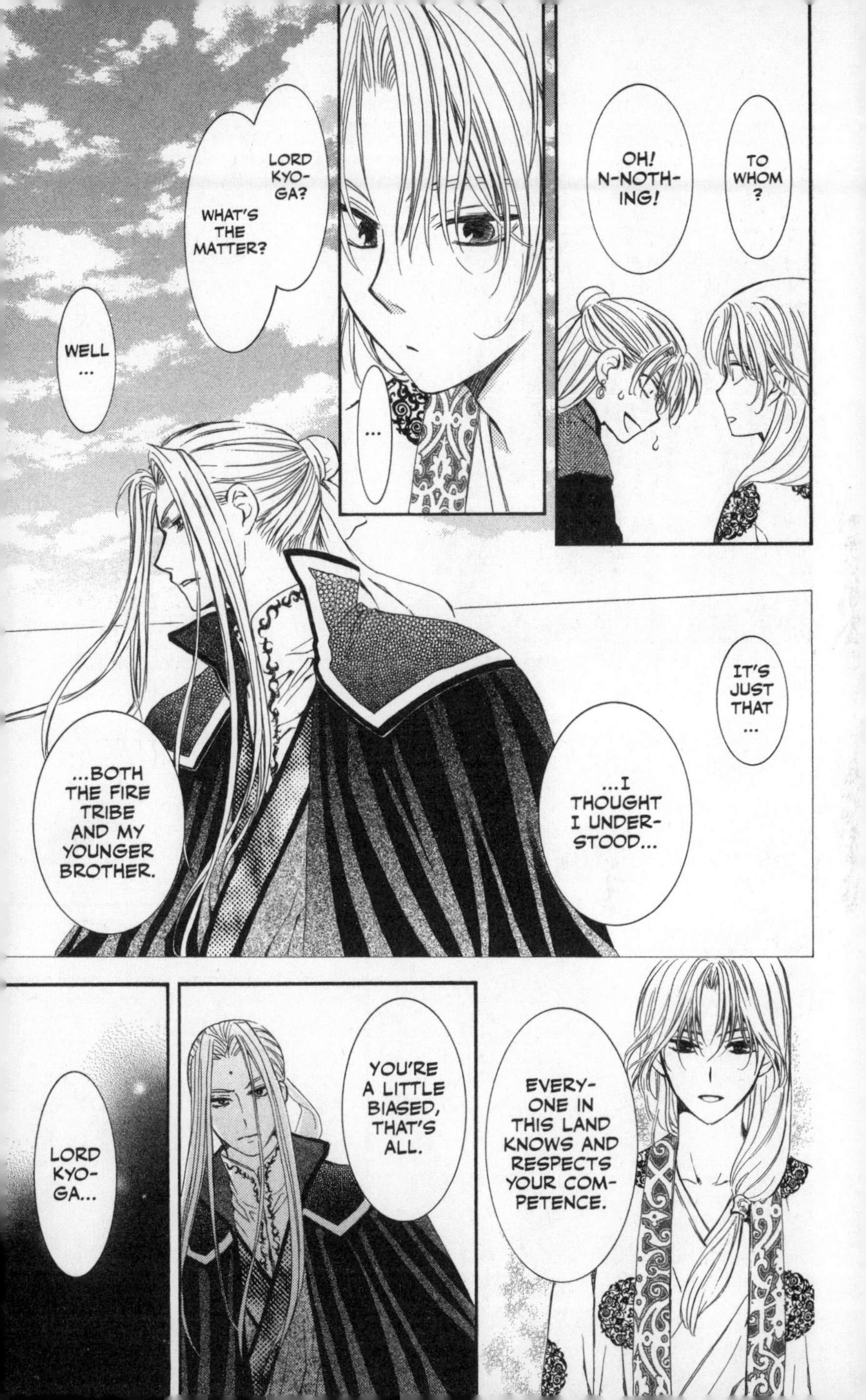
TO WHOM?
OH! N-NOTHING!
LORD KYO-GA? WHAT'S THE MATTER?
...
WELL...
IT'S JUST THAT...
...I THOUGHT I UNDERSTOOD...
...BOTH THE FIRE TRIBE AND MY YOUNGER BROTHER.
EVERYONE IN THIS LAND KNOWS AND RESPECTS YOUR COMPETENCE.
YOU'RE A LITTLE BIASED, THAT'S ALL.
LORD KYO-GA...

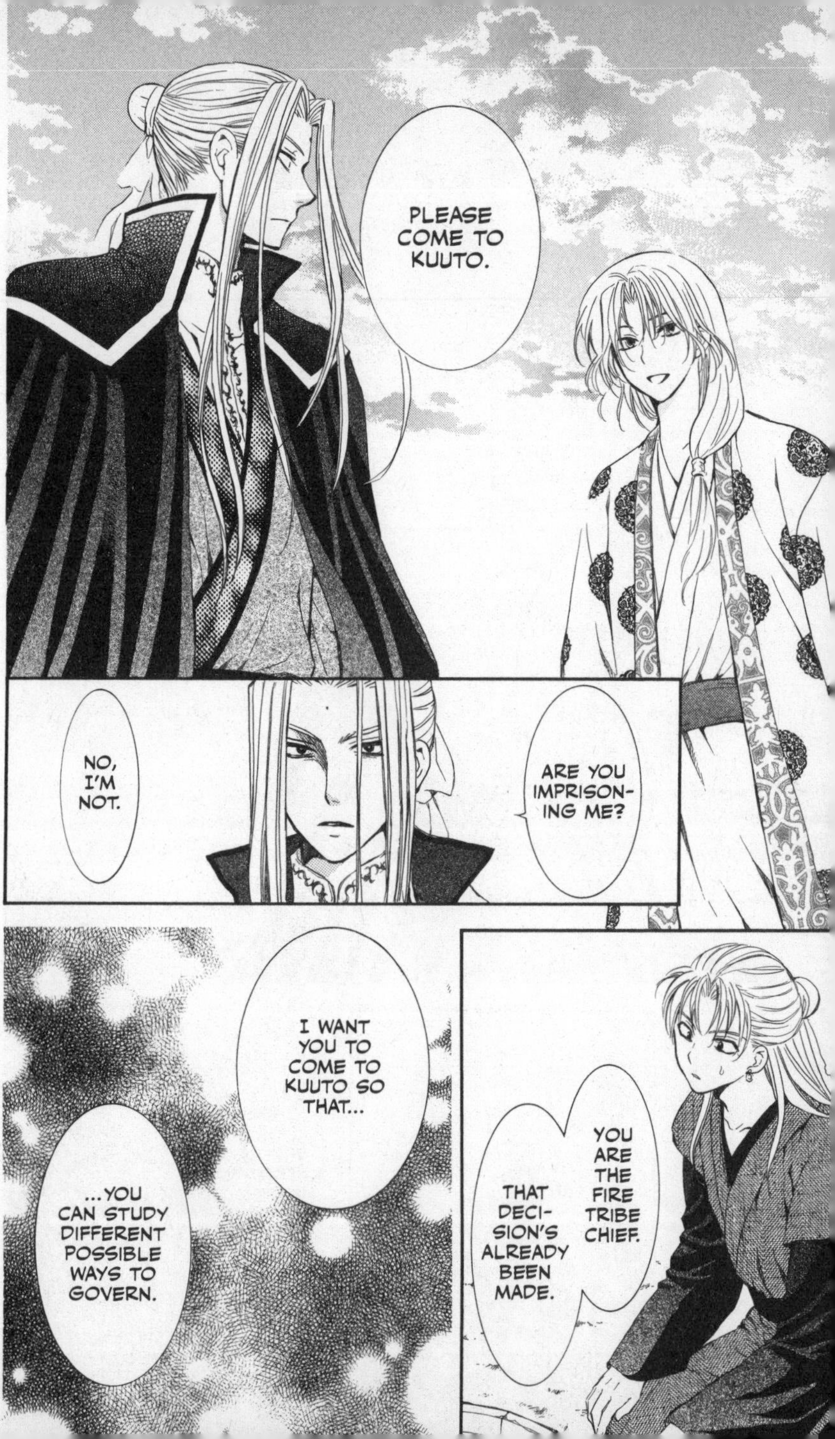
PLEASE COME TO KUUTO.
ARE YOU IMPRISON-ING ME?
NO, I'M NOT.
YOU ARE THE FIRE TRIBE CHIEF.
THAT DECI-SION'S ALREADY BEEN MADE.
I WANT YOU TO COME TO KUUTO SO THAT...
...YOU CAN STUDY DIFFERENT POSSIBLE WAYS TO GOVERN.

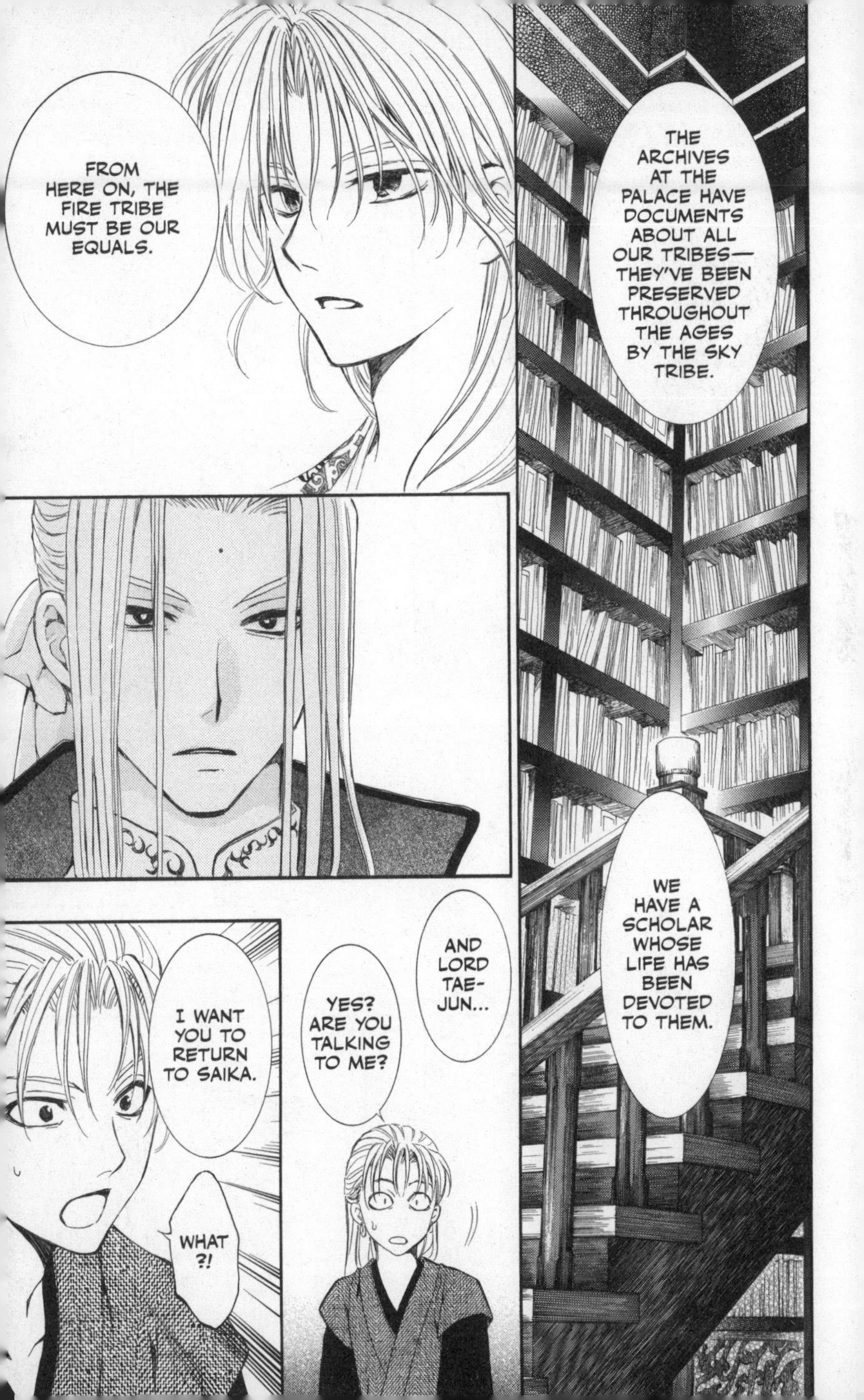
THE ARCHIVES AT THE PALACE HAVE DOCUMENTS ABOUT ALL OUR TRIBES—THEY'VE BEEN PRESERVED THROUGHOUT THE AGES BY THE SKY TRIBE.
WE HAVE A SCHOLAR WHOSE LIFE HAS BEEN DEVOTED TO THEM.
FROM HERE ON, THE FIRE TRIBE MUST BE OUR EQUALS.
AND LORD TAE-JUN...
YES? ARE YOU TALKING TO ME?
I WANT YOU TO RETURN TO SAIKA.
WHAT?!

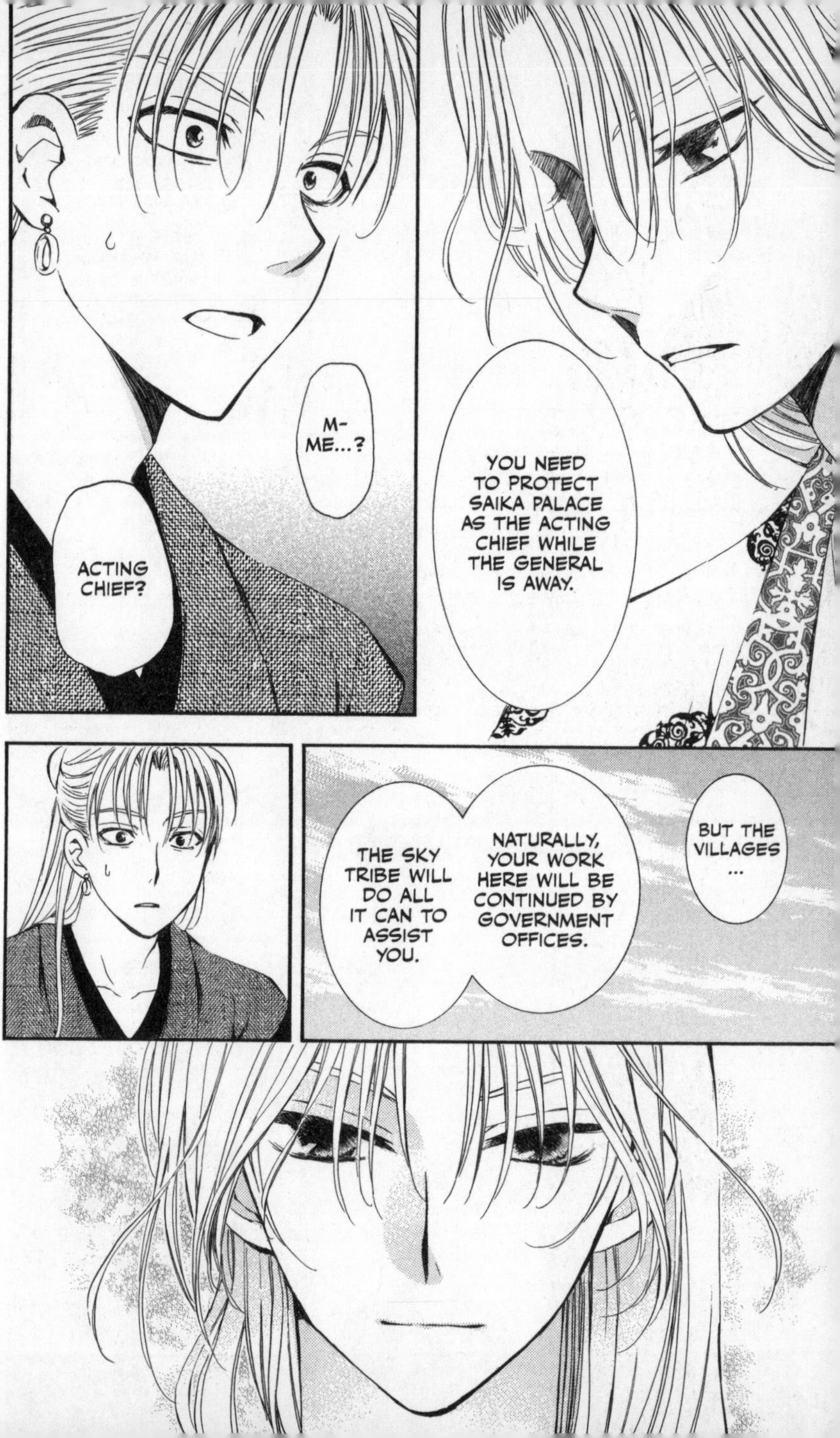
YOU NEED TO PROTECT SAIKA PALACE AS THE ACTING CHIEF WHILE THE GENERAL IS AWAY.
M- ME...?
ACTING CHIEF?
BUT THE VILLAGES ...
NATURALLY, YOUR WORK HERE WILL BE CONTINUED BY GOVERNMENT OFFICES.
THE SKY TRIBE WILL DO ALL IT CAN TO ASSIST YOU.

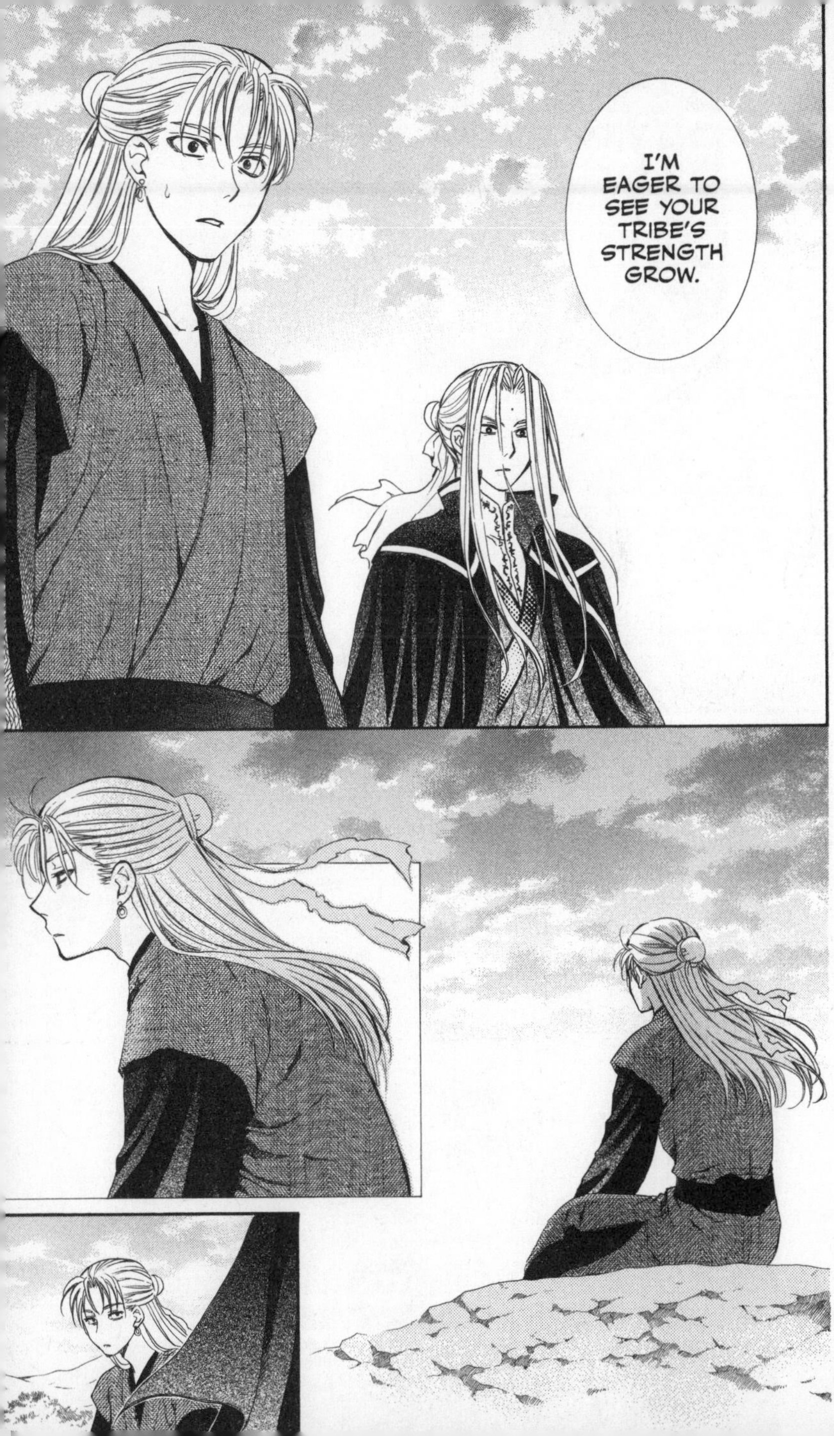
I'M EAGER TO SEE YOUR TRIBE'S STRENGTH GROW.

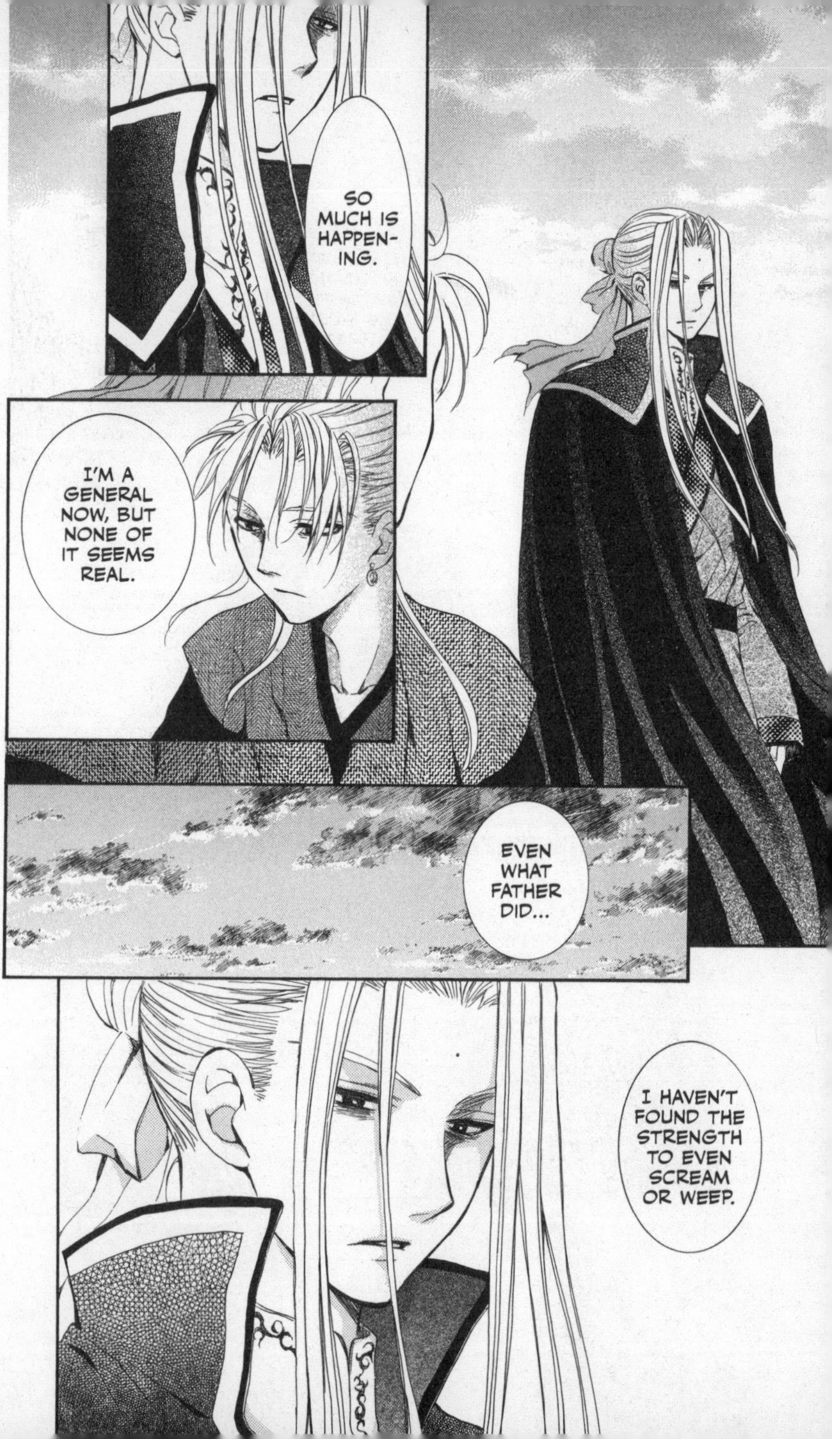
SO MUCH IS HAPPEN-ING.
I'M A GENERAL NOW, BUT NONE OF IT SEEMS REAL.
EVEN WHAT FATHER DID...
I HAVEN'T FOUND THE STRENGTH TO EVEN SCREAM OR WEEP.

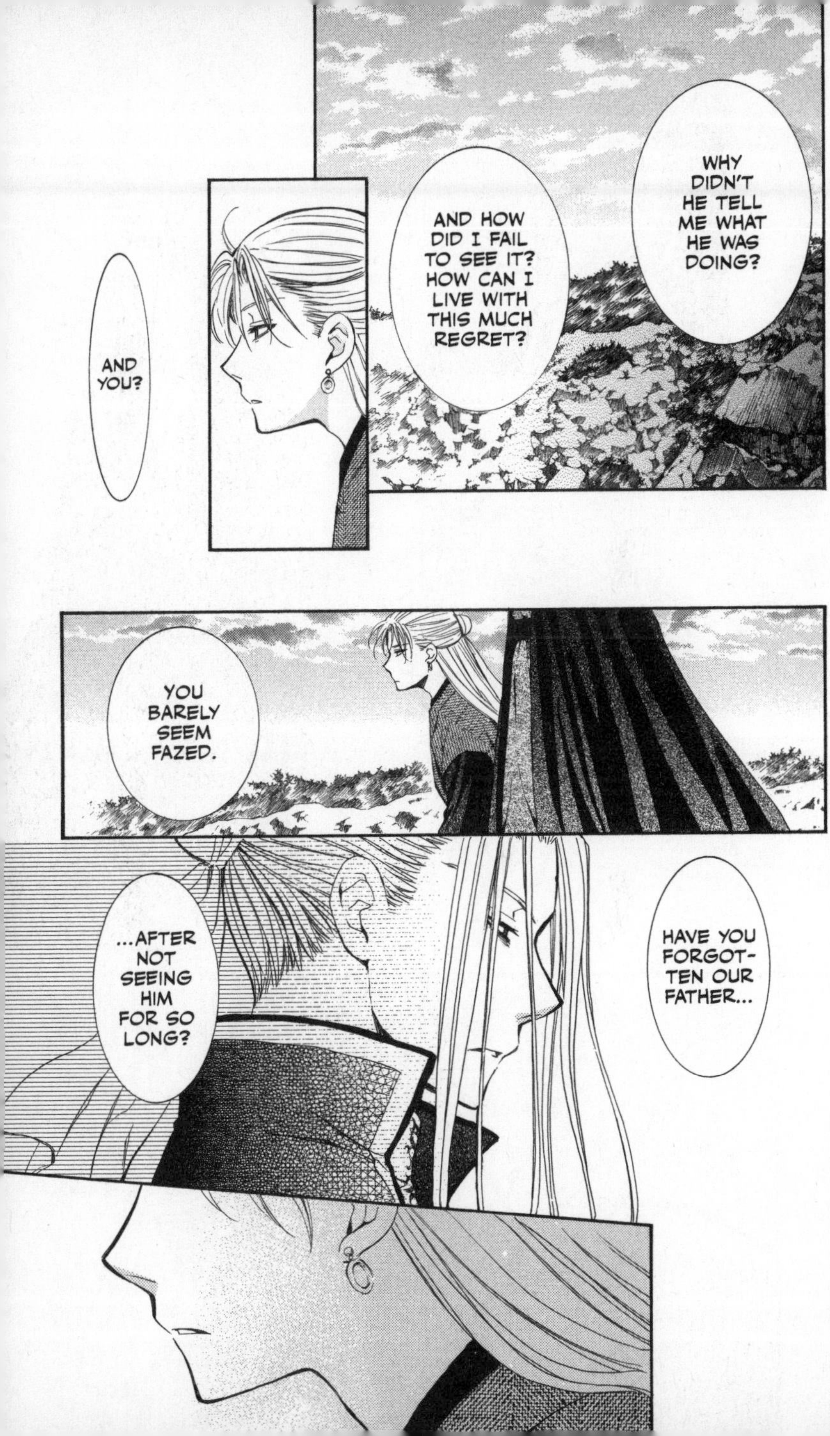
WHY DIDN'T HE TELL ME WHAT HE WAS DOING?
AND HOW DID I FAIL TO SEE IT? HOW CAN I LIVE WITH THIS MUCH REGRET?
AND YOU?
YOU BARELY SEEM FAZED.
HAVE YOU FORGOT-TEN OUR FATHER...
...AFTER NOT SEEING HIM FOR SO LONG?

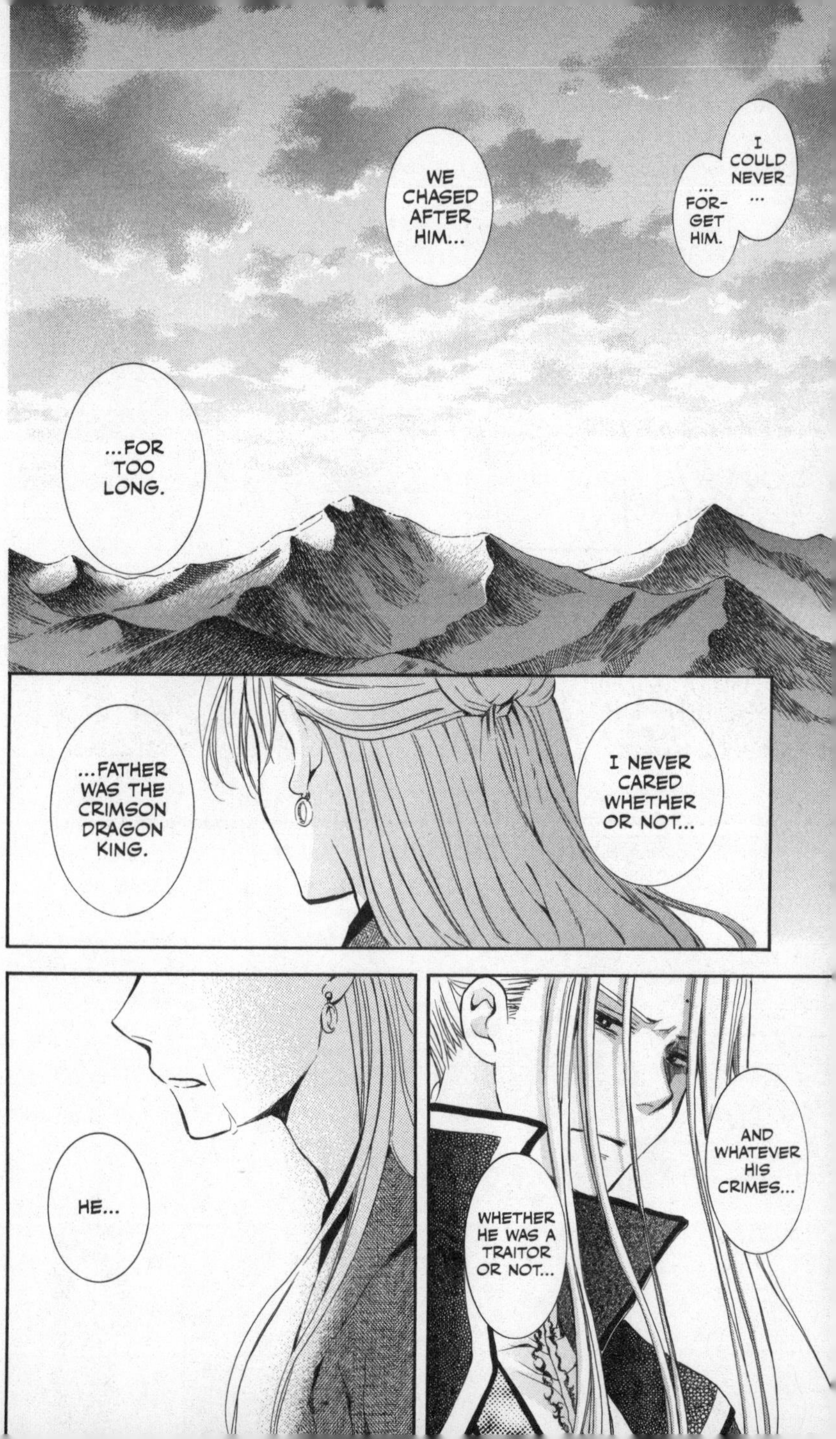
I COULD NEVER ...
... FOR-GET HIM.
WE CHASED AFTER HIM...
...FOR TOO LONG.
I NEVER CARED WHETHER OR NOT...
...FATHER WAS THE CRIMSON DRAGON KING.
AND WHATEVER HIS CRIMES...
WHETHER HE WAS A TRAITOR OR NOT...
HE...

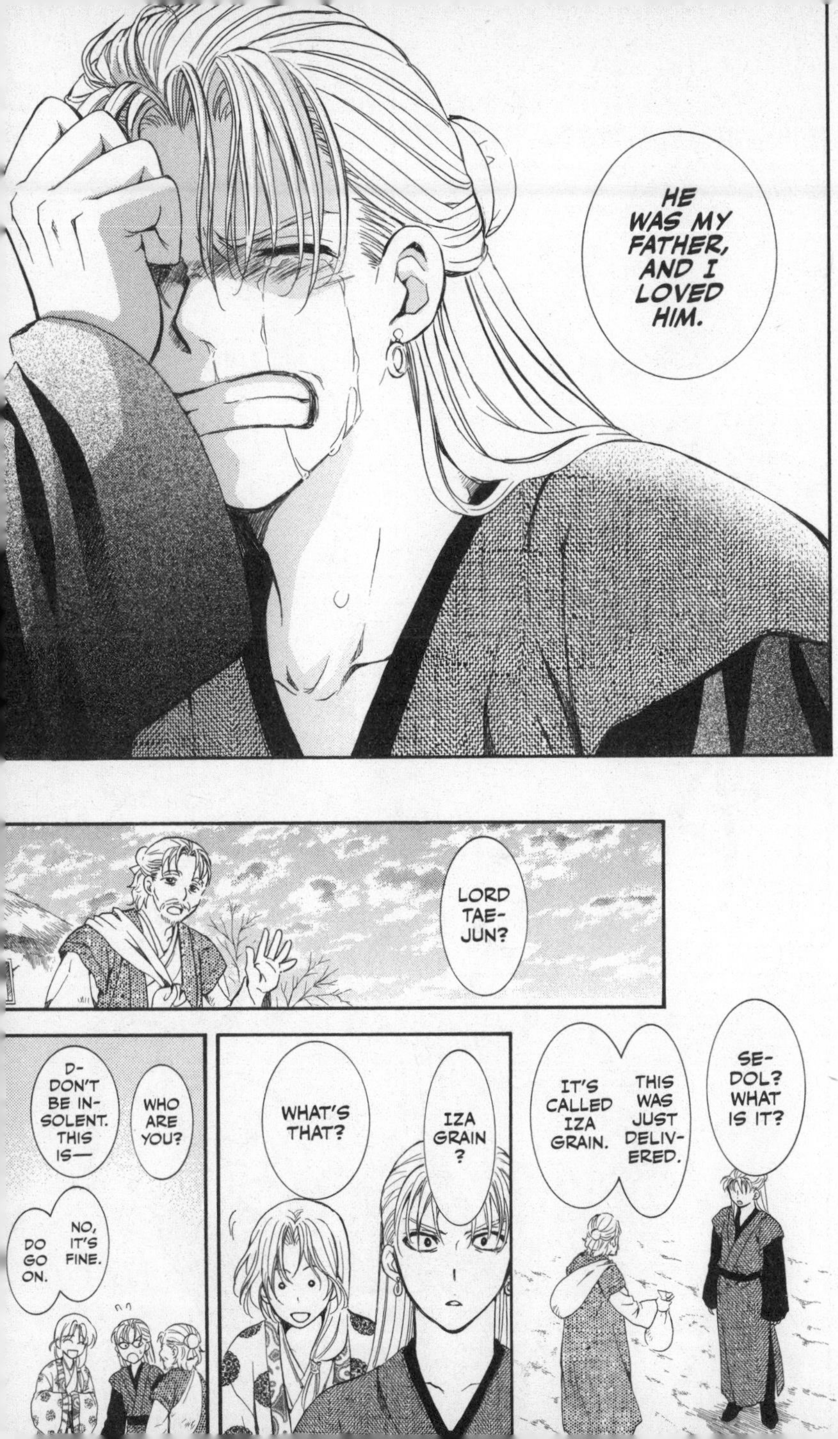
HE WAS MY FATHER, AND I LOVED HIM.
LORD TAE-JUN?
SE-DOL? WHAT IS IT?
THIS WAS JUST DELIV-ERED.
IT'S CALLED IZA GRAIN.
IZA GRAIN?
WHAT'S THAT?
WHO ARE YOU?
D-DON'T BE IN-SOLENT. THIS IS—
NO, IT'S FINE.
DO GO ON.

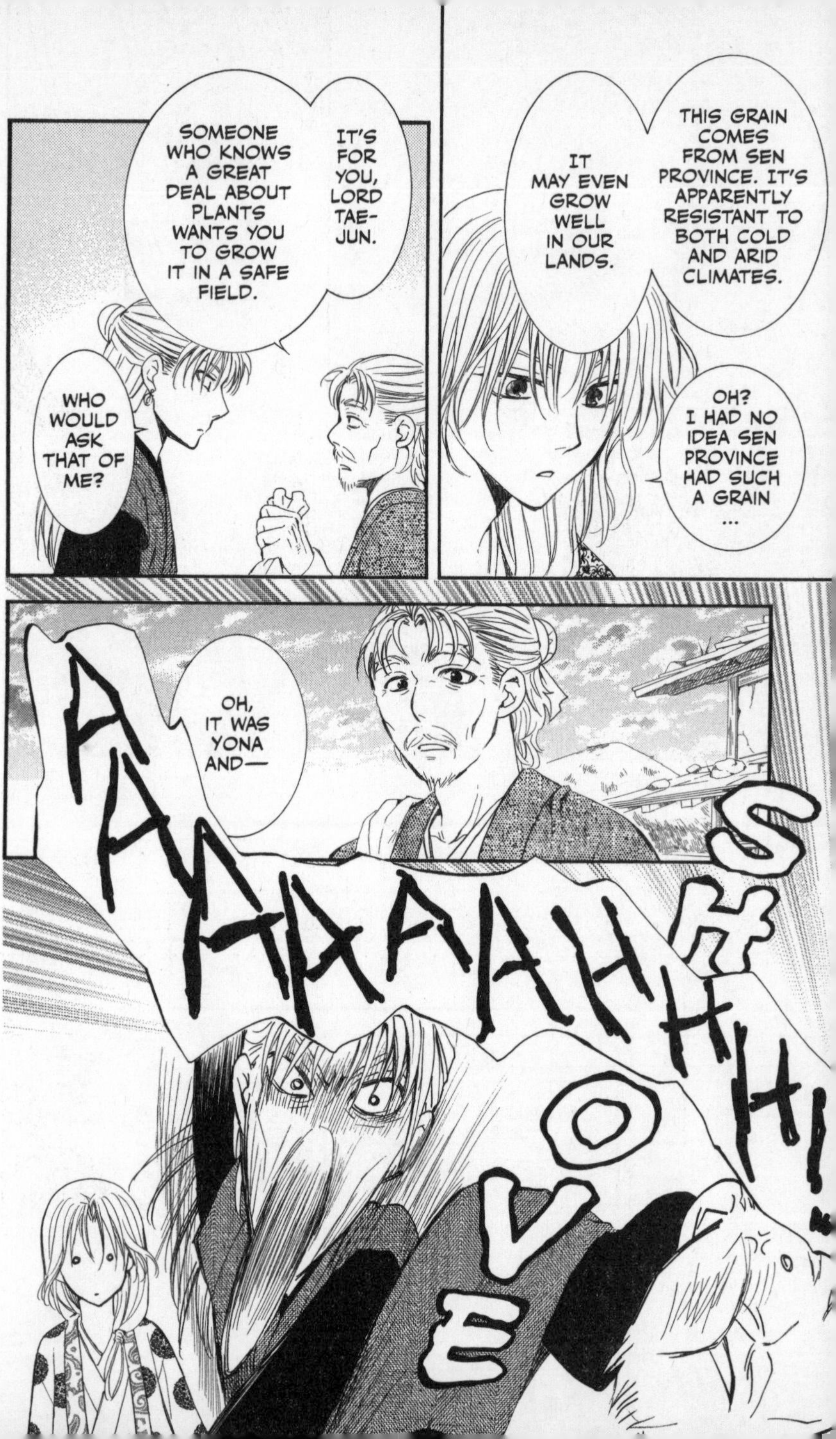
THIS GRAIN COMES FROM SEN PROVINCE. IT'S APPARENTLY RESISTANT TO BOTH COLD AND ARID CLIMATES.
IT MAY EVEN GROW WELL IN OUR LANDS.
OH? I HAD NO IDEA SEN PROVINCE HAD SUCH A GRAIN...
IT'S FOR YOU, LORD TAE-JUN.
SOMEONE WHO KNOWS A GREAT DEAL ABOUT PLANTS WANTS YOU TO GROW IT IN A SAFE FIELD.
WHO WOULD ASK THAT OF ME?
OH, IT WAS YONA AND—
AAAAAHHHH!
SHOVE!

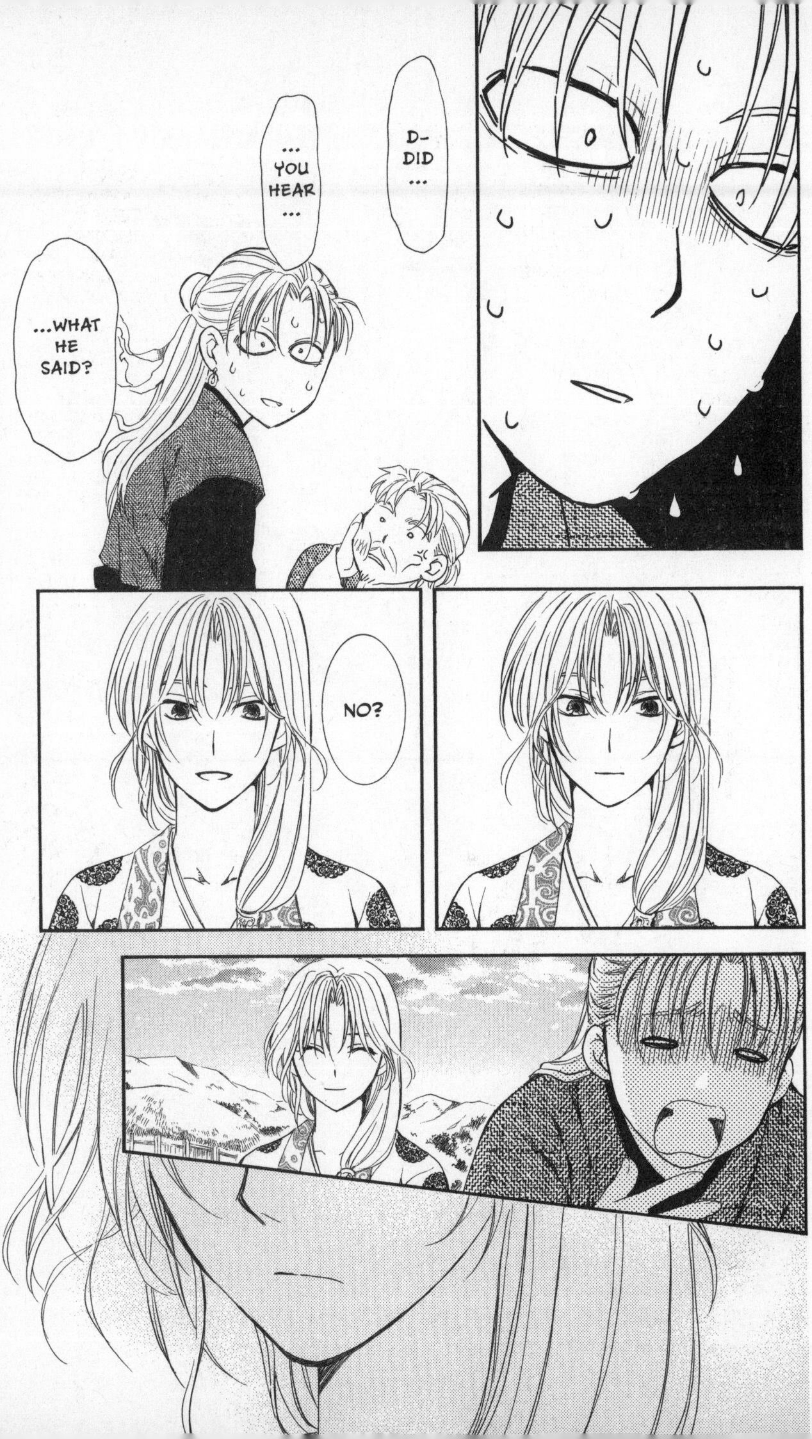
D-DID...
...YOU HEAR...
...WHAT HE SAID?
NO?

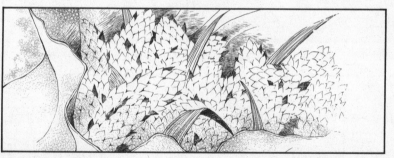

HER...

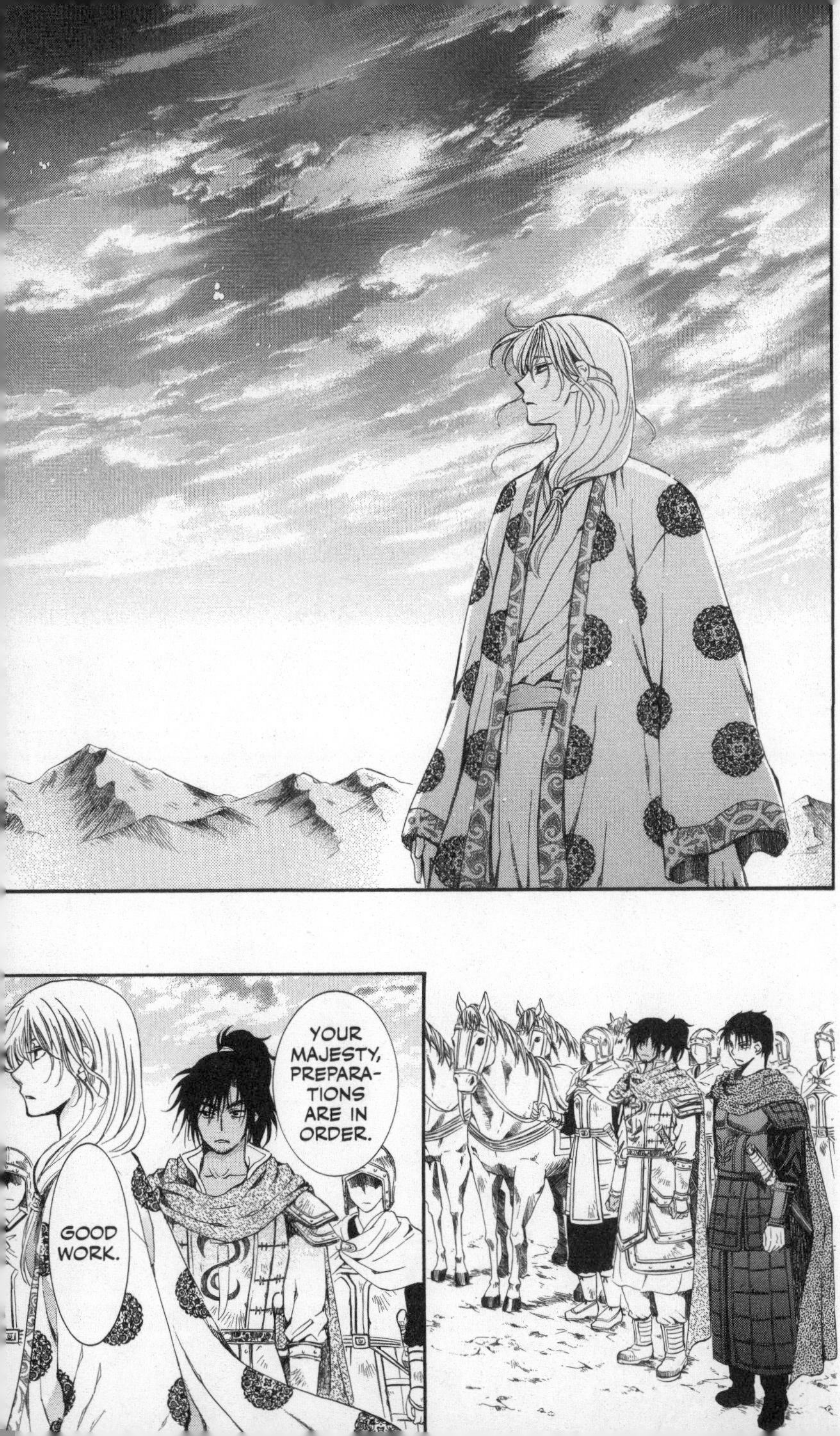
YOUR MAJESTY, PREPARATIONS ARE IN ORDER.
GOOD WORK.

WELL, SHALL WE GET GOING?
OUR NEXT STOP IS SEN PROVINCE ...
...IN THE KAI EMPIRE.
CHAPTER 74 / THE END

CHAPTER 75: THREE CONDITIONS

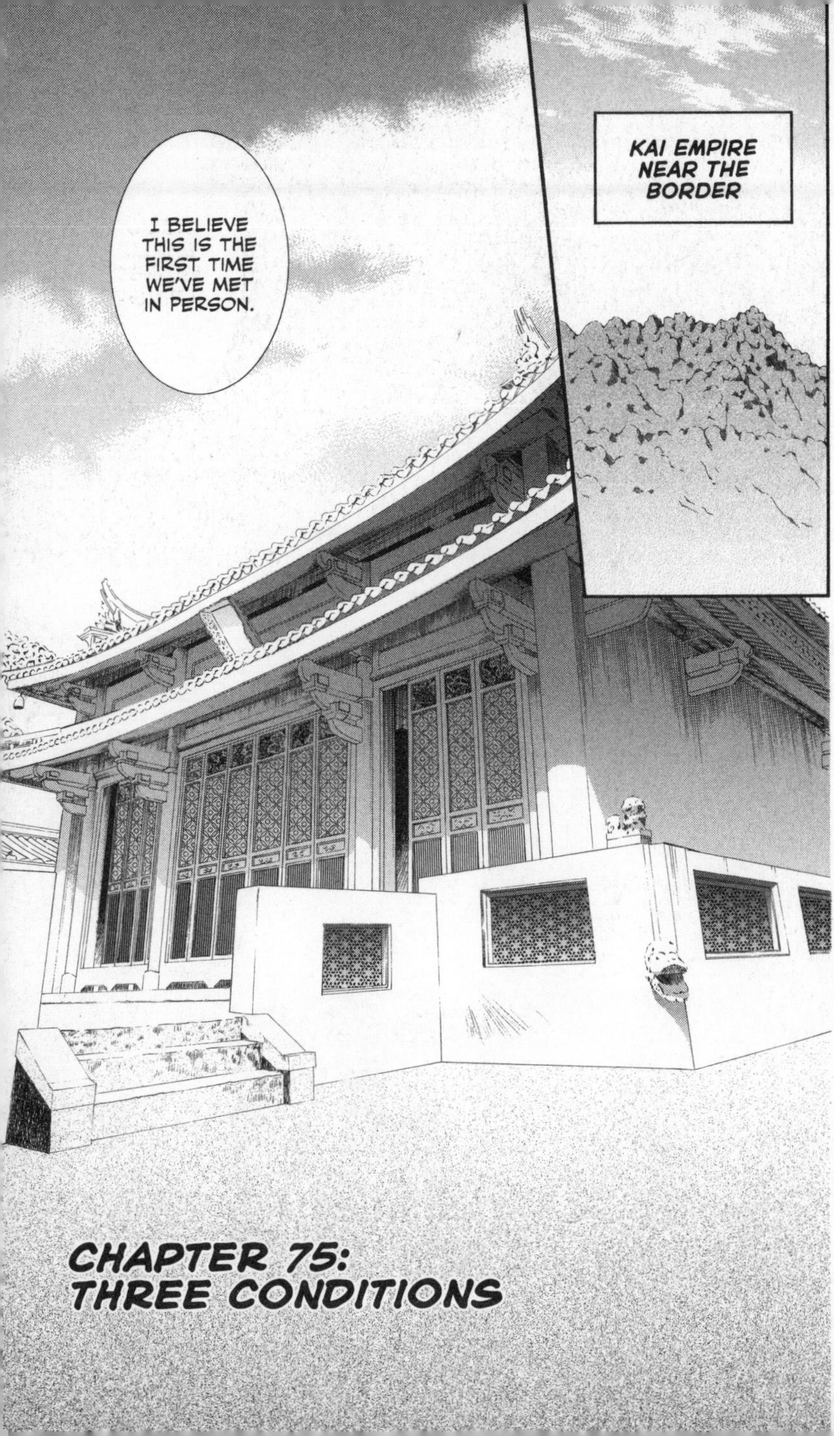
KAI EMPIRE NEAR THE BORDER
I BELIEVE THIS IS THE FIRST TIME WE'VE MET IN PERSON.

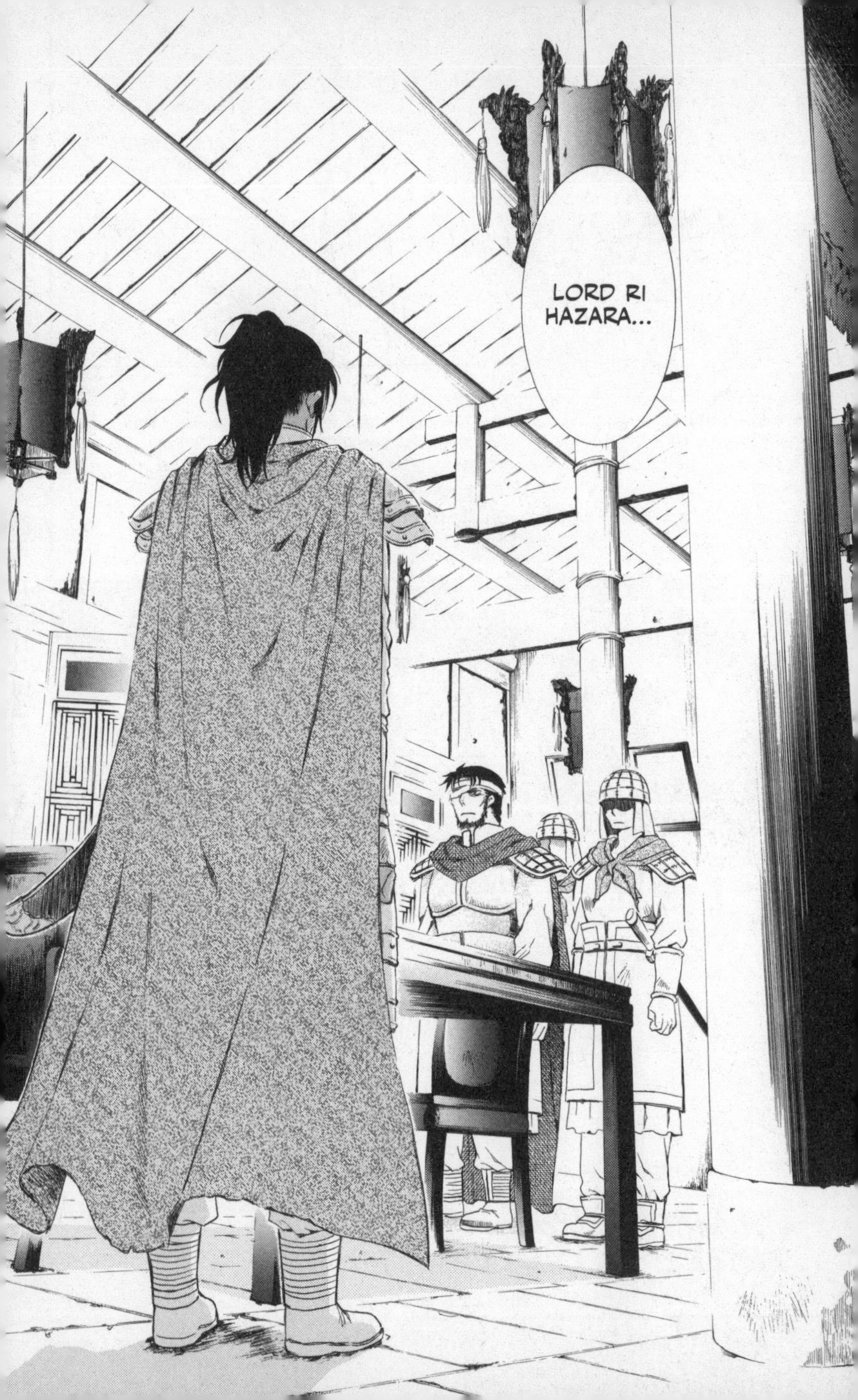
LORD RI HAZARA...

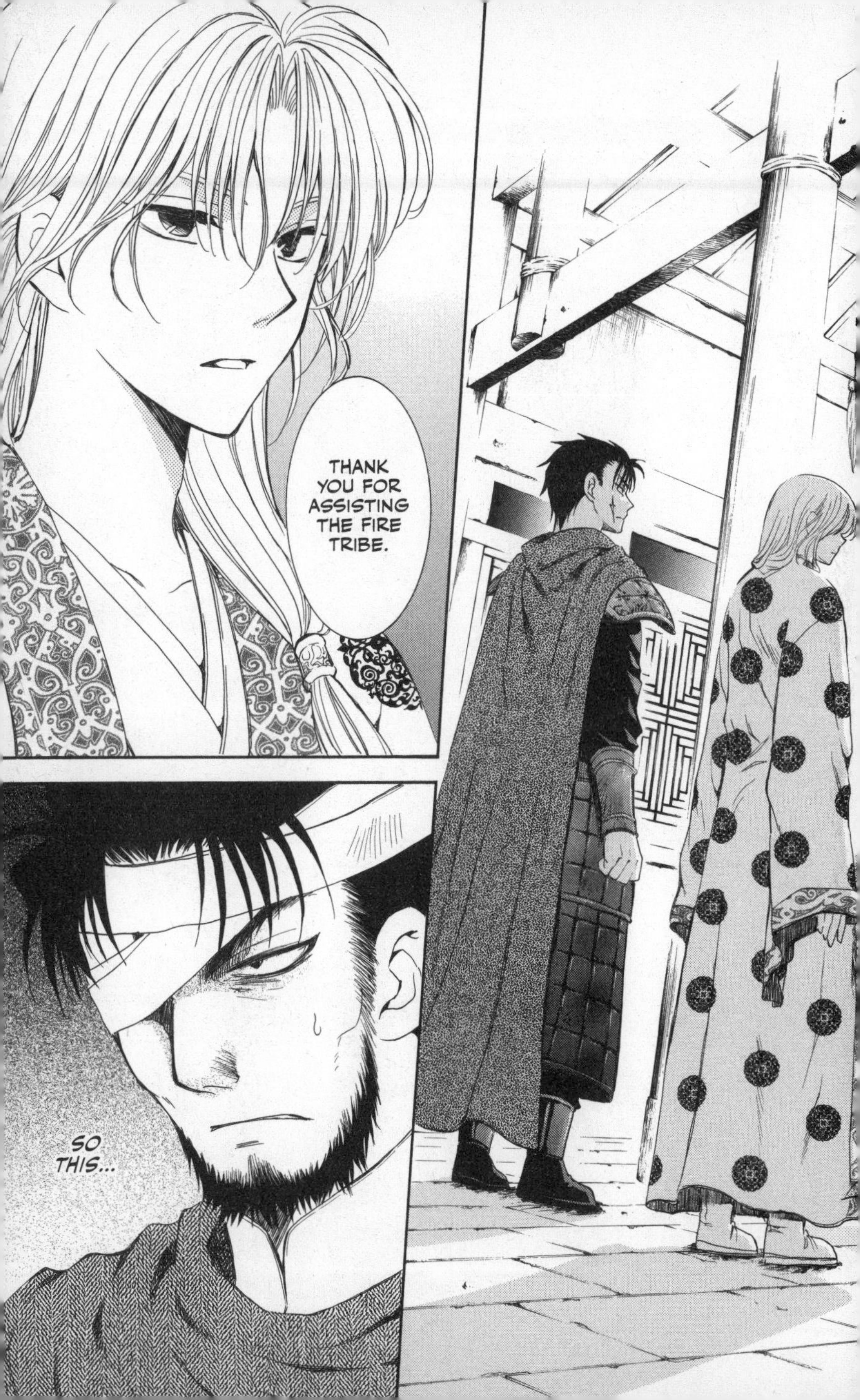
THANK YOU FOR ASSISTING THE FIRE TRIBE.
SO THIS...

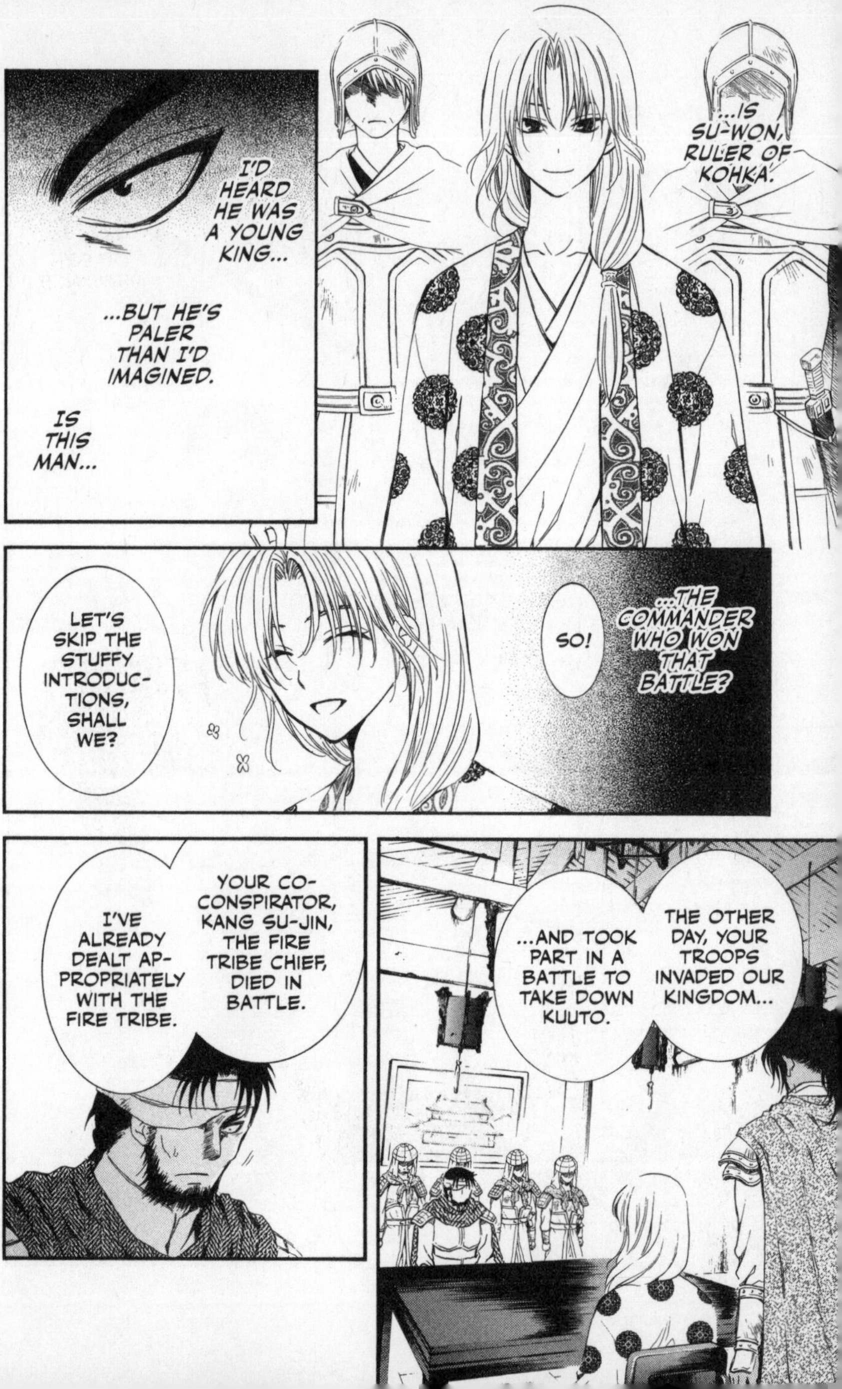
I'D HEARD HE WAS A YOUNG KING...
...BUT HE'S PALER THAN I'D IMAGINED.
IS THIS MAN...
...IS SU-WON, RULER OF KOHKA.
...THE COMMANDER WHO WON THAT BATTLE?
SO!
LET'S SKIP THE STUFFY INTRODUC-TIONS, SHALL WE?
THE OTHER DAY, YOUR TROOPS INVADED OUR KINGDOM...
...AND TOOK PART IN A BATTLE TO TAKE DOWN KUUTO.
YOUR CO-CONSPIRATOR, KANG SU-JIN, THE FIRE TRIBE CHIEF, DIED IN BATTLE.
I'VE ALREADY DEALT AP-PROPRIATELY WITH THE FIRE TRIBE.

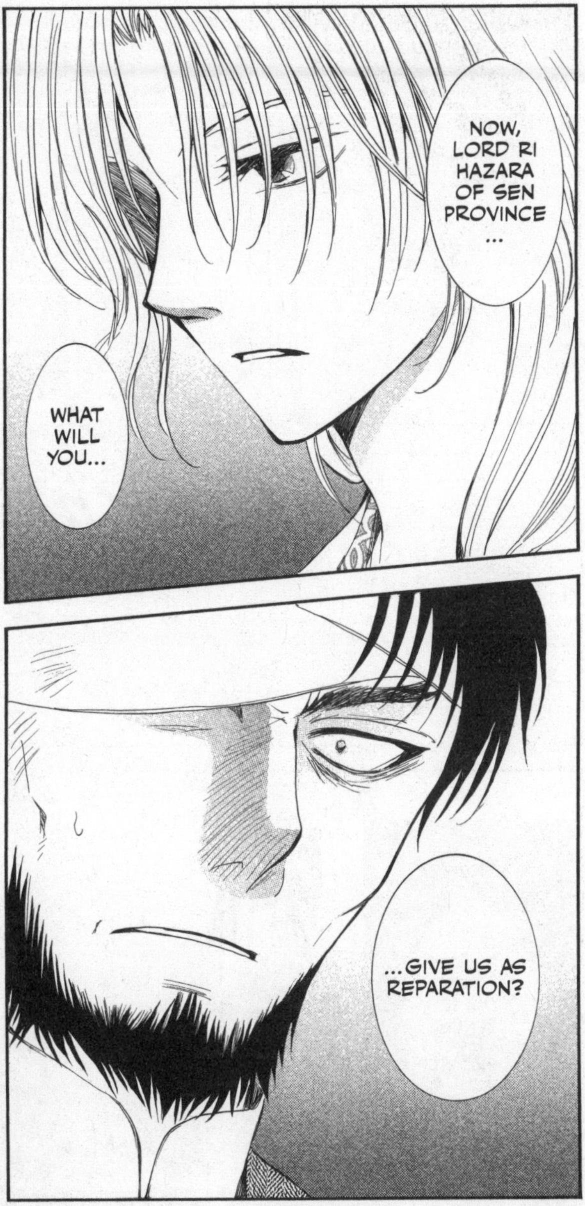
NOW, LORD RI HAZARA OF SEN PROVINCE ...
WHAT WILL YOU...
...GIVE US AS REPARATION?

The Fire Tribe Arc (a.k.a. the "Tae-jun Works Hard in the Fields Arc") has come to an end. This story's purpose was to showcase Su-won, so I didn't focus on the Happy Hungry Bunch's fighting. The fact is, while they did have battles, I couldn't have squeezed everything into a single chapter if I'd given them much page time. Drawing the battle scenes was hard work, but I'd like to do it again someday.

This is a trivial detail, but in chapter 74, Tae-jun says, "Is Granny Kune all right?" Granny Kune is the old lady Tae-jun massaged in chapter 59 (volume 10). ↓

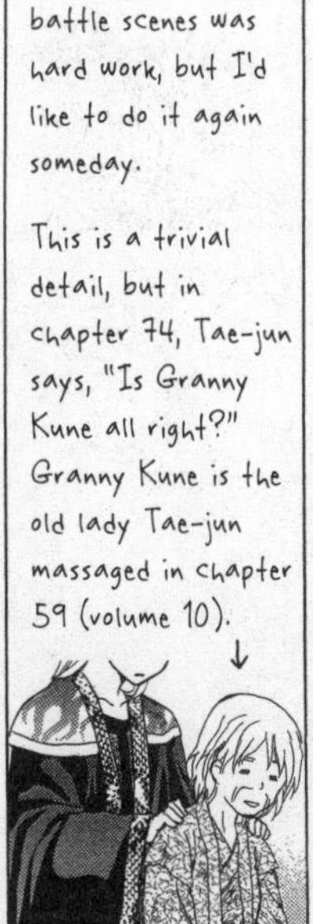

That really was trivial, wasn't it?

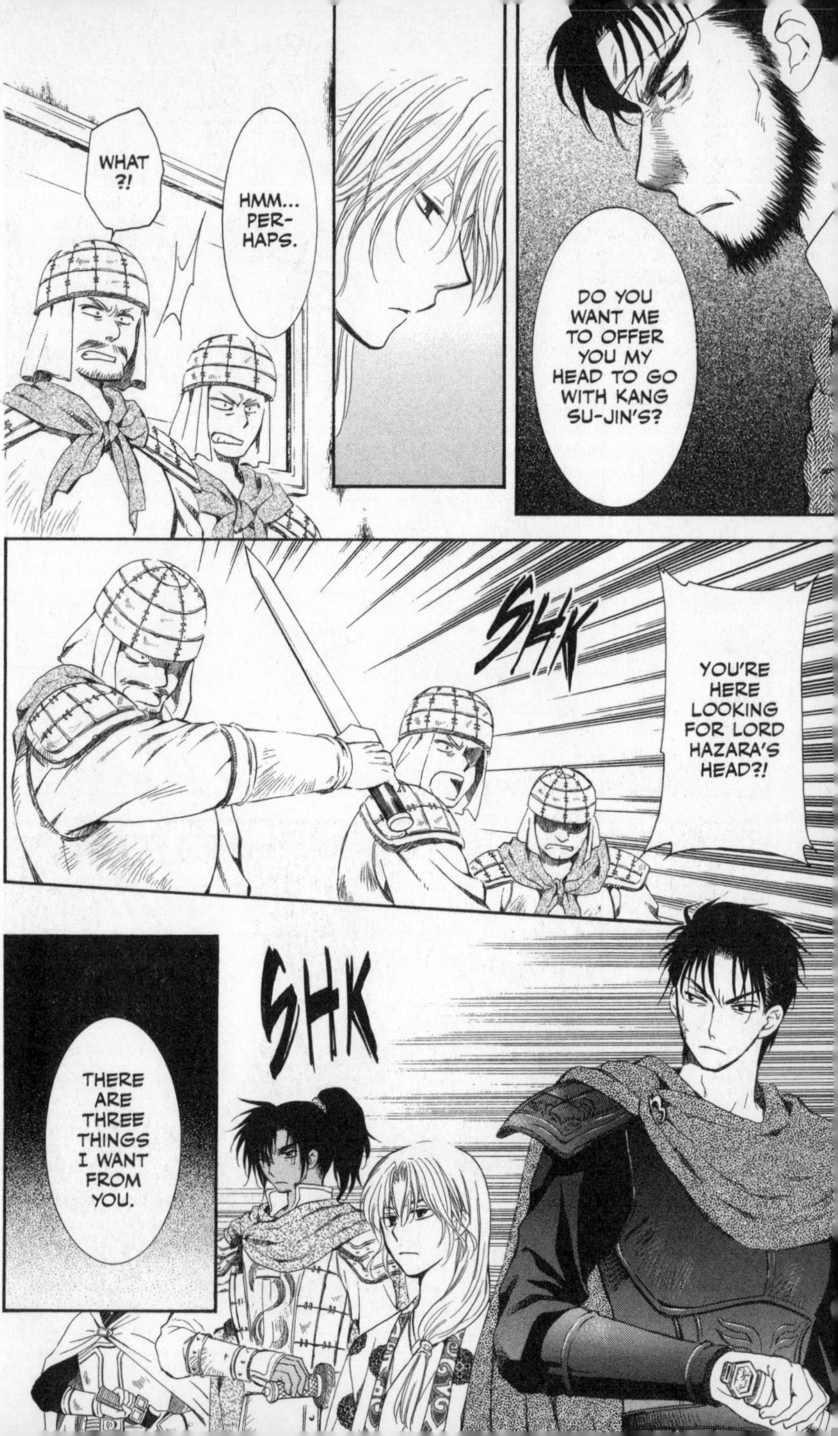
DO YOU WANT ME TO OFFER YOU MY HEAD TO GO WITH KANG SU-JIN'S?
HMM... PER-HAPS.
WHAT?!
SHK
YOU'RE HERE LOOKING FOR LORD HAZARA'S HEAD?!
SHK
THERE ARE THREE THINGS I WANT FROM YOU.

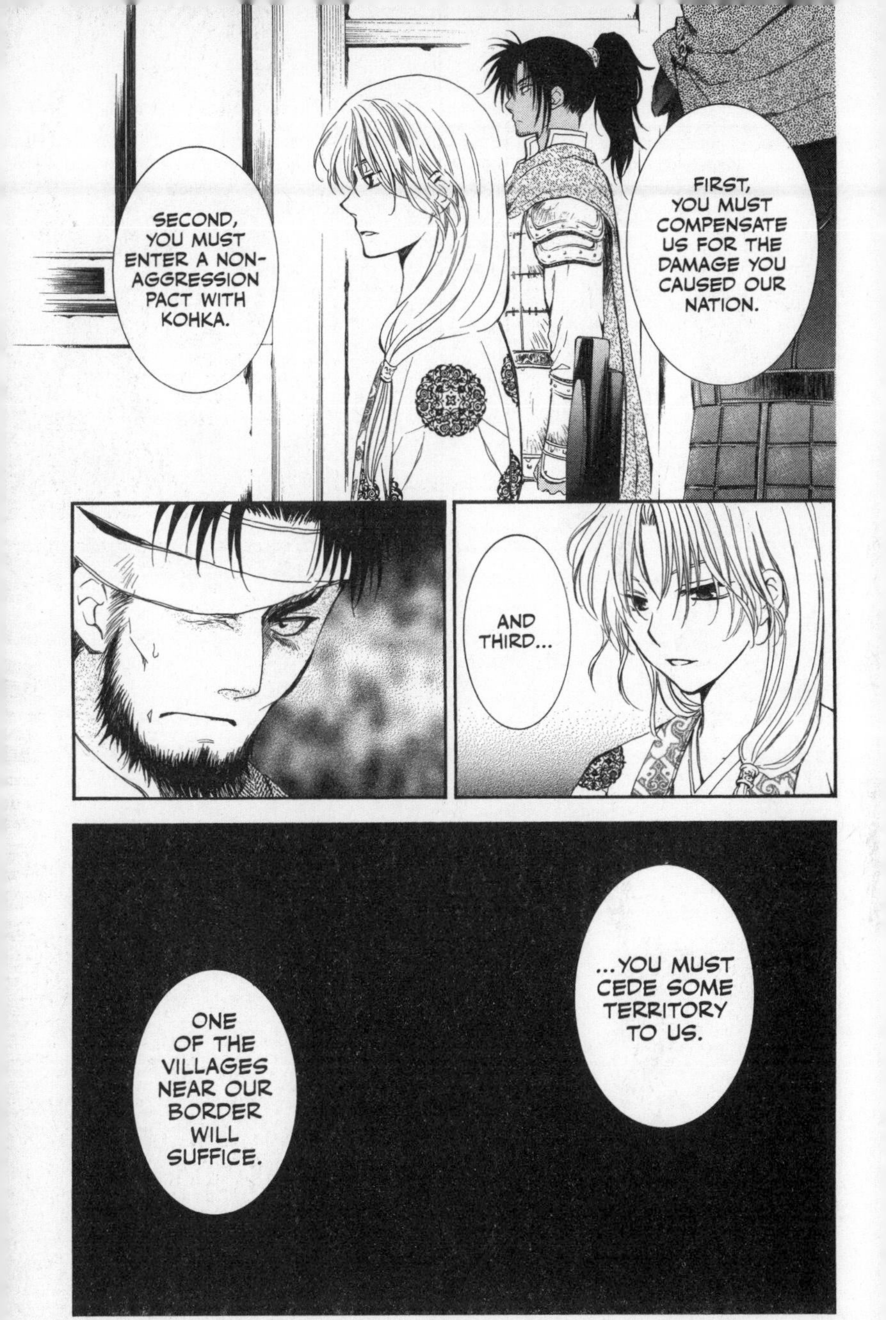
FIRST, YOU MUST COMPENSATE US FOR THE DAMAGE YOU CAUSED OUR NATION.
SECOND, YOU MUST ENTER A NON-AGGRESSION PACT WITH KOHKA.
AND THIRD...
...YOU MUST CEDE SOME TERRITORY TO US.
ONE OF THE VILLAGES NEAR OUR BORDER WILL SUFFICE.

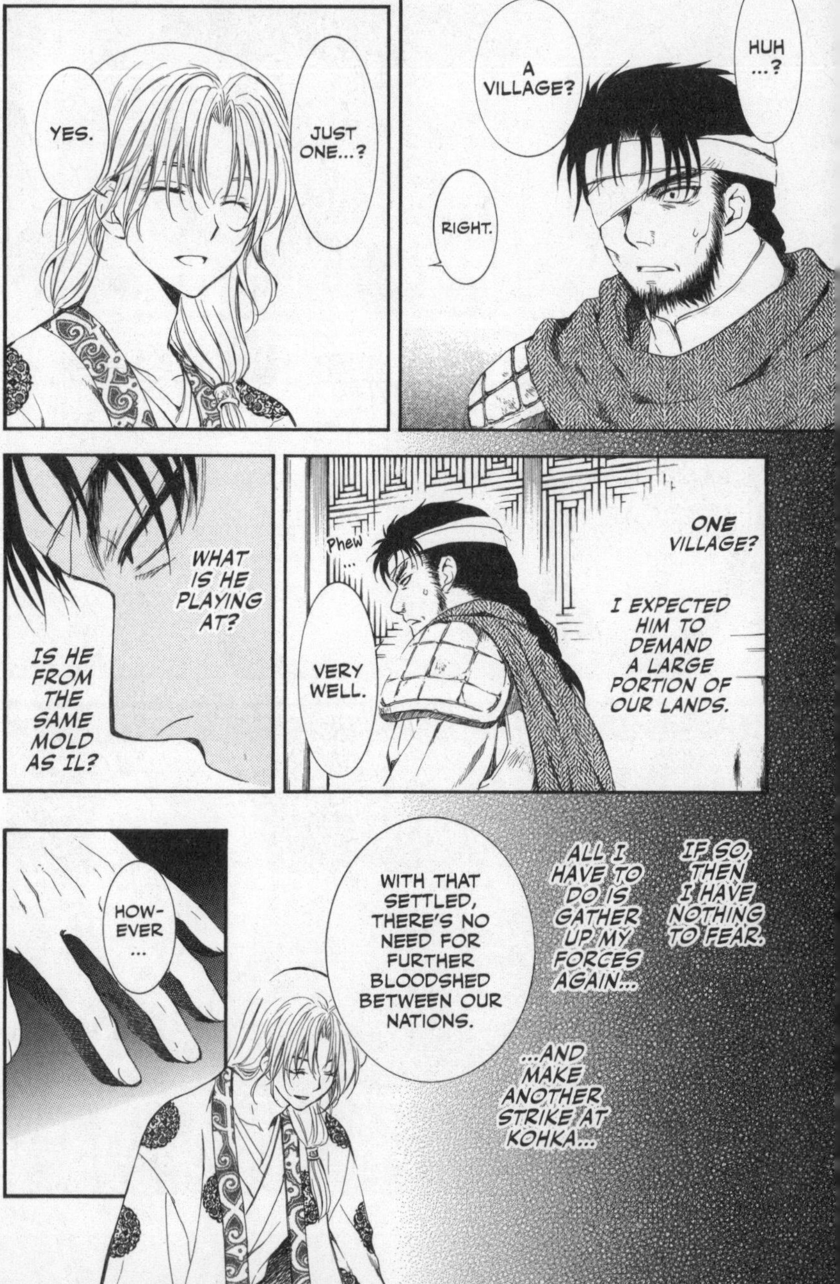
HUH ...?
A VILLAGE?
RIGHT.
JUST ONE...?
YES.
ONE VILLAGE?
I EXPECTED HIM TO DEMAND A LARGE PORTION OF OUR LANDS.
Phew ...
VERY WELL.
WHAT IS HE PLAYING AT?
IS HE FROM THE SAME MOLD AS IL?
IF SO, THEN I HAVE NOTHING TO FEAR.
ALL I HAVE TO DO IS GATHER UP MY FORCES AGAIN...
...AND MAKE ANOTHER STRIKE AT KOHKA...
WITH THAT SETTLED, THERE'S NO NEED FOR FURTHER BLOODSHED BETWEEN OUR NATIONS.
HOW-EVER ...

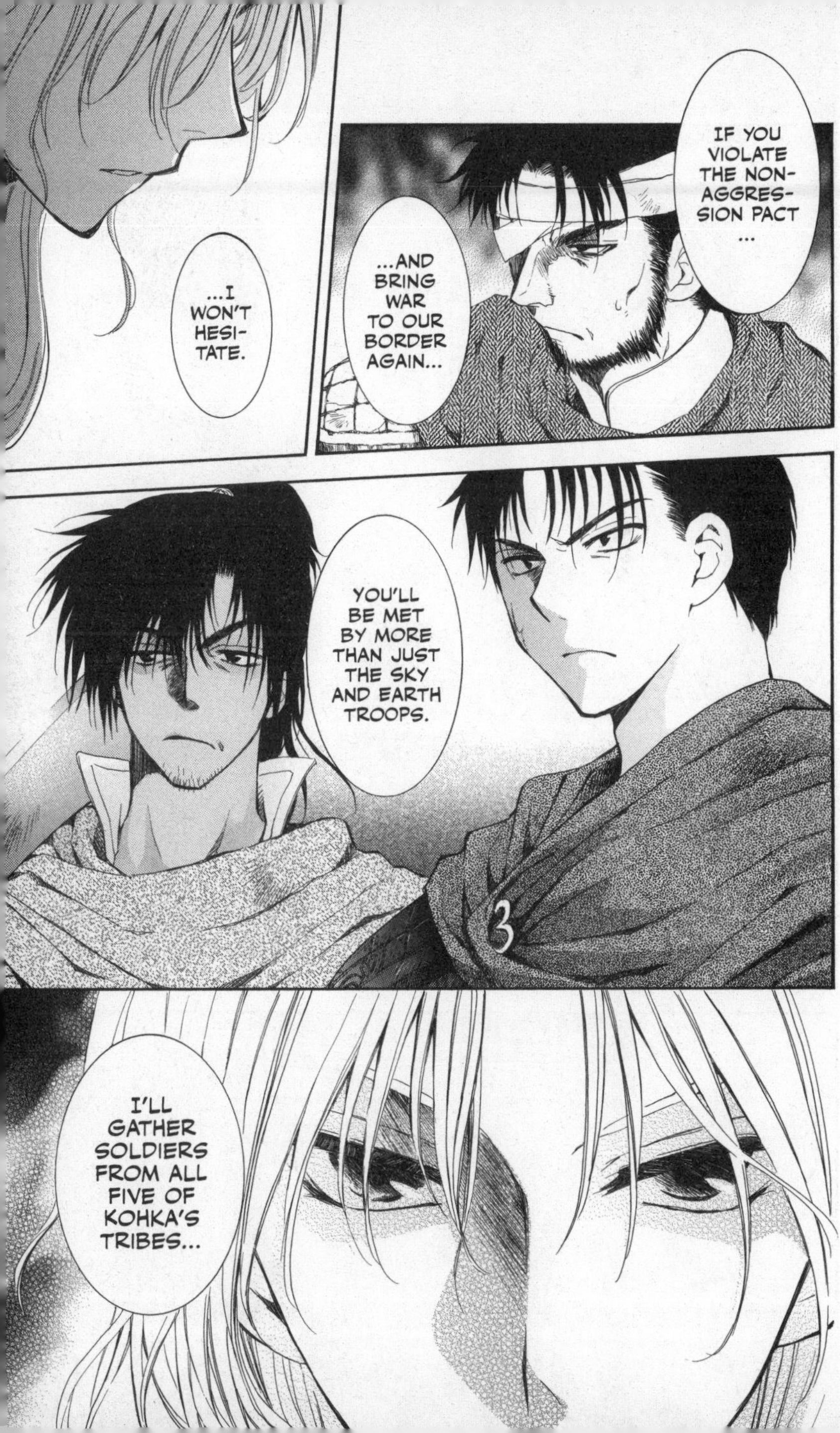
IF YOU VIOLATE THE NON-AGGRESSION PACT ...
...AND BRING WAR TO OUR BORDER AGAIN...
...I WON'T HESITATE.
YOU'LL BE MET BY MORE THAN JUST THE SKY AND EARTH TROOPS.
I'LL GATHER SOLDIERS FROM ALL FIVE OF KOHKA'S TRIBES...

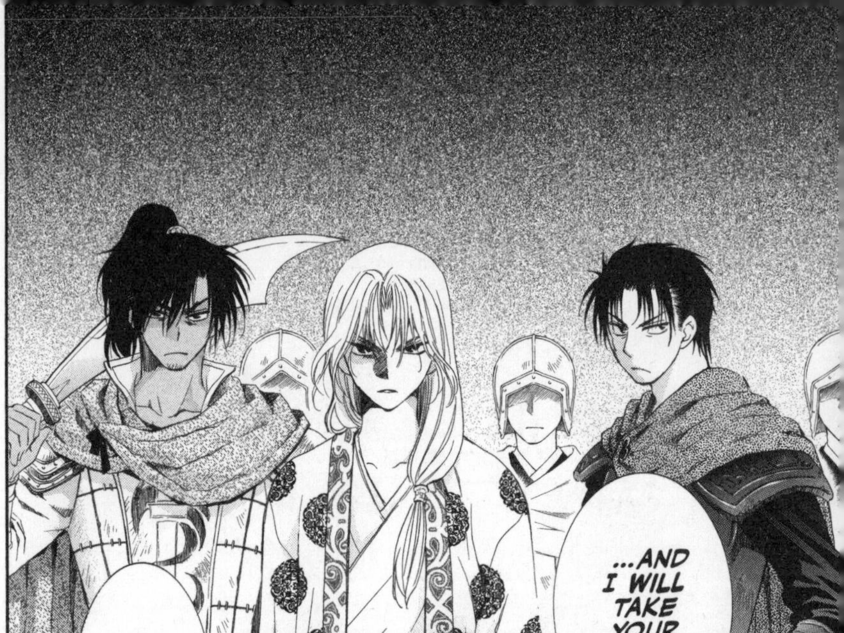
...AND I WILL TAKE YOUR HEAD.
CHOOSE WISELY.

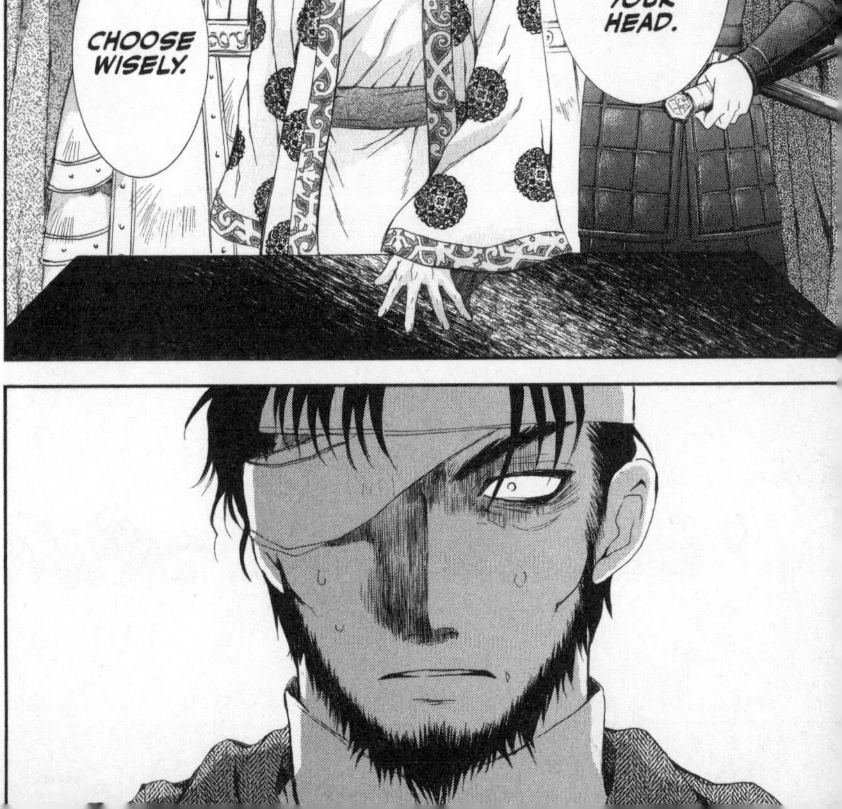

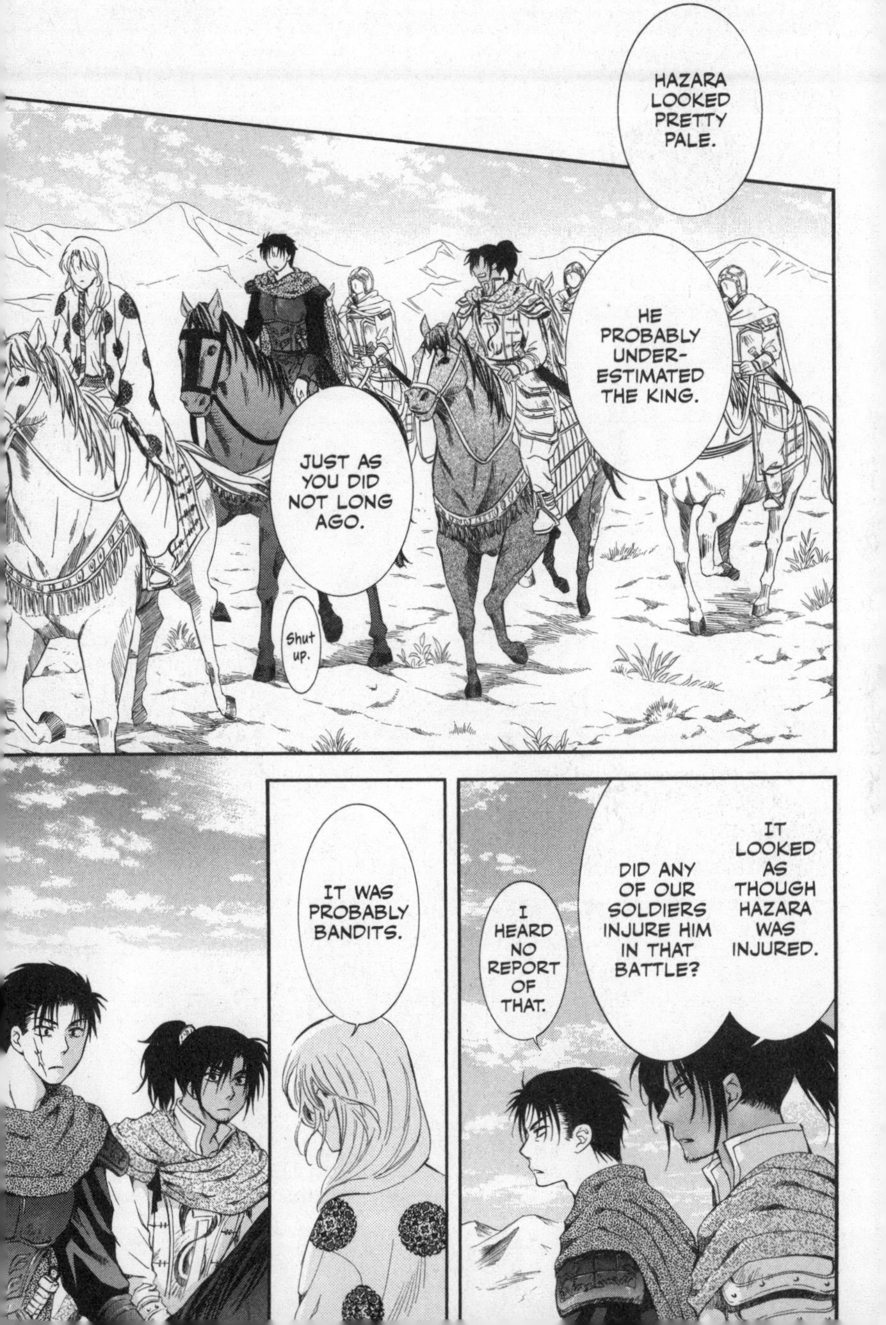
HAZARA LOOKED PRETTY PALE.
HE PROBABLY UNDER-ESTIMATED THE KING.
JUST AS YOU DID NOT LONG AGO.
Shut up.
IT LOOKED AS THOUGH HAZARA WAS INJURED.
DID ANY OF OUR SOLDIERS INJURE HIM IN THAT BATTLE?
I HEARD NO REPORT OF THAT.
IT WAS PROBABLY BANDITS.

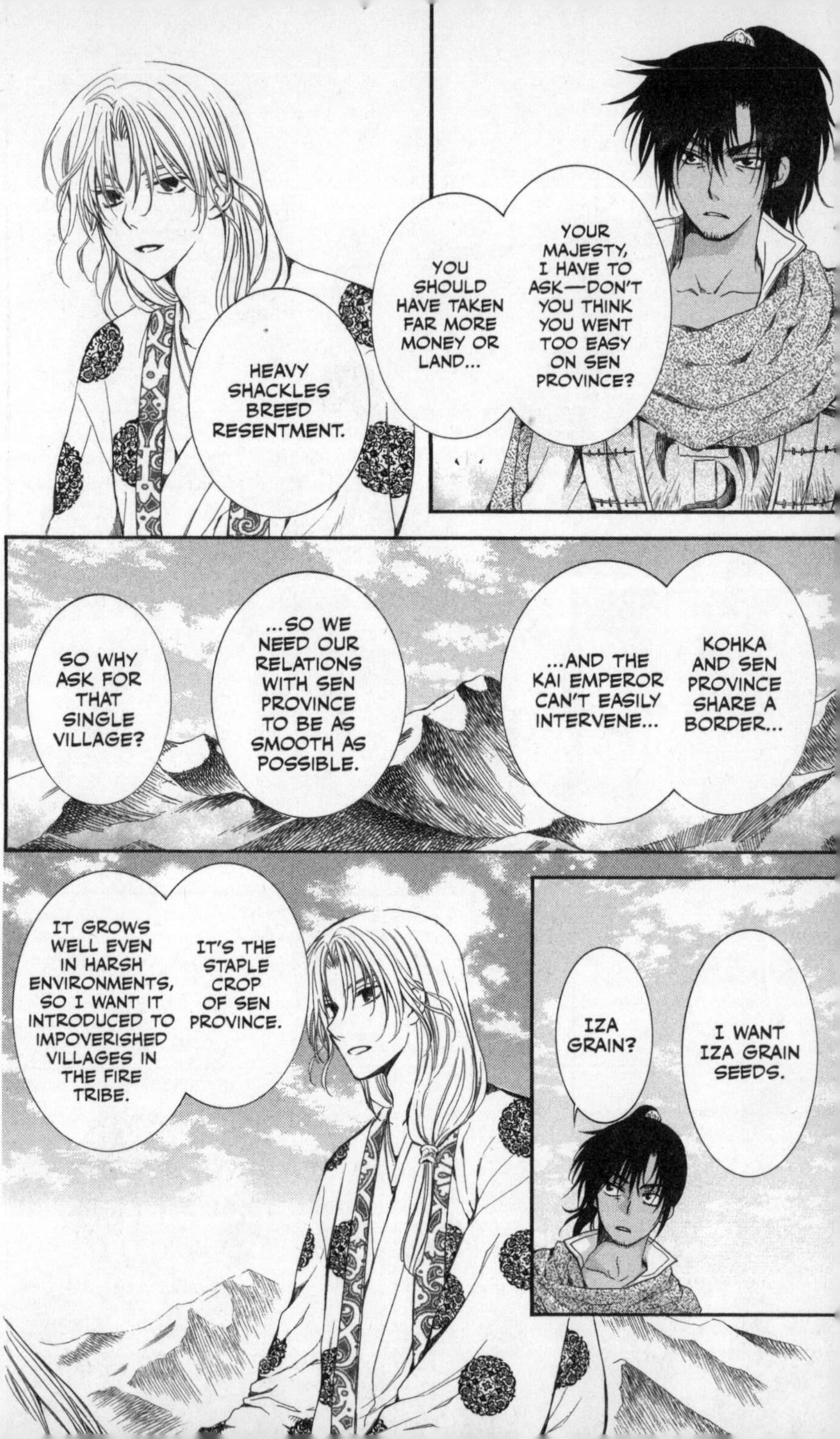
YOUR MAJESTY, I HAVE TO ASK—DON'T YOU THINK YOU WENT TOO EASY ON SEN PROVINCE?
YOU SHOULD HAVE TAKEN FAR MORE MONEY OR LAND...
HEAVY SHACKLES BREED RESENTMENT.
KOHKA AND SEN PROVINCE SHARE A BORDER...
...AND THE KAI EMPEROR CAN'T EASILY INTERVENE...
...SO WE NEED OUR RELATIONS WITH SEN PROVINCE TO BE AS SMOOTH AS POSSIBLE.
SO WHY ASK FOR THAT SINGLE VILLAGE?
I WANT IZA GRAIN SEEDS.
IZA GRAIN?
IT'S THE STAPLE CROP OF SEN PROVINCE.
IT GROWS WELL EVEN IN HARSH ENVIRONMENTS, SO I WANT IT INTRODUCED TO IMPOVERISHED VILLAGES IN THE FIRE TRIBE.

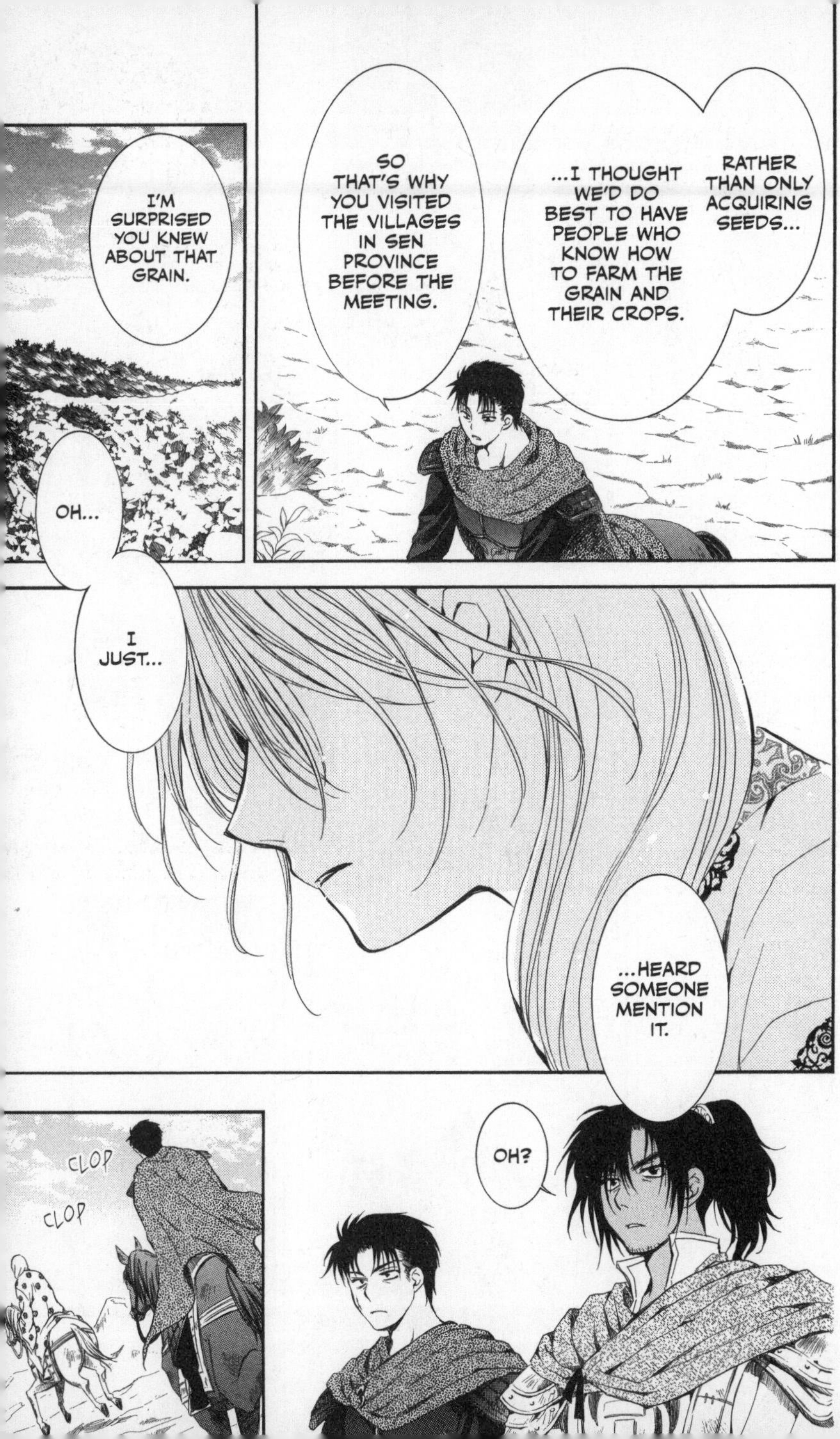
RATHER THAN ONLY ACQUIRING SEEDS...
...I THOUGHT WE'D DO BEST TO HAVE PEOPLE WHO KNOW HOW TO FARM THE GRAIN AND THEIR CROPS.
SO THAT'S WHY YOU VISITED THE VILLAGES IN SEN PROVINCE BEFORE THE MEETING.
I'M SURPRISED YOU KNEW ABOUT THAT GRAIN.
OH...
I JUST...
...HEARD SOMEONE MENTION IT.
OH?
CLOP
CLOP

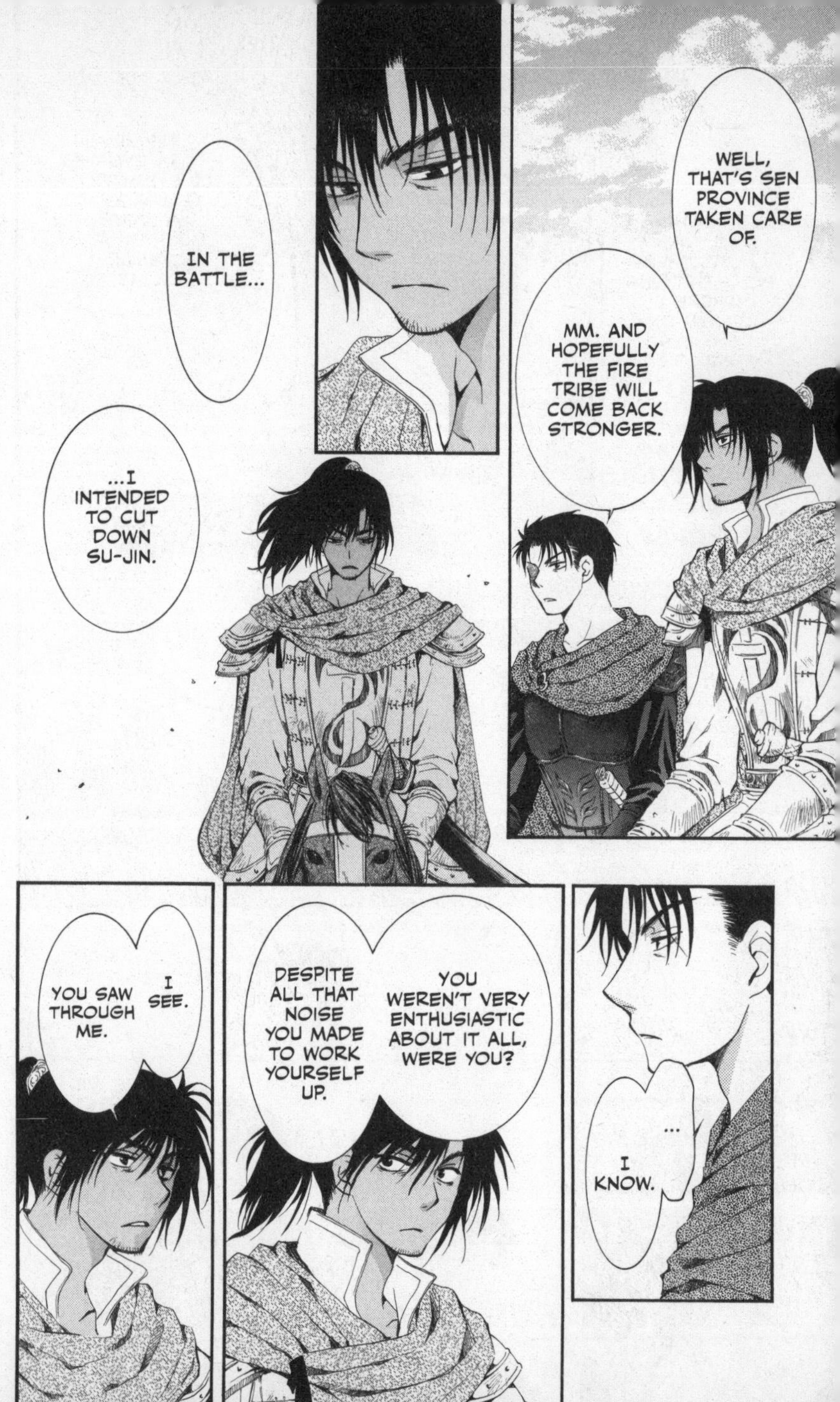
WELL, THAT'S SEN PROVINCE TAKEN CARE OF.
MM. AND HOPEFULLY THE FIRE TRIBE WILL COME BACK STRONGER.
IN THE BATTLE...
...I INTENDED TO CUT DOWN SU-JIN.
... I KNOW.
YOU WEREN'T VERY ENTHUSIASTIC ABOUT IT ALL, WERE YOU?
DESPITE ALL THAT NOISE YOU MADE TO WORK YOURSELF UP.
I SEE.
YOU SAW THROUGH ME.

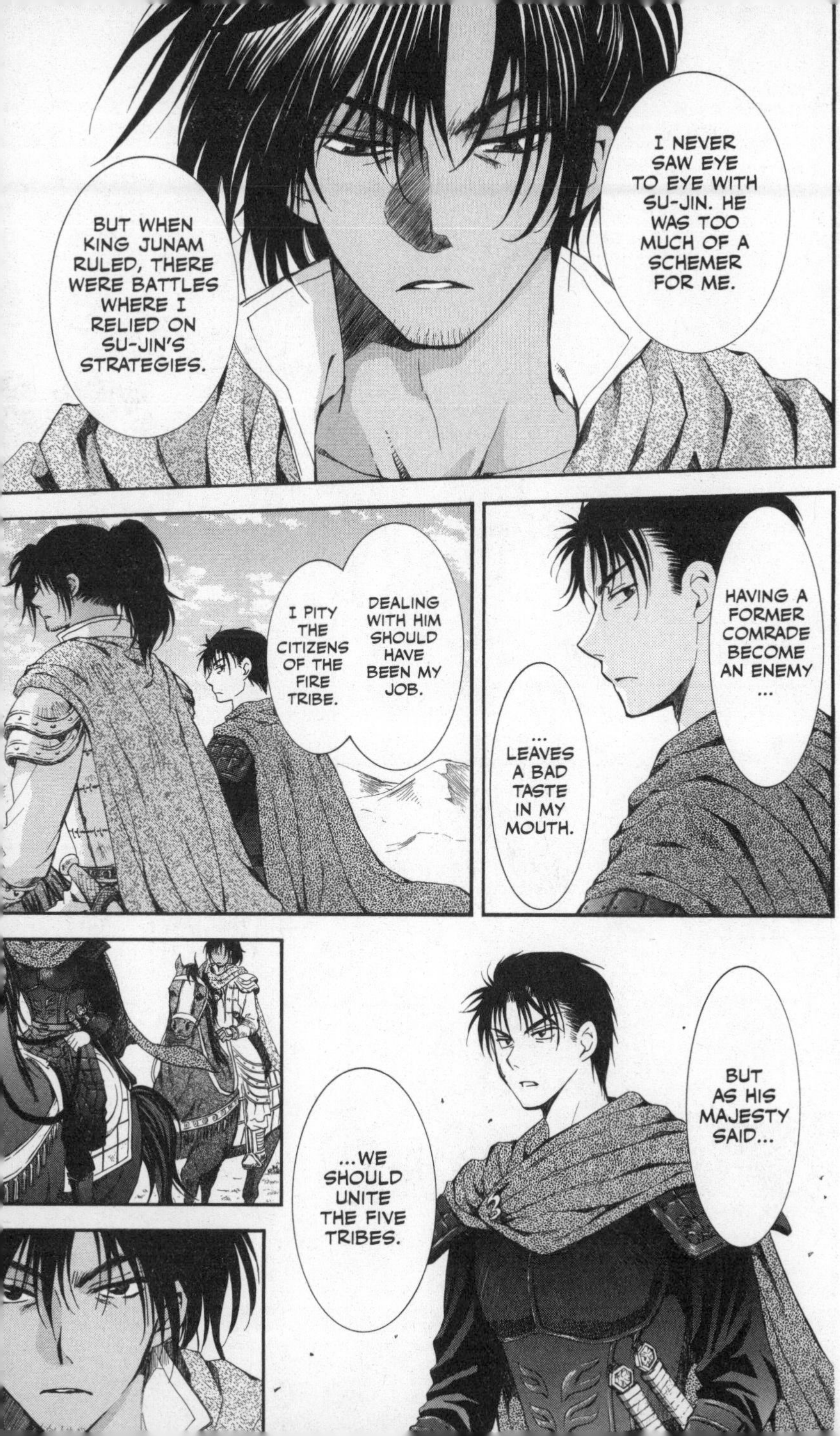
I NEVER SAW EYE TO EYE WITH SU-JIN. HE WAS TOO MUCH OF A SCHEMER FOR ME.
BUT WHEN KING JUNAM RULED, THERE WERE BATTLES WHERE I RELIED ON SU-JIN'S STRATEGIES.
HAVING A FORMER COMRADE BECOME AN ENEMY ...
... LEAVES A BAD TASTE IN MY MOUTH.
DEALING WITH HIM SHOULD HAVE BEEN MY JOB.
I PITY THE CITIZENS OF THE FIRE TRIBE.
BUT AS HIS MAJESTY SAID...
...WE SHOULD UNITE THE FIVE TRIBES.

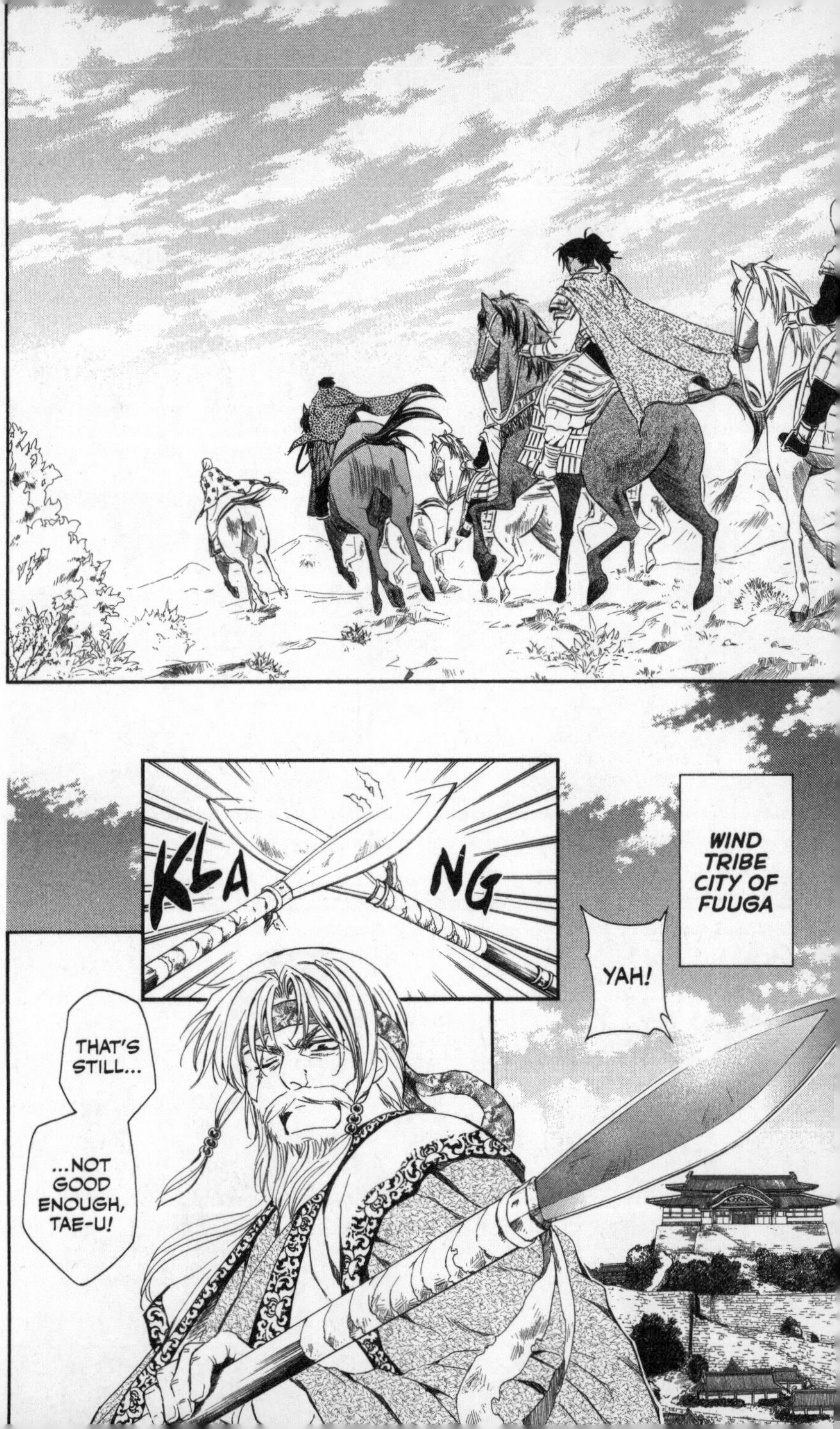
WIND TRIBE CITY OF FUUGA
YAH!
KLANG
THAT'S STILL...
...NOT GOOD ENOUGH, TAE-U!

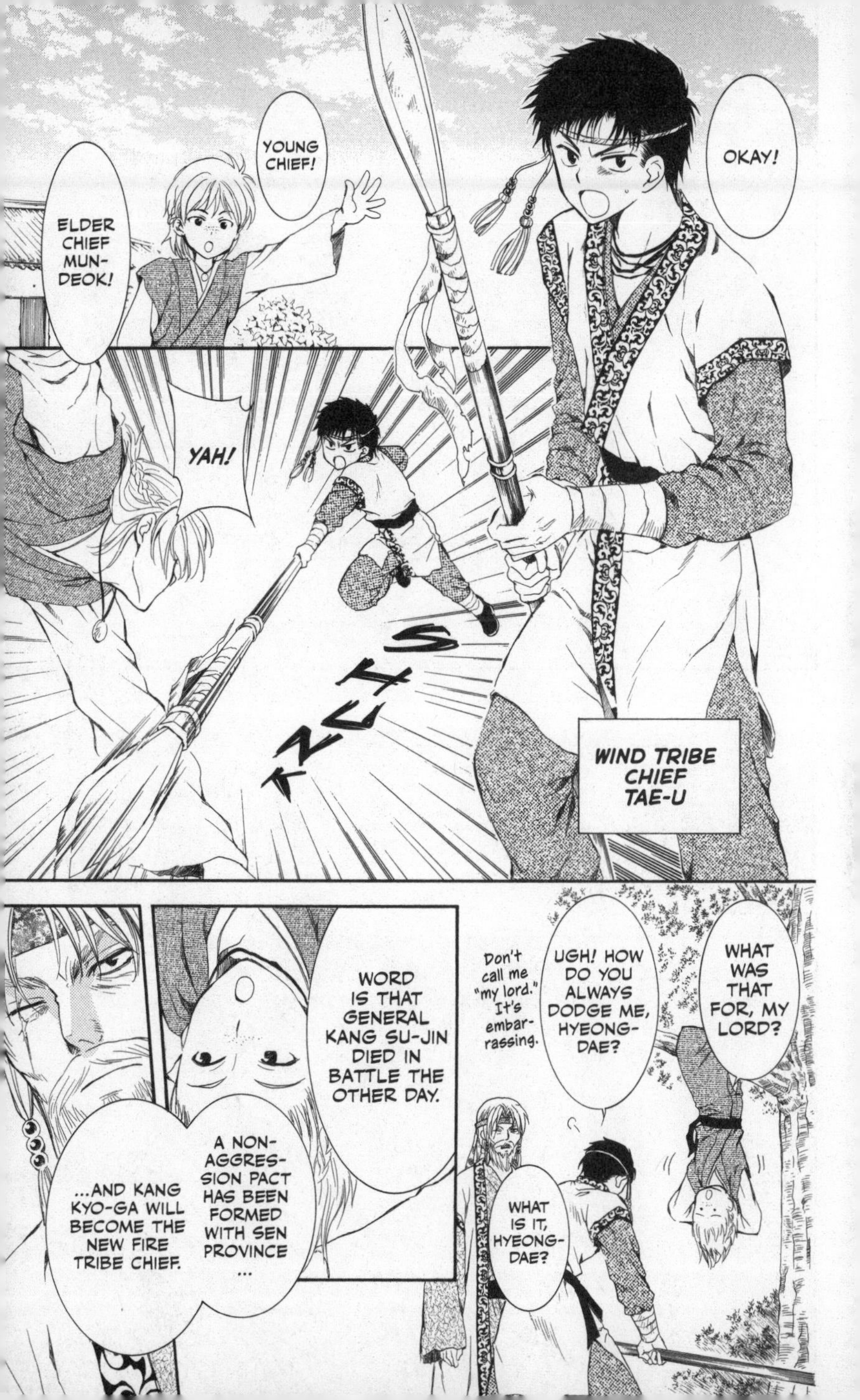
YOUNG CHIEF!
ELDER CHIEF MUN-DEOK!
OKAY!
YAH!
SHUNK
WIND TRIBE CHIEF TAE-U
WHAT WAS THAT FOR, MY LORD?
UGH! HOW DO YOU ALWAYS DODGE ME, HYEONG-DAE?
Don't call me "my lord." It's embarrassing.
WHAT IS IT, HYEONG-DAE?
WORD IS THAT GENERAL KANG SU-JIN DIED IN BATTLE THE OTHER DAY.
A NON-AGGRESSION PACT HAS BEEN FORMED WITH SEN PROVINCE ...
...AND KANG KYO-GA WILL BECOME THE NEW FIRE TRIBE CHIEF.

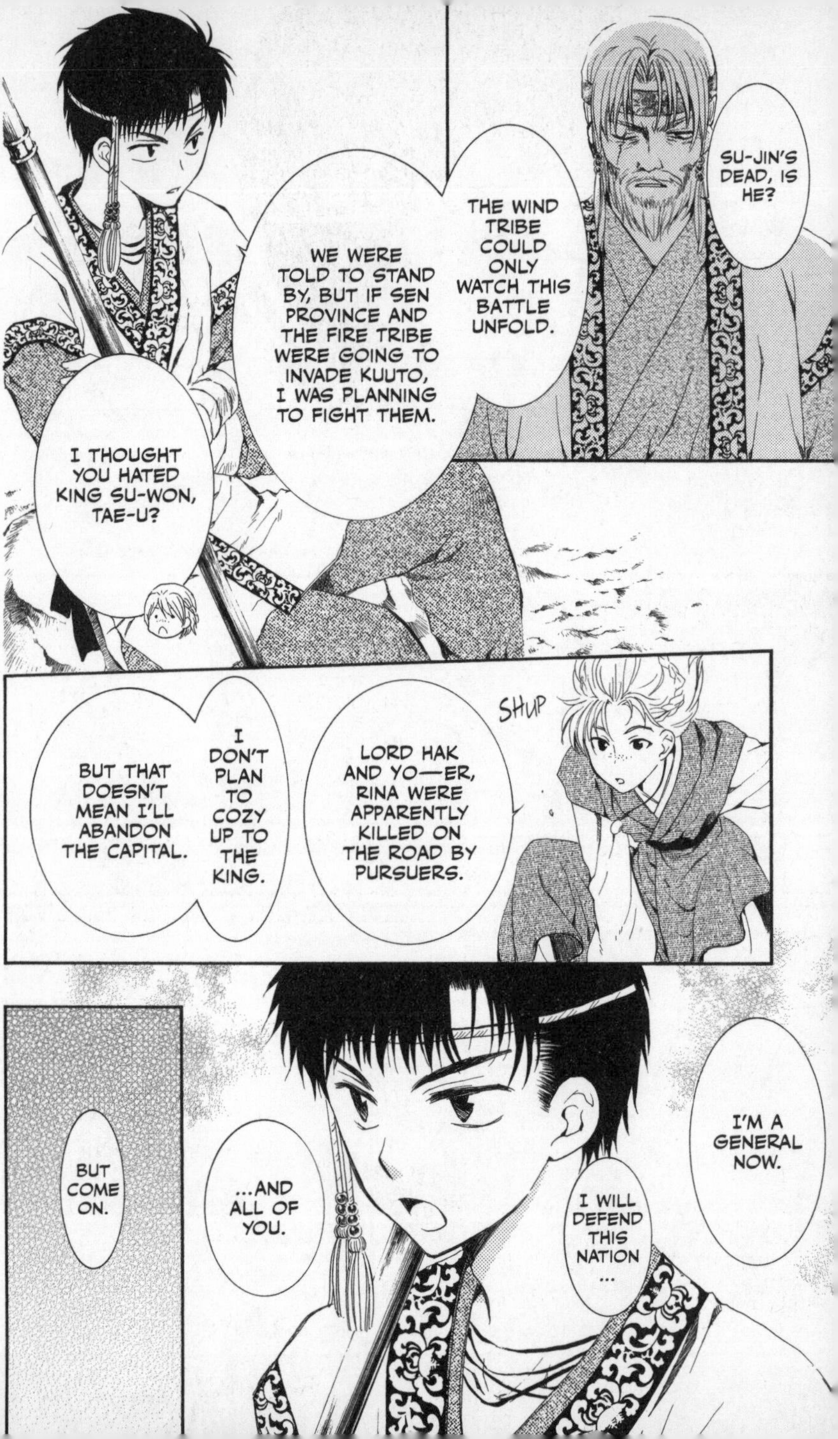
SU-JIN'S DEAD, IS HE?
THE WIND TRIBE COULD ONLY WATCH THIS BATTLE UNFOLD.
WE WERE TOLD TO STAND BY, BUT IF SEN PROVINCE AND THE FIRE TRIBE WERE GOING TO INVADE KUUTO, I WAS PLANNING TO FIGHT THEM.
I THOUGHT YOU HATED KING SU-WON, TAE-U?
SHUP
LORD HAK AND YO—ER, RINA WERE APPARENTLY KILLED ON THE ROAD BY PURSUERS.
I DON'T PLAN TO COZY UP TO THE KING.
BUT THAT DOESN'T MEAN I'LL ABANDON THE CAPITAL.
I'M A GENERAL NOW.
I WILL DEFEND THIS NATION ...
...AND ALL OF YOU.
BUT COME ON.

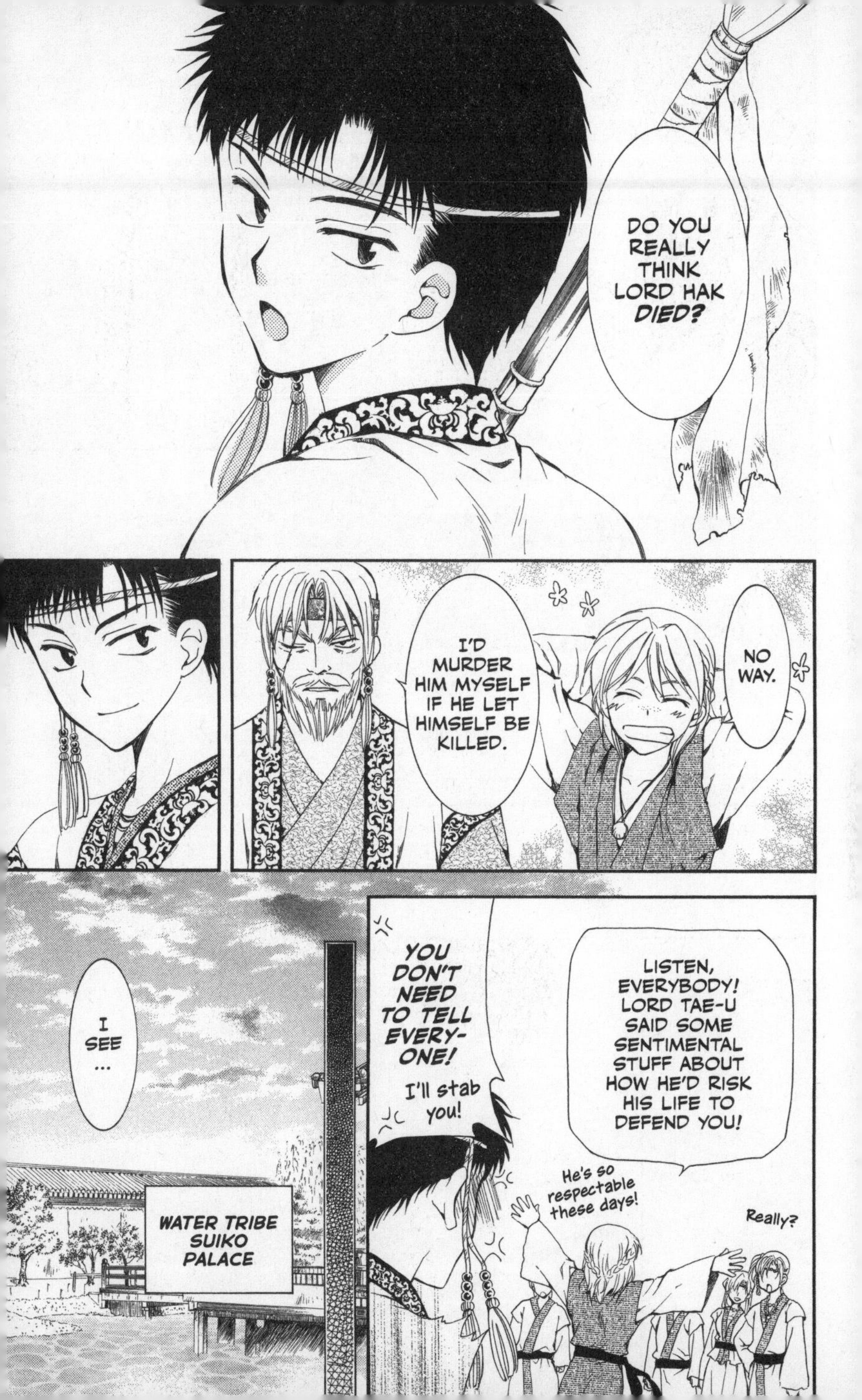

DO YOU REALLY THINK LORD HAK *DIED?*
NO WAY.
I'D MURDER HIM MYSELF IF HE LET HIMSELF BE KILLED.
LISTEN, EVERYBODY! LORD TAE-U SAID SOME SENTIMENTAL STUFF ABOUT HOW HE'D RISK HIS LIFE TO DEFEND YOU!
YOU DON'T NEED TO TELL EVERY-ONE!
I'll stab you!
He's so respectable these days!
Really?
I SEE ...
WATER TRIBE SUIKO PALACE

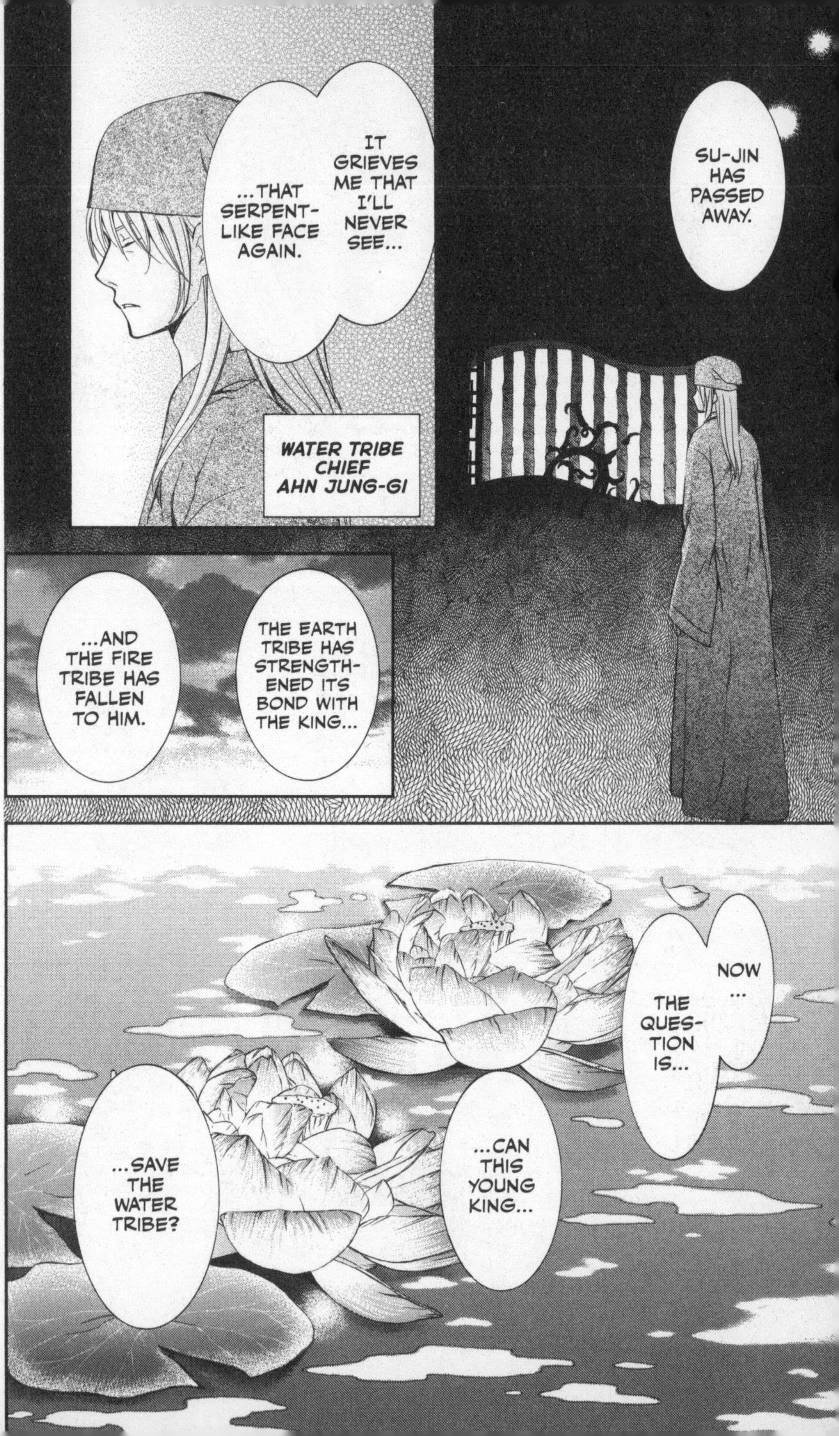
SU-JIN HAS PASSED AWAY.
IT GRIEVES ME THAT I'LL NEVER SEE...
...THAT SERPENT-LIKE FACE AGAIN.
WATER TRIBE CHIEF AHN JUNG-GI
THE EARTH TRIBE HAS STRENGTHENED ITS BOND WITH THE KING...
...AND THE FIRE TRIBE HAS FALLEN TO HIM.
NOW...
THE QUESTION IS...
...CAN THIS YOUNG KING...
...SAVE THE WATER TRIBE?

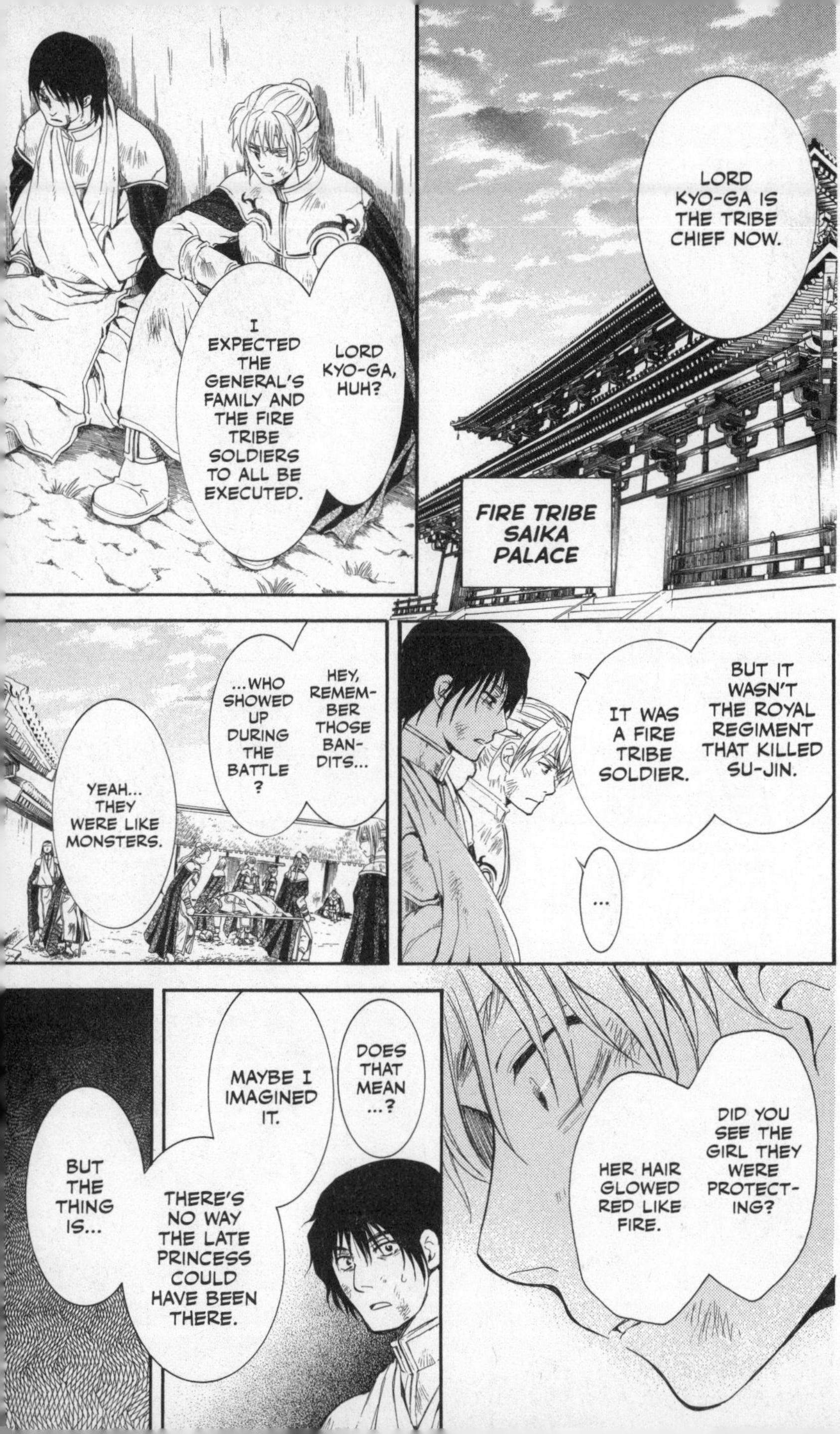
LORD KYO-GA IS THE TRIBE CHIEF NOW.
FIRE TRIBE SAIKA PALACE
LORD KYO-GA, HUH?
I EXPECTED THE GENERAL'S FAMILY AND THE FIRE TRIBE SOLDIERS TO ALL BE EXECUTED.
BUT IT WASN'T THE ROYAL REGIMENT THAT KILLED SU-JIN.
IT WAS A FIRE TRIBE SOLDIER.
...
HEY, REMEMBER THOSE BANDITS...
...WHO SHOWED UP DURING THE BATTLE?
YEAH... THEY WERE LIKE MONSTERS.
DID YOU SEE THE GIRL THEY WERE PROTECTING?
HER HAIR GLOWED RED LIKE FIRE.
DOES THAT MEAN...?
MAYBE I IMAGINED IT.
BUT THE THING IS...
THERE'S NO WAY THE LATE PRINCESS COULD HAVE BEEN THERE.

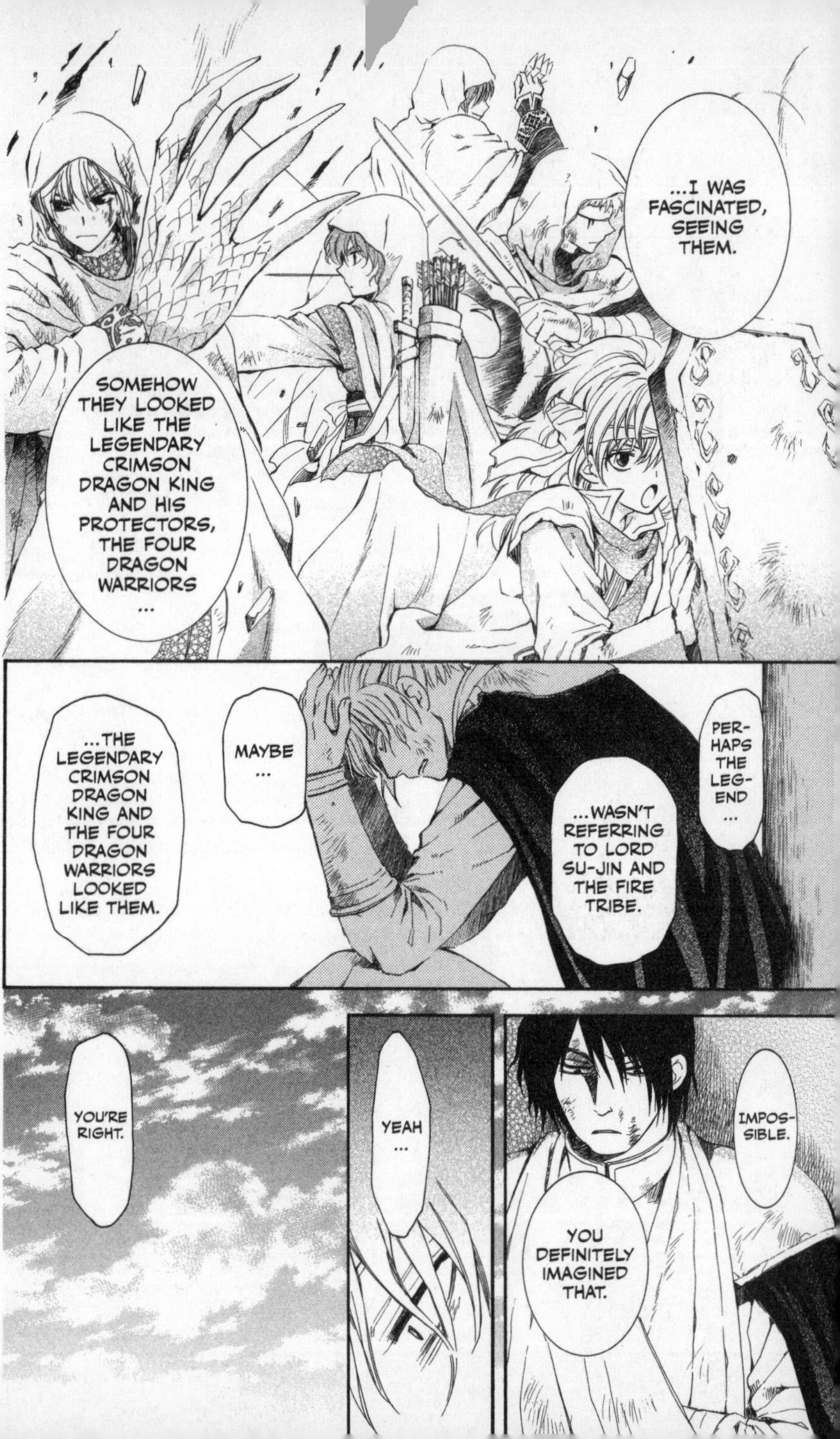
...I WAS FASCINATED, SEEING THEM.
SOMEHOW THEY LOOKED LIKE THE LEGENDARY CRIMSON DRAGON KING AND HIS PROTECTORS, THE FOUR DRAGON WARRIORS ...
PER-HAPS THE LEG-END ...
...WASN'T REFERRING TO LORD SU-JIN AND THE FIRE TRIBE.
MAYBE ...
...THE LEGENDARY CRIMSON DRAGON KING AND THE FOUR DRAGON WARRIORS LOOKED LIKE THEM.
IMPOS-SIBLE.
YOU DEFINITELY IMAGINED THAT.
YEAH ...
YOU'RE RIGHT.

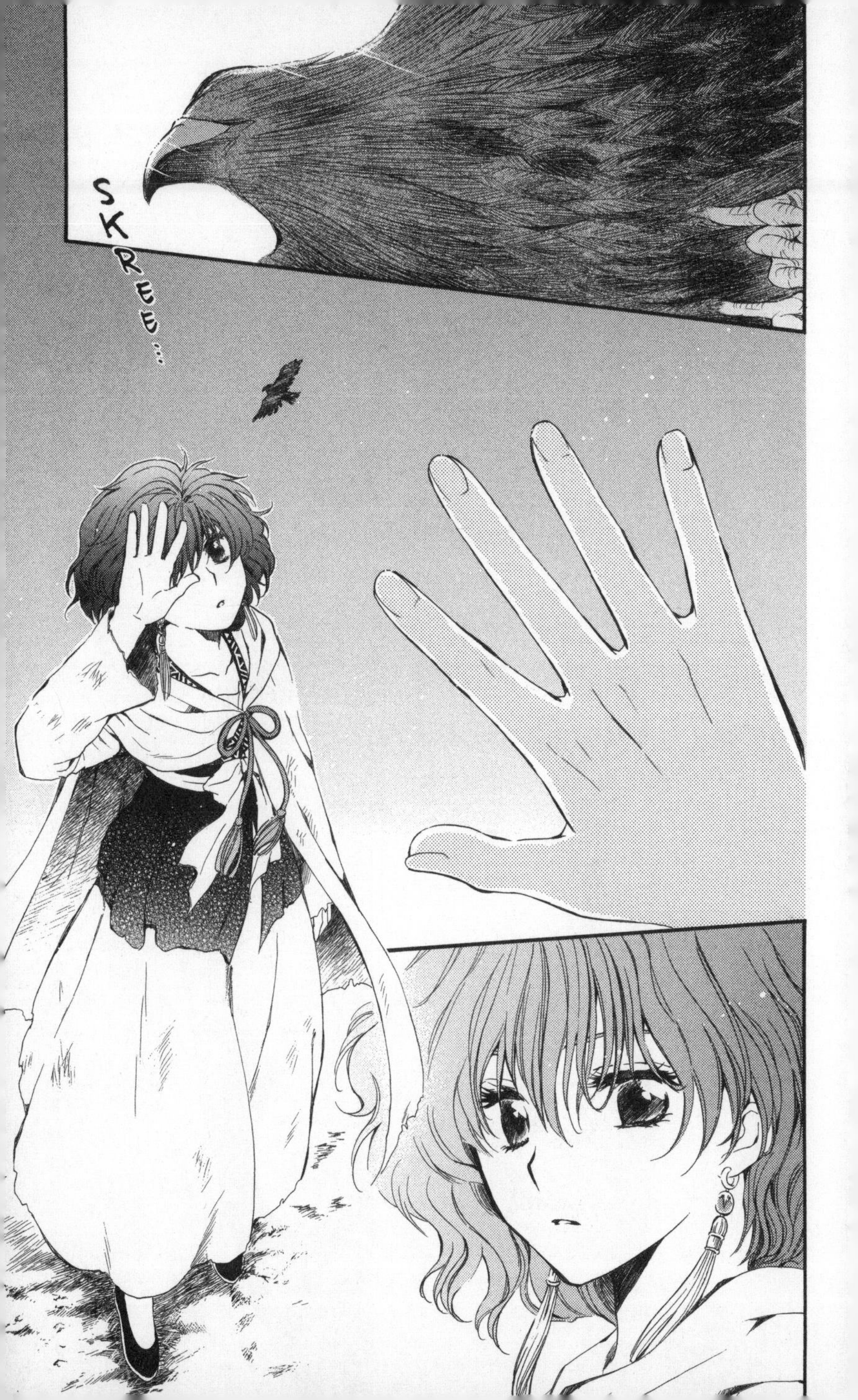
SKREE...

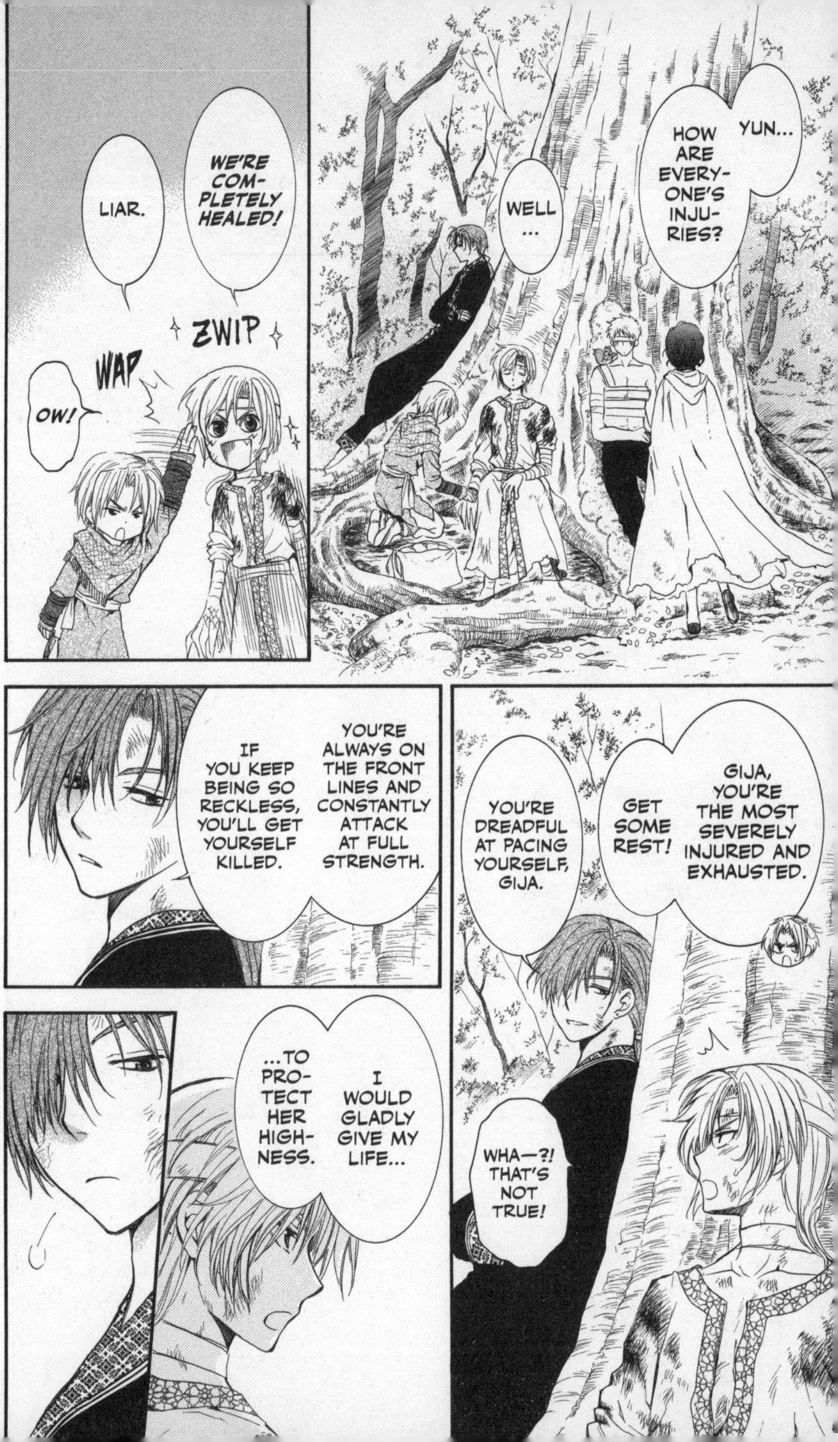
YUN...
HOW ARE EVERY-ONE'S INJU-RIES?
WELL ...
WE'RE COM-PLETELY HEALED!
LIAR.
ZWIP
WAP
OW!
GIJA, YOU'RE THE MOST SEVERELY INJURED AND EXHAUSTED.
GET SOME REST!
YOU'RE DREADFUL AT PACING YOURSELF, GIJA.
WHA—?! THAT'S NOT TRUE!
YOU'RE ALWAYS ON THE FRONT LINES AND CONSTANTLY ATTACK AT FULL STRENGTH.
IF YOU KEEP BEING SO RECKLESS, YOU'LL GET YOURSELF KILLED.
I WOULD GLADLY GIVE MY LIFE...
...TO PROTECT HER HIGH-NESS.

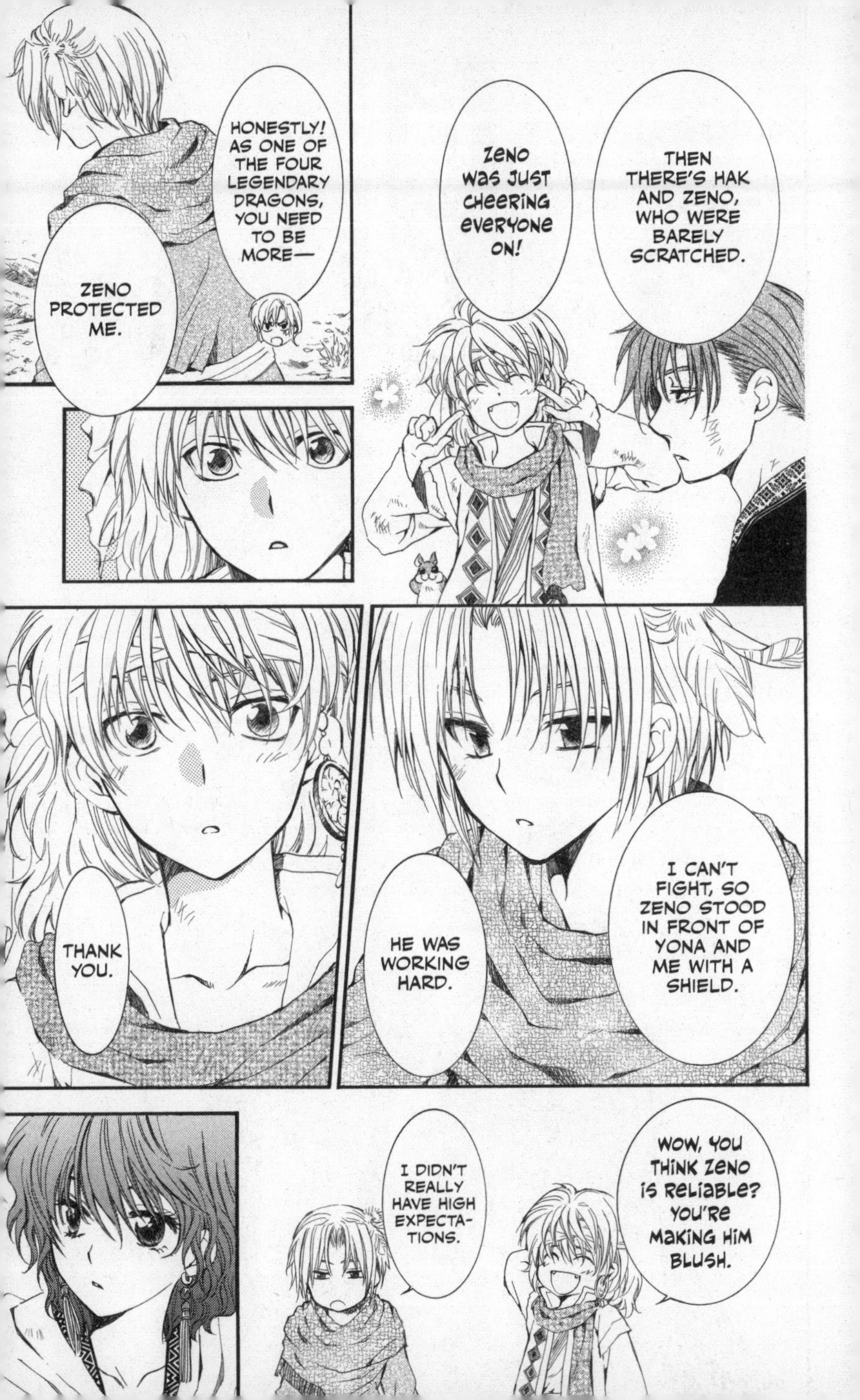
THEN THERE'S HAK AND ZENO, WHO WERE BARELY SCRATCHED.
Zeno was just cheering everyone on!
HONESTLY! AS ONE OF THE FOUR LEGENDARY DRAGONS, YOU NEED TO BE MORE—
ZENO PROTECTED ME.
I CAN'T FIGHT, SO ZENO STOOD IN FRONT OF YONA AND ME WITH A SHIELD.
HE WAS WORKING HARD.
THANK YOU.
Wow, you think Zeno is reliable? You're making him blush.
I DIDN'T REALLY HAVE HIGH EXPECTA-TIONS.

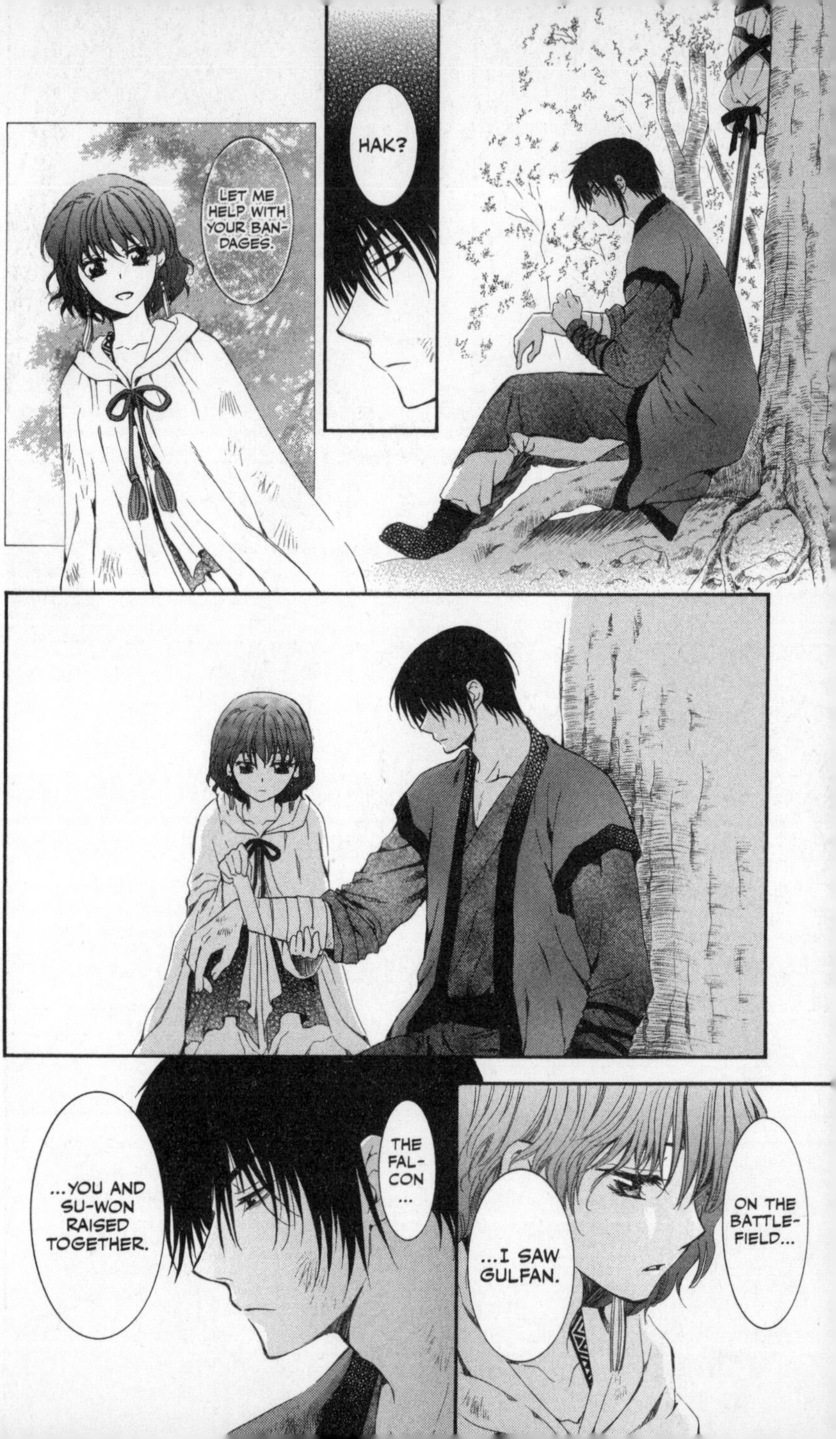
HAK?
LET ME HELP WITH YOUR BAN-DAGES.
ON THE BATTLE-FIELD...
...I SAW GULFAN.
THE FAL-CON...
...YOU AND SU-WON RAISED TOGETHER.

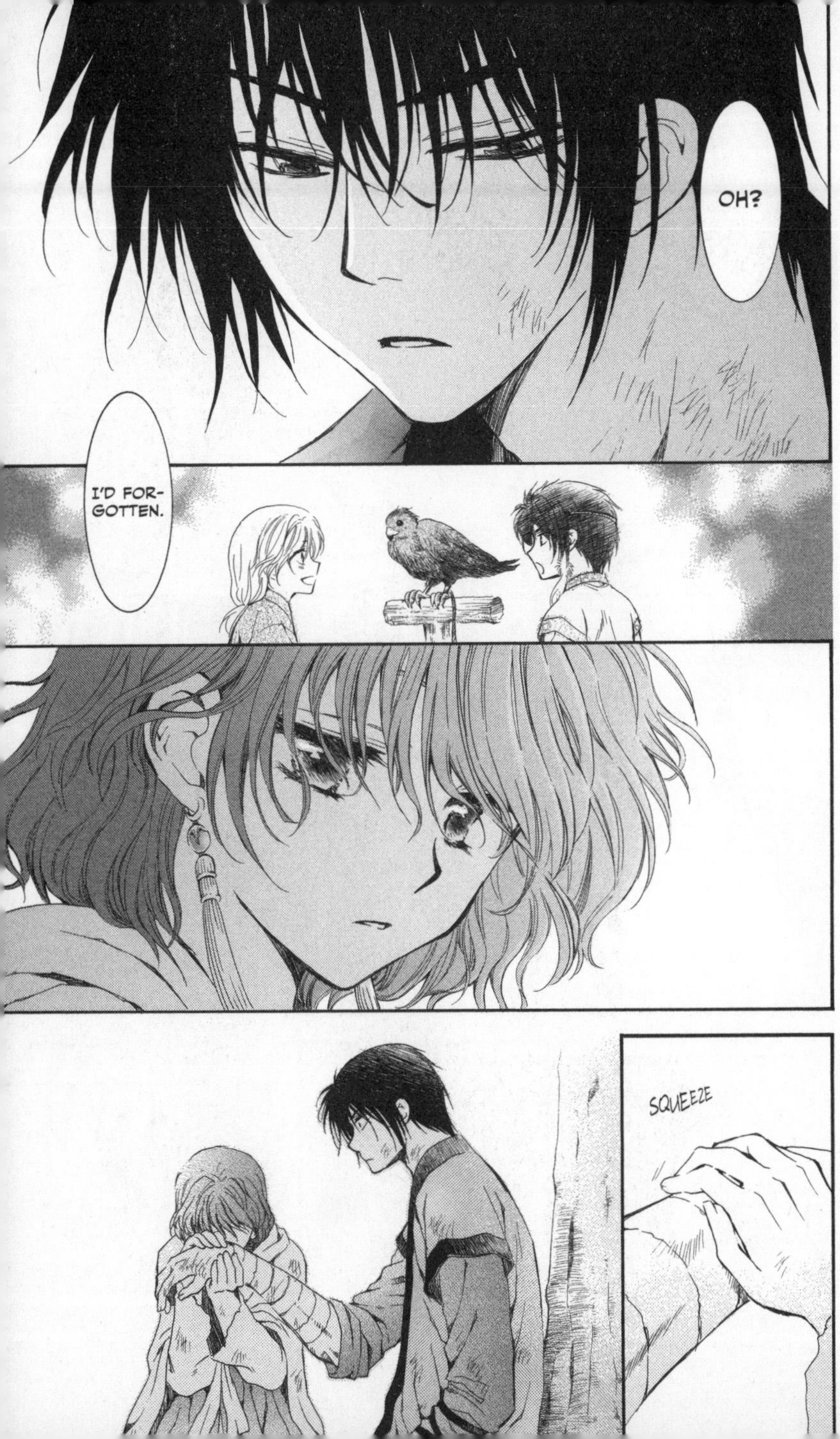
OH?
I'D FOR-GOTTEN.
SQUEEZE

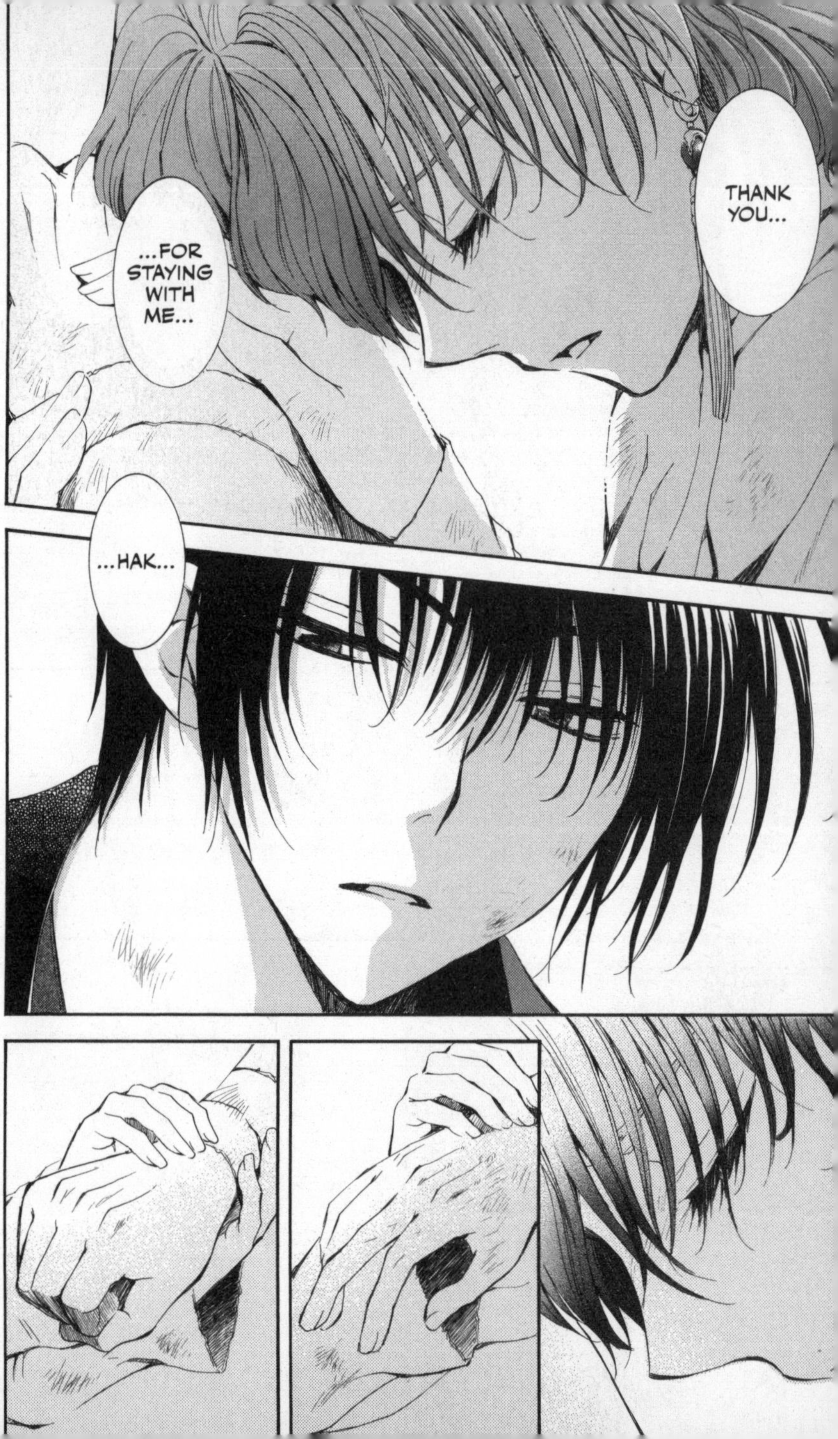
THANK YOU...
...FOR STAYING WITH ME...
...HAK...

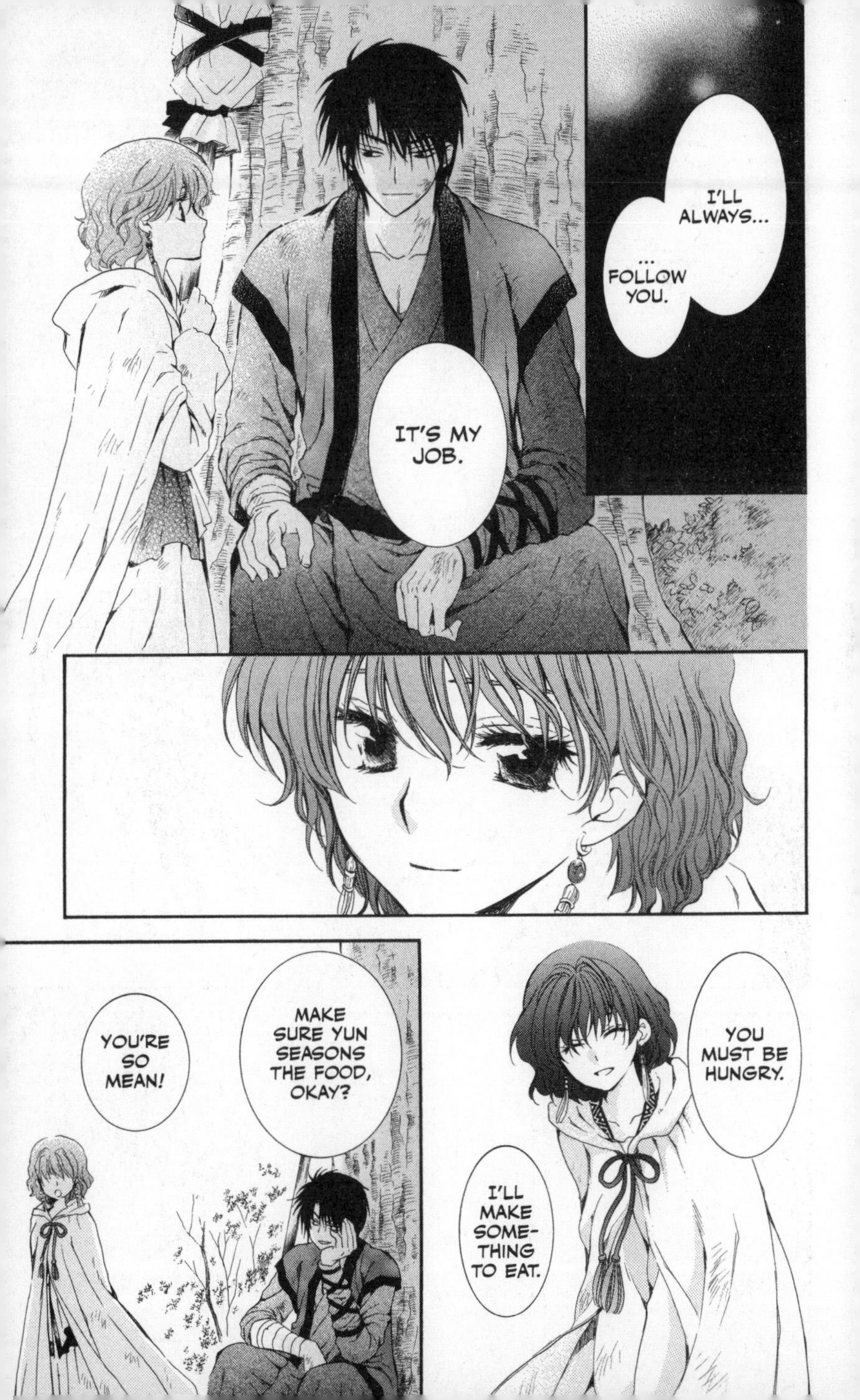
I'LL ALWAYS...
...FOLLOW YOU.
IT'S MY JOB.
YOU MUST BE HUNGRY.
I'LL MAKE SOME-THING TO EAT.
MAKE SURE YUN SEASONS THE FOOD, OKAY?
YOU'RE SO MEAN!

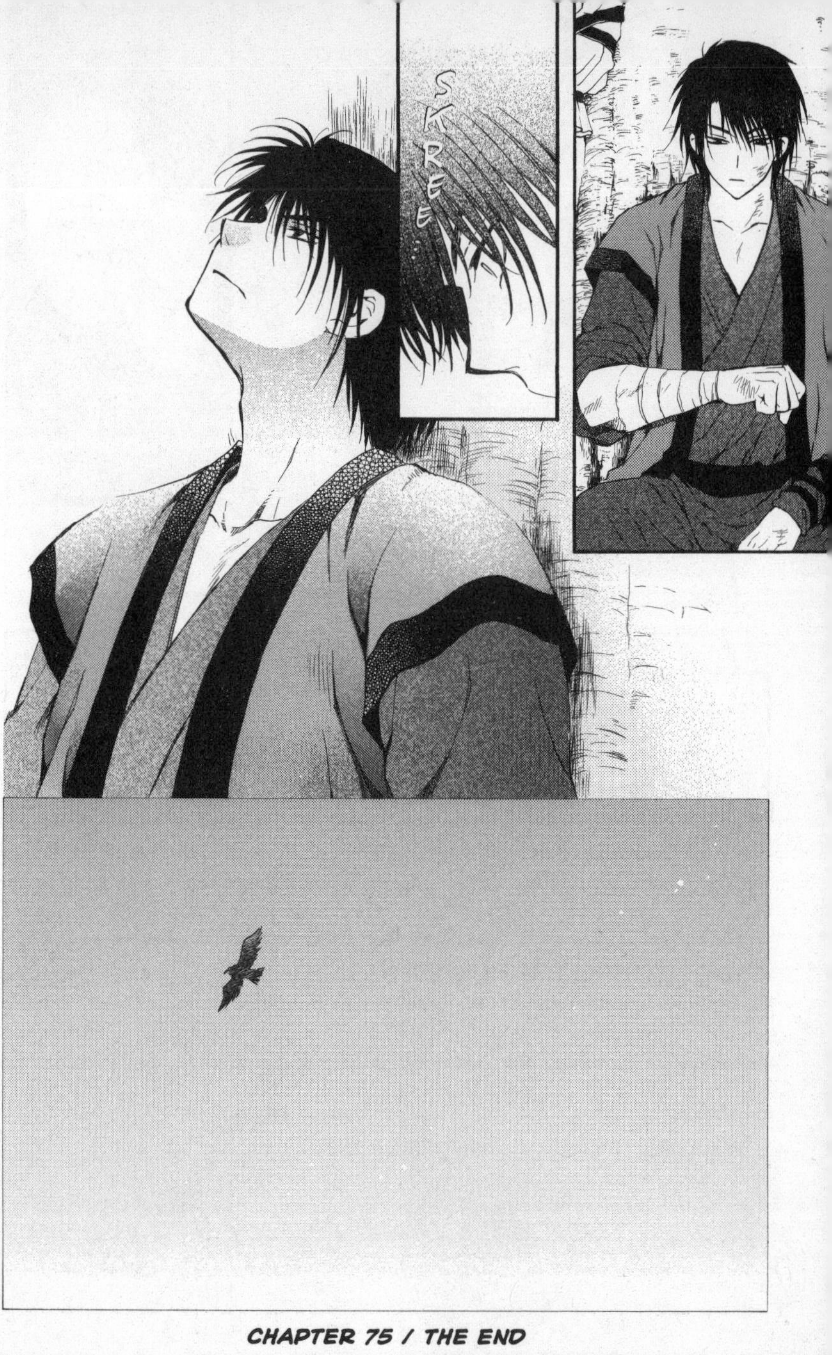
SKREE

CHAPTER 75 / THE END

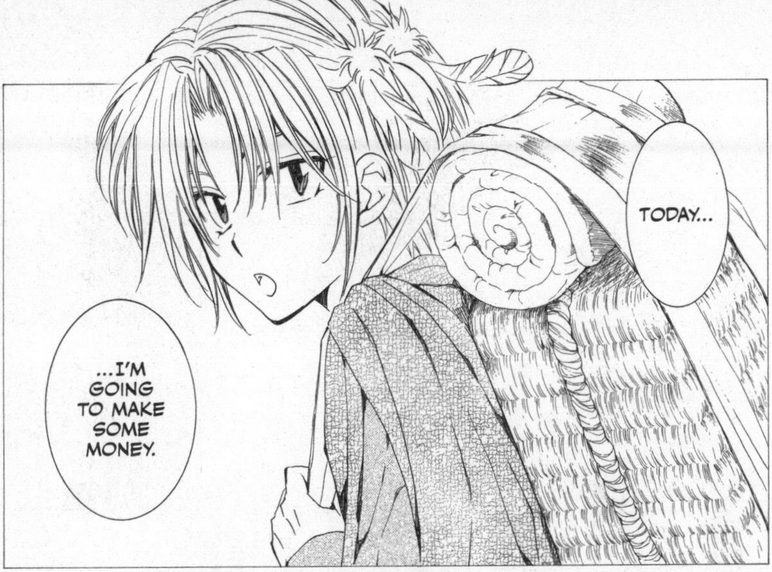
TODAY...
...I'M GOING TO MAKE SOME MONEY.

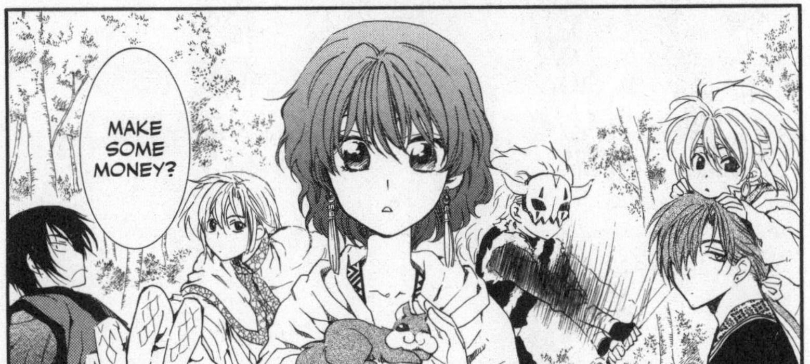
MAKE SOME MONEY?

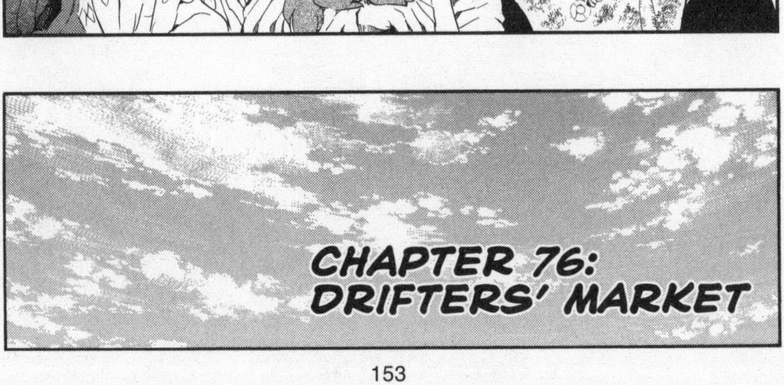
CHAPTER 76:
DRIFTERS' MARKET

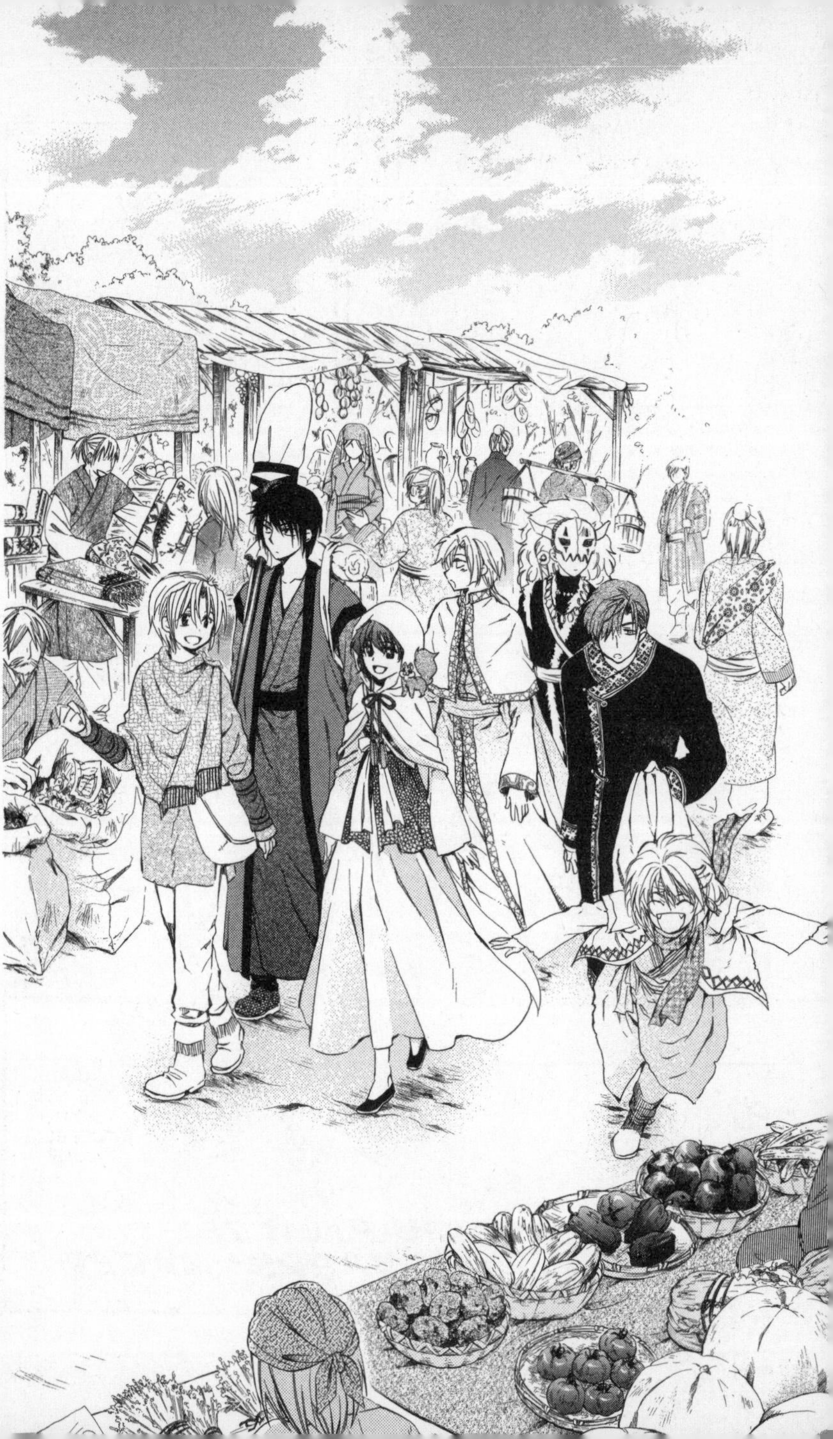

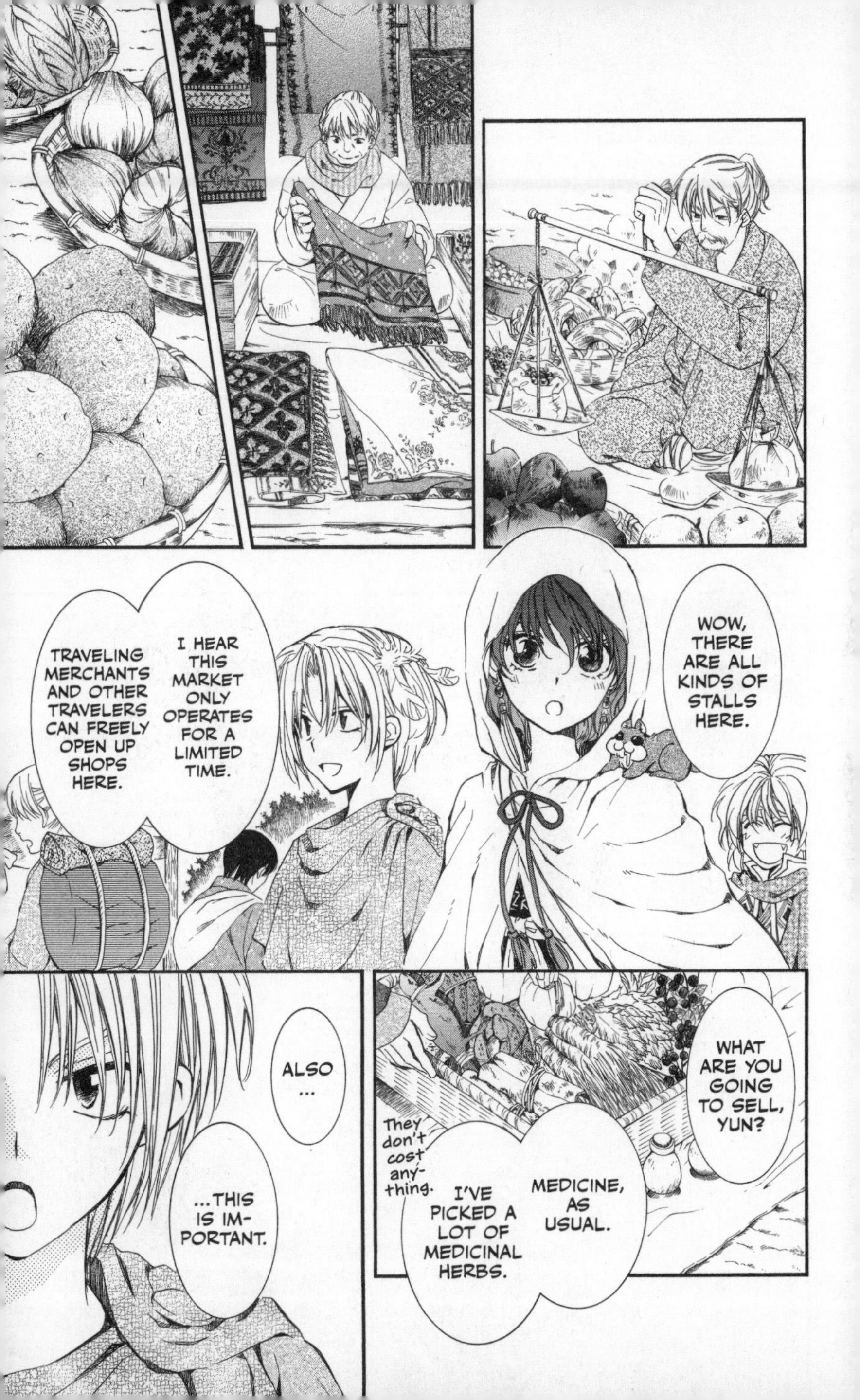
WOW, THERE ARE ALL KINDS OF STALLS HERE.
I HEAR THIS MARKET ONLY OPERATES FOR A LIMITED TIME.
TRAVELING MERCHANTS AND OTHER TRAVELERS CAN FREELY OPEN UP SHOPS HERE.
WHAT ARE YOU GOING TO SELL, YUN?
MEDICINE, AS USUAL.
I'VE PICKED A LOT OF MEDICINAL HERBS.
They don't cost any-thing.
ALSO ...
...THIS IS IM-PORTANT.

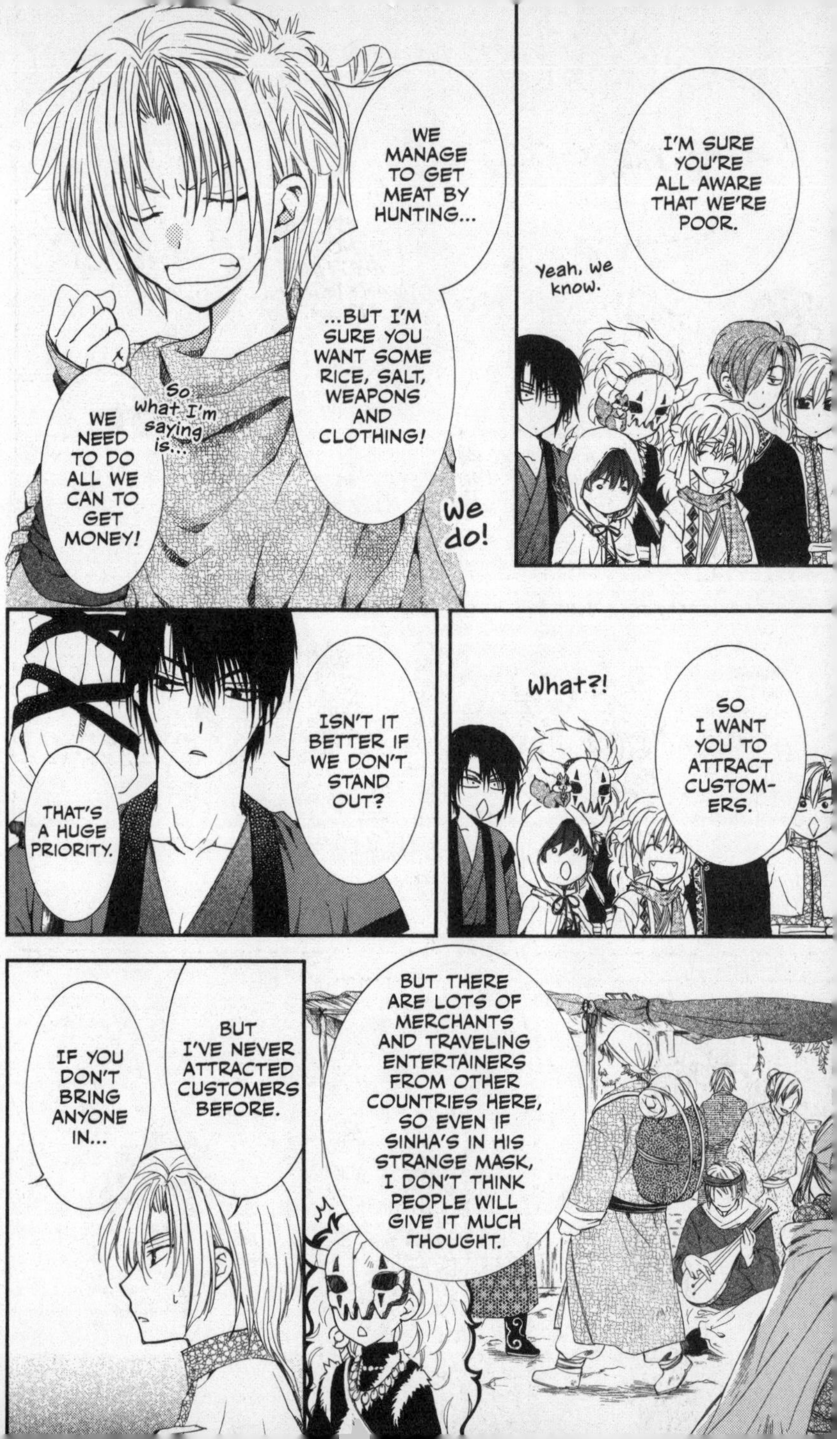
I'M SURE YOU'RE ALL AWARE THAT WE'RE POOR.
Yeah, we know.
WE MANAGE TO GET MEAT BY HUNTING...
...BUT I'M SURE YOU WANT SOME RICE, SALT, WEAPONS AND CLOTHING!
We do!
So what I'm saying is...
WE NEED TO DO ALL WE CAN TO GET MONEY!
SO I WANT YOU TO ATTRACT CUSTOM-ERS.
What?!
ISN'T IT BETTER IF WE DON'T STAND OUT?
THAT'S A HUGE PRIORITY.
BUT THERE ARE LOTS OF MERCHANTS AND TRAVELING ENTERTAINERS FROM OTHER COUNTRIES HERE, SO EVEN IF SINHA'S IN HIS STRANGE MASK, I DON'T THINK PEOPLE WILL GIVE IT MUCH THOUGHT.
BUT I'VE NEVER ATTRACTED CUSTOMERS BEFORE.
IF YOU DON'T BRING ANYONE IN...

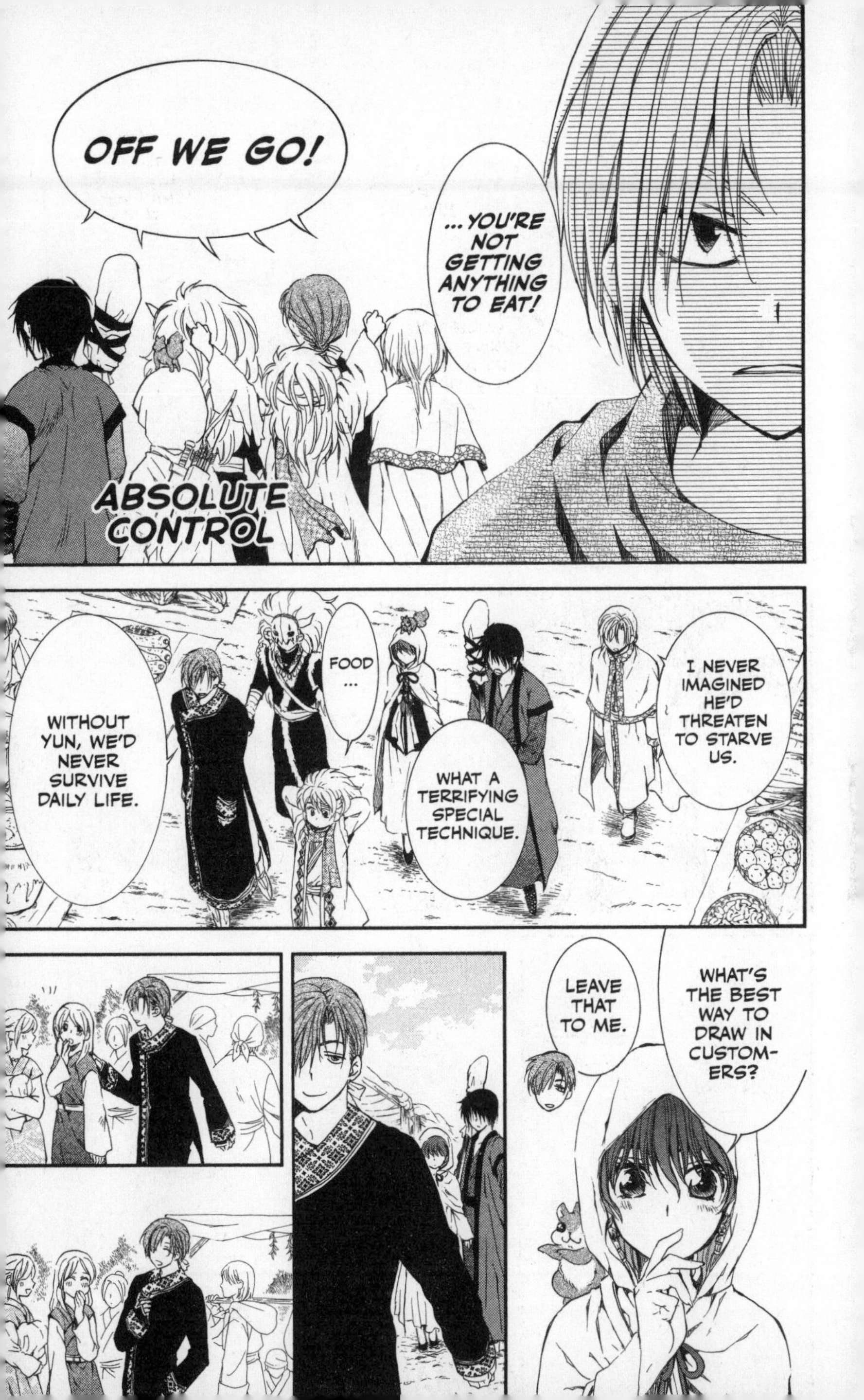
...YOU'RE NOT GETTING ANYTHING TO EAT!
OFF WE GO!
ABSOLUTE CONTROL
I NEVER IMAGINED HE'D THREATEN TO STARVE US.
WHAT A TERRIFYING SPECIAL TECHNIQUE.
FOOD ...
WITHOUT YUN, WE'D NEVER SURVIVE DAILY LIFE.
WHAT'S THE BEST WAY TO DRAW IN CUSTOM-ERS?
LEAVE THAT TO ME.

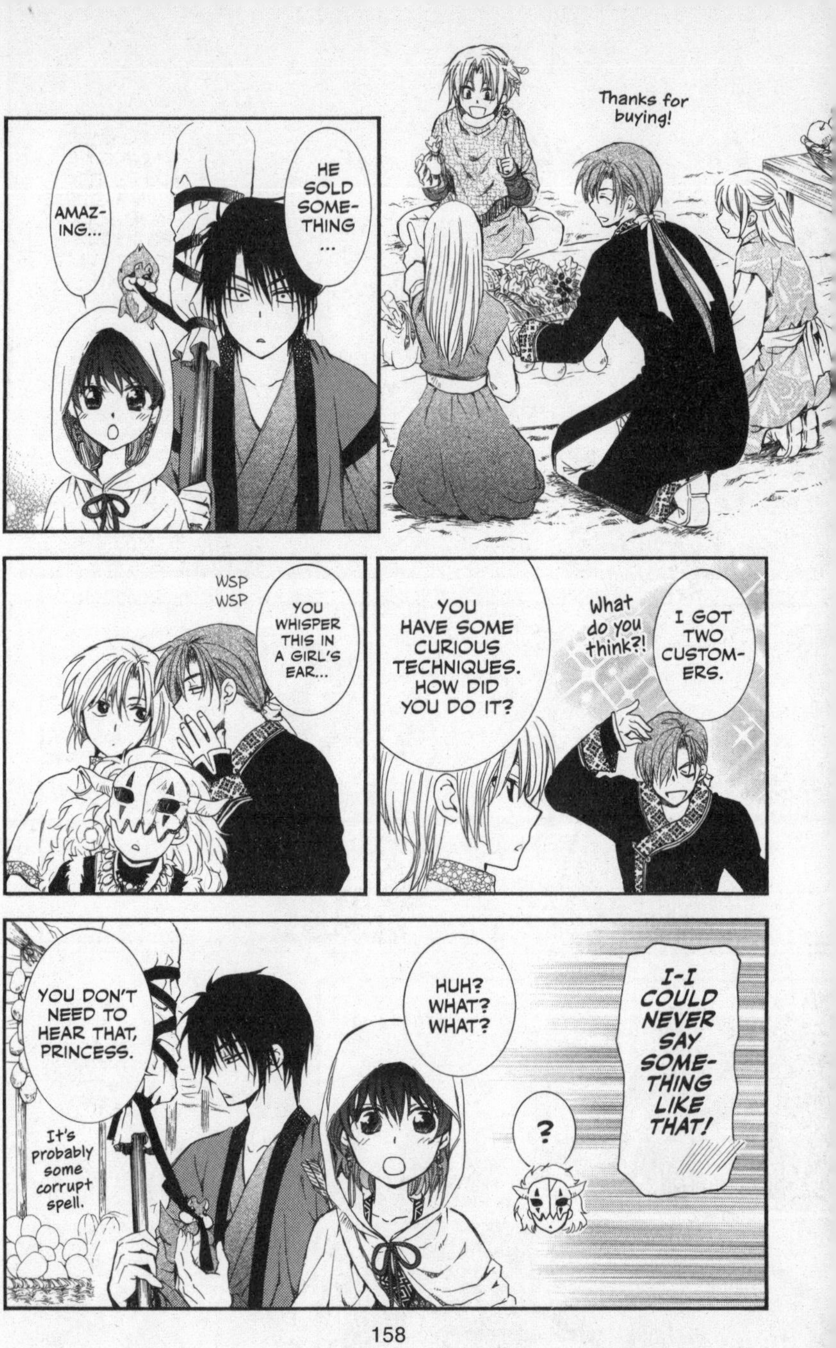
Thanks for buying!
HE SOLD SOMETHING...
AMAZING...
I GOT TWO CUSTOMERS.
What do you think?!
YOU HAVE SOME CURIOUS TECHNIQUES. HOW DID YOU DO IT?
WSP WSP
YOU WHISPER THIS IN A GIRL'S EAR...
I-I COULD NEVER SAY SOMETHING LIKE THAT!
?
HUH? WHAT? WHAT?
YOU DON'T NEED TO HEAR THAT, PRINCESS.
It's probably some corrupt spell.

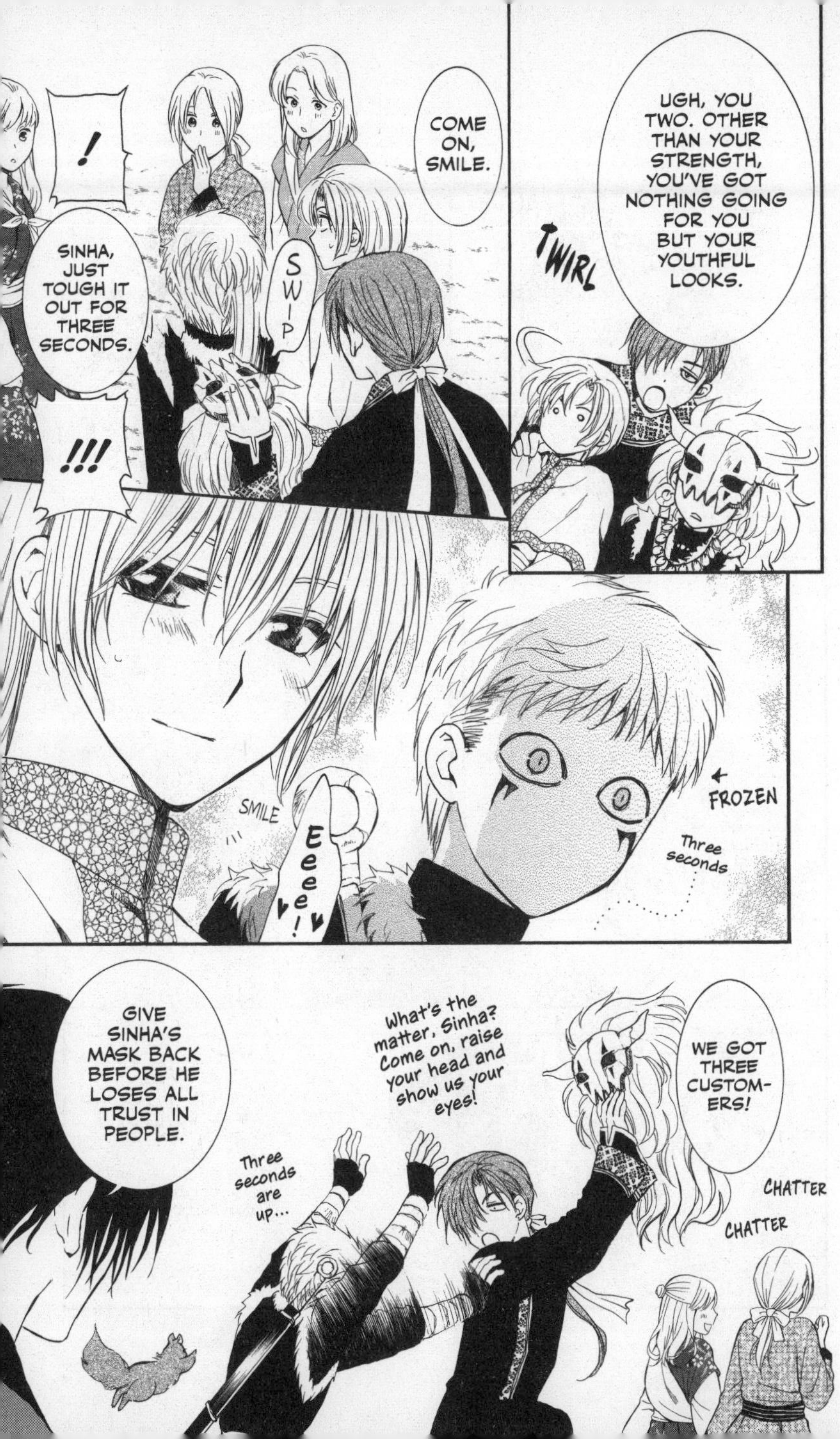
UGH, YOU TWO. OTHER THAN YOUR STRENGTH, YOU'VE GOT NOTHING GOING FOR YOU BUT YOUR YOUTHFUL LOOKS.
TWIRL
COME ON, SMILE.
SWIP
!
SINHA, JUST TOUGH IT OUT FOR THREE SECONDS.
!!!
FROZEN
Three seconds
SMILE
Eeee!
WE GOT THREE CUSTOMERS!
CHATTER
CHATTER
What's the matter, Sinha? Come on, raise your head and show us your eyes!
Three seconds are up...
GIVE SINHA'S MASK BACK BEFORE HE LOSES ALL TRUST IN PEOPLE.

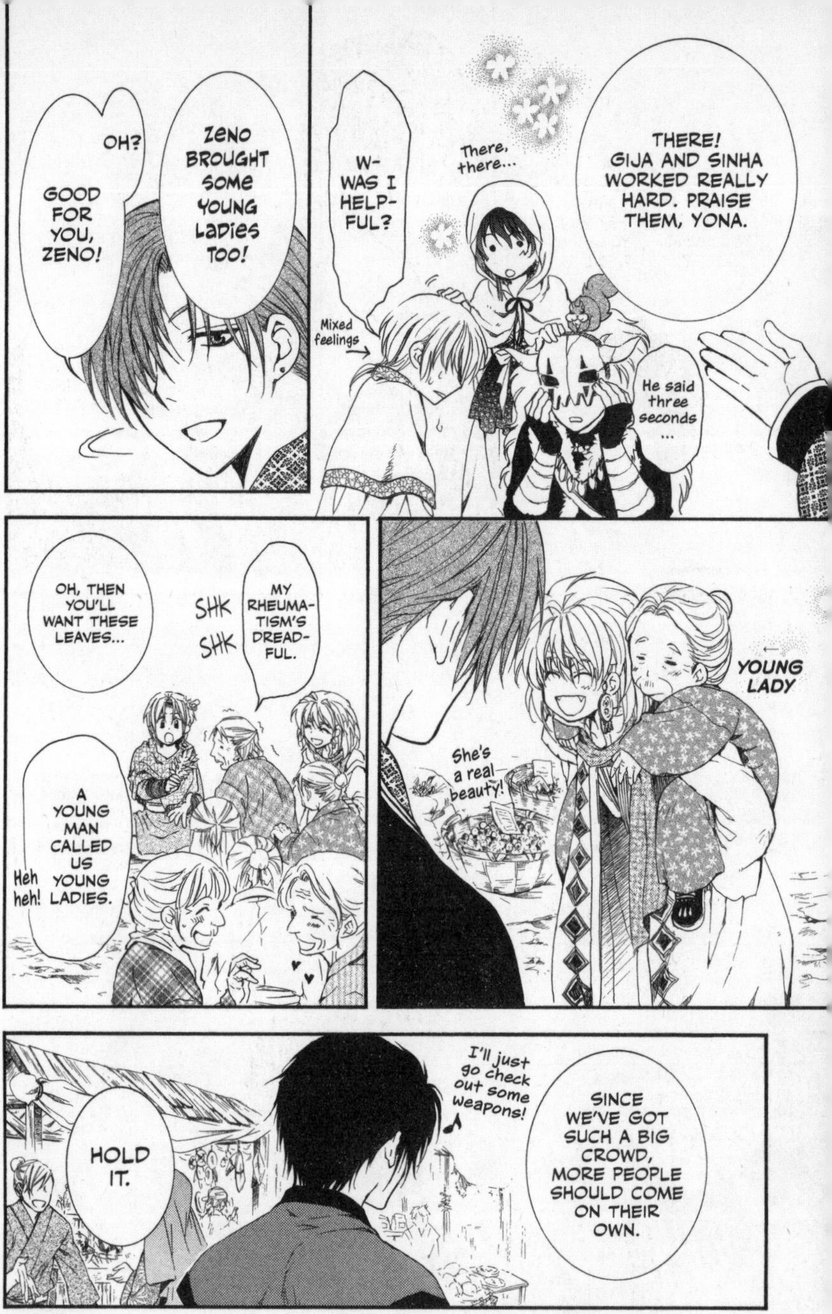
THERE! GIJA AND SINHA WORKED REALLY HARD. PRAISE THEM, YONA.
There, there...
He said three seconds ...
W-WAS I HELP-FUL?
Mixed feelings
ZENO BROUGHT SOME YOUNG LADIES TOO!
OH? GOOD FOR YOU, ZENO!
YOUNG LADY
She's a real beauty!
MY RHEUMA-TISM'S DREAD-FUL.
SHK SHK
OH, THEN YOU'LL WANT THESE LEAVES...
A YOUNG MAN CALLED US YOUNG LADIES.
Heh heh!
SINCE WE'VE GOT SUCH A BIG CROWD, MORE PEOPLE SHOULD COME ON THEIR OWN.
I'll just go check out some weapons!
HOLD IT.

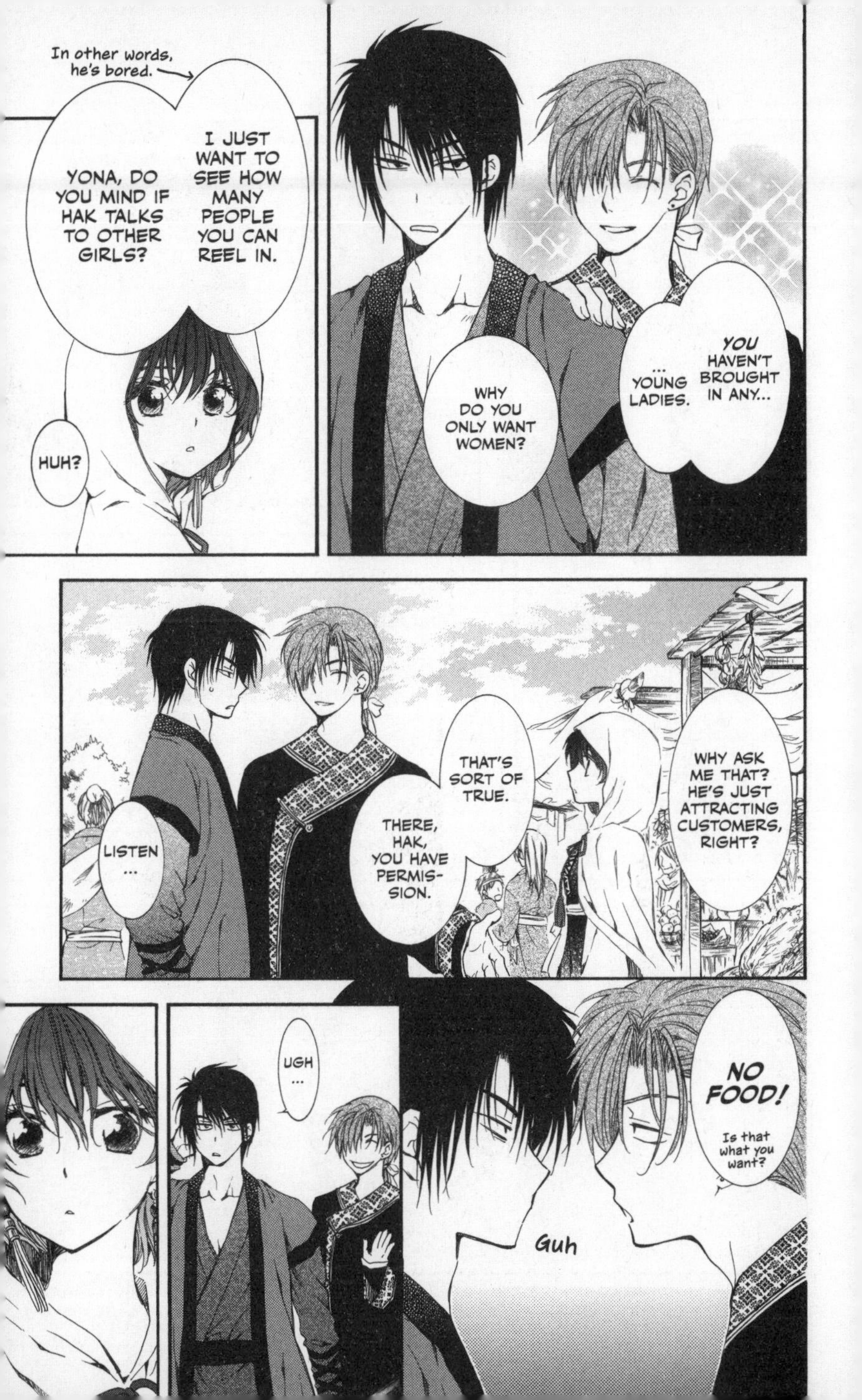
YOU HAVEN'T BROUGHT IN ANY...
... YOUNG LADIES.
WHY DO YOU ONLY WANT WOMEN?
I JUST WANT TO SEE HOW MANY PEOPLE YOU CAN REEL IN.
In other words, he's bored.
YONA, DO YOU MIND IF HAK TALKS TO OTHER GIRLS?
HUH?
WHY ASK ME THAT? HE'S JUST ATTRACTING CUSTOMERS, RIGHT?
THAT'S SORT OF TRUE.
THERE, HAK, YOU HAVE PERMIS-SION.
LISTEN ...
NO FOOD!
Is that what you want?
Guh
UGH ...

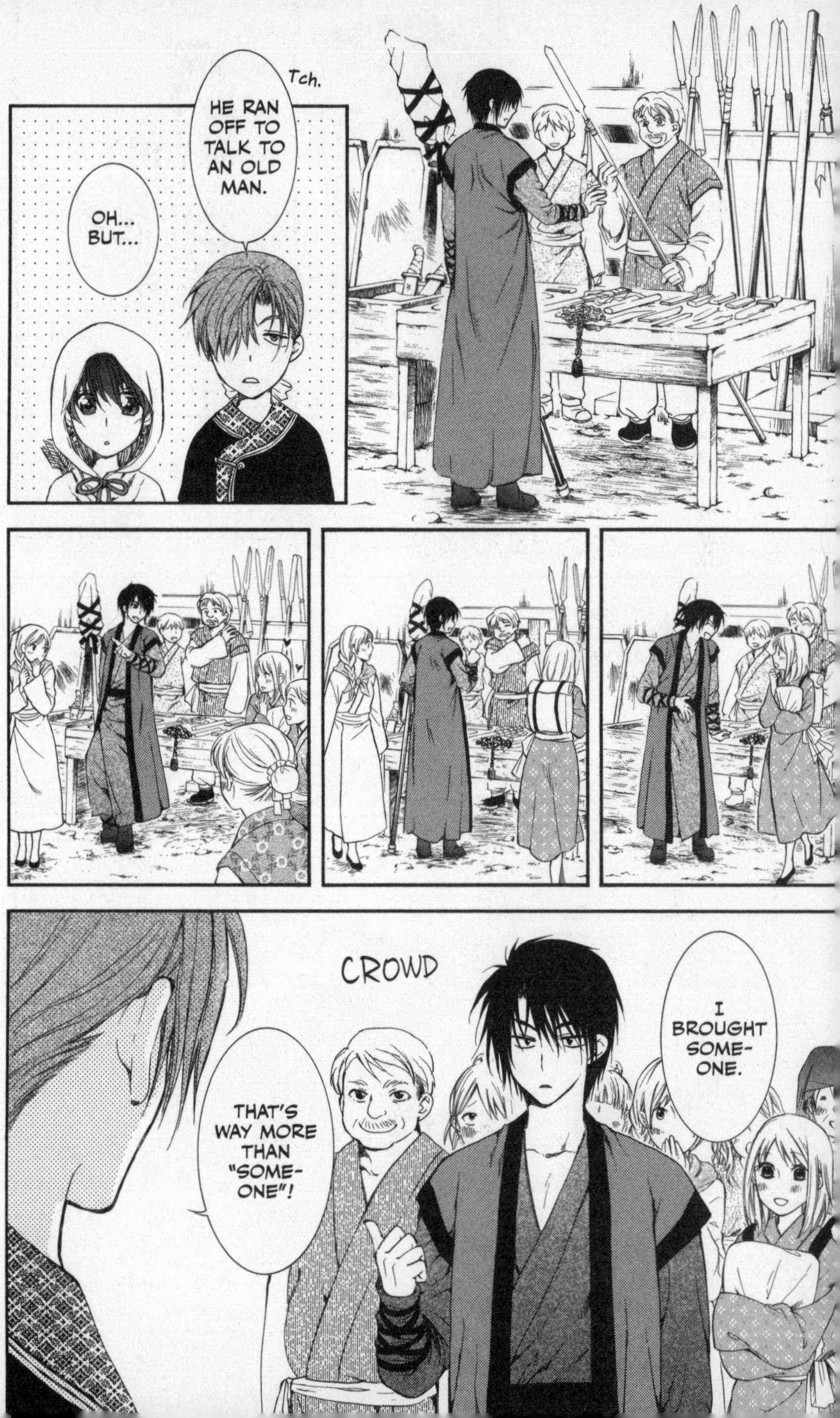
Tch.
HE RAN OFF TO TALK TO AN OLD MAN.
OH... BUT...
I BROUGHT SOME-ONE.
CROWD
THAT'S WAY MORE THAN "SOME-ONE"!

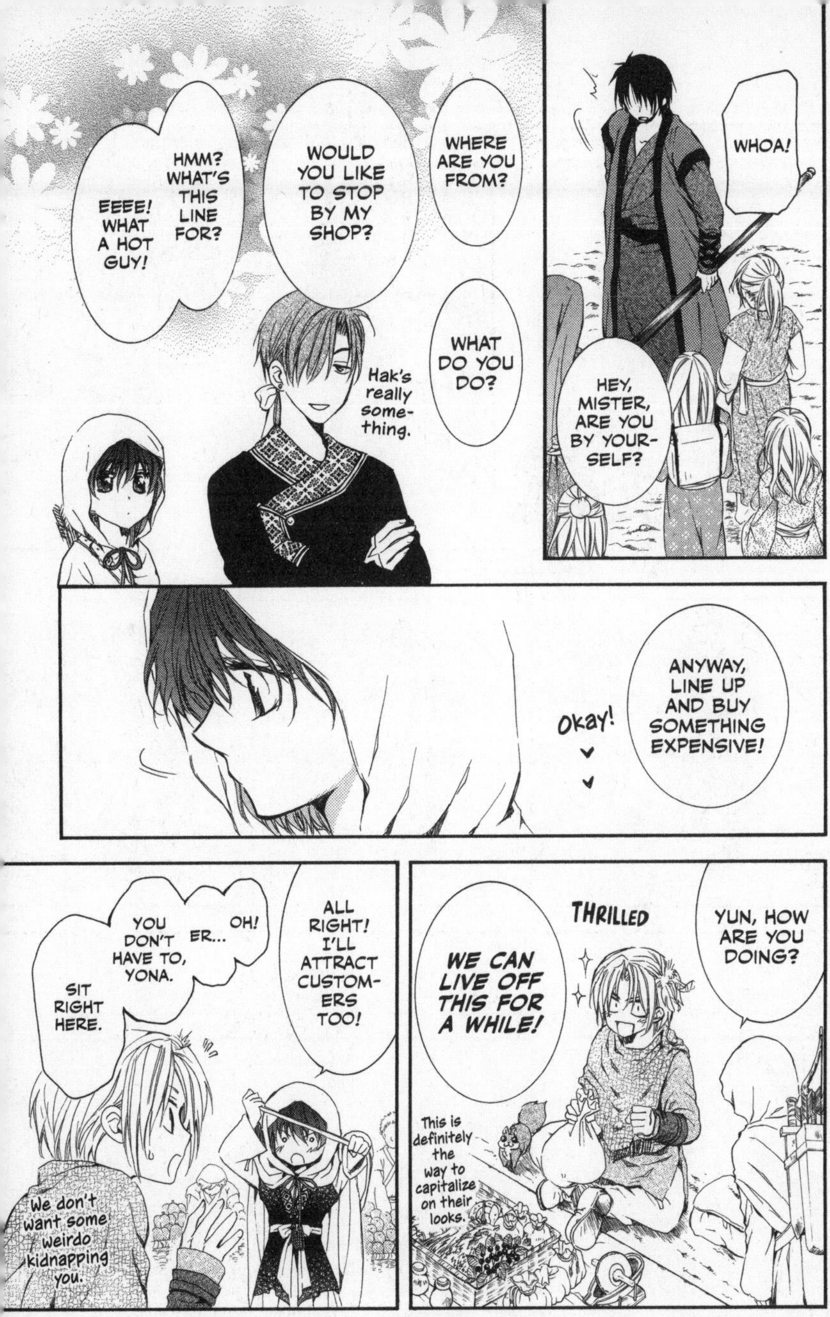
WHOA!
HEY, MISTER, ARE YOU BY YOURSELF?
WHERE ARE YOU FROM?
WOULD YOU LIKE TO STOP BY MY SHOP?
WHAT DO YOU DO?
HMM? WHAT'S THIS LINE FOR?
EEEE! WHAT A HOT GUY!
Hak's really something.
ANYWAY, LINE UP AND BUY SOMETHING EXPENSIVE!
Okay!
YUN, HOW ARE YOU DOING?
THRILLED
WE CAN LIVE OFF THIS FOR A WHILE!
This is definitely the way to capitalize on their looks.
ALL RIGHT! I'LL ATTRACT CUSTOMERS TOO!
OH!
ER...
YOU DON'T HAVE TO, YONA.
SIT RIGHT HERE.
We don't want some weirdo kidnapping you.

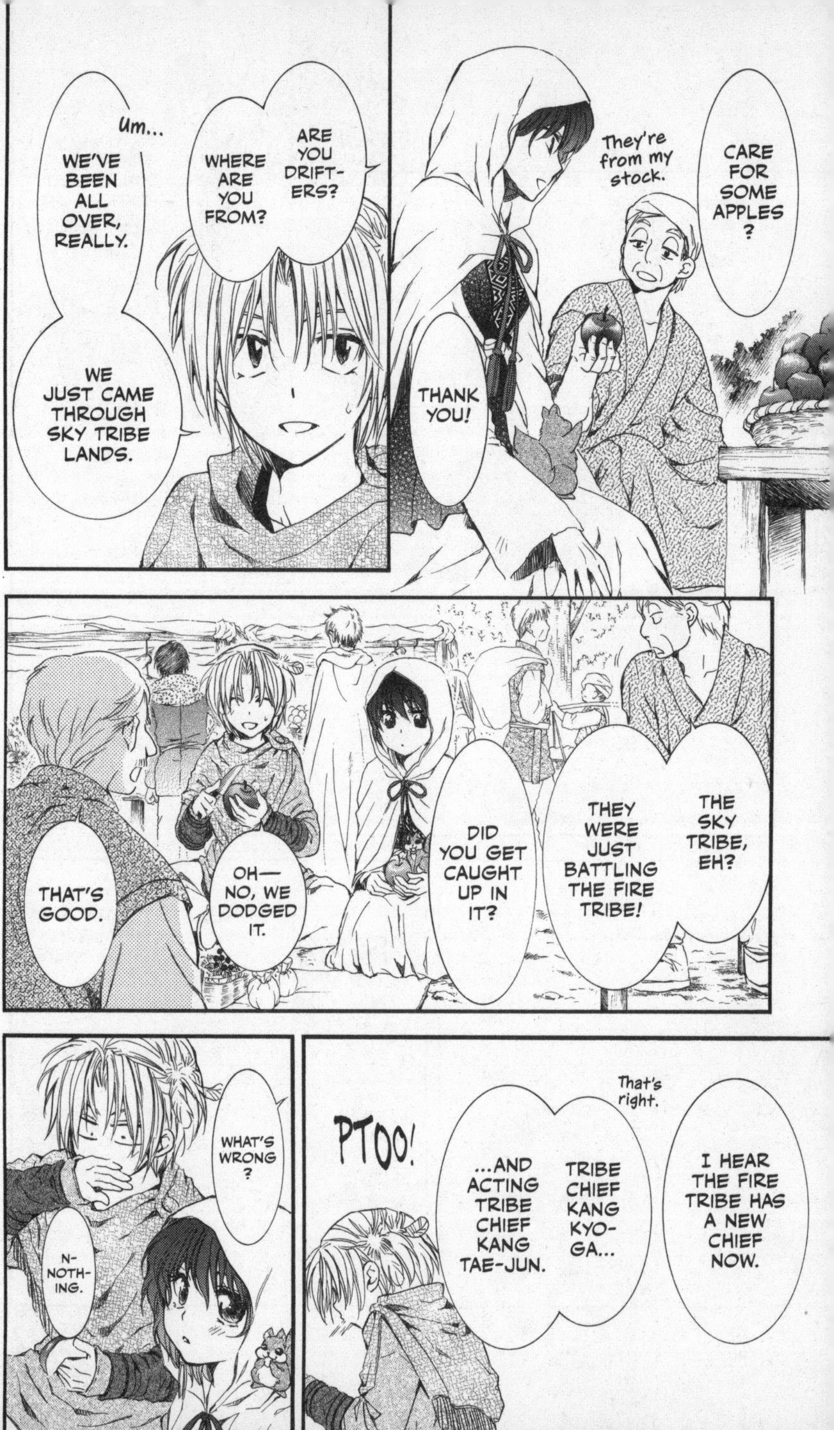
CARE FOR SOME APPLES?
They're from my stock.
THANK YOU!
ARE YOU DRIFTERS?
WHERE ARE YOU FROM?
Um...
WE'VE BEEN ALL OVER, REALLY.
WE JUST CAME THROUGH SKY TRIBE LANDS.
THE SKY TRIBE, EH?
THEY WERE JUST BATTLING THE FIRE TRIBE!
DID YOU GET CAUGHT UP IN IT?
OH— NO, WE DODGED IT.
THAT'S GOOD.
I HEAR THE FIRE TRIBE HAS A NEW CHIEF NOW.
That's right.
TRIBE CHIEF KANG KYO-GA...
...AND ACTING TRIBE CHIEF KANG TAE-JUN.
PTOO!
WHAT'S WRONG?
N-NOTHING.

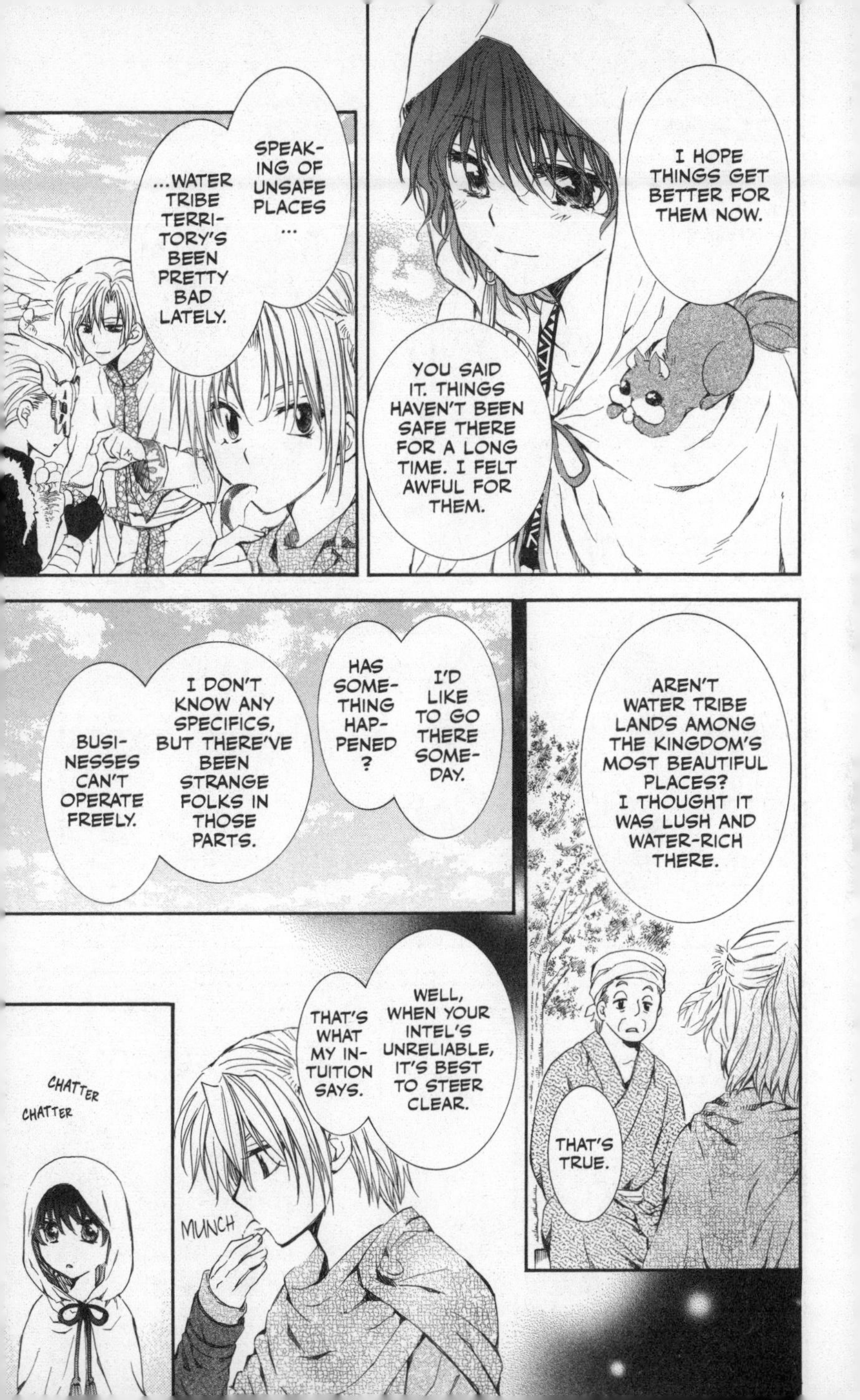
I HOPE THINGS GET BETTER FOR THEM NOW.
YOU SAID IT. THINGS HAVEN'T BEEN SAFE THERE FOR A LONG TIME. I FELT AWFUL FOR THEM.
SPEAK-ING OF UNSAFE PLACES ...
...WATER TRIBE TERRI-TORY'S BEEN PRETTY BAD LATELY.
AREN'T WATER TRIBE LANDS AMONG THE KINGDOM'S MOST BEAUTIFUL PLACES? I THOUGHT IT WAS LUSH AND WATER-RICH THERE.
THAT'S TRUE.
I'D LIKE TO GO THERE SOME-DAY.
HAS SOME-THING HAP-PENED?
I DON'T KNOW ANY SPECIFICS, BUT THERE'VE BEEN STRANGE FOLKS IN THOSE PARTS.
BUSI-NESSES CAN'T OPERATE FREELY.
WELL, WHEN YOUR INTEL'S UNRELIABLE, IT'S BEST TO STEER CLEAR.
THAT'S WHAT MY IN-TUITION SAYS.
MUNCH
CHATTER
CHATTER

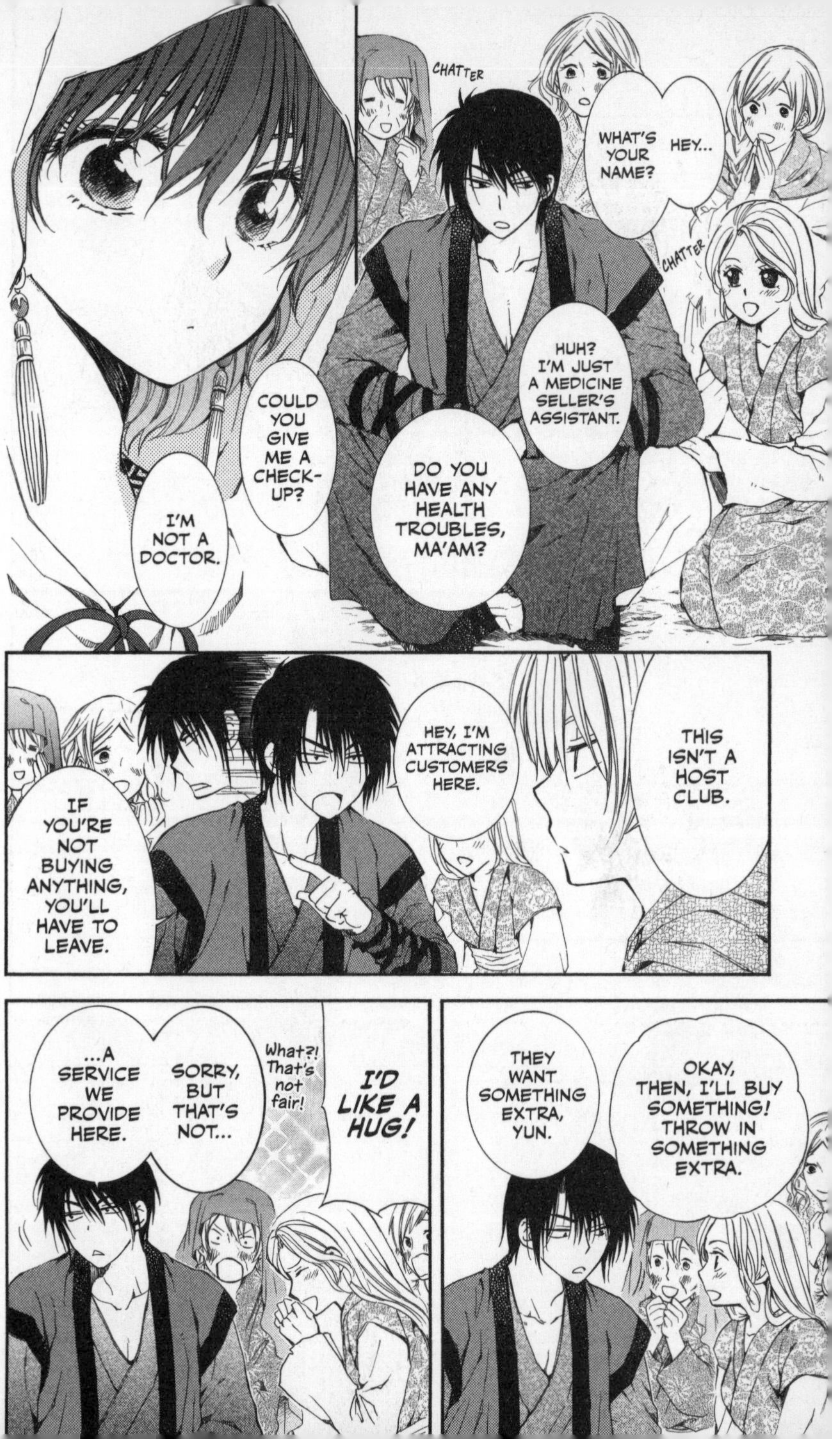
CHATTER
HEY...
WHAT'S YOUR NAME?
CHATTER
HUH? I'M JUST A MEDICINE SELLER'S ASSISTANT.
DO YOU HAVE ANY HEALTH TROUBLES, MA'AM?
COULD YOU GIVE ME A CHECK-UP?
I'M NOT A DOCTOR.
THIS ISN'T A HOST CLUB.
HEY, I'M ATTRACTING CUSTOMERS HERE.
IF YOU'RE NOT BUYING ANYTHING, YOU'LL HAVE TO LEAVE.
OKAY, THEN, I'LL BUY SOMETHING! THROW IN SOMETHING EXTRA.
THEY WANT SOMETHING EXTRA, YUN.
I'D LIKE A HUG!
What?! That's not fair!
SORRY, BUT THAT'S NOT...
...A SERVICE WE PROVIDE HERE.

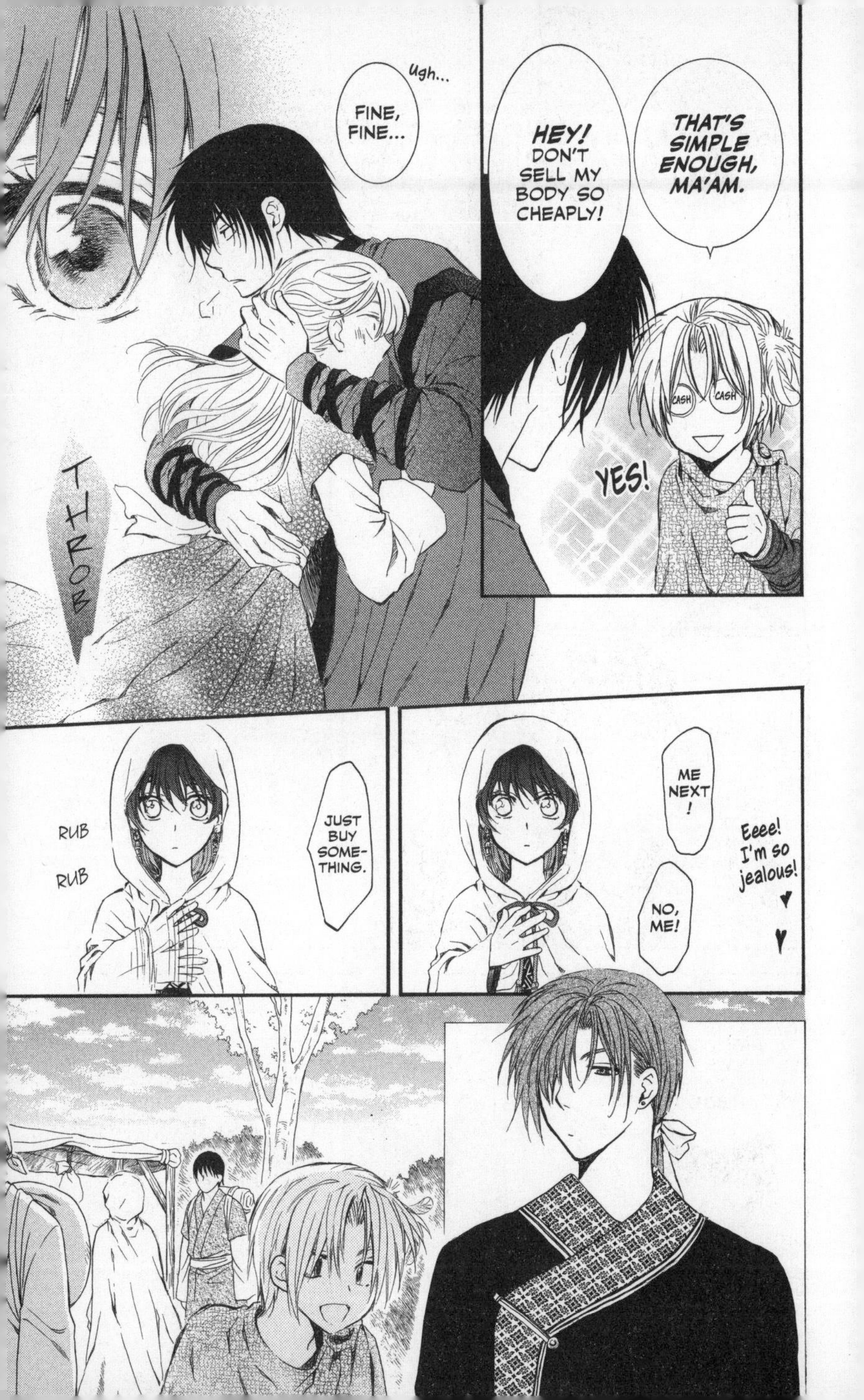
THAT'S SIMPLE ENOUGH, MA'AM.
HEY! DON'T SELL MY BODY SO CHEAPLY!
CASH CASH
YES!
Ugh...
FINE, FINE...
THROB
ME NEXT!
NO, ME!
Eeee! I'm so jealous!
JUST BUY SOME-THING.
RUB RUB

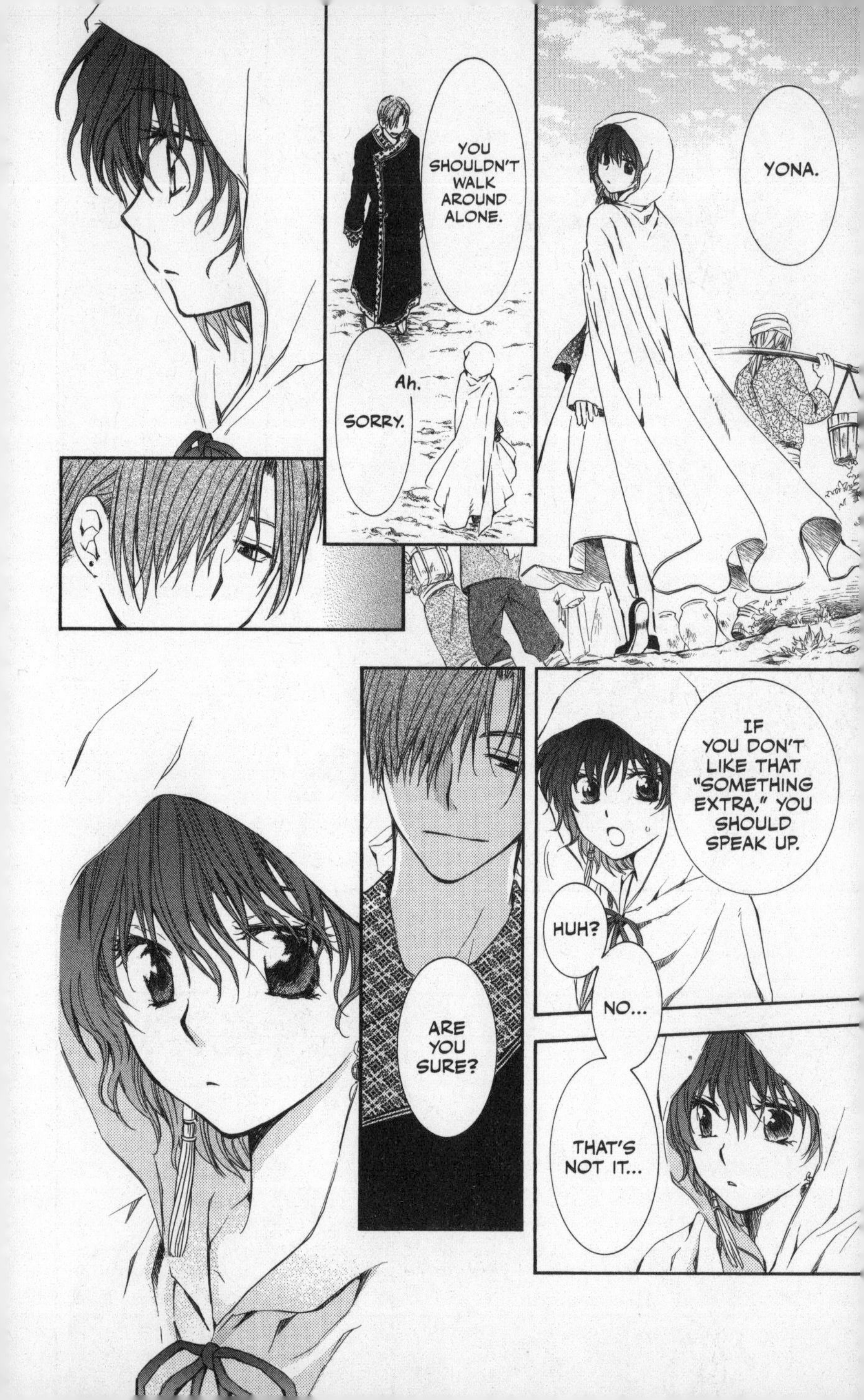
YONA.
YOU SHOULDN'T WALK AROUND ALONE.
Ah.
SORRY.
IF YOU DON'T LIKE THAT "SOMETHING EXTRA," YOU SHOULD SPEAK UP.
HUH?
NO...
THAT'S NOT IT...
ARE YOU SURE?

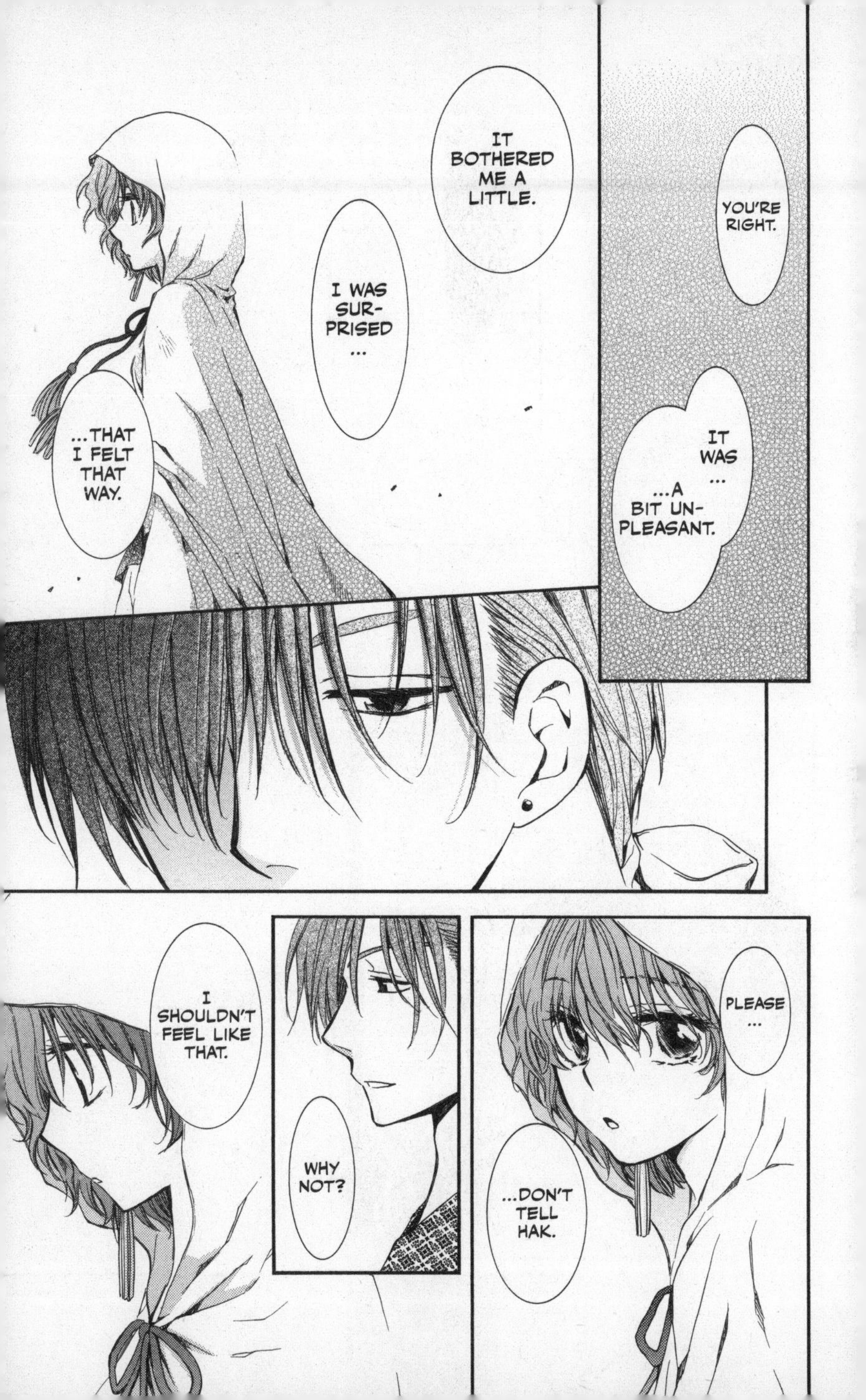
YOU'RE RIGHT.
IT WAS ...
...A BIT UN-PLEASANT.
IT BOTHERED ME A LITTLE.
I WAS SUR-PRISED ...
...THAT I FELT THAT WAY.
PLEASE ...
...DON'T TELL HAK.
WHY NOT?
I SHOULDN'T FEEL LIKE THAT.

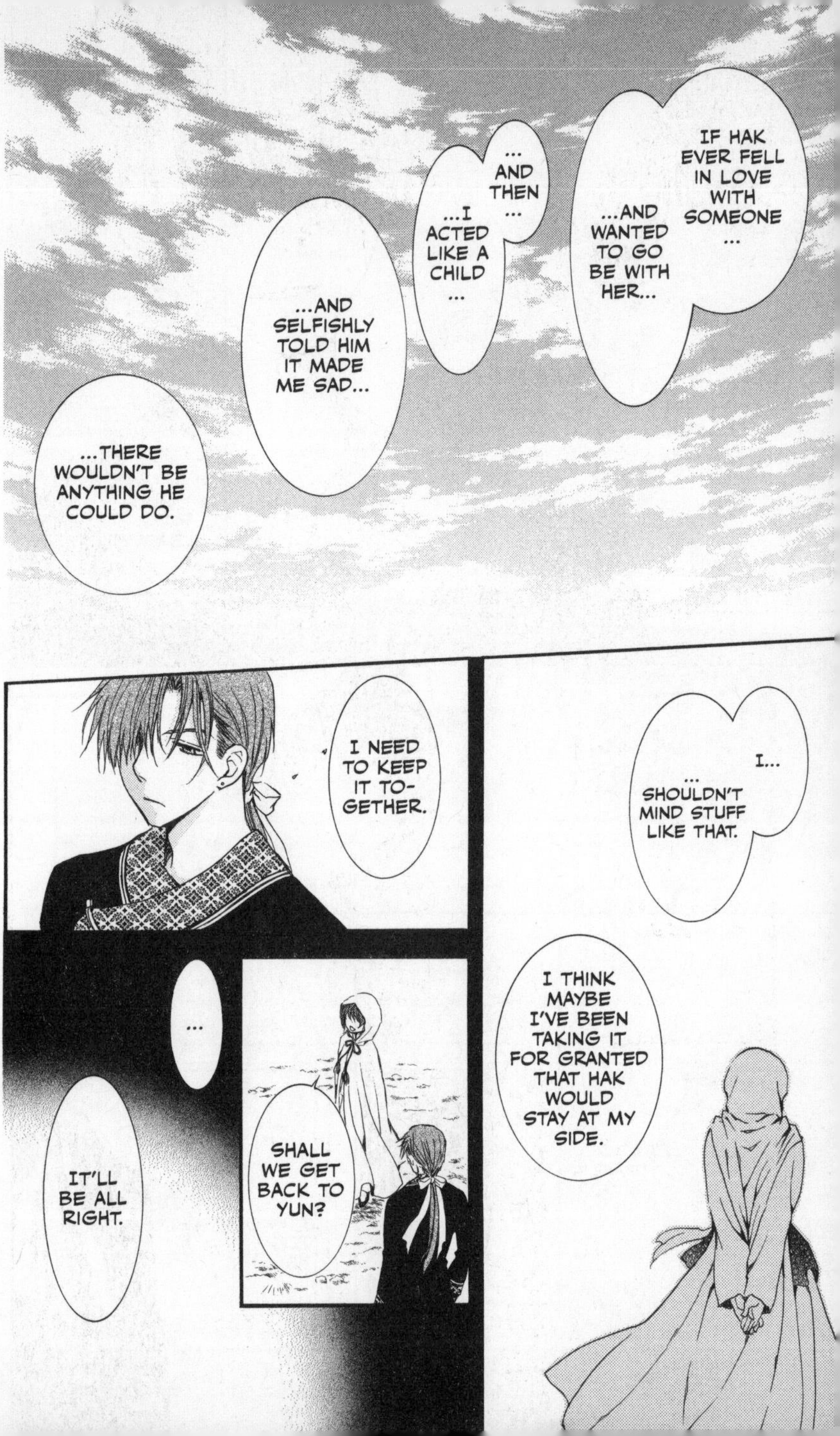
IF HAK EVER FELL IN LOVE WITH SOMEONE...
...AND WANTED TO GO BE WITH HER...
...AND THEN...
...I ACTED LIKE A CHILD...
...AND SELFISHLY TOLD HIM IT MADE ME SAD...
...THERE WOULDN'T BE ANYTHING HE COULD DO.
I... ... SHOULDN'T MIND STUFF LIKE THAT.
I THINK MAYBE I'VE BEEN TAKING IT FOR GRANTED THAT HAK WOULD STAY AT MY SIDE.
I NEED TO KEEP IT TO- GETHER.
SHALL WE GET BACK TO YUN?
...
IT'LL BE ALL RIGHT.

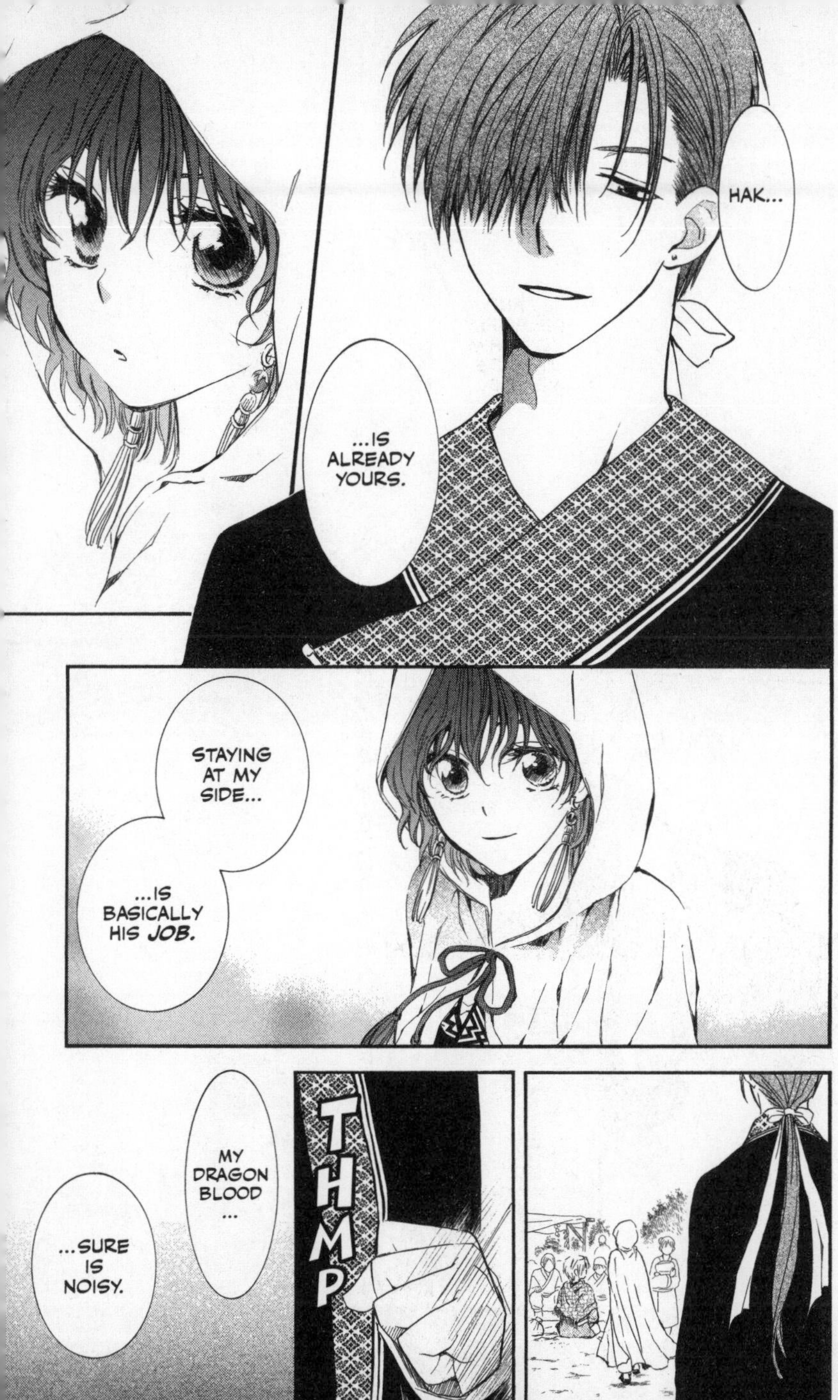
HAK...
...IS ALREADY YOURS.
STAYING AT MY SIDE...
...IS BASICALLY HIS *JOB.*
THMP
MY DRAGON BLOOD ...
...SURE IS NOISY.

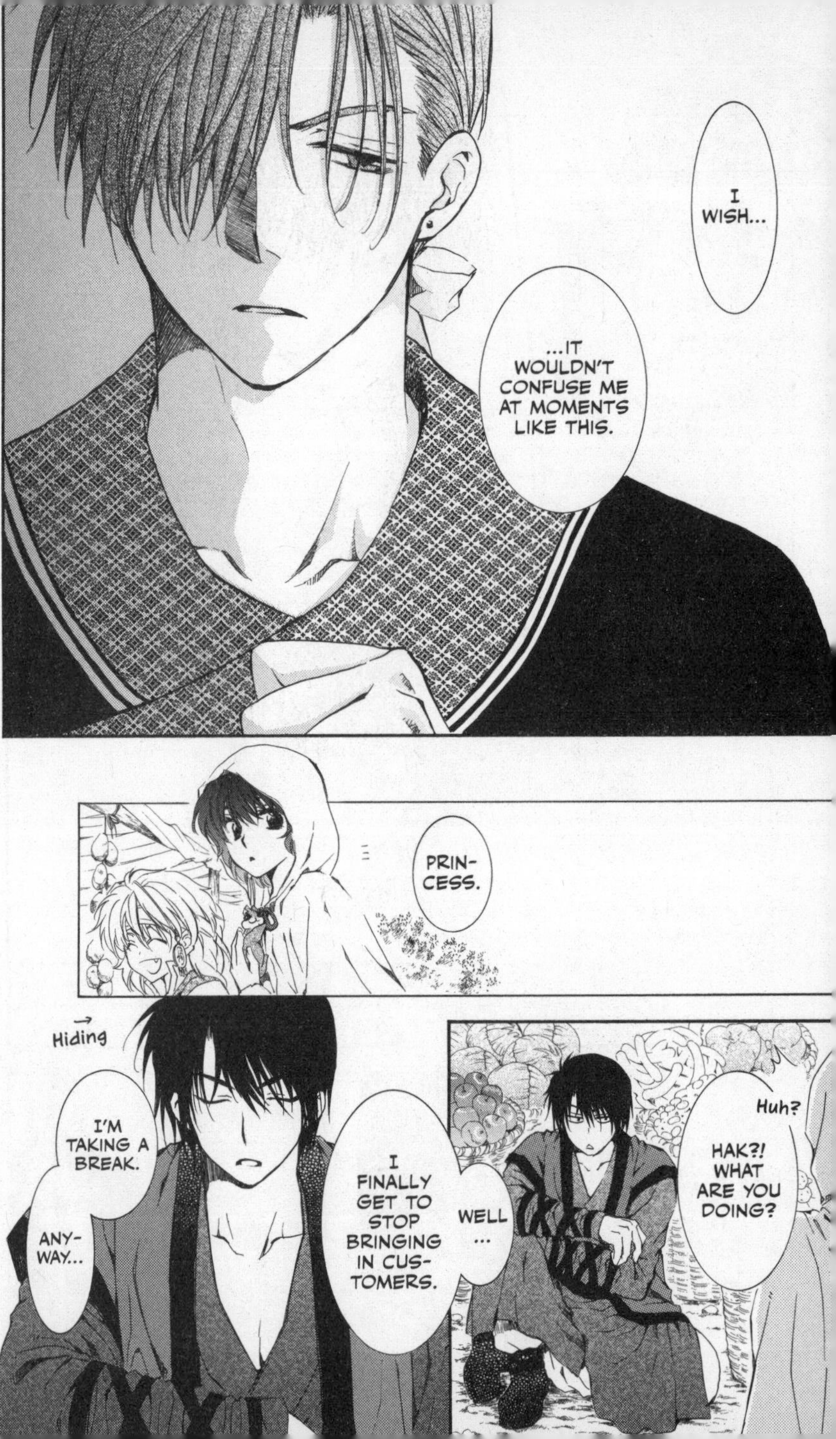
I WISH...
...IT WOULDN'T CONFUSE ME AT MOMENTS LIKE THIS.
PRIN-CESS.
Huh?
HAK?! WHAT ARE YOU DOING?
WELL ...
→ Hiding
I FINALLY GET TO STOP BRINGING IN CUS-TOMERS.
I'M TAKING A BREAK.
ANY-WAY...

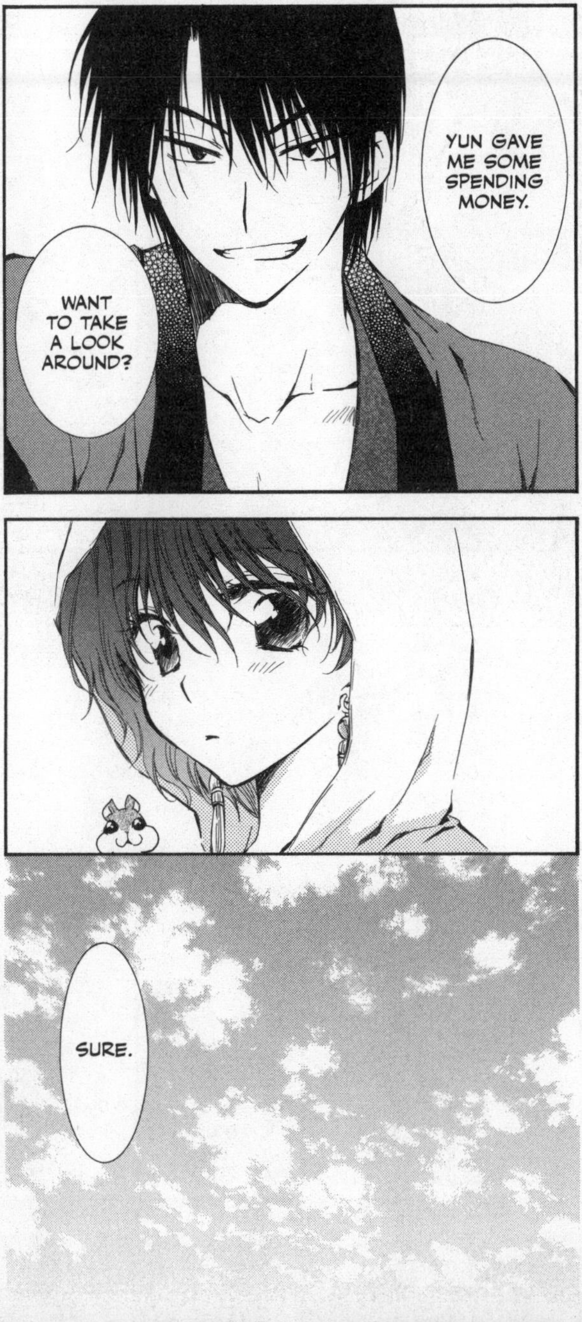
YUN GAVE ME SOME SPENDING MONEY.
WANT TO TAKE A LOOK AROUND?
SURE.

About a year ago, I visited Taiwan to take pictures of buildings. The local guide was very friendly and the buildings were interesting. It's a wonderful country. During the Tohoku earthquake, Taiwan gave us a lot of help, and I'm very grateful. If I ever have the opportunity, I'd like to go back there.

Yuno awaiting Geun-tae's return

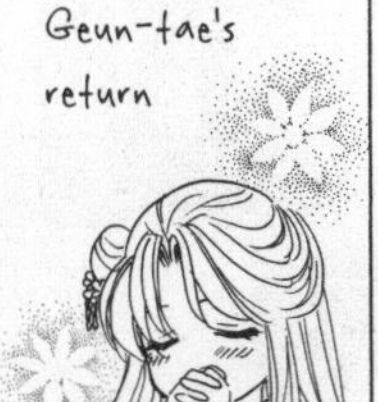

I hope to see you in volume 14!

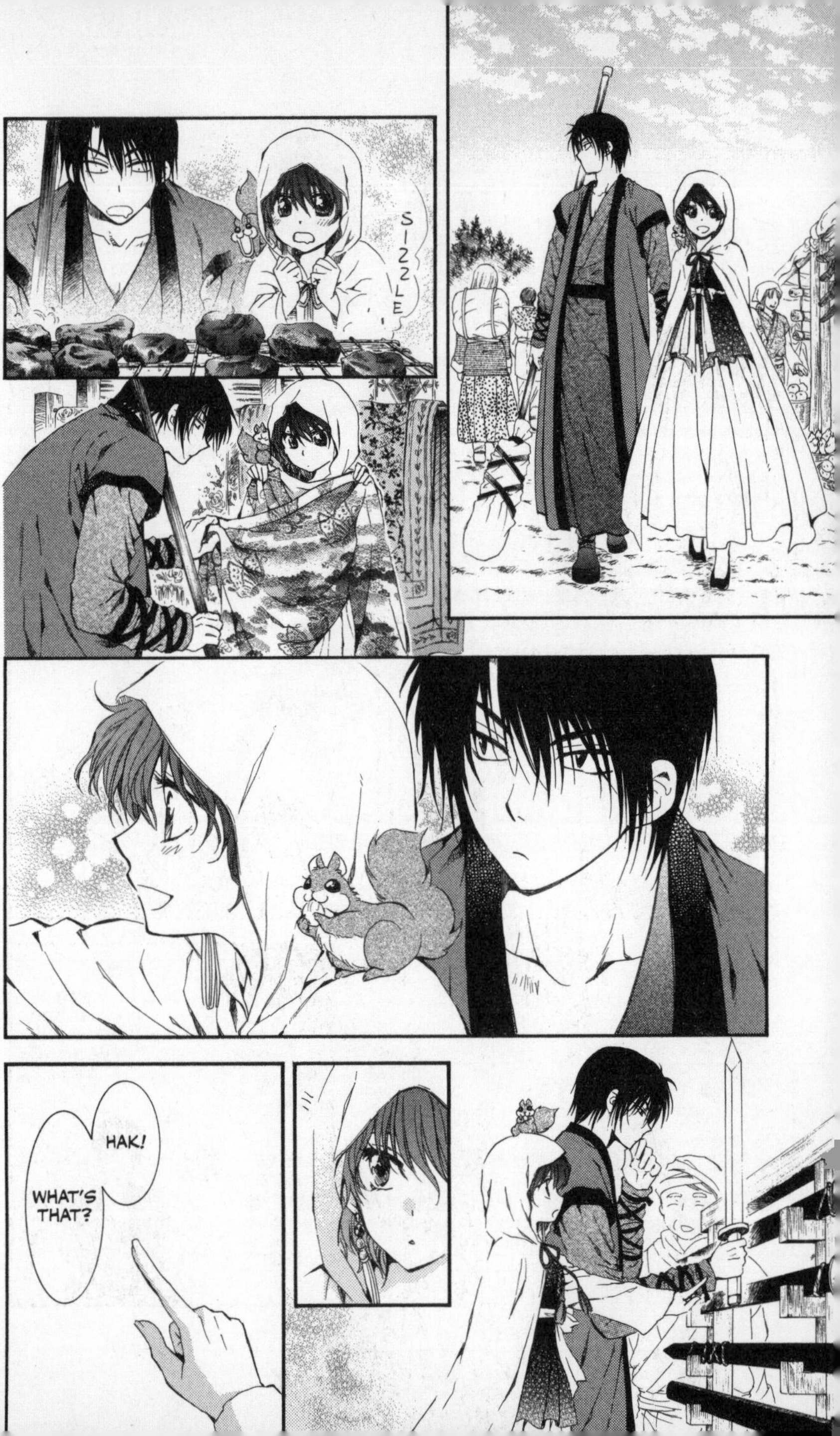
SIZZLE
HAK!
WHAT'S THAT?

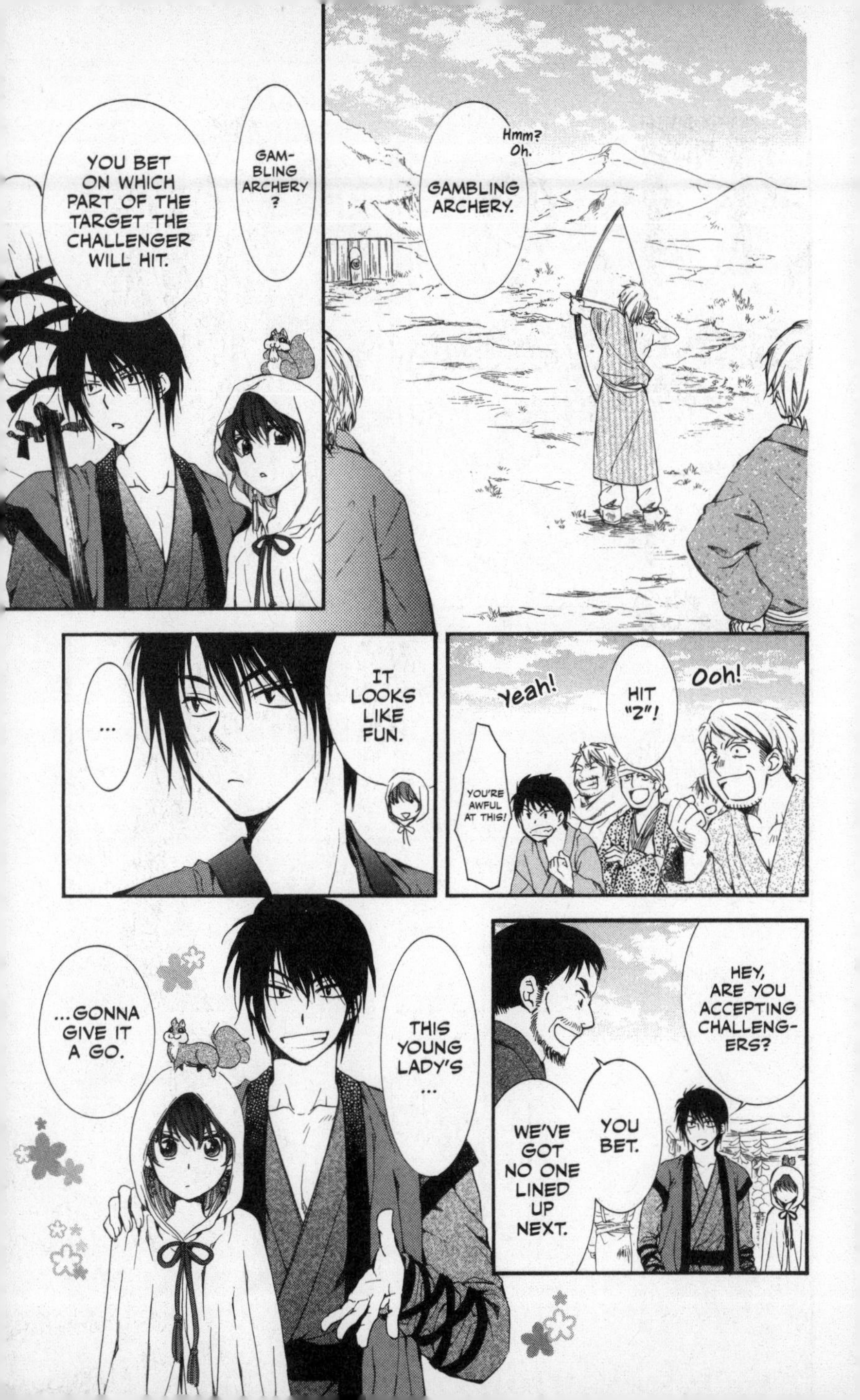
Hmm? Oh.
GAMBLING ARCHERY.
GAMBLING ARCHERY?
YOU BET ON WHICH PART OF THE TARGET THE CHALLENGER WILL HIT.
Ooh!
HIT "2"!
Yeah!
YOU'RE AWFUL AT THIS!
IT LOOKS LIKE FUN.
...
HEY, ARE YOU ACCEPTING CHALLENGERS?
YOU BET.
WE'VE GOT NO ONE LINED UP NEXT.
THIS YOUNG LADY'S...
...GONNA GIVE IT A GO.

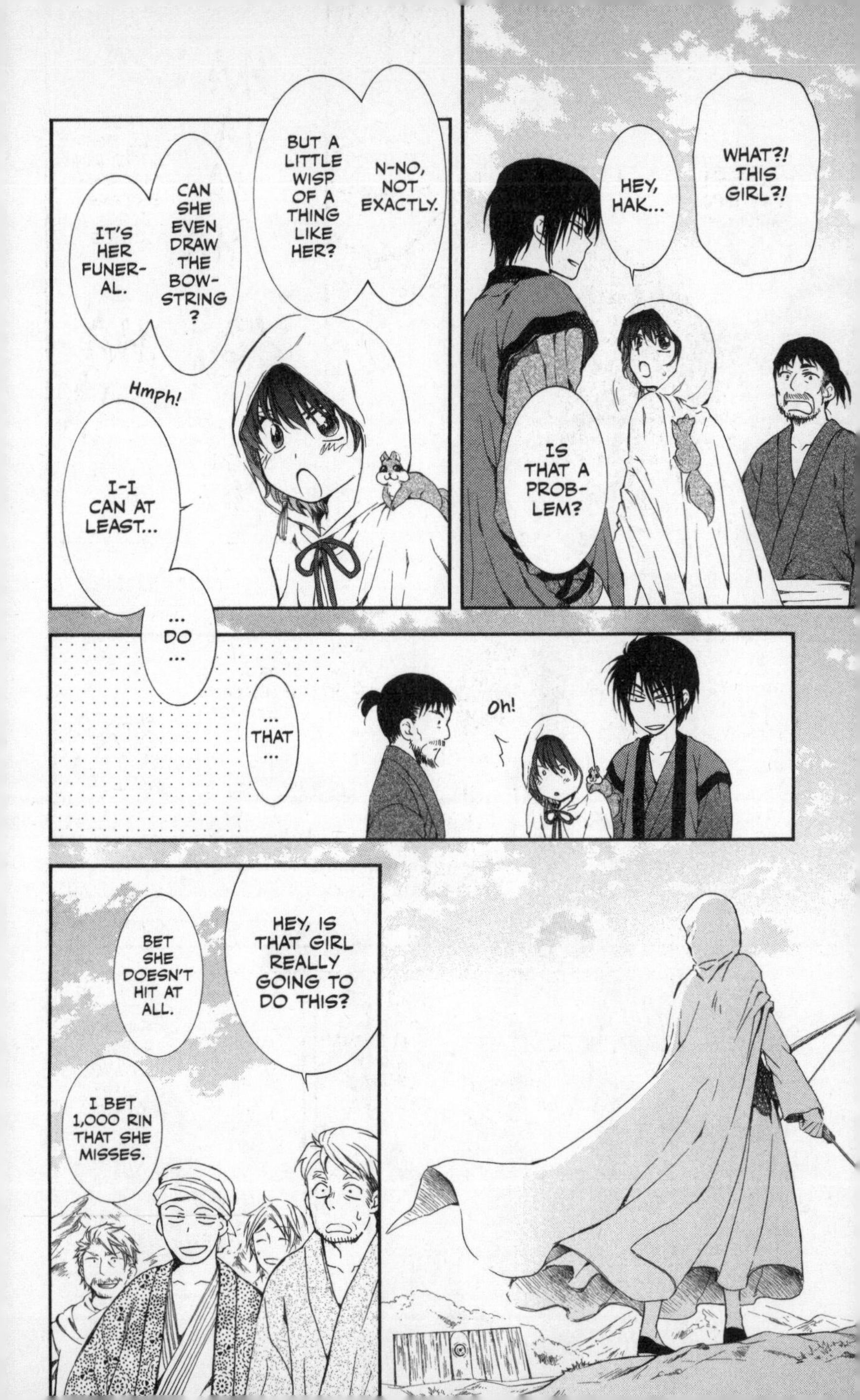
WHAT?! THIS GIRL?!
HEY, HAK...
IS THAT A PROB-LEM?
N-NO, NOT EXACTLY.
BUT A LITTLE WISP OF A THING LIKE HER?
CAN SHE EVEN DRAW THE BOW-STRING?
IT'S HER FUNER-AL.
Hmph!
I-I CAN AT LEAST...
...DO...
Oh!
...THAT...
HEY, IS THAT GIRL REALLY GOING TO DO THIS?
BET SHE DOESN'T HIT AT ALL.
I BET 1,000 RIN THAT SHE MISSES.

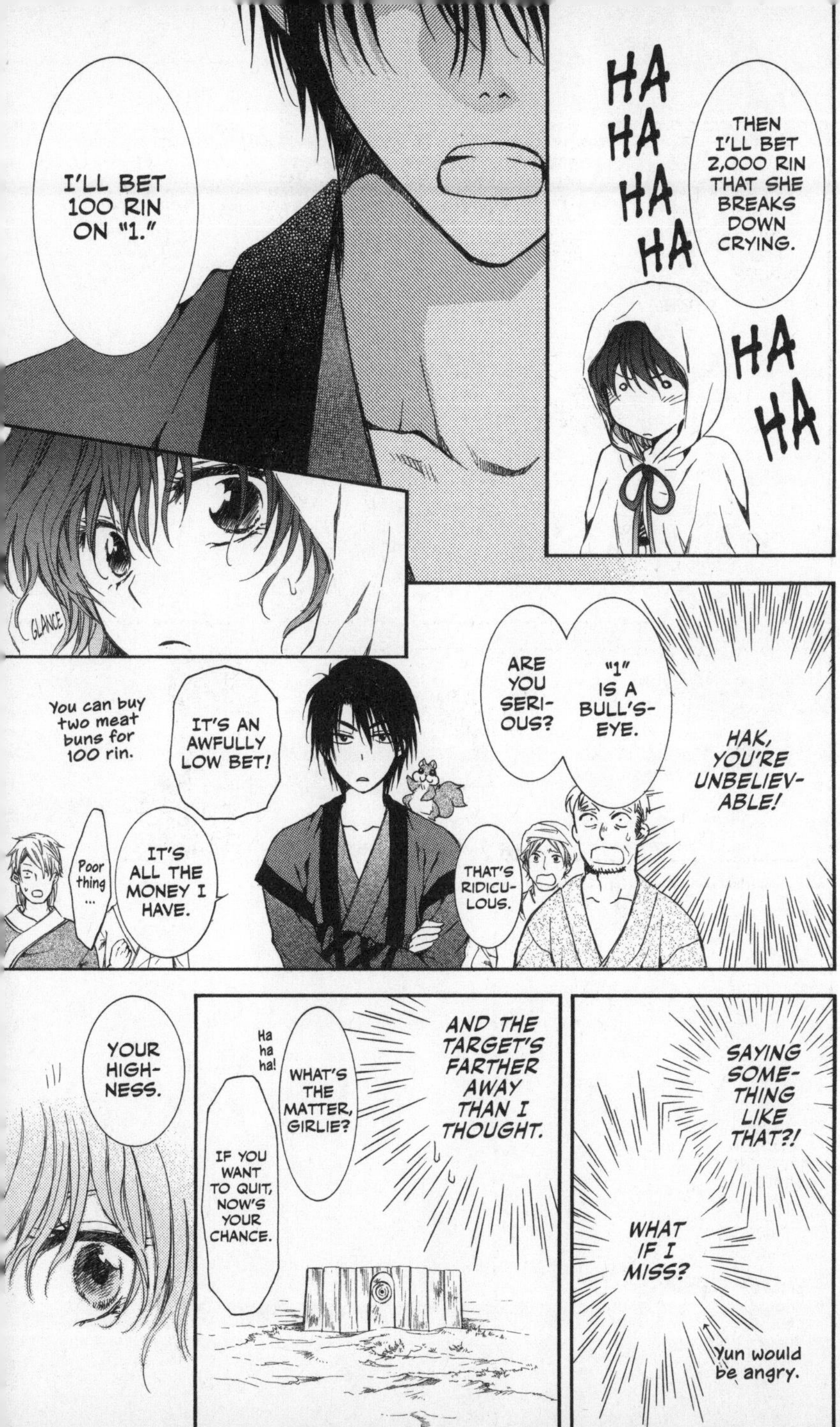
HA HA HA HA
THEN I'LL BET 2,000 RIN THAT SHE BREAKS DOWN CRYING.
HA HA
I'LL BET 100 RIN ON "1."
GLANCE
HAK, YOU'RE UNBELIEV-ABLE!
"1" IS A BULL'S-EYE.
ARE YOU SERI-OUS?
THAT'S RIDICU-LOUS.
IT'S AN AWFULLY LOW BET!
You can buy two meat buns for 100 rin.
IT'S ALL THE MONEY I HAVE.
Poor thing...
SAYING SOME-THING LIKE THAT?!
WHAT IF I MISS?
Yun would be angry.
AND THE TARGET'S FARTHER AWAY THAN I THOUGHT.
WHAT'S THE MATTER, GIRLIE?
Ha ha ha!
IF YOU WANT TO QUIT, NOW'S YOUR CHANCE.
YOUR HIGH-NESS.

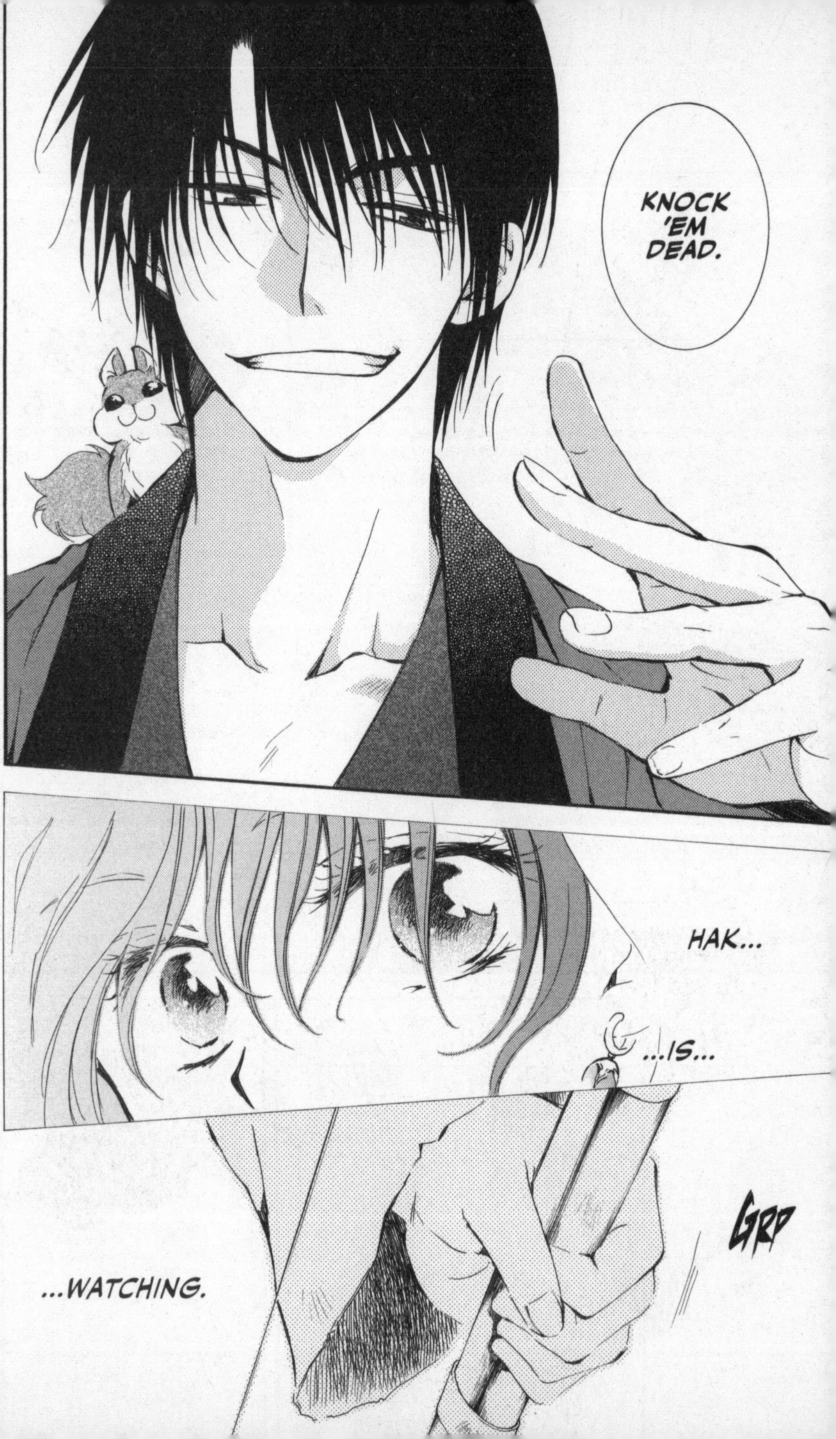
KNOCK 'EM DEAD.
HAK...
...IS...
GRP
...WATCHING.

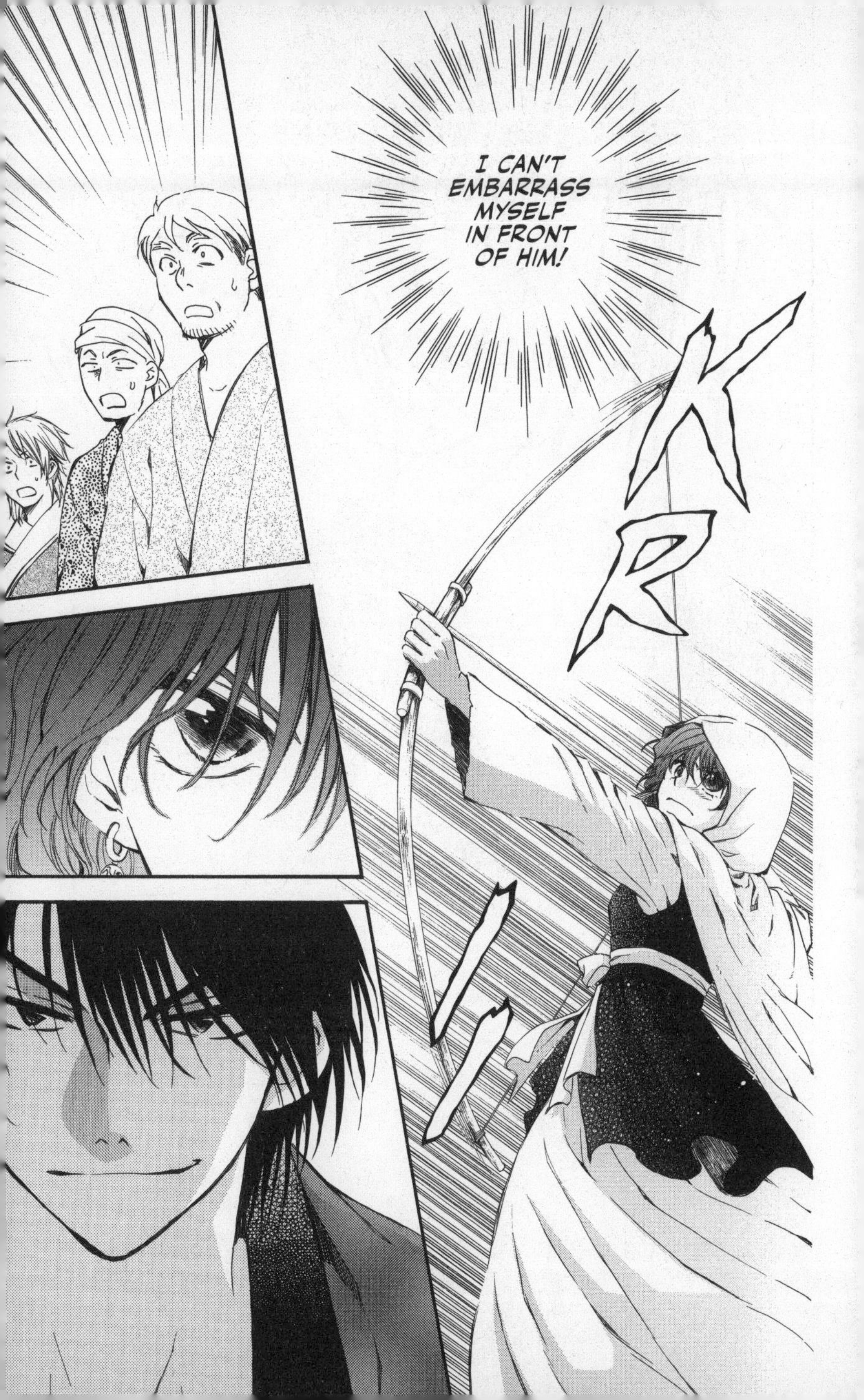
I CAN'T EMBARRASS MYSELF IN FRONT OF HIM!
KR
I I

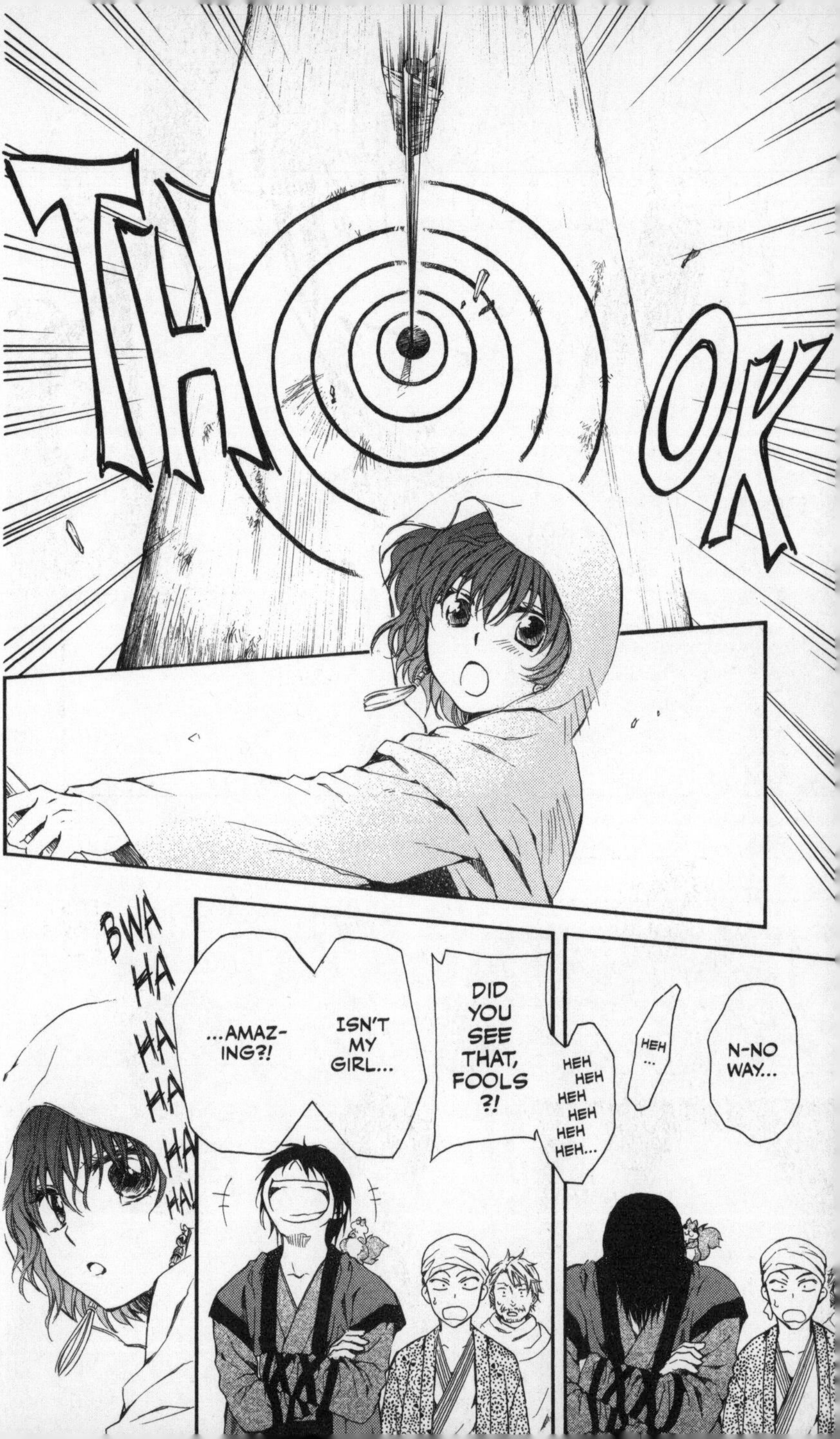
THOOK
N-NO WAY...
HEH...
HEH HEH HEH HEH HEH HEH...
DID YOU SEE THAT, FOOLS?!
ISN'T MY GIRL...
...AMAZING?!
BWA HA HA HA HA HA HA!

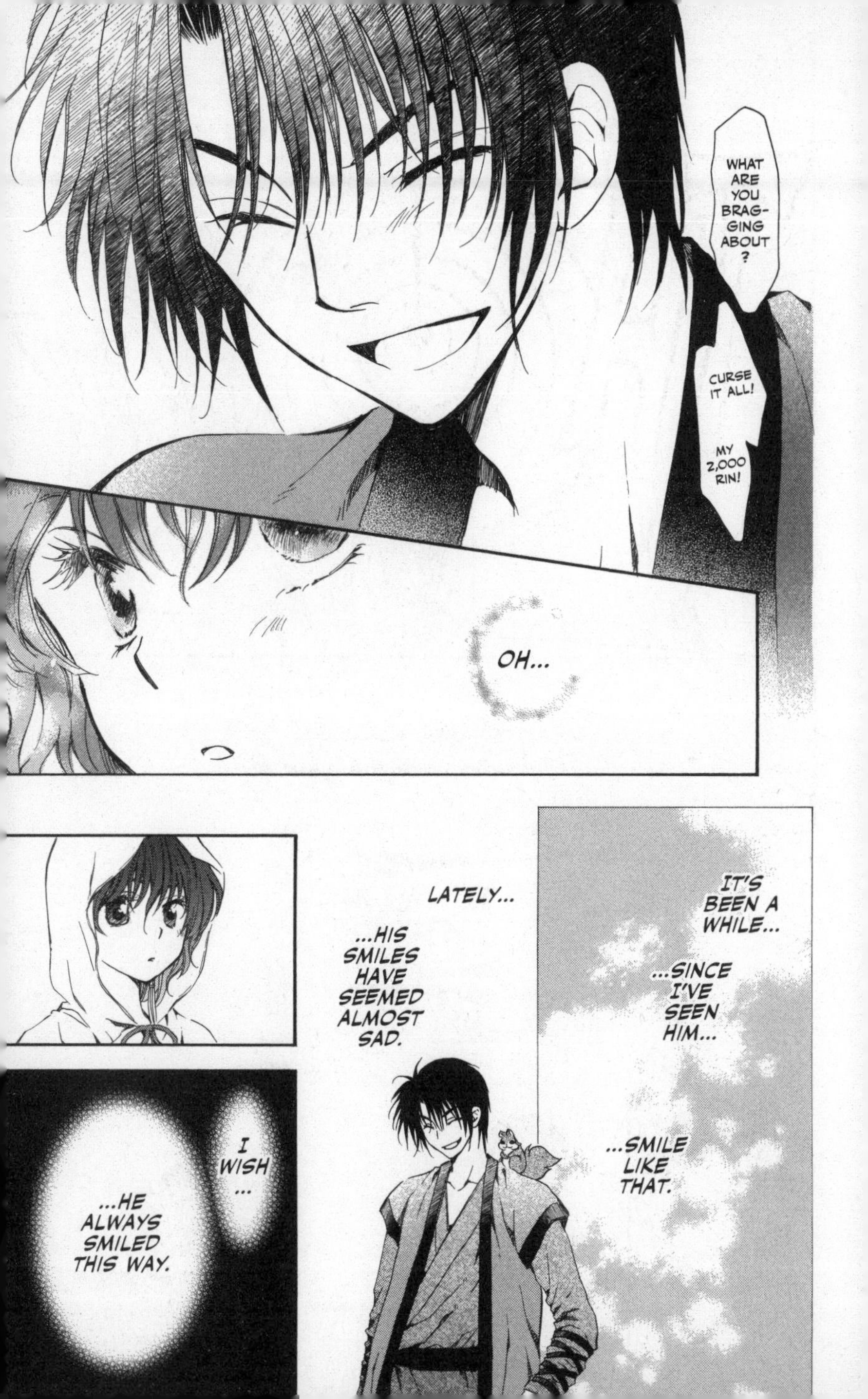
WHAT ARE YOU BRAGGING ABOUT?
CURSE IT ALL!
MY 2,000 RIN!
OH...
IT'S BEEN A WHILE...
...SINCE I'VE SEEN HIM...
...SMILE LIKE THAT.
LATELY...
...HIS SMILES HAVE SEEMED ALMOST SAD.
I WISH...
...HE ALWAYS SMILED THIS WAY.

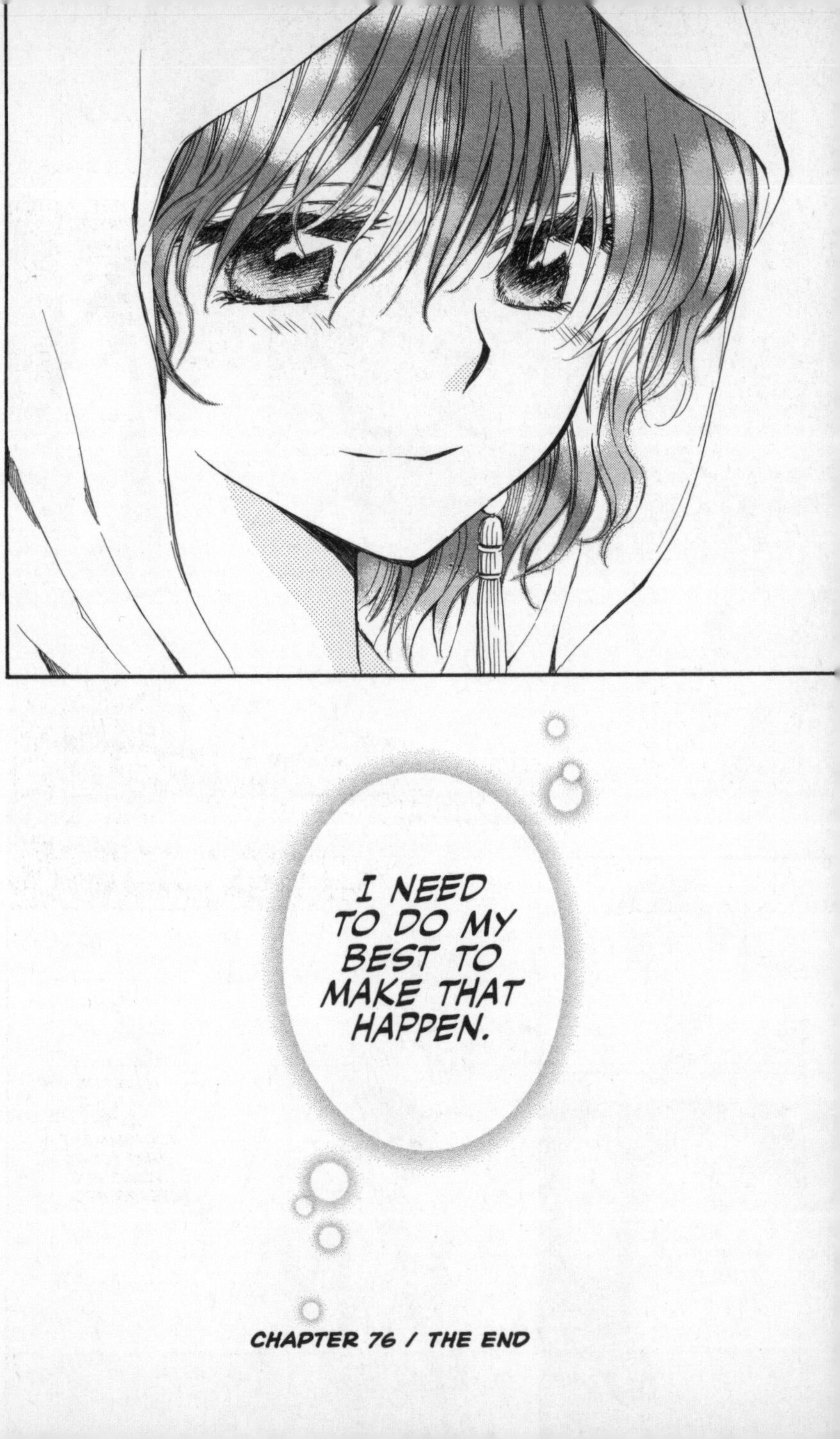
I NEED TO DO MY BEST TO MAKE THAT HAPPEN.
CHAPTER 76 / THE END

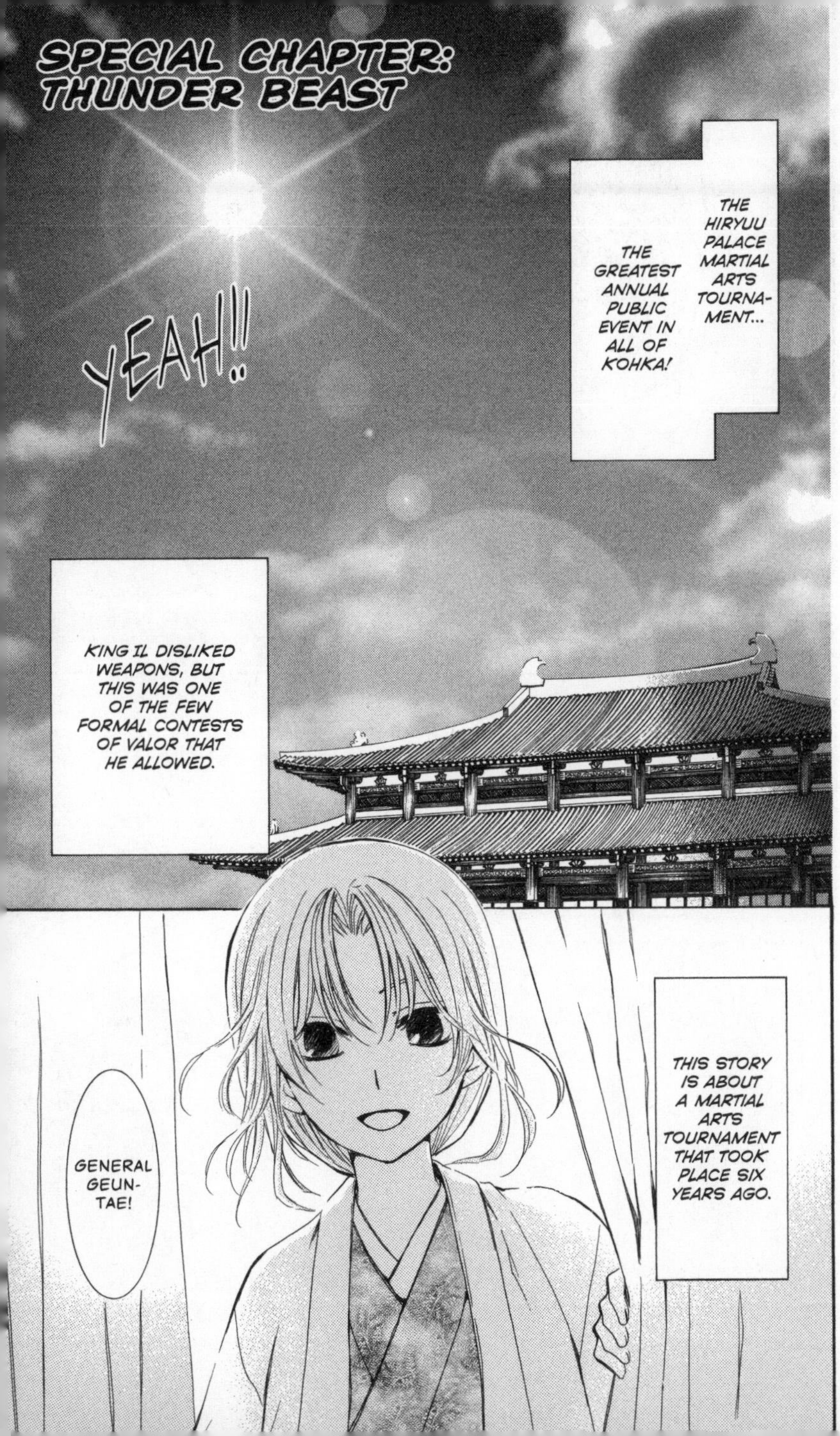
SPECIAL CHAPTER: THUNDER BEAST
THE HIRYUU PALACE MARTIAL ARTS TOURNAMENT...
THE GREATEST ANNUAL PUBLIC EVENT IN ALL OF KOHKA!
YEAH!!
KING IL DISLIKED WEAPONS, BUT THIS WAS ONE OF THE FEW FORMAL CONTESTS OF VALOR THAT HE ALLOWED.
THIS STORY IS ABOUT A MARTIAL ARTS TOURNAMENT THAT TOOK PLACE SIX YEARS AGO.
GENERAL GEUN-TAE!

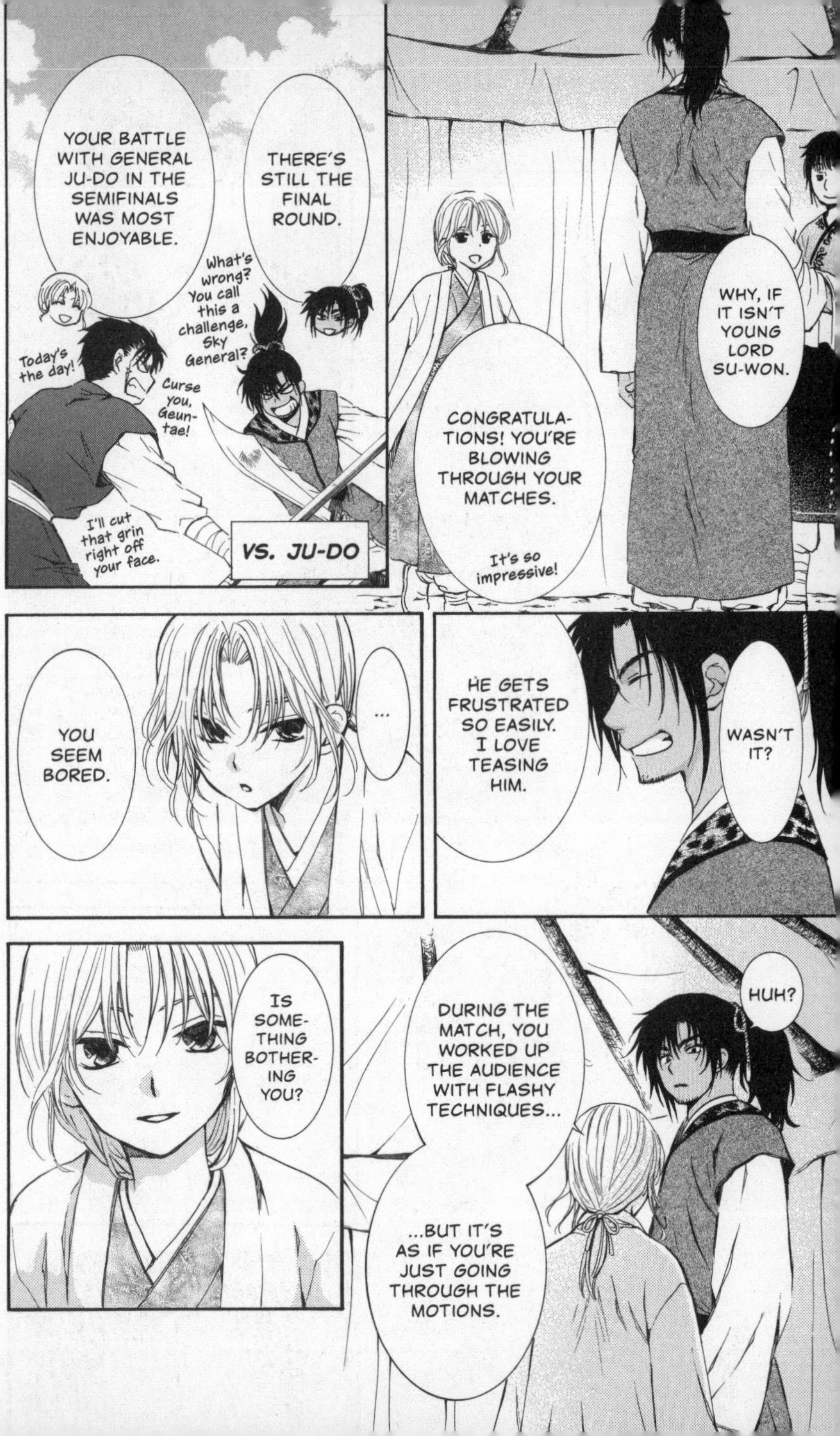
WHY, IF IT ISN'T YOUNG LORD SU-WON.
CONGRATULATIONS! YOU'RE BLOWING THROUGH YOUR MATCHES.
It's so impressive!
THERE'S STILL THE FINAL ROUND.
YOUR BATTLE WITH GENERAL JU-DO IN THE SEMIFINALS WAS MOST ENJOYABLE.
What's wrong? You call this a challenge, Sky General?
Curse you, Geun-tae!
Today's the day!
I'll cut that grin right off your face.
VS. JU-DO
WASN'T IT?
HE GETS FRUSTRATED SO EASILY. I LOVE TEASING HIM.
...
YOU SEEM BORED.
HUH?
DURING THE MATCH, YOU WORKED UP THE AUDIENCE WITH FLASHY TECHNIQUES...
...BUT IT'S AS IF YOU'RE JUST GOING THROUGH THE MOTIONS.
IS SOMETHING BOTHERING YOU?

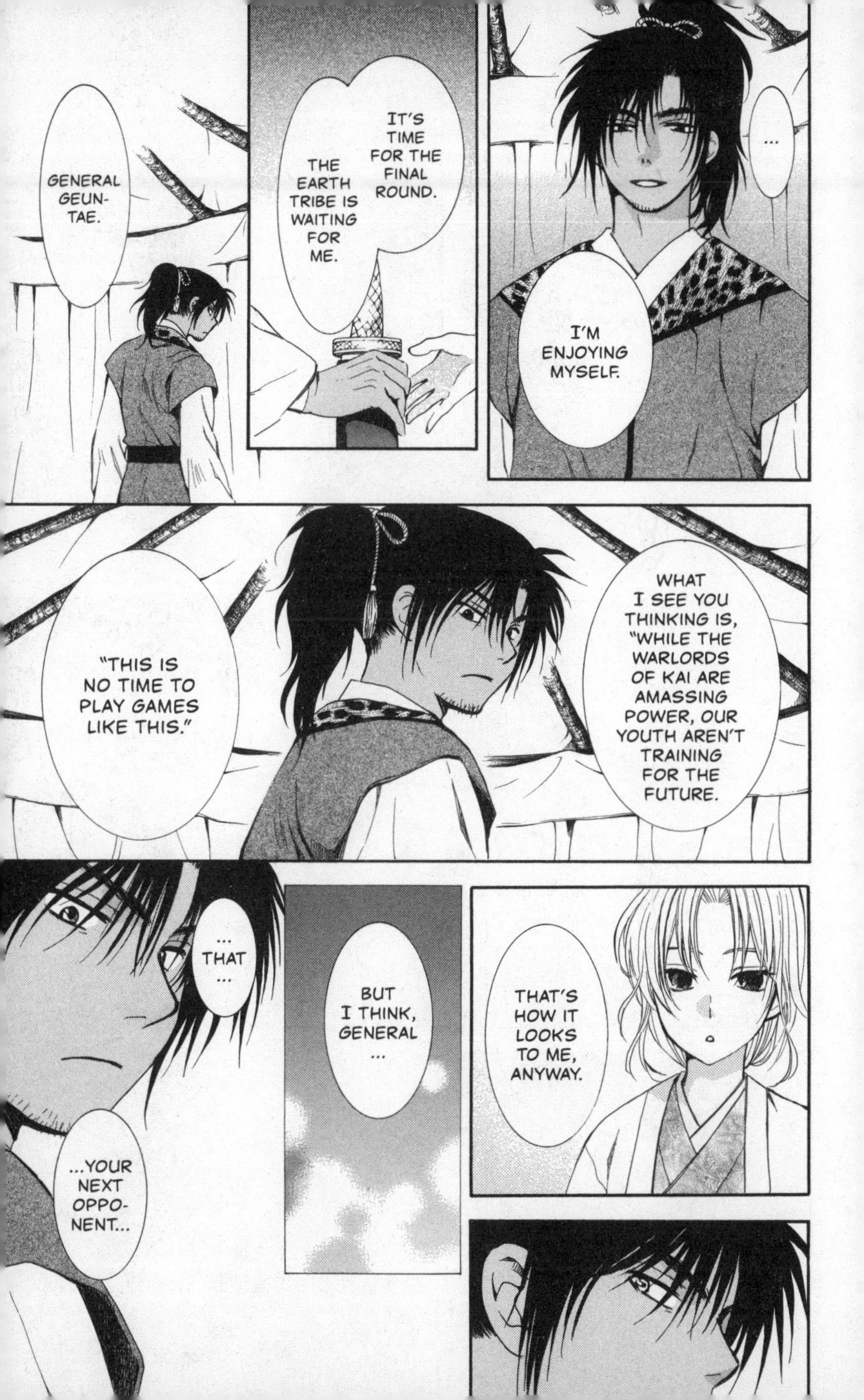
...
I'M ENJOYING MYSELF.
IT'S TIME FOR THE FINAL ROUND.
THE EARTH TRIBE IS WAITING FOR ME.
GENERAL GEUN-TAE.
WHAT I SEE YOU THINKING IS, "WHILE THE WARLORDS OF KAI ARE AMASSING POWER, OUR YOUTH AREN'T TRAINING FOR THE FUTURE.
"THIS IS NO TIME TO PLAY GAMES LIKE THIS."
THAT'S HOW IT LOOKS TO ME, ANYWAY.
BUT I THINK, GENERAL ...
... THAT ...
...YOUR NEXT OPPO-NENT...

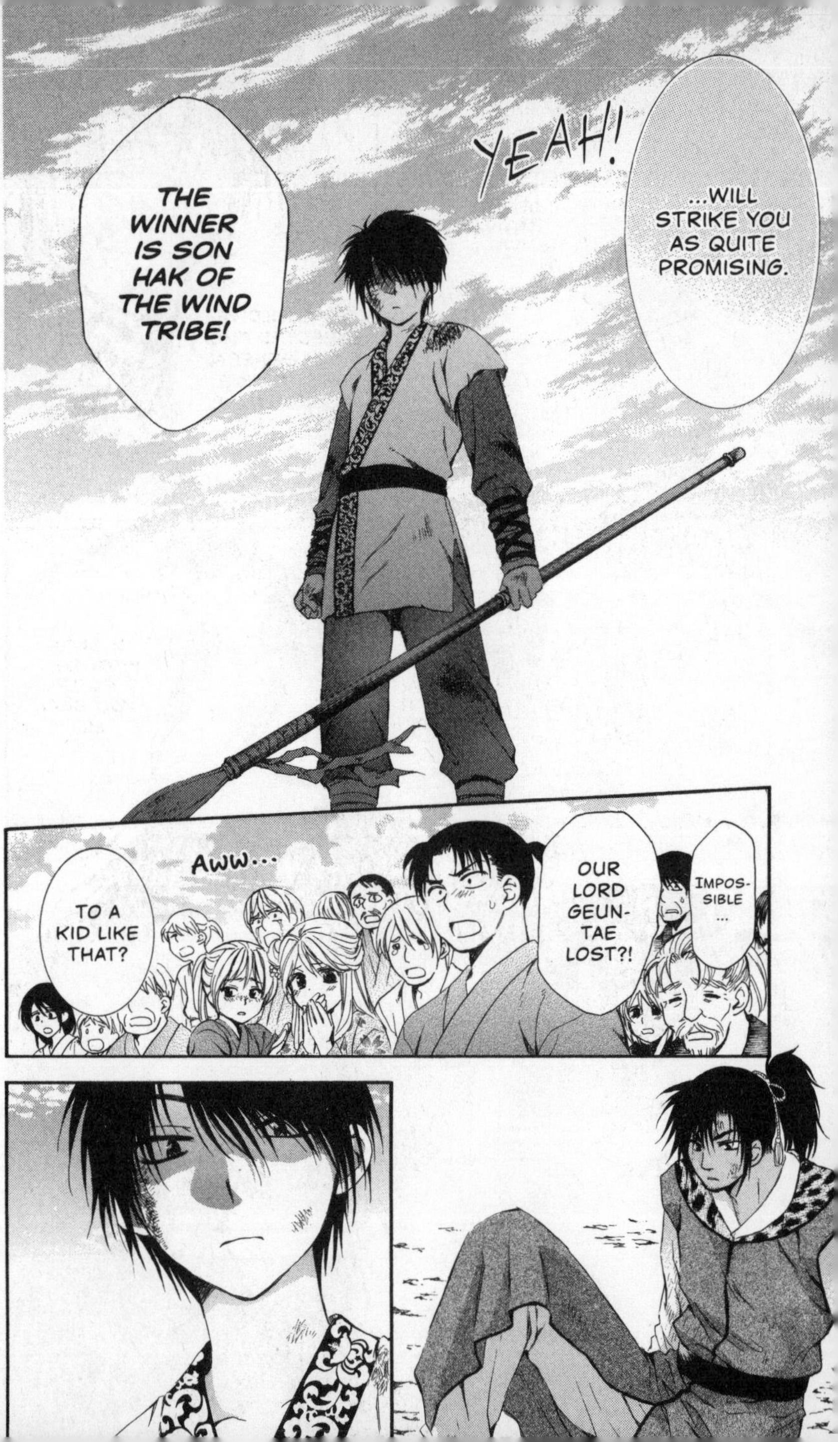
...WILL STRIKE YOU AS QUITE PROMISING.
YEAH!
THE WINNER IS SON HAK OF THE WIND TRIBE!
IMPOSSIBLE...
OUR LORD GEUN-TAE LOST?!
AWW...
TO A KID LIKE THAT?

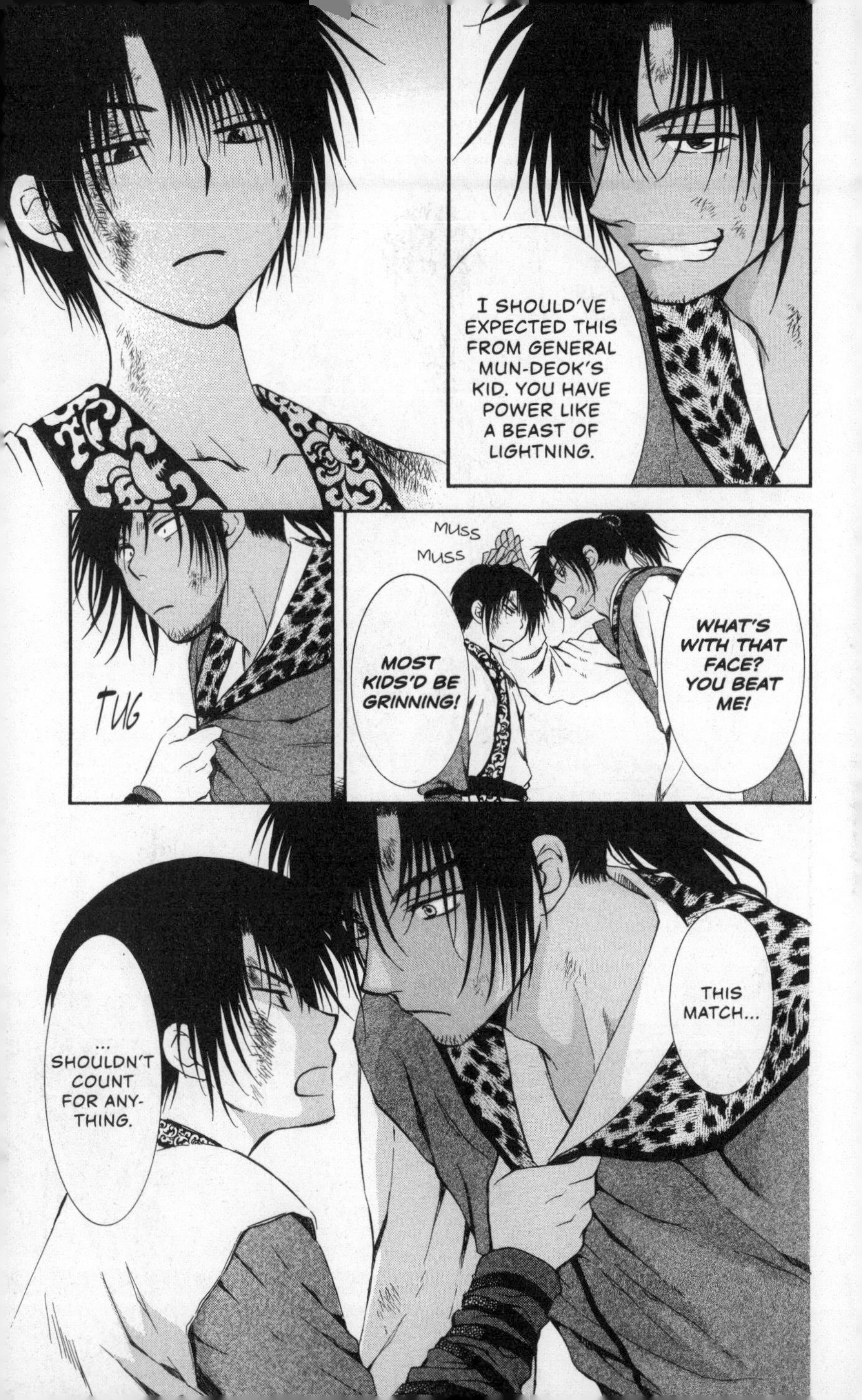
I SHOULD'VE EXPECTED THIS FROM GENERAL MUN-DEOK'S KID. YOU HAVE POWER LIKE A BEAST OF LIGHTNING.
WHAT'S WITH THAT FACE? YOU BEAT ME!
MUSS MUSS
MOST KIDS'D BE GRINNING!
TUG
THIS MATCH...
...SHOULDN'T COUNT FOR ANY-THING.

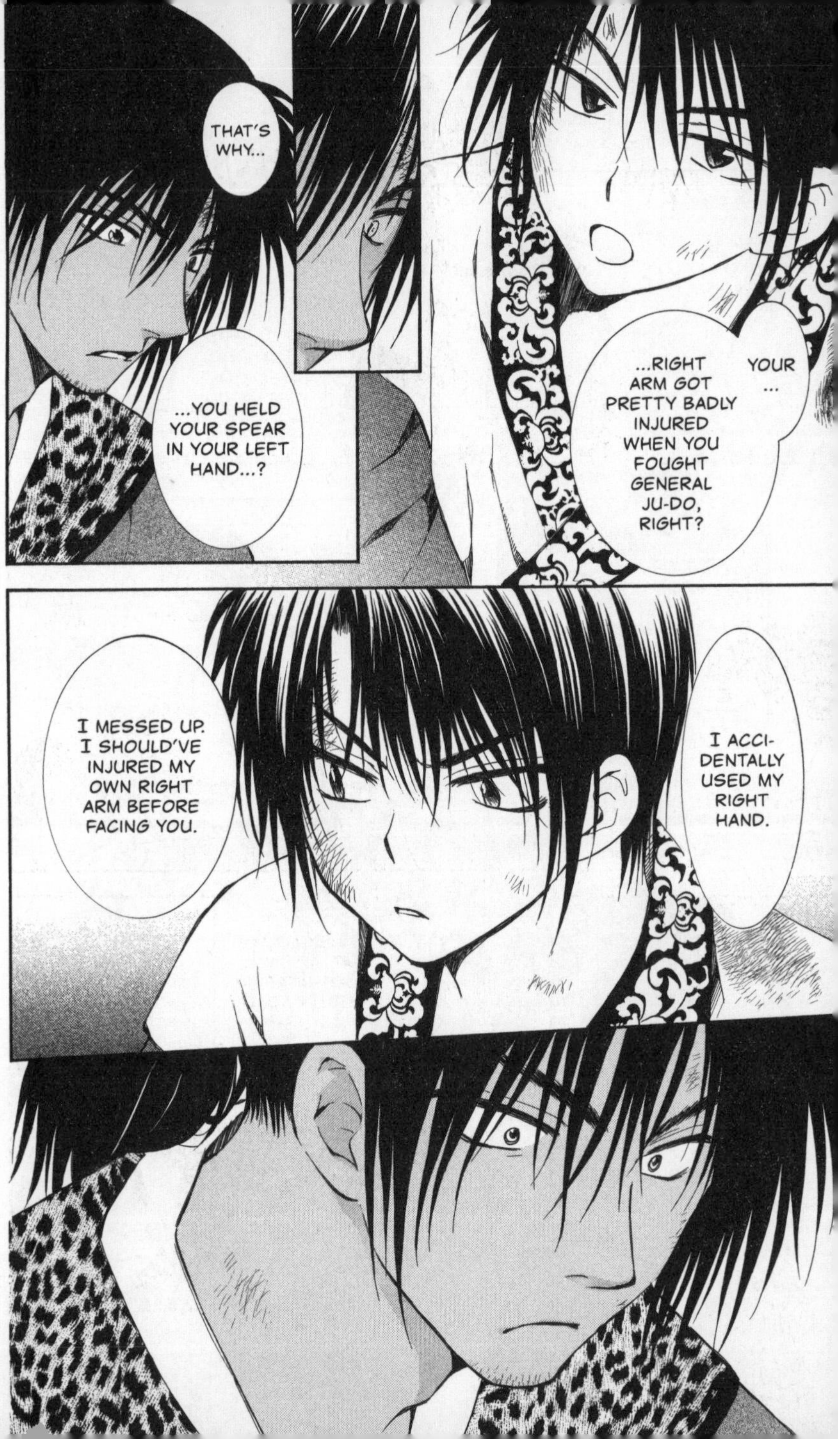
YOUR ...
...RIGHT ARM GOT PRETTY BADLY INJURED WHEN YOU FOUGHT GENERAL JU-DO, RIGHT?
THAT'S WHY...
...YOU HELD YOUR SPEAR IN YOUR LEFT HAND...?
I ACCI-DENTALLY USED MY RIGHT HAND.
I MESSED UP. I SHOULD'VE INJURED MY OWN RIGHT ARM BEFORE FACING YOU.

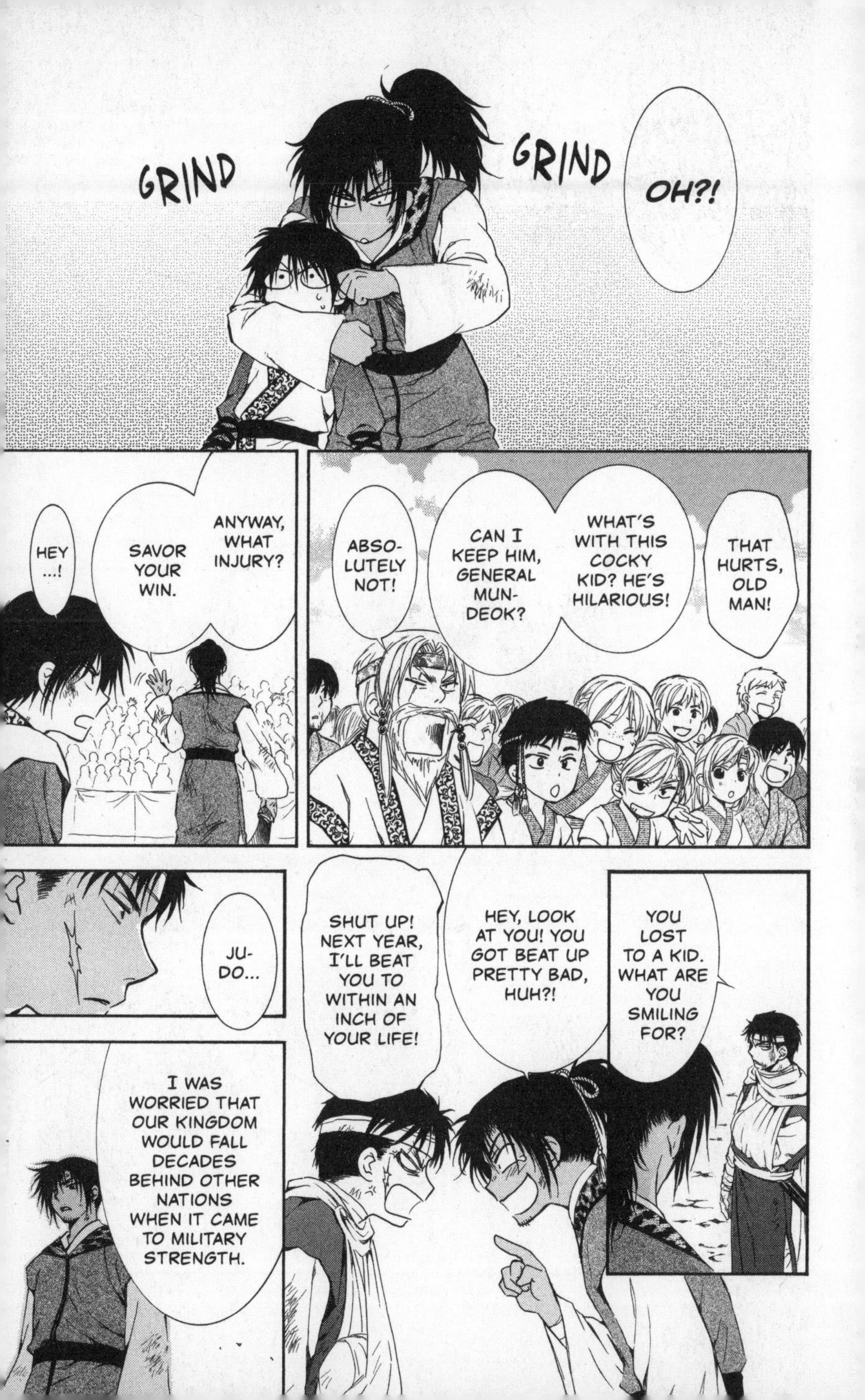
OH?!
GRIND
GRIND
THAT HURTS, OLD MAN!
WHAT'S WITH THIS COCKY KID? HE'S HILARIOUS!
CAN I KEEP HIM, GENERAL MUN-DEOK?
ABSO-LUTELY NOT!
ANYWAY, WHAT INJURY?
SAVOR YOUR WIN.
HEY ...!
YOU LOST TO A KID. WHAT ARE YOU SMILING FOR?
HEY, LOOK AT YOU! YOU GOT BEAT UP PRETTY BAD, HUH?!
SHUT UP! NEXT YEAR, I'LL BEAT YOU TO WITHIN AN INCH OF YOUR LIFE!
JU-DO...
I WAS WORRIED THAT OUR KINGDOM WOULD FALL DECADES BEHIND OTHER NATIONS WHEN IT CAME TO MILITARY STRENGTH.

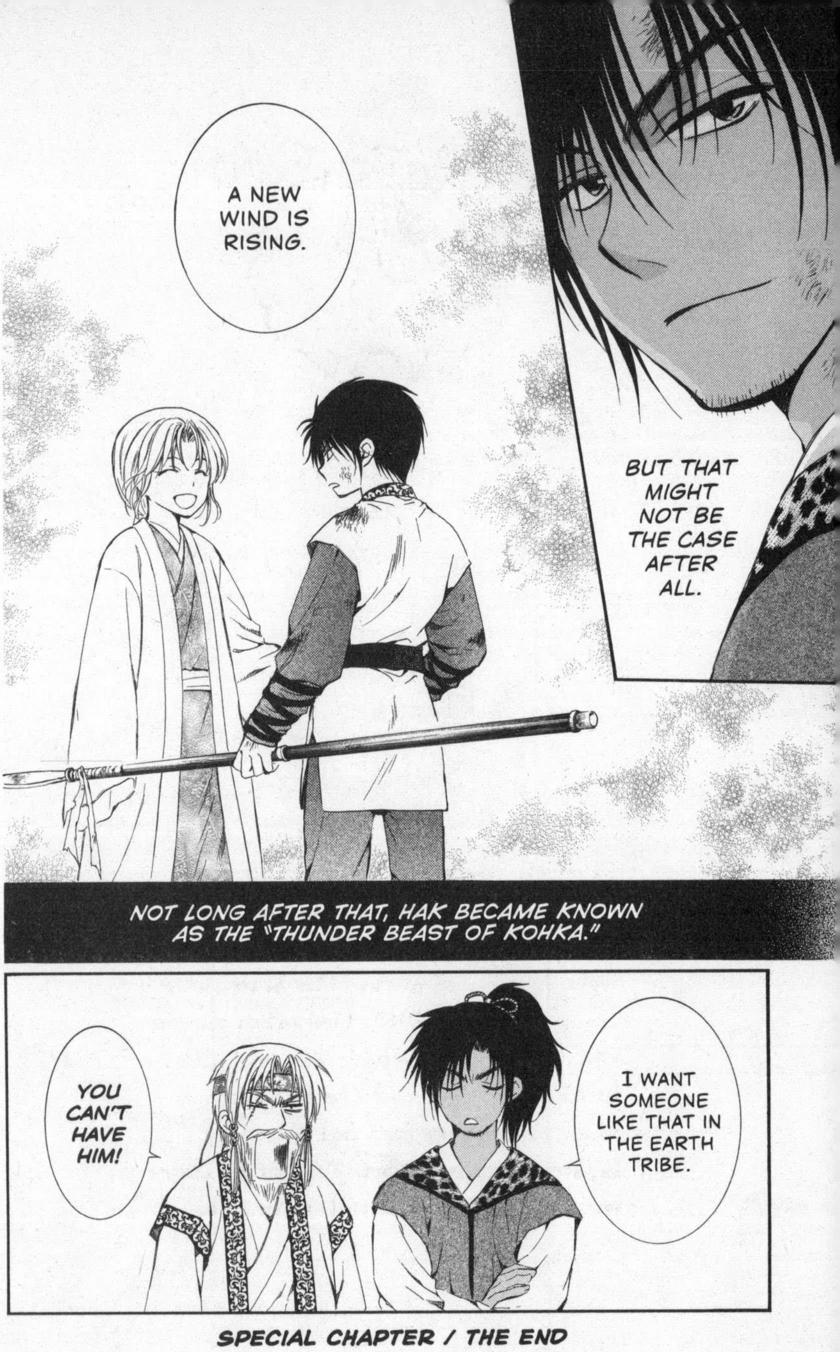
BUT THAT MIGHT NOT BE THE CASE AFTER ALL.
A NEW WIND IS RISING.
NOT LONG AFTER THAT, HAK BECAME KNOWN AS THE "THUNDER BEAST OF KOHKA."
I WANT SOMEONE LIKE THAT IN THE EARTH TRIBE.
YOU CAN'T HAVE HIM!

SPECIAL CHAPTER / THE END

Because of the (original Japanese) cover design change in the last volume, some people couldn't find *Yona* at the bookstore. In this volume, I'm not featuring Yona or Hak on the cover, but rather the old men. I'm afraid that people will be even more likely to overlook this volume at the bookstore.

—Mizuho Kusanagi

Born on February 3 in Kumamoto Prefecture in Japan, Mizuho Kusanagi began her professional manga career with *Yoiko no Kokoroe* (The Rules of a Good Child) in 2003. Her other works include *NG Life*, which was serialized in *Hana to Yume* and *The Hana to Yume* magazines and published by Hakusensha in Japan. *Yona of the Dawn* was adapted into an anime in 2014.

YONA OF THE DAWN
VOL.13
Shojo Beat Edition

✤

STORY AND ART BY
MIZUHO KUSANAGI

English Adaptation/Ysabet Reinhardt MacFarlane
Translation/JN Productions
Touch-Up Art & Lettering/Lys Blakeslee
Design/Yukiko Whitley
Editor/Amy Yu

Akatsuki no Yona by Mizuho Kusanagi
© Mizuho Kusanagi 2013
All rights reserved.
First published in Japan in 2013 by HAKUSENSHA, Inc., Tokyo.
English language translation rights arranged with
HAKUSENSHA, Inc., Tokyo.

Printed in Canada

Published by VIZ Media, LLC
P.O. Box 77010
San Francisco, CA 94107

10 9 8 7 6 5 4 3 2 1
First printing, August 2018

viz.com

shojobeat.com